Structural Equation Modeling with M*plus*

Basic Concepts, Applications, and Programming

Multivariate Applications Series

Sponsored by the Society of Multivariate Experimental Psychology, the goal of this series is to apply complex statistical methods to significant social or behavioral issues, in such a way so as to be accessible to a nontechnical-oriented readership (e.g., nonmethodological researchers, teachers, students, government personnel, practitioners, and other professionals). Applications from a variety of disciplines such as psychology, public health, sociology, education, and business are welcome. Books can be single- or multiple-authored or edited volumes that (a) demonstrate the application of a variety of multivariate methods to a single, major area of research; (b) describe a multivariate procedure or framework that could be applied to a number of research areas; or (c) present a variety of perspectives on a topic of interest to applied multivariate researchers.

There are currently 19 books in the series:

- *What if There Were No Significance Tests?* coedited by Lisa L. Harlow, Stanley A. Mulaik, and James H. Steiger (1997)
- *Structural Equation Modeling With LISREL, PRELIS, and SIMPLIS: Basic Concepts, Applications, and Programming*, written by Barbara M. Byrne (1998)
- *Multivariate Applications in Substance Use Research: New Methods for New Questions*, coedited by Jennifer S. Rose, Laurie Chassin, Clark C. Presson, and Steven J. Sherman (2000)
- *Item Response Theory for Psychologists*, coauthored by Susan E. Embretson and Steven P. Reise (2000)
- *Structural Equation Modeling With AMOS: Basic Concepts, Applications, and Programming*, written by Barbara M. Byrne (2001)
- *Conducting Meta-Analysis Using SAS*, written by Winfred Arthur, Jr., Winston Bennett, Jr., and Allen I. Huffcutt (2001)
- *Modeling Intraindividual Variability With Repeated Measures Data: Methods and Applications*, coedited by D. S. Moskowitz and Scott L. Hershberger (2002)
- *Multilevel Modeling: Methodological Advances, Issues, and Applications*, coedited by Steven P. Reise and Naihua Duan (2003)
- *The Essence of Multivariate Thinking: Basic Themes and Methods*, written by Lisa Harlow (2005)
- *Contemporary Psychometrics: A Festschrift for Roderick P. McDonald*, coedited by Albert Maydeu-Olivares and John J. McArdle (2005)

- *Structural Equation Modeling With EQS: Basic Concepts, Applications, and Programming*, 2nd ed., by Barbara M. Byrne (2006)
- *A Paul Meehl Reader: Essays on the Practice of Scientific Psychology*, coedited by Niels G. Waller, Leslie J. Yonce, William M. Grove, David Faust, and Mark F. Lenzenweger (2006)
- *Introduction to Statistical Mediation Analysis*, written by David P. MacKinnon (2008)
- *Applied Data Analytic Techniques for Turning Points Research*, edited by Patricia Cohen (2008)
- *Cognitive Assessment: An Introduction to the Rule Space Method*, written by Kikumi K. Tatsuoka (2009)
- *Structural Equation Modeling With AMOS: Basic Concepts, Applications, and Programming*, 2nd ed., written by Barbara M. Byrne (2010)
- *Handbook of Ethics in Quantitative Methodology*, coedited by Abigail T. Panter and Sonya K. Sterba (2011)
- *Longitudinal Data Analysis: A Practical Guide for Researchers in Aging, Health, and Social Sciences*, coedited by Jason T. Newsom, Richard N. Jones, and Scott M. Hofer (2011)
- *Structural Equation Modeling With Mplus: Basic Concepts, Applications, and Programming*, written by Barbara M. Byrne (2012)

Anyone wishing to submit a book proposal should send the following: (a) the author and title; (b) a timeline, including the completion date; (c) a brief overview of the book's focus, including a table of contents and, ideally, a sample chapter (or chapters); (d) a brief description of competing publications; and (e) targeted audiences.

For more information, please contact the series editor, Lisa Harlow, at Department of Psychology, University of Rhode Island, 10 Chafee Road, Suite 8, Kingston, RI 02881-0808; phone (401) 874-4242; fax (401) 874-5562; or LHarlow@uri.edu. Information may also be obtained from members of the editorial and advisory board: Leona Aiken (Arizona State University), Daniel Bauer (University of North Carolina), Jeremy Biesanz (University of British Columbia), Gwyneth Boodoo (Educational Testing Services), Barbara M. Byrne (University of Ottawa), Scott Maxwell (University of Notre Dame), Liora Schmelkin (Hofstra University), and Stephen West (Arizona State University).

Structural Equation Modeling with M*plus*

Basic Concepts, Applications, and Programming

Barbara M. Byrne

University of Ottawa

Routledge
Taylor & Francis Group
New York   London

Routledge
Taylor & Francis Group
711 Third Avenue
New York, NY 10017

Routledge
Taylor & Francis Group
27 Church Road
Hove, East Sussex BN3 2FA

Printed in the United States of America on acid-free paper
Version Date: 20110627

International Standard Book Number: 978-0-8058-5986-7 (Hardback) 978-1-84872-839-4 (Paperback)

Library of Congress Cataloging-in-Publication Data

Byrne, Barbara M.
    Structural equation modeling with Mplus : basic concepts,
    applications, and programming / Barbara M. Byrne.
        p. cm. -- (Multivariate applications series)
    Summary: "This text aims to provide readers with a nonmathematical introduction
to the basic concepts associated with structural equation modeling, and to illustrate
its basic applications using the Mplus program"-- Provided by publisher.
    ISBN-13: 978-0-8058-5986-7 (hardback)
    ISBN-10: 0-8058-5986-1 (hardcover)
    ISBN-13: 978-1-84872-839-4 (pbk.)
    1. Structural equation modeling. 2. Multivariate analysis. 3. Mplus. 4. Social
sciences--Statistical methods. I. Title.

QA278.B974 2011
519.5'3--dc23   2011018745

Visit the Taylor & Francis Web site at
http://www.taylorandfrancis.com

and the Psychology Press Web site at
http://www.psypress.com

Contents

Preface

As with each of my previous introductory structural equation modeling (SEM) books, my overall goal here is to provide my readers with a
nonmathematical introduction to the basic concepts associated with this
methodology, and to illustrate its basic applications using the M*plus* program. Most applications in this volume are based on M*plus* 6*, the most current version of the program at the time this book went to press. Although
it is inevitable that newer versions of the program will emerge at some
later date, the basic principles covered in this first edition of the book
remain fully intact.

This book is specifically designed and written for readers who may
have little to no knowledge of either SEM or the M*plus* program. It is
intended neither as a text on the topic of SEM, nor as a comprehensive
review of the many statistical and graphical functions available in the
M*plus* program. Rather, my primary aim is to provide a practical guide
to SEM using M*plus*. As such, readers are "walked through" a diversity of
SEM applications that include confirmatory factor analytic (CFA) and full
latent variable models tested on a wide variety of data (single/multiple-
group; normal/non-normal; complete/incomplete; continuous/ordinal),
and based on either the analysis of covariance structures, or on the analysis of mean and covariance structures. Throughout the book, each application is accompanied by numerous illustrative "how to" examples related
to particular procedural aspects of the program. All of the data files used
for the applications in this book can be downloaded from http://www.
psypress.com/9781848728394 or http://www.psypress.com/sem-with-
mplus/datasets. In summary, each application is accompanied by the
following:

- statement of the hypothesis to be tested
- schematic representation of the model under study
- full explanation bearing on related Mplus model specification input
  files
- full explanation and interpretation of related Mplus output files
- published reference from which the application is drawn

*The applications in chapters 3, 4, 5, and 11 are based on Mplus 5. *xi*

- illustrated use and function of the Language Generator option
- data file upon which the application is based

The book is divided into four major sections. A brief outline of each section and of its encompassing chapters is as follows:

Section I

This initial section comprises two introductory chapters. In *Chapter 1*, I introduce you to the basic concepts associated with SEM methodology, and then familiarize you with SEM symbol notation, the process of model-building, visible and nonvisible model components, and the formulation of covariance and mean structure modeling. Finally, I provide you with a general overview of M*plus* notation and illustrate its application to three very simple models.

Chapter 2 focuses solely on the M*plus* program. Here, I familiarize you with the lexicon and structuring of Mplus input files, identify the 10 key commands used in building these files, note the availability of several analytic and output options, acquaint you with the M*plus* Language Generator facility, identify important default settings, and alert you to the provision of a graphics module designed for use in displaying observed data and analytic results. Along the way, I address the issue of model (or statistical) identification, demonstrate the calculation of degrees of freedom based on covariance, as well as mean structures, and distinguish between over-, just-, and under-identified models and their resulting implications. Finally, because I consider it imperative that you fully comprehend the link between model specification as described in the M*plus* input, as well as schematically portrayed in its related model, I walk you through specifications associated with three simple, albeit diverse model examples: (a) a first-order CFA model, (b) a second-order CFA model, and (c) a full latent variable model.

Section II

This section is devoted to applications involving only single-group analyses. Chapter 3 involves specification of a first-order CFA model representing the multidimensional structure of a theoretical construct and outlines the steps involved in testing the validity of its postulated structure. In this first application, I walk you through each stage involved in building the related M*plus* input file based on use of the Language Generator, illustrate how to run the job, and provide a detailed explanation of all results presented in the output file. Included here is a description of each goodness-of-fit statistic reported by M*plus*, together with a complete breakdown of its computation.

In *Chapter 4*, we examine another first-order CFA model, albeit this time, as it relates to the hypothesized structure of a well-established measuring instrument. In contrast to the model tested in Chapter 3, the one tested here exhibits strong evidence of model misspecification. As such, I subsequently walk you through various stages of the post hoc model-fitting process in an attempt to establish a better-fitting model that is not only statistically viable and substantively meaningful, but also addresses the issue of scientific parsimony. Important caveats are noted throughout this model-fitting phase. Given that the data used here are non-normally distributed, I alert you to use and specification of the appropriate estimator and also outline how to obtain values related to skewness and kurtosis in M*plus*.

Chapter 5 introduces you to the testing of a second-order CFA model representing the hypothesized structure of a measuring instrument based on data that are both ordinal and non-normally distributed. The basic concepts, underlying theory and statistical assumptions associated with the analysis of categorical data are described, and the general analytic strategies involving various estimators are reviewed. In the interest of both completeness and relevance (given a review of SEM applications in the literature), I walk you through two analyses of the same data: (a) with the categorical variables treated as if they are of a continuous scale, and (b) with the categorical nature of the variables taken into account. Along the way, I introduce you to the presence of a condition code error and illustrate how and why it relates to a problem of model identification.

Chapter 6 presents the final single-group application in this section. Here, I walk you through the various stages involved in testing the validity of a full latent variable model that represents an empirically-derived causal structure. In dissecting component parts of this model, I introduce and briefly address the topic of parceling. Finally, as part of a lengthy set of post hoc model-fitting analyses, I address the issue of model comparison and work through a detailed computation breakdown of the robust chi-square difference test that must be used when data are non-normally distributed.

Section III

Three applications related to multiple-group analyses are presented in this section - two are rooted in the analysis of covariance structures and one in the analysis of mean and covariance structures. In *Chapter 7*, I introduce you to the basic notion of measurement and structural invariance (i.e., equivalence), as well as to the basic testing strategy. Based only on the analysis of covariance structures, I show you how to test for measurement and structural equivalence across groups with respect to a measuring error residuals, as well as factor variances and covariances. In addition, given a slightly different slant to the same idea, I once again walk you through computation of the robust chi-square difference test.

In *Chapter 8,* we work from a somewhat different perspective that encompasses the analysis of mean and covariance structures. Here, I first outline basic concepts associated with the analysis of latent mean structures and then continue on to illustrate the various stages involved in testing for latent mean differences across groups. Given that one group comprises incomplete data, I address the issue of missingness and outline the many estimation options available in M*plus.* Along the way, I introduce you to the issues of partial measurement invariance, under-identification pertinent to the number of estimated intercepts, and evaluation of invariance based on a practical, rather than statistical, perspective.

Chapter 9 addresses the issue of cross-validation and illustrates tests for the equivalence of causal structure across calibration and validation samples. In this chapter, as well as elsewhere in the book, I discuss the issue of a Heywood case and, in the interest of parameter clarification, urge specification of a particular TECH option in the **OUTPUT** command.

Section IV

In this final section, we examine three models that increasingly are becoming of substantial interest to SEM practitioners and researchers. *Chapter 10* addresses the issue of construct validity and illustrates the specification and testing of a *multitrait*-multimethod (MTMM) model. More specifically, we work through two CFA approaches to MTMM analyses based on (a) the general CFA approach, and (b) the correlated uniquenesses CFA approach.

Chapter 11 focuses on longitudinal data and presents a latent growth curve (LGC) model. Following an introduction to the general notion of measuring change over time, I walk you through the testing of a dual domain LGC model that is tested with and without predictor variables. Along the way, we examine application of the Plot option in the **OUTPUT** command, and interpret results from several different perspectives.

Finally, in *Chapter 12,* I acquaint you with the notion of multilevel SEM analyses. Following an overview of multilevel modeling (MLV) in general, comparison of single-level and multilevel approaches to the analyses, and review of recent advances in the estimation of MLVs, we test for the validity of a two-level model representing the hypothesized structure of a measuring instrument based on data for 27 geographically diverse cultural groups.

Although there are now several SEM texts available, the present book distinguishes itself from the rest in a number of ways. *First,* it is the only book to demonstrate, by application to actual data, a wide range of CFA and full latent variable models drawn from published studies and accompanied by a detailed explanation of each model tested, as well as the resulting output file. *Second*, it is the only book to incorporate applications based solely on the M*plus* program. *Third*, it is the only book to literally "walk" readers through: (a) model specification, estimation, evaluation, and post hoc modification decisions and processes associated with a variety of applications, (b) competing approaches to the analysis of multiple-group and MTMM models, and of categorical/continuous data, based on the M*plus* program, (c) illustrated applications of the optional M*plus* Plot and Tech **OUTPUT** commands, together with interpretation of their results, and (d) a step-by-step application of the M*plus* Language Generator facility. Overall, this volume serves well as a companion book to the M*plus* user's guide (Muthén & Muthén, 2007-2010), as well as to any statistics textbook devoted to the topic of SEM.

In writing a book of this nature, it is essential that I have access to a number of different data sets capable of lending themselves to various applications. To facilitate this need, all examples presented throughout the book are drawn from my own research. Related journal references are cited for readers who may be interested in a more detailed discussion of theoretical frameworks, aspects of the methodology, and/or substantive issues and findings. It is important to emphasize that, although all applications are based on data that are of a social/psychological nature, they could just as easily have been based on data representative of the health sciences, leisure studies, marketing, or a multitude of other disciplines; my data, then, serve only as one example of each application. Indeed, I urge you to seek out and examine similar examples as they relate to other subject areas.

Although I have now written seven of these introductory SEM books pertinent to particular programs (Byrne, 1989, 1994c, 1998, 2001, 2006, 2009), including the present volume (2011), I must say that each provides its own unique learning experience. Without question, such a project demands seemingly endless time and is certainly not without its frustrations. However, thanks to the incredibly rapid and efficient support provided by Linda Muthén via the M*plus* Support Services (http://www.statmodel. com/support), such difficulties were always quickly resolved. In weaving together the textual, graphical, and statistical threads that form the fabric of this book, I hope that I have provided my readers with a comprehensive understanding of basic concepts and applications of SEM, as well as with an extensive working knowledge of the M*plus* program. Achievement of this goal has necessarily meant the concomitant juggling of word processing, "grabber", and statistical programs in order to produce the end result. It has been an incredible editorial journey, but one that has left me feeling truly enriched for having had yet another wonderful learning experience. I can only hope that, as you wend your way through the chapters of this book, you will find the journey to be equally exciting and fulfilling.

Acknowledgments

As with the writing of each of my other books, there are several people to whom I owe a great deal of thanks. First and foremost, I wish to express my sincere appreciation to Albert Maydeu-Olivares and Kris Preacher for both their time and invaluable suggestions related to several chapters. I am also very grateful to Ron Heck and Ke-Hai Yuan for lending their expertise to assist me in addressing particular issues related to multilevel modeling.

As has been the case for my last four books, I have had the great fortune to have Debra Riegert as my editor. As always, I wish to express my very special thanks to Debra, whom I consider to be the crème de la crème of editors and, in addition, a paragon of patience! As a chronic list maker and deadline setter, my perspective of the ideal editor is one who allows me to set and meet my own deadlines without the impingement of editorial pressure; this, Debra has done in spades! Indeed, for the same reason, I am additionally grateful to Suzanne Lassandro who truly has been the best production editor with whom I have ever had the pleasure of working. Thank you both so much for your pressure-free approach to the editorial process.

I wish also to extend sincere gratitude to my multitude of loyal readers around the globe. Many of you have introduced yourselves to me at conferences, at one of my SEM workshops, or via email correspondence. I truly value these brief, yet incredibly warm exchanges and thank you so much for taking the time to share with me your many achievements and accomplishments following your walk through my selected SEM applications. Thank you all for your continued loyalty over the years. I hope you enjoy this latest addition of the M*plus* book to my series of introductory books and look forward to hearing from you!

Last, but certainly far from the least, I am grateful to my husband, Alex, for his continued patience, support, and understanding of the incredible number of hours that my computer and I necessarily spend together working through a project of this sort. I consider myself to be fortunate indeed!

section I

Introduction

chapter 1

Structural Equation Models
The Basics

Structural tequation modeling (SEvaM) is a statistical methodology that takes a confirmatory (i.e., hypothesis-testing) approach to the analysis of a structural theory bearing on some phenomenon. Typically, this theory represents "causal" processes that generate observations on multiple variables (Bentler, 1988). The term *structural equation modeling* conveys two important aspects of the procedure: (a) that the causal processes under study are represented by a series of structural (i.e., regression) equations, and (b) that these structural relations can be modeled pictorially to enable a clearer conceptualization of the theory under study. The hypothesized model can then be tested statistically in a simultaneous analysis of the entire system of variables to determine the extent to which it is consistent with the data. If goodness-of-fit is adequate, the model argues for the plausibility of postulated relations among variables; if it is inadequate, the tenability of such relations is rejected.

Several aspects of SEM set it apart from the older generation of multivariate procedures. First, as noted above, it takes a confirmatory, rather than exploratory, approach to the data analysis (although aspects of the latter can be addressed). Furthermore, by demanding that the pattern of intervariable relations be specified a priori, SEM lends itself well to the analysis of data for inferential purposes. By contrast, most other multivariate procedures are essentially descriptive by nature (e.g., exploratory factor analysis), so that hypothesis testing is difficult, if not impossible. Second, whereas traditional multivariate procedures are incapable of either assessing or correcting for measurement error, SEM provides explicit estimates of these error variance parameters. Indeed, alternative methods (e.g., those rooted in regression, or the general linear model) assume that an error or errors in the explanatory (i.e., independent) variables vanish. Thus, applying those methods when there is error in the explanatory variables is tantamount to ignoring error, which may lead, ultimately, to serious inaccuracies—especially when the errors are sizeable. Such mistakes are avoided when corresponding SEM analyses (in general terms) are used. Third, although data analyses using the former methods are based on observed measurements only, those using SEM procedures can incorporate both unobserved (i.e., latent) and observed variables. Finally, there are no widely and easily applied alternative methods for modeling multivariate relations, or for estimating point and/or interval indirect effects; these important features are available using SEM methodology.

Given these highly desirable characteristics, SEM has become a popular methodology for nonexperimental research where methods for testing theories are not well developed and ethical considerations make experimental design unfeasible (Bentler, 1980). Structural equation modeling can be utilized very effectively to address numerous research problems involving nonexperimental research; in this book, I illustrate the most common applications (e.g., in Chapters 3, 4, 6, 7, and 9), as well as some that are less frequently found in the substantive literatures (e.g., in Chapters 5, 8, 10, 11, and 12). Before showing you how to use the M*plus* program (Muthén & Muthén, 2007–2010), however, it is essential that I first review key concepts associated with the methodology. We turn now to their brief explanation.

Basic Concepts

Latent Versus Observed Variables

In the behavioral sciences, researchers are often interested in studying theoretical constructs that cannot be observed directly. These abstract phenomena are termed *latent variables*.[1] Examples of latent variables in psychology are depression and motivation; in sociology, professionalism and anomie; in education, verbal ability and teacher expectancy; and in economics, capitalism and social class.

Because latent variables are not observed directly, it follows that they cannot be measured directly. Thus, the researcher must operationally define the latent variable of interest in terms of behavior believed to represent it. As such, the unobserved variable is linked to one that is observable, thereby making its measurement possible. Assessment of the behavior, then, constitutes the *direct* measurement of an observed variable, albeit the *indirect* measurement of an unobserved variable (i.e., the underlying construct). It is important to note that the term *behavior* is used here in the very broadest sense to include scores derived from any measuring instrument. Thus, observation may include, for example, self-report responses to an attitudinal scale, scores on an achievement test, in vivo observation scores representing some physical task or activity, coded responses to interview questions, and the like. These measured scores (i.e., the measurements) are termed *observed* or *manifest* variables; within the context of SEM methodology, they serve as *indicators* of the underlying construct that they are presumed to represent. Given this necessary bridging process between observed variables and unobserved latent variables, it should now be clear why methodologists urge researchers to be circum-spect in their selection of assessment measures. Although the choice of psychometrically sound instruments bears importantly on the credibility of all study findings, such selection becomes even more critical when the observed measure is presumed to represent an underlying construct.[2]

Exogenous Versus Endogenous Latent Variables

It is helpful in working with SEM models to distinguish between latent vari-ables that are exogenous and those that are endogenous. *Exogenous* latent variables are synonymous with independent variables; they "cause" fluctua-tions in the values of other latent variables in the model. Changes in the values of exogenous variables are not explained by the model. Rather, they are con-sidered to be influenced by other factors external to the model. Background variables such as gender, age, and socioeconomic status are examples of such external factors. *Endogenous* latent variables are synonymous with depen-dent variables and, as such, are influenced by the exogenous variables in the model, either directly or indirectly. Fluctuation in the values of endogenous variables is said to be explained by the model because all latent variables that influence them are included in the model specification.

The Factor Analytic Model

The oldest and best known statistical procedure for investigating relations between sets of observed and latent variables is that of *factor analysis*. In using this approach to data analyses, the researcher examines the covaria-tion among a set of observed variables in order to gather information on their underlying latent constructs, commonly termed *factors* within the context of a factor analysis. There are two basic types of factor analyses: exploratory factor analysis (EFA) and confirmatory factor analysis (CFA). We turn now to a brief description of each.

EFA is designed for the situation where links between the observed and latent variables are unknown or uncertain. The analysis thus proceeds in an exploratory mode to determine how, and to what extent, the observed variables are linked to their underlying factors. Typically, the researcher wishes to identify the minimal number of factors that underlie (or account for) covariation among the observed variables. For example, suppose a researcher develops a new instrument designed to measure five facets of physical self-concept (e.g., [self-perceived] Health, Sport Competence, Physical Appearance, Coordination, and Body Strength). Following the formulation of questionnaire items designed to measure these five latent constructs, he or she would then conduct an EFA to determine the extent to which the item measurements (the observed variables) were related to the five latent constructs. In factor analysis, these relations are represented by *factor loadings*. The researcher would hope that items designed to measure health, for example, exhibited high loadings on that factor, and low or negligible loadings on the other four factors. This factor analytic approach is considered to be exploratory in the sense that the researcher has no prior knowledge that the items do, indeed, measure the intended factors. (For texts dealing with EFA, see Comrey, 1992; Gorsuch, 1983; McDonald, 1985; Mulaik, 2009. For informative articles on EFA, see Byrne, 2005a; Fabrigar, Wegener, MacCallum, & Strahan, 1999; MacCallum, Widaman, Zhang, & Hong, 1999; Preacher & MacCallum, 2003; Wood, Tataryn, & Gorsuch, 1996. For a detailed discussion of EFA, see Brown, 2006.)

In contrast to EFA, CFA is appropriately used when the researcher has some knowledge of the underlying latent variable structure. Based on knowledge of the theory, empirical research, or both, he or she postulates relations between the observed measures and the underlying factors a priori and then tests this hypothesized structure statistically. For example, based on the proposed measuring instrument cited earlier, the researcher would argue for the loading of items designed to measure sport competence self-concept on that specific factor, and *not* on the health, physical appearance, coordination, or body strength self-concept dimensions. Accordingly, a priori specification of the CFA model would allow all sport competence self-concept items to be free to load on that factor, but restricted to have zero loadings on the remaining factors. The model would then be evaluated by statistical means to determine the adequacy of its goodness-of-fit to the sample data. (For a text devoted to CFA, see Brown, 2006. And for more detailed discussions of CFA, see, e.g., Bollen, 1989; Byrne, 2003, 2005b; Cudeck & MacCallum, 2007; Long, 1983a.)

In summary, then, the factor analytic model (EFA or CFA) focuses solely on how, and to what extent, observed variables are linked to their underlying latent factors. More specifically, it is concerned with the extent to which the observed variables are generated by the underlying latent constructs, and thus the strength of the regression paths from the factors to the observed variables (the factor loadings) is of primary interest. Although interfactor relations are also of interest, any regression structure among them is not considered in the factor analytic model. Because the CFA model focuses solely on the link between factors and their measured variables, within the framework of SEM, it represents what has been termed a *measurement model*.

The Full Latent Variable Model

In contrast to the factor analytic model, the full latent variable, otherwise referred to in this book as the *full SEM model*, allows for the specification of regression structure among the latent variables. That is to say, the researcher can hypothesize the impact of one latent construct on another in the modeling of causal direction. This model is termed *full* (or *complete*) because it comprises both a measurement model and a structural model: the measurement model depicting the links between the latent variables and their observed measures (i.e., the CFA model), and the structural model depicting the links among the latent variables themselves.

A full SEM model that specifies direction of cause from only one direction is termed a *recursive model*; one that allows for reciprocal or feedback effects is termed a *nonrecursive model*. Only applications of recursive models are considered in this volume.

General Purpose and Process of Statistical Modeling

Statistical models provide an efficient and convenient way of describing the latent structure underlying a set of observed variables. Expressed either diagrammatically or mathematically via a set of equations, such models explain how the observed and latent variables are related to one another.

Typically, a researcher postulates a statistical model based on his or her knowledge of the related theory, empirical research in the area of study, or some combination of both. Once the model is specified, the researcher then tests its plausibility based on sample data that comprise all observed variables in the model. The primary task in this model-testing procedure is to determine the goodness-of-fit between the hypothesized model and the sample data. As such, the researcher imposes the structure of the hypothesized model on the sample data, and then tests how well the observed data fit this restricted structure. Because it is highly unlikely that a perfect fit will exist between the observed data and the hypothesized model, there will necessarily be a differential between the two; this differential is termed the *residual*. The model-fitting process can therefore be summarized as follows:

$$\text{Data} = \text{Model} + \text{Residual}$$

where:

data represent score measurements related to the observed variables as derived from persons comprising the sample;

model represents the hypothesized structure linking the observed variables to the latent variables, and, in some models, linking particular latent variables to one another; and

residual represents the discrepancy between the hypothesized model and the observed data.

In summarizing the general strategic framework for testing structural equation models, Jöreskog (1993) distinguished among three scenarios, which he termed *strictly confirmatory* (SC), *alternative models* (AM), and *model generating* (MG). In the SC scenario, the researcher postulates a single model based on theory, collects the appropriate data, and then tests the fit of the hypothesized model to the sample data. From the results of this test, the researcher either rejects or fails to reject the model; no further modifications to the model are made. In the AM case, the researcher proposes several alternative (i.e., competing) models, all of which are grounded in theory. Following analysis of a single set of empirical data, he or she selects one model as most appropriate in representing the sample data. Finally, the MG scenario represents the case where the researcher, having postulated and rejected a theoretically derived model on the basis of its poor fit to the sample data, proceeds in an exploratory (rather than confirmatory) fashion to modify and reestimate the model. The primary focus, in this instance, is to locate the source of misfit in the model and to determine a model that better describes the sample data. Jöreskog (1993) noted that, although respecification may be either theory or data driven, the ultimate objective is to find a model that is both substantively meaningful and statistically well fitting. He further posited that despite the fact that "a model is tested in each round, the whole approach is model generating, rather than model testing" (Jöreskog, 1993, p. 295).

Of course, even a cursory review of the empirical literature will clearly show the MG situation to be the most common of the three scenarios, and for good reason. Given the many costs associated with the collection of data, it would be a rare researcher indeed who could afford to terminate his or her research on the basis of a rejected hypothesized model! As a consequence, the SC case is not commonly found in practice. Although the AM approach to modeling has also been a relatively uncommon practice, at least two important papers on the topic (e.g., MacCallum, Roznowski, & Necowitz, 1992; MacCallum, Wegener, Uchino, & Fabrigar, 1993) have precipitated more activity with respect to this analytic strategy.

Statistical theory related to these model-fitting processes can be found in (a) texts devoted to the topic of SEM (e.g., Bollen, 1989; Kaplan, 2000; Kline, 2011; Loehlin, 1992; Long, 1983b; Raykov & Marcoulides, 2000; Saris & Stronkhurst, 1984; Schumacker & Lomax, 2004); (b) edited books devoted to the topic (e.g., Bollen & Long, 1993; Cudeck, du Toit, & Sörbom, 2001; Hoyle, 1995a, in press; Marcoulides & Schumacker, 1996); and (c) methodologically oriented journals such as *Applied Psychological Measurement, Applied Measurement in Education, British Journal of Mathematical and Statistical Psychology, Journal of Educational and Behavioral Statistics, Multivariate Behavioral Research, Psychological Methods, Psychometrika, Sociological Methodology, Sociological Methods & Research*, and *Structural Equation Modeling.*

The General Structural Equation Model
Symbol Notation

Structural equation models are schematically portrayed using particular configurations of four geometric symbols—a circle (or ellipse; ◯), a square (or rectangle; ▭), a single-headed arrow (→), and a double-headed arrow (↔). By convention, circles (or ellipses) represent unobserved latent factors, squares (or rectangles) represent observed variables, single-headed arrows represent the impact of one variable on another, and double-headed arrows represent covariances or correlations between pairs of variables. In building a model of a particular structure under study, researchers use these symbols within the framework of four basic configurations, each of which represents an important component in the analytic process. These configurations, each accompanied by a brief description, are as follows:

- Path coefficient for regression of an observed variable onto an unobserved latent variable (or factor)
- Path coefficient for regression of one factor onto another factor
- Measurement error associated with an observed variable
- Residual error in the prediction of an unobserved factor

The Path Diagram

Schematic representations of models are termed *path diagrams* because they provide a visual portrayal of relations that are assumed to hold among the variables under study. Essentially, as you will see later, a path diagram depicting a particular SEM model is actually the graphical equivalent of its mathematical representation whereby a set of equations relates dependent variables to their explanatory variables. As a means of illustrating how the above four symbol configurations may represent a particular causal process, let me now walk you through the simple model shown in Figure 1.1. To facilitate interpretation related to this initial SEM model, all variables are identified by their actual label, rather than by their parameter label.

In reviewing the model shown in Figure 1.1, we see that there are two unobserved latent factors—social self-concept as it relates to one's peers (SSC PEERS) and peer relations (PEER RELATIONS). These factors (i.e., constructs) are measured by seven observed variables—three considered to measure SSC PEERS (*SDQSSCPR*, *APISSCPR*, and *SPPCSSCPR*) and four to measure PEER RELATIONS (*peer activity, peer attachment, peer*

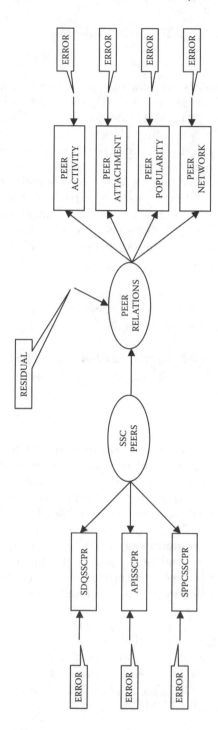

Figure 1.1. A general structural equation model.

popularity, and *peer network).* These seven observed variables function as indicators of their respective underlying latent factors. For purposes of example, let's suppose that (a) the three indicators of SSC PEERS represent subscale scores of social self-concept (i.e., self-perceived relations with peers) as measured by three different measuring instruments (SDQ, API, and SPPC, as previously underlined), and (b) the four indicators of PEER RELATIONS represent total scores based on four different approaches to measuring peer relations (e.g., a sociometric scale, in vivo observations, a self-report, and a teacher rating scale).

Associated with each observed variable, and with the factor being predicted (PEER RELATIONS), is a single-headed arrow. However, there is an important distinction between these two sets of single-headed arrows. Error associated with observed variables represents *measurement error,* which reflects on their adequacy in measuring the related underlying factors (SSC PEERS and PEER RELATIONS). Measurement error derives from two sources: *random measurement error* (in the psychometric sense) and *error uniqueness,* a term used to describe error variance arising from some characteristic that is considered to be specific (or unique) to a particular indicator variable. Such error often represents *nonrandom* (or *systematic*) measurement error. In contrast, error associated with the prediction of endogenous factors from exogenous factors represents the extent to which this predicted value is in error; it is commonly termed *residual error.*[3] For example, the residual error implied by the related single-headed arrow in Figure 1.1 represents error in the prediction of PEER RELATIONS (the endogenous factor) from SSC PEERS (the exogenous factor).

It is important to note that although both types of errors are termed *residuals* in M*plus,* their distinction is evidenced from their linkage to either a factor or an observed variable. For simplicity, however, I maintain use of the terms *error* and *residual* throughout this introductory chapter. Further clarification of these distinctions will emerge as we work our way through the applications presented in Chapters 3 through 12.

It is worth noting that, consistent with the representation of factors in SEM, measurement error and residual error actually represent unobserved variables. Thus, it would seem perfectly reasonable to indicate their presence by means of a small circle. However, I am aware of only one SEM program (AMOS) that actually models error in this way.

In addition to symbols that represent variables, certain others are used in path diagrams to denote hypothesized processes involving the entire system of variables. In particular, one-way arrows leading from one variable to another represent structural regression coefficients and thus indicate the impact of one variable on another. In Figure 1.1, for example, the unidirectional arrow leading from the exogenous factor, SSC PEERS, to the endogenous factor, PEER RELATIONS, implies that peer social self-concept "causes" peer relations.[4] Likewise, the three unidirectional arrows leading from SSC PEERS to each of the three observed variables (*SDQSSCPR, APISSCPR,* and *SPPCSSCPR*), and those leading from PEER RELATIONS to each of its indicators (*peer activity, peer attachment, peer popularity,* and *peer network*), suggest that their score values are each influenced by their respective underlying factors. These path coefficients represent the magnitude of expected change in the observed variables for every change in the related latent variable (or factor). It is important to note that these observed variables typically represent item scores (see, e.g., Chapter 4), item pairs (see, e.g., Chapter 3), subscale scores (see, e.g., Chapter 11), and/or carefully formulated item parcels (see, e.g., Chapter 6).

The one-way arrows leading from the ERROR callouts to each of the observed variables indicate the impact of measurement error (random and unique) on the observed variables. Likewise, the single-headed arrow leading from the RESIDUAL callout to the endogenous factor represents the impact of error in the prediction of PEER RELATIONS.

Structural Equations

As noted in the initial paragraph of this chapter, in addition to lending themselves to pictorial description via a schematic presentation of the causal processes under study, structural equation models can also be represented by a series of regression (i.e., structural) equations. Because (a) regression equations represent the influence of one or more variables on another, and (b) this influence, conventionally in SEM, is symbolized by a single-headed arrow pointing from the variable of influence to the variable of interest, we can think of each equation as summarizing the impact of all relevant variables in the model (observed and unobserved) on one specific variable (observed or unobserved). Thus, one relatively simple approach to formulating these equations is to note each variable that has one or more arrows pointing toward it, and then record the summation of all such influences for each of these dependent variables.

To illustrate this conversion of regression processes into structural equations, let's turn again to Figure 1.1. We can see that there are eight variables with arrows pointing toward them; seven represent observed variables (from *SDQSSCPR* to *SPPCSSCPR* on the left, and from *peer activity* to *peer network* on the right), and one represents an unobserved latent variable (or factor: PEER RELATIONS). Thus, we know that the regression functions symbolized in the model shown in Figure 1.1 can be summarized in terms of eight separate equation-like representations of linear dependencies as follows:

PEER RELATIONS = SSC PEERS + residual

SDQSSCPR = SSC PEERS + error

APISSCPR = SSC PEERS + error

SPPCSSCPR = SSC PEERS + error

peer activity = PEER RELATIONS + error

peer attachment = PEER RELATIONS + error

peer popularity = PEER RELATIONS + error

peer network = PEER RELATIONS + error

Nonvisible Components of a Model

Although, in principle, there is a one-to-one correspondence between the schematic presentation of a model and its translation into a set of structural equations, it is important to note that neither one of these model representations tells the whole story; some parameters critical to the estimation of the model are not explicitly shown and thus may not be obvious to the novice structural equation modeler. For example, in both the path diagram and the equations just shown, there is no indication that the *variance* of the exogenous latent variable, SSC PEERS, is a parameter in the model; indeed, such parameters are essential to all structural equation models. Although researchers must be mindful of this inadequacy of path diagrams in building model input files related to other SEM programs, M*plus* facilitates this specification by automatically incorporating the estimation of variances by default for all independent factors in a model.[5]

Likewise, it is equally important to draw your attention to the specified *nonexistence* of certain parameters in a model. For example, in Figure 1.1, we detect no curved arrow between the error associated with the observed variable, *peer activity*, and the error associated with *peer popularity*, which suggests the lack of covariance between the error terms. Similarly, there is no hypothesized covariance between SSC PEERS and the residual; absence of this path addresses the common, and most often necessary, assumption that the predictor (or exogenous) variable is in no way associated with any error arising from the prediction of the criterion (or endogenous) variable. In the case of both examples cited here, M*plus*, once again, makes it easy for the novice structural equation modeler by automatically assuming these specifications to be nonexistent. These important default assumptions will be addressed in Chapter 2, where I review the basic elements of M*plus* input files, as well as throughout remaining chapters in the book.

Basic Composition

The general SEM model can be decomposed into two submodels: a measurement model and a structural model. The *measurement model* defines relations between the observed and unobserved variables. In other words, it provides the link between scores on a measuring instrument (i.e., the observed indicator variables) and the underlying constructs they are designed to measure (i.e., the unobserved latent variables). The measurement model, then, represents the CFA model described earlier in that it specifies the pattern by which each observed measure loads on a particular factor. In contrast, the *structural model* defines relations among the unobserved (or latent) variables. Accordingly, it specifies the manner by which particular latent variables directly or indirectly influence (i.e., "cause") changes in the values of certain other latent variables in the model.

For didactic purposes in clarifying this important aspect of SEM composition, let's now examine Figure 1.2, in which the same model presented in Figure 1.1 has been demarcated into measurement and structural components.

Considered separately, the elements modeled within each rectangle in Figure 1.2 represent two CFA models.[6] Enclosure of the two factors within the ellipse represents a full latent variable model and thus would not be of interest in CFA research. The CFA model to the left of the diagram represents a one-factor model (SSC PEERS) measured by three observed variables (from *SDQSSCPR* to *SPPCSSCPR*), whereas the CFA model on the right represents a one-factor model (PEER RELATIONS) measured by four observed variables (from *peer activity* to *peer network*). In both cases, (a) the regression of the observed variables on each factor and (b) the variances of both the factor and the errors of measurement are of primary interest.

It is perhaps important to note that, although both CFA models described in Figure 1.2 represent first-order factor models, second- and higher order CFA models can also be analyzed using M*plus*. Such hierarchical CFA models, however, are less commonly found in the literature. Discussion and application of CFA models in the present book are limited to first- and second-order models only. (For a more comprehensive discussion and explanation of first- and second-order CFA models, see Bollen, 1989; Brown, 2006; Byrne, 2005a; Kerlinger, 1984.)

The Formulation of Covariance and Mean Structures

The core parameters in structural equation models that focus on the analysis of covariance structures are the regression coefficients, and the variances and covariances of the independent variables. When the focus extends to the analysis of mean structures, the means and intercepts also

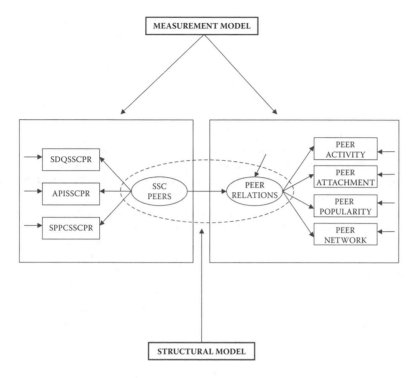

Figure 1.2. A general structural equation model demarcated into measurement and structural components.

become central parameters in the model. However, given that sample data comprise observed scores only, there needs to be some internal mechanism whereby the data are transposed into parameters of the model. This task is accomplished via a mathematical model representing the entire system of variables. Such representation systems vary with each SEM computer program. In contrast to other SEM programs, M*plus*, by default, estimates the observed variable intercepts. However, if the model under study involves no structure on the means (i.e., tests involving the latent factor means are of no interest), these values are automatically fixed to zero. Details related to means and covariance structural models are addressed in Chapter 8.

The General Mplus Structural Equation Model

Mplus Notation

In general, M*plus* regards all variables as falling into one of two categories—measured (observed) variables or unmeasured (unobserved, latent) variables. Measured variables are considered to be either *background* variables or *outcome* (i.e., dependent) variables (as determined by the model of interest). Expressed generically, background variables are labeled as *x*, whereas outcome variables are labeled according to type as follows: Continuous and censored outcome variables are labeled as *y*, and binary, ordinal (ordered categorical), and nominal (unordered categorical) variables as *u*. Only continuous and ordinal variables are used in data comprising models discussed in this book.

Likewise, M*plus* distinguishes between labels used in the representation of unobserved latent variables, with continuous latent variables being labeled as *f* and categorical latent variables as *c*. Finally, unlike most other SEM programs, M*plus* models do not explicitly label measurement and residual errors; these parameters are characterized simply by a single-headed arrow. For a comprehensive and intriguing schematic representation of how these various components epitomize the many models capable of being tested using the M*plus* program, see Muthén and Muthén (2007–2010).

To ensure a clear understanding of this labeling schema, let's turn to Figure 1.3, a replication of Figure 1.1, recast as an M*plus*-specified model within the framework of a generically labeled schema. Given the detailed description of this path diagram presented earlier, no further explanation of the model per se is provided here. However, I would like to present another perspective on the observed variables labeled as *y1* through *y7*. I noted earlier that M*plus* labels continuous observed variables as *y*'s, and this is what we can see in Figure 1.3. However, another way of conceptualizing the labeling of these observed variables is to think of them as *dependent* variables in the model. Consistent with my earlier explanation regarding the formulation of linear structural equations, each observed variable shown in Figure 1.3 has two arrows pointing toward it, thereby making it a dependent variable (in the model). Possibly due to our earlier training in traditional statistical procedures, we tend automatically, and perhaps subconsciously, to associate the term *dependent variable* with the label *y* (as opposed to *x*). Thus, this generically labeled model may serve to provide you with another way of conceptualizing this full SEM structure.

In this chapter, I have presented you with a few of the basic concepts associated with SEM. Now that you are familiar with these critical underpinnings of this methodology, we can turn our attention to the specification and analysis of models within the framework of M*plus*. In Chapter 2, then, I introduce you to the language of M*plus* needed in the structuring of input files that result in the correct analyses being conducted. Because a picture is worth a thousand words, I exemplify this input information within the context of three very simple models: a first-order CFA model, a second-order CFA model, and a full SEM model. Further elaboration,

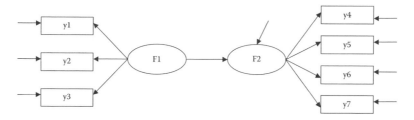

Figure 1.3. A general structural equation model generically labeled within the framework of M*plus*.

together with details related to the analytic process, is addressed as I walk you through particular models in each of the remaining 10 chapters. As you work your way through the applications included in this book, you will become increasingly more confident both in your understanding of SEM and in using the M*plus* program. So, let's move on to Chapter 2 and a more comprehensive look at SEM modeling with M*plus*.

Notes

1. Within the context of factor analytic modeling, latent variables are commonly termed *factors*.
2. Throughout the remainder of the book, the terms *latent*, *unobserved*, or *unmeasured* variable are used synonymously to represent a hypothetical construct or factor; the terms *observed*, *manifest*, and *measured* variable are also used interchangeably.
3. Residual terms are often referred to as *disturbance terms*.
4. In this book, the term *cause* implies a direct effect of one variable on another within the context of a complete model. Its magnitude and direction are given by the partial regression coefficient. If the complete model contains all relevant influences on a given dependent variable, its causal precursors are correctly specified. In practice, however, models may omit key predictors and may be misspecified, so that it may be inadequate as a "causal model" in the philosophical sense.
5. More specifically, the M*plus* program, by default, estimates all independent *continuous* factors in the model.
6. The residual error, of course, would not be a part of the CFA model as it represents predictive error.

chapter 2

Using the Mplus Program

The purpose of this chapter is to introduce you to the general format of the Mplus structural equation modeling (SEM) program so that you can more easily comprehend the applications presented and discussed in Chapters 3 through 12. More specifically, my intent is to (a) familiarize you with the Mplus language used in structuring input files, (b) identify the availability of several analytic and output options, (c) acquaint you with the language generator facility, (d) note important default settings, and (e) alert you to the provision of a graphics module designed for use in displaying observed data and analytic results.

Although Mplus provides for the specification and testing of a broad array of models based on a wide choice of estimators and algorithms for analyses of continuous, categorical (ordinal and nominal), binary (i.e., dichotomous), and censored data, the selection of models illustrated and discussed in this book is necessarily limited only to those considered of most interest to researchers and practitioners wishing to know and understand the basic concepts and applications of SEM analyses. Based on my own experience in conducting close to 100 introductory SEM workshops worldwide, I have found the 10 applications presented in the remaining chapters consistently to have generated the largest number of queries from individuals eager to know more about the rapidly expanding world of SEM. In particular, all models are based on data comprising variables that have either a continuous or an ordinal scale. Readers wishing more specific information related to nominal, censored, or binary data are referred to the Mplus *User's Guide* (Muthén & Muthén, 2007–2010) and/or website (http://www.statmodel.com).

As with any form of communication, one must first understand the language before being able to interpret the message conveyed. So it is in comprehending the specification of SEM models, as each computer program has its own language and set of rules for structuring an input file that describes the model to be tested. We turn now to this important feature of the Mplus program.

Mplus Notation and Input File Components and Structure

The building of input files using Mplus is relatively easy and straightforward, mainly because its language consists of a maximum of only 10 command statements. As would be expected, however, each of these commands provides for several options that can further refine model specification and desired outcome information. These options notwithstanding, even specification of very complex models requires only minimal input. What makes the structuring of M*plus* input files so easy is that in most cases, you will need to use only a small subset of these 10 commands and their options. This minimization of input structure has been made possible largely as a consequence of numerous programmed defaults chosen on the basis of models that are the most commonly tested in practice. Where applicable, these defaults will be brought to your attention; some are noted in this current chapter, and others will be highlighted where applicable in the remaining chapters. It is important for you to know, however, that all programmed defaults can be overridden. Example applications of this option are illustrated in Chapters 5, 9, and 10.

There are several important aspects of these commands and their options that are essential in learning to work with M*plus*. Being an inveterate list maker, I always find it most convenient to work from a list when confronted with this type of information. Thus, with the hope of making your foray into the world of SEM a little easier, I now list what I consider to be key characteristics of the M*plus* input file. It is important to note, however, that this list is necessarily limited as space considerations weigh heavily on the amount of information I can include here. Thus, for additional and more specific details related to input, readers are referred to the M*plus User's Guide* (Muthén & Muthén, 2007–2010).

- Each command must appear on a new line and be followed by a colon.
- With the exception of the TITLE command, information provided for each must always be terminated with a semicolon.
- Command options are separated and terminated by a semicolon.
- There can be more than one option per line of input.
- With the exception of two (to be noted below), a command may or may not be specified.
- Commands can be placed in any order.
- Commands, options, and option settings can be shortened to four or more letters.
- Records comprising the input file can contain upper- and/or lowercase letters and tabs and cannot exceed a length of 90 columns.
- Comments can be included anywhere in the input but must be preceded by an exclamation mark (!); all information that follows is ignored by the program.
- Command options often include the use of keywords critical to appropriate model specification and estimation; these keywords (and one symbol) are IS, ARE, and =, which in most cases can be used interchangeably.

Of the 10 commands, at least four are consistently specified for all applications detailed in this book. Thus, following a description of these four commands, I consider it instructive to stop at that point and show you an example input file before completing descriptions for the remaining commands. Let's turn now to a listing and elaboration of these first four key commands.

TITLE

This command, of course, gives you the opportunity to identify a particular analysis through the creation of a title. In contrast to simply assigning a brief label to the analysis, I strongly recommend that you be generous in the amount of information included in the title. Not uncommon to each of us is the situation where what might have seemed obvious when we conducted the initial analysis of a model may seem not quite so obvious several months later when, for whatever reason, we wish to reexamine the data using the same input files. Liberal use of title information is particularly helpful in the case where numerous *Mplus* runs were executed for a particular analytic project. *Mplus* allows you to use as many lines as you wish in this title section.

DATA

This command is *always required* as it conveys information about the data to the program. Specifically, it provides both the name of the data file and its location in the computer. Of critical note is that the data must be numeric except for certain missing value flags (Muthén & Muthén, 2007–2010) and must reside in an external ASCII file containing not more than 500 variables and with a maximum record length of 5,000. If, for example, your data are in SPSS file format, all you need to do is to save the data as a .dat file. In addition, however, you will need to delete the initial line of data containing all variable names.

In specifying data information, this command typically includes one of the three keywords noted earlier (File IS …). Although there are several options that can be included in this command, three of the most common relate to (a) type of data (e.g., individual, covariance matrix, or correlation matrix), (b) format of data (e.g., free or fixed), and (c) number of observations (or groups, if applicable). If the data comprise individual scores and are of free format, there is no need to specify this optional information as it is already programmed by default. However, if the data are in summary form (i.e., covariance or correlation matrices) the number of observations must be specified (NOBSERVATIONS ARE).

VARIABLE

Consistent with the DATA command, this one too, along with its NAMES option, is *always required* as it identifies the names of all variables in the data set, as well as which variables are to be included in the analysis (if applicable). Specification of these variables typically includes one of the three keywords noted earlier (e.g., NAMES <u>ARE</u>).

A second important aspect of this command is that all observed data are assumed to be complete (i.e., no missing data) and all observed variables are assumed to be measured on a continuous scale. In other words, these assumptions represent default information. Should this not be the case, then the appropriate information must be entered via a related option statement (e.g., CATEGORICAL <u>ARE</u>).

There are three additional aspects of this command and its options that are worthy of mention here: (a) When the variables in a data file have been entered consecutively, a hyphen can be used to indicate the set of variables to be used in the analysis (e.g., ITEM1–ITEM8); (b) individual words, letters, or numbers in a list can be separated either by blanks or by commas; and (c) a special keyword, ALL, can be used to indicate that all variables are included in the analysis.

MODEL

This command, of course, is *always required* as it provides for specification of the model to be estimated. In other words, it identifies which parameters are involved in the estimation process. Critical to this process are three essential pieces of information that must be conveyed to the program: (a) whether the variables are observed or unobserved (i.e., latent); (b) whether they serve as independent or dependent (i.e., exogenous or endogenous)[1] variables in the model; and (c) in the case of observed variables, identification of their scale. The latter, as shown earlier, is specified under the VARIABLE command.

Specification of a model is accomplished through the use of three single-word options: BY, ON, and WITH. The BY option is an abbreviation for *measured by* and is used to define the regression link between an underlying (continuous) latent factor and its related observed indicator variables in, say, a confirmatory factor analysis (CFA) model or measurement model in a full path analytic SEM model. Taken together, the BY option defines the continuous latent variables in the model. The ON option represents the expression *regressed on* and defines any regression paths in a full SEM model. Finally, the WITH option is short for *correlated with*. It is used to identify covariance (i.e., correlational) relations between latent variables in either the measurement or structural models; these can include, for example, error covariances.

Despite this textual explanation of these MODEL options, a full appreciation of their specification is likely possible only from inspection and from related explanation of a schematic portrayal of postulated variable relations. To this end, following a description of all M*plus* commands, as well as the language generator, I close out this chapter by presenting you with three different very simple models, at which time I walk you through the linkage between each model and its related input file. Thus, how these BY, ON, and WITH options are used should become clarified at that time.

Following description of these first four M*plus* commands, let's now review this simple input file:

TITLE: A simple example of the first four commands

DATA: File is "C:\Mplus\Files\FRBDI2.dat";
VARIABLE: Names are FBD1 – FBD30;
      Use variables are FBD8 – FBD12, FBD14, FBD19, FBD23;
MODEL: F1 by FBD8 – FBD12;
      F2 by FBD14, FBD19, FBD23;

Turning first to the DATA command, we can see both the name of the data file (FRBDI2.dat) and its location on the computer. Note that this entire string is encased within double quotation marks. Equivalently, we could also have stated this command as follows: File = "C:\Mplus\Files\ FRBDI2.dat" (i.e., use of an equal sign [=] in lieu of *is*). Finally, the fact that there is no mention of either the type or format of data indicates that they comprise individual raw data observations and have a free format.[2]

Turning next to the VARIABLE command, we see that there is a string of 30 similarly labeled variables ranging from FBD1 through FBD30. However, the next line under this command alerts us that not all 30 variables are to be used in the analysis. As indicated by the *Use Variables* option, only variables FBD1 through FBD12, plus FBD14, FBD19, and FBD23, will be included.

The MODEL command informs us that Factor 1 will be measured by five indicator variables (*FBD8* through *FBD12*), and Factor 2 measured by three indicator variables (*FBD14*, *FBD19*, and *FBD23*). As such, *FBD8* through *FBD12* are each regressed onto Factor 1, whereas variables *FBD14*, *FBD19*, and *FBD23* are regressed onto Factor 2. These regression paths represent the factor loadings of a CFA model or, equivalently, of the measurement model of a full SEM model.

Let's move on to an overview of the remaining M*plus* commands, each of which is now described.

DEFINE

The primary purpose of this command is to request transformation of an existing variable and to create new variables. Such operations can be applied to all observed variables or can be limited to only a select group of variables via use of a conditional statement.

ANALYSIS

The major function of this command is to describe technical details of the analysis, which are as follows: type of analysis to be conducted, statistical estimator to be used, parameterization of the model, and specifics of the computational algorithms. M*plus* considers four types of analyses—GENERAL, MIXTURE, TWOLEVEL, and EFA. The GENERAL type represents the default analysis; included here are regression analysis, path analysis, CFA, SEM, latent growth curve analysis, discrete-time survival analysis, and continuous-time analysis. Only CFA, SEM, and latent growth curve modeling are included in this book. With respect to statistical estimators, this choice necessarily varies with the particular type of analysis to be conducted. However, for TYPE = GENERAL, maximum likelihood (ML) estimation is default. The PARAMETERIZATION and ALGORITHM options are of no particular concern with the modeling applications to be presented in this book and, thus, are not elaborated upon here.

OUTPUT

The purpose of the OUTPUT command is to request information over and beyond that which is provided by default. Because I include various examples of these OUTPUT options and their related material in all applications presented in this book, I include here only a listing of the usual defaulted output information provided. Accordingly, the default output for all analyses includes a record of the input file, along with summaries of both the analytic specifications and analytic results. This information will be detailed for the first application (Chapter 3) and additionally inspected and reported for all subsequent applications in the book.

The initial information provided in the M*plus* output file represents a replication of the input file. This repeated listing of the command statements can be extremely helpful, particularly in the face of unexpected results, as it enables you to double-check your specification commands pertinent to the model under study.

The next set of information in the output file is a summary of the analytic specifications. The importance of this section is that it enables you to see how the program interpreted your instructions regarding the reading of data and requested analytic procedures. In particular, it is essential to note here whether or not the reported number of observations is correct. Finally, in the event that M*plus* encountered difficulties with your input instructions and/or the data file, any warnings or error messages generated by the program will appear in this section of the output. Thus, it is important to always check out any such messages as they will be critical to you for resolving the analytic roadblock.

The third and final block of M*plus* output information, by default, summarizes results of the analysis conducted. Here we find (a) the model goodness-of-fit results, (b) the parameter estimates, (c) the standard errors, and (d) parameter significance test results as represented by a ratio of the parameter estimate divided by its standard error (referred to in other programs as *t*-values [LISREL], *z*-values [EQS], and C.R. [critical ratio] values [AMOS]. As noted earlier, examination and discussion of these defaulted output components will accompany all applications in this book, and thus further elaboration is not detailed here.

SAVEDATA

The primary function of this command is to enable the user to save a variety of information to separate files that can be used in subsequent analyses. In general terms, this command allows for the saving of analytic data, auxiliary variables, and a range of analytic results. Three common and popular examples include the saving of matrix data (correlation, covariance), factor scores, and outliers. Readers are referred to the M*plus User's Guide* (Muthén & Muthén, 2007–2010) for a perusal of additional options.

PLOT

Inclusion of this command in the input file requests the graphical display of observed data and analytic results. These visual presentations can be inspected after the analysis is completed using a dialog-based postprocessing graphics module. Although a few of these graphical displays will be presented with various applications in this book, a brief description of the PLOT options is provided here.

The PLOT command has three primary options: TYPE, SERIES, and OUTLIERS. There are three types of plots, labeled as PLOT1, PLOT2, and PLOT3, each of which produces a different set of graphical displays. Thus, specification of the TYPE option allows the user to select a plot pertinent to a particular aspect of his or her data and/or analytic results.

The SERIES option allows for the listing of names related to a set of variables to be used in plots in which the values are connected by a line. This specification also requires that the *x*-axis values for each variable be provided. Of important note is that non–series plots (e.g., histograms and scatterplots) are available for all analyses.

Finally, the OUTLIERS option is specified when the user wishes to select and save outliers for use in graphical displays. Accordingly, M*plus* provides the choice of four methods by which outliers are identified: the Mahalanobis distance plus its *p*-value (MAHALANOBIS), Cook's D parameter estimate influence measure (COOKS), the loglikelihood contribution (LOGLIKELIHOOD), and the loglikelihood distance influence measure (INFLUENCE).

MONTECARLO

As is evident from its label, the MONTECARLO command is used for the purposes of specifying and conducting a Monte Carlo simulation study. M*plus* has extensive Monte Carlo capabilities used for data generation as well as data analysis. However, given that no Monte Carlo analyses are illustrated in this introductory book, no further information will be presented on this topic.

Having reviewed the 10 possible commands that constitute the major building blocks of M*plus* input files, along with some of the many options associated with these commands, let's move on now to the M*plus* language generator.

The Mplus Language Generator

The language generator is a very helpful feature of the M*plus* program as it makes the building of input files very easy. Not only does it reduce the time involved in structuring the file, but also it ensures the correct formulation of all commands and their options. The language generator functions by taking users through a series of screens that prompt for related information pertinent to their data and analyses. However, one caveat worthy of note is that this facility contains all M*plus* commands except for DEFINE, MODEL, PLOT, and MONTECARLO.

Let's now review Figures 2.1 and 2.2, where we can see how easy it is to work with the language generator in structuring an M*plus* input file.[3] Turning first to Figure 2.1, note that once you click on the M*plus* tab, this action opens a dialog box containing the language generator. By clicking on the latter option, as shown in Figure 2.2, you are then presented with a list of choices from which to select the correct type of analysis for the model under study. In Chapter 3, we will proceed through the steps that necessarily follow, at which time I walk you through this automated file-building process as it pertains to the first application of this book. Thus, further details related to the language generator will be presented at that time.

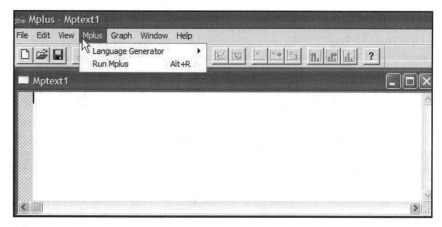

Figure 2.1. Selecting the M*plus* language generator.

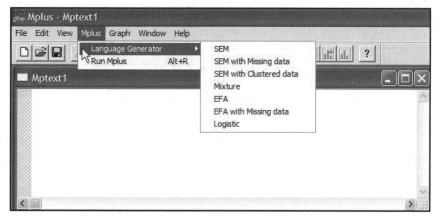

Figure 2.2. The M*plus* language generator menu options.

Model Specification From Two Perspectives

Newcomers to SEM methodology often experience difficulty in making the link between specification of a model as documented in a programmed input file and as presented in a related graphical schema. In my experience, I have always found it easiest to work *from* the schematic model *to* the input file. In other words, translate what you see in the model into the command language of the SEM program with which you are working. To help you in developing an understanding of the link between these two forms of model specification, I now walk you through the specification of three simple, albeit diverse model examples: (a) a first-order CFA model (Figure 2.3), (b) a second-order CFA model (Figure 2.4), and (c) a full SEM model (Figure 2.5).

Example 1: A First-Order CFA Model

In reviewing Figure 2.3, we observe a model that is hypothesized to have four factors—Sense of Humor (Factor 1), Trustworthiness (Factor 2), Sociability (Factor 3), and Emotional Stability (Factor 4). Let's say that these factors represent four subscales of an instrument designed to measure Social Acceptance. As indicated by the configuration of the 16 rectangles, each factor is measured by four observed (indicator) variables, which in this case represent items comprising the assessment scale: Items 1–4 measure Factor 1, Items 5–8 measure Factor 2, Items 9–12 measure Factor 3, and Items 13–16 measure Factor 4. The double-headed arrows linking the four factors indicate their postulated intercorrelation; the single-headed arrows leading from each factor to its related indicator variables represent the regression of this set of item scores onto their underlying constructs (i.e., the factor loadings); and the single-headed arrows pointing to each of the observed variables represent measurement error. Recall, however, that these errors are termed *residuals* in M*plus*.

Although this review of the model thus far should seem somewhat familiar to you, there are two features that are worthy of some elaboration. The first of these relates to the double labeling of each indicator variable shown in the model. Recall from Chapter 1 that M*plus* notation designates outcome continuous variables as *y*. For purposes of clarification in helping you understand the rationale for this labeling, I have assigned a *y* label to each indicator variable, in addition to its more general variable label.[4] We can think of the item scores as representing outcome variables as they are influenced by both their underlying latent factor and measurement error. Another way of thinking about them is as *dependent* variables. In SEM, all variables, regardless of whether they are observed or latent, are either dependent or independent variables in the model. An easy way of determining this designation is as follows: Any variable having a single-headed arrow pointing at it represents a dependent variable in the model; otherwise, it is an independent variable in the model. As is evident from the model shown in Figure 2.3, all of the observed item scores have two arrows pointing at them, thereby indicating that they are dependent variables in the model.

The second important point relates to the "1's" (shown here within callouts) assigned to the first factor loading in each set of factor loadings. These 1's represent fixed parameters in the model. That is to say, the factor loadings to which they are assigned are not freely estimated; rather, they remain fixed to a value of 1.0.[5] There are at least three important points to be made here. First, the value assigned to these parameters need not be 1.0. Although any numeral may be assigned to these parameters, a value of 1.0 typically has been the assignment of choice. Second, the constrained parameter need *not* be limited to the first indicator variable; any one of

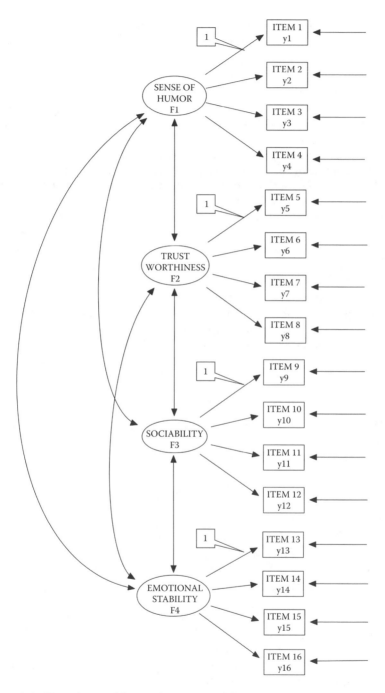

Figure 2.3. Hypothesized first-order CFA model.

a congeneric[6] set of parameters may be chosen. Finally, over and above these technical notations, however, there are two critically important points to be made regarding these fixed factor loadings: They address the issues of (a) *model identification* (also termed *statistical identification*) and (b) *latent variable scaling*, topics to which we turn shortly.

Critical to knowing whether or not a model is statistically identified is your understanding of the number of estimable parameters in the model. Thus, one extremely important caveat in working with structural equation models is to always tally the number of freely estimated parameters prior to running the analyses. As a prerequisite to the discussion of model identification, then, let's count the number of parameters to be estimated for the model portrayed in Figure 2.3. From a review of this figure, we ascertain that there are 16 regression coefficients (factor loadings), 20 variances (16 error variances and 4 factor variances), and 6 factor covariances. The 1's assigned to one of each set of the regression path parameters represent a fixed value of 1.00; as such, these parameters are not estimated. In total, then, there are 38 parameters to be estimated for the CFA model depicted in Figure 2.3; these are 12 factor loadings, 16 error variances, 4 factor variances, and 6 factor covariances. By default, however, M*plus* also estimates the observed variable intercepts, thereby making the number of parameters estimated to be 54 (38 + 16).

Before addressing the issues of model identification and latent variable scaling, let's first review the M*plus* input file pertinent to this CFA model:

TITLE: Example 1st-order CFA Input File (Figure 2.3)
DATA:
    FILE IS "C:\Mplus\Files\Example 1.dat";
VARIABLE:
    NAMES ARE ITEM1 – ITEM16;
MODEL:
F1 by ITEM1 – ITEM4;
F2 by ITEM5 – ITEM8;
F3 by ITEM9 – ITEM12;
F4 by ITEM13 – ITEM16;

As is evident from this file, the amount of text input is minimal. Three important aspects of this file are worthy of note. First, given that (a) the data file comprises only 16 variables (*ITEM1–ITEM16*), (b) the variables have been entered into the data file consecutively beginning with *ITEM1*, and (c) all variables are used in the analysis, there is no need to include the option USE VARIABLES. Second, the MODEL command provides for information that defines how the observed variables load onto each of the four factors; in other words, which observed variable measures which factor. This information is conveyed through use of the word *by*. A review of each option comprising the word *by* indicates that F1 is to be measured by the variables *ITEM1* through *ITEM4*, F2 by *ITEM5* through *ITEM8*, F3 by *ITEM9* through *ITEM12*, and F4 by *ITEM13* through *ITEM16*. Finally, three important programmed defaults come into play in this model: (a) As noted earlier, by default, M*plus* fixes the first factor loading in each congeneric set of indicator variables to 1.0 in CFA models and/or the measurement portion of other SEM models, (b) variances of and covariances among independent latent variables (i.e., the variances of F1–F4) are freely estimated,[7] and (c) residual variances of dependent observed variables (i.e., the error variances associated with each observed variable) are freely estimated. Due to defaults (b) and (c) noted here, no specifications for these parameters are needed, and therefore are not shown in the input file related to the CFA model in Figure 2.3.

That M*plus* makes no distinction in terminology between factor variance and residual variance can be confusing for new users. Furthermore, the fact that they are both estimated by default for continuous variables (as in this case) may exacerbate the situation. Thus, I consider it important to both clarify and emphasize the approach taken in this regard. Specifically, M*plus* distinguishes between these two types of variance based on their function in the model; that is, in terms of whether the variance parameter is associated with an independent or dependent variable in the model. If the former (i.e., there are no single-headed arrows pointing at it), then M*plus* considers the parameter to represent a factor variance. If, on the other hand, the parameter is associated with a dependent variable in the model (i.e., there is a single-headed arrow pointing at it), then M*plus* interprets the variance as representing residual variance. In short, factor variances are estimated for independent variables, whereas residual variances are estimated for dependent variables (see note 3).

Now that you have made the link in model specification between the graphical presentation of the model and its related program input file, let's return to a brief discussion of the two important concepts of model identification and latent variable scaling.

The Concept of Model Identification

Model identification is a complex topic that is difficult to explain in nontechnical terms. Although a thorough explanation of the identification principle exceeds the scope of the present book, it is not critical to the reader's understanding and use of the book. Nonetheless, because some insight into the general concept of the identification issue will undoubtedly help you to better understand why, for example, particular parameters are specified as having certain fixed values, I attempt now to give you a brief, nonmathematical explanation of the basic idea underlying this concept. However, I strongly encourage you to expand your knowledge of the topic via at least one or two of the following references. For a very clear and readable description of issues underlying the concept of model identification, I highly recommend the book chapter by MacCallum (1995) and monographs by Long (1983a, 1983b). For a more comprehensive treatment of the topic, I refer you to the following texts: Bollen (1989), Brown (2006), Kline (2011), and Little (in press). Finally, for an easy-to-read didactic overview of identification issues related mostly to exploratory factor analysis, see Hayashi and Marcoulides (2006); and for a more mathematical discussion pertinent to specific rules of identification, see Bollen and Davis (2009).

In broad terms, the issue of identification focuses on whether or not there is a unique set of parameters consistent with the data. This question bears directly on the transposition of the variance–covariance matrix of observed variables (the data) into the structural parameters of the model under study. If a unique solution for the values of the structural parameters can be found, the model is considered identified. As a consequence, the parameters are considered to be estimable, and the model therefore testable. If, on the other hand, a model cannot be identified, it indicates that the parameters are subject to arbitrariness, thereby implying that different parameter values define the same model; such being the case, attainment of consistent estimates for all parameters is not possible, and, thus, the model cannot be evaluated empirically. By way of a simple example, the process would be conceptually akin to trying to determine unique values for X and Y, when the only information you have is that $X + Y = 15$. Generalizing this example to covariance structure analysis, then, the model identification issue focuses on the extent to which a unique set of values can be inferred for the unknown parameters from a given covariance matrix of analyzed variables that is reproduced by the model.

Structural models may be just identified, overidentified, or underidentified. A *just-identified* model is one in which there is a one-to-one correspondence between the data and the structural parameters. That is to say, the number of data variances and covariances equals the number of parameters to be estimated. However, despite the capability of the model to yield a unique solution for all parameters, the just-identified model is not scientifically interesting because it has no degrees of freedom and therefore can never be rejected. An *overidentified* model is one in which the number of estimable parameters is less than the number of data points (i.e., variances and covariances of the observed variables). This situation results in positive degrees of freedom that allow for rejection of the model, thereby rendering it of scientific use. The aim in SEM, then, is to specify a model such that it meets the criterion of overidentification. Finally, an *underidentified* model is one in which the number of parameters to be estimated exceeds the number of variances and covariances (i.e., data points). As such, the model contains insufficient information (from the input data) for the purpose of attaining a determinate solution of parameter estimation; that is, an infinite number of solutions are possible for an underidentified model.

Reviewing the CFA model in Figure 2.3, let's now determine how many data points we have to work with (i.e., how much information do we have with respect to our data?). As noted above, these constitute the variances and covariances of the observed variables. Let's say we have p variables with which to work; the number of elements comprising the variance–covariance matrix will be p (p + 1) / 2. Given that there are 16 observed variables shown in Figure 2.3, this means that we have 16 (16 + 1) / 2 = 136 data points. In addition, however, because Mplus estimates the observed variable intercepts by default, the observed means also contribute to information upon which the analysis is based. Pertinent to this example, then, we add 16 means to this total, thereby giving us 152 (136 + 16) data points. Prior to this discussion of identification, we determined a total of 54 unknown parameters (including the intercepts). Thus, with 152 data points and 54 parameters to be estimated, we have an overidentified model with 98 degrees of freedom.

It is important to point out, however, that the specification of an overidentified model is a *necessary* but *not sufficient* condition to resolve the identification problem. Indeed, the imposition of constraints on particular parameters can sometimes be beneficial in helping the researcher to attain an overidentified model. An example of such a constraint is illustrated in Chapter 5 with the application of a second-order CFA model.

The Concept of Latent Variable Scaling

Linked to the issue of identification is the requirement that every latent variable have its scale determined. This requirement arises because latent variables are unobserved and therefore have no definite metric scale; this requirement can be accomplished in one of three ways. The first and most commonly applied approach is termed the *reference variable method*. This approach is tied to specification of the measurement model whereby the unmeasured latent variable is mapped onto its related observed indicator variable. This scaling requisite is satisfied by constraining to some non-zero value (typically 1.0), one factor-loading parameter in each congeneric set of loadings. This constraint holds for both independent and dependent latent variables in a model. In reviewing Figure 2.3, this means that, for one of the three regression paths leading from each Social Acceptance factor to a set of observed indicators, some fixed value should be specified; this fixed parameter is termed a *reference variable* (or *reference indicator*).

With respect to the model in Figure 2.3, for example, the scale has been established by constraining to a value of 1.0, the first parameter in each congeneric set of observed variables. Thus, there is no need to specify this constraint in the input file. However, should you wish instead to constrain another factor loading within the same congeneric set as the reference variable, the specified constraint would need to be included in the input file. This alternate specification is demonstrated in Chapters 5 and 10.

The second approach to establishing scale for latent variables is termed the *fixed factor method*. Using this procedure of scaling, the factor variances are constrained to 1.0. Should this be the preferred approach, then all factor loadings are freely estimated. These first two scale-setting approaches have generated some debate in the literature regarding the advantages and disadvantages of each (see, e.g., Gonzalez & Griffin, 2001; Little, Slegers, & Card, 2006). More recently, however, Little et al. (2006) have proposed a third approach, which they term the "effects coding" method. These authors posited that, of the three approaches, the latter is the only scale-setting constraint that both is nonarbitrary and provides a real scale. Regardless of the reported pros and cons related to these three scale-setting approaches, the reference variable method, at this point in time, is the procedure most widely used (Brown, 2006).

Now that you have a better idea of important aspects of the specification of a CFA model in general, specification using the Mplus program in particular, and the basic notions associated with model identification and latent variable scaling, let's move on to inspect the remaining two models to be reviewed in this chapter.

Example 2: A Second-Order CFA Model

This second example model, shown in Figure 2.4, supports the notion that one's sense of humor, trustworthiness, sociability, and emotional stability are influenced by some higher order global construct, which we might term *self-perceived social competence*. Thus, although the first-order structure of this model remains basically the same as in Figure 2.3, there are four important differential features that need to be noted. First, in contrast to the first-order CFA example in which only regression paths between the observed variables and their related underlying factors are specified, this second-order model also includes regression paths between these first-order factors and the higher order factor. Specifically, these parameters represent the impact of $F5$ (an independent variable in the model) on $F1$, $F2$, $F3$, and $F4$. Second, consistent with the first-order CFA structure, whereby one factor loading from each congeneric set of indicator variables was constrained to 1.0 for purposes of model identification and latent variable scaling, so too this concern needs to be addressed at the

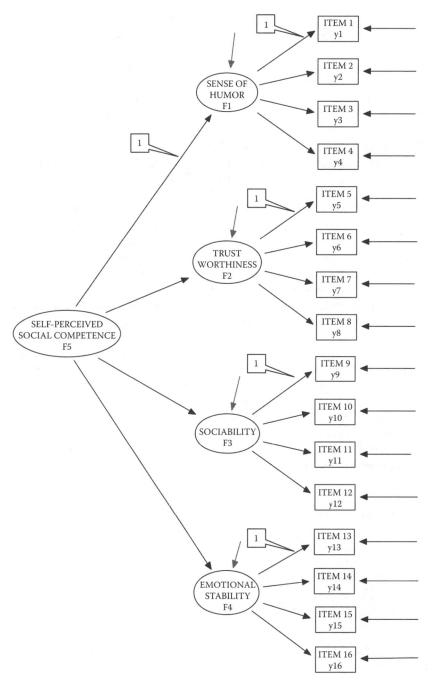

Figure 2.4. Hypothesized second-order CFA model.

higher order level. Once again, by default, M*plus* automatically fixes the value of the first higher order factor loading to a value of 1.0, as shown in the callout in Figure 2.4. More typically, however, researchers tend to fix the variance of the higher order factor to 1.0, rather than one of the higher order loadings, as estimation of the factor loadings is of more interest. Again, this alternate specification is demonstrated in Chapter 5. Third, given that SELF-PERCEIVED SOCIAL COMPETENCE is hypothesized to cause each of the four first-order factors, *F1* through *F4* now represent dependent variables in the model. Accordingly, SENSE OF HUMOR, TRUSTWORTHINESS, SOCIABILITY, and EMOTIONAL STABILITY are hypothesized as being predicted from self-perceived social competence, but with some degree of error, which is captured by the residual term, as indicated in Figure 2.4 by the single-headed arrow pointing toward each of these four factors. Finally, in second-order models, any covariance among the first-order factors is presumed to be explained by the higher order factor(s). Thus, note the absence of double-headed arrows linking the four first-order factors in the path diagram.

Turning now to the M*plus* input file pertinent to this higher order model, the only difference between this specification and the one for the first-order CFA model is the added statement of "*F5* by *F1–F4*." This statement, of course, indicates that *F1* through *F4* are regressed onto the higher order factor, *F5*. Importantly, with one exception, the M*plus* defaults noted for Figure 2.3 also hold for Figure 2.4. The one differing default relates to the factor variances for *F1* through *F4*, which now are not estimated. More specifically, given that in this second-order model, *F5* (Social Competence) is postulated to "cause" the first-order factors (*F1–F4*), these four factors are now dependent variables in the model. As a consequence, this specification triggers M*plus* to estimate their residuals by default, thereby negating any need to include their specification in the input file.

TITLE: Example 2ⁿᵈ-order CFA Input File (Figure 2.4)
DATA:
        FILE IS "C:\Mplus\Files\Example 2.dat";
VARIABLE:
        NAMES ARE ITEM1 – ITEM16;
MODEL:
F1 by ITEM1 – ITEM4;
F2 by ITEM5 – ITEM8;
F3 by ITEM9 – ITEM12;
F4 by ITEM13 – ITEM16;
F5 by F1–F4;

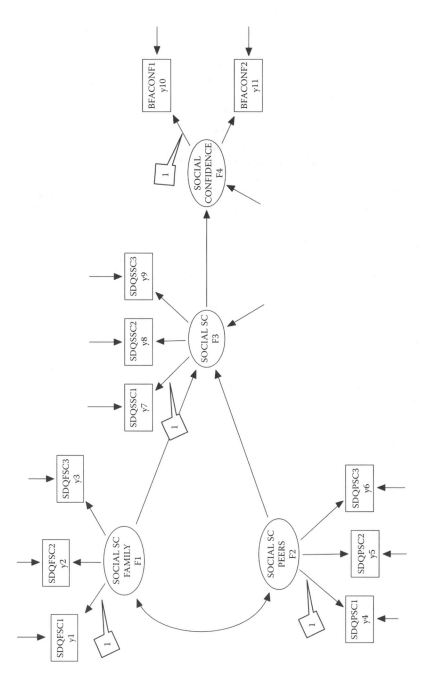

Figure 2.5. Hypothesized full structural equation model.

Example 3: A Full Structural Equation Model

The path diagram shown in Figure 2.5, considered within the context of an adolescent population, postulates that one's social self-concept (SC), in general, is influenced by two more specific-type SCs: social SC as it relates to the family and social SC as it relates to peers. (General) social SC, in turn, is postulated to predict one's sense of social confidence. In reviewing this full SEM model, shown in Figure 2.5, I wish to draw your attention to three particular specifications. First, note that, of the four factors comprising this model, only *F1* and *F2* are independent variables in the model (i.e., they have no single-headed arrows pointing at them); all other factors operate as dependent variables in the model. Thus, only the variances for *F1* and *F2*, together with their covariance (indicated by the double-headed arrow), are freely estimated parameters in the model. Second, as with the second-order model shown in Figure 2.4, here again we have regression equations involving two factors. In the present case, equations are specified for *F3* and *F4* only, as each is explained by other factors in the model. More specifically, *F1* and *F2* are hypothesized to predict *F3*, which in turn predicts *F4*. Third, given the dependent variable status of *F3* and *F4* in the model, note the presence of their residual variances, represented by the short single-headed arrows pointing toward each of these factors. Finally, it is worth noting that, although Factor 3 would appear to operate as both an independent and a dependent variable in the model, this is not so. Once a variable is defined as a dependent variable in a model, it maintains that designation throughout all analyses bearing on the hypothesized model.

Let's look now at this final example of an *Mplus* input file:

TITLE: Example Full SEM Model (Figure 2.5)
DATA:
    FILE IS "C:\Mplus\Files\Example 3.dat";
VARIABLE:
    NAMES ARE SDQFSC1 – BFACONF2;
MODEL:
F1 by SDQFSC1 – SDQFSC3;
F2 by SDQPSC1 – SDQPSC3;
F3 by SDQSSC1 – SDQSSC3;
F4 by BFACONF1 – BFACONF2;
F4 on F3;
F3 on F1 F2;

Three aspects of this input file are worthy of elaboration here. First, turning to the MODEL command, we look first at the measurement portion of the model. Accordingly, "F1 by SDQFSC1–SDQFSC3" indicates that *F1* is measured by three observed variables—*SDQFSC1* through *SDQFSC3*; likewise, this pattern follows for the next three specifications, albeit *F4* is measured by only two observed measures. Third, the structural portion of the model is described by the last two lines of input. The specification "F4 on F3" states that *F4* is regressed on *F3*; likewise, the statement "F3 on F1, F2" advises that *F3* is regressed on both *F1* and *F2*. Finally, the defaults noted earlier for the other two models likewise hold for this full SEM model. That is, (a) the first factor loading of each congeneric set of indicator variables is constrained to 1.0, (b) the factor variances for *F1* and *F2* are freely estimated, (c) the factor covariance between *F1* and *F2* is freely estimated, (d) residual variances associated with the observed variables are freely estimated, and (e) residual variances associated with *F3* and *F4* are freely estimated. Thus, specification regarding these parameters is not included in the input file.

Overview of Remaining Chapters

Thus far, I have introduced you to the bricks and mortar of SEM applications using the M*plus* program. As such, you have learned the basics regarding the (a) concepts underlying SEM procedures, (b) components of the CFA and full SEM models, (c) elements and structure of the M*plus* program, (d) creation of M*plus* input files, and (e) major program defaults related to the estimation of parameters. Now it's time to see how these bricks and mortar can be combined to build a variety of other SEM models. The remainder of this book, then, is directed toward helping you understand the application and interpretation of a variety of CFA and full SEM models using the M*plus* program.

In presenting these applications from the literature, I have tried to address the diverse needs of my readers by including a potpourri of basic models and M*plus* setups. All data related to these applications are included at the publisher's website http://www.psypress.com/sem-with-mplus. Given that personal experience is always the best teacher, I encourage you to work through these applications on your own computer. Taken together, the applications presented in the next 10 chapters should provide you with a comprehensive understanding of how M*plus* can be used to analyze a variety of structural equation models. Let's move on, then, to the remaining chapters, where we explore the analytic processes involved in SEM using M*plus*.

Notes

1. The terms *independent* and *dependent* will be used throughout the remainder of the book.
2. Importantly, if the data file resides in the same folder as the input file(s) for which it will be used, it is not necessary to specify the path string.
3. It is important to note that in order to activate the language generator, you must first indicate to the program that you are creating a new file. This is accomplished by clicking on the "FILE" tab and selecting the "NEW" option.
4. The labeling of *y1*, of course, presumes that it is the first variable in the data set. If, on the other hand, it had been the fifth variable in the data set, it would rightfully be labeled *y5*.
5. In M*plus*, these parameters are automatically fixed to 1.0 by default. That is, if you intend the first factor loading in each set to be fixed to 1.0, there is no need to specify this constraint.
6. A set of measures is said to be *congeneric* if each measure in the set purports to assess the same construct, except for errors of measurement (Jöreskog, 1971a). For example, as indicated in Figure 2.3, ITEM1, ITEM2, ITEM3, and ITEM4 all serve as measures of the factor SENSE OF HUMOR; they therefore represent a congeneric set of indicator variables.
7. An important tenet in SEM is that variances and covariances of only independent variables in the model (in the SEM sense) are eligible to be freely estimated.

section II

Single-Group Analyses

Confirmatory Factor Analytic Models

The Full Latent Variable Model

chapter 3

Testing the Factorial Validity of a Theoretical Construct
First-Order Confirmatory Factor Analysis Model

Our first application examines a first-order confirmatory factor analysis (CFA) model designed to test the multidimensionality of a theoretical construct. Specifically, this application tests the hypothesis that self-concept (SC), for early adolescents (grade 7), is a multidimensional construct composed of four factors—General SC (GSC), Academic SC (ASC), English SC (ESC), and Mathematics SC (MSC). The theoretical underpinning of this hypothesis derives from the hierarchical model of SC proposed by Shavelson, Hubner, and Stanton (1976). The example is taken from a study by Byrne and Worth Gavin (1996) in which four hypotheses related to the Shavelson et al. model were tested for three groups of children—preadolescents (grade 3), early adolescents (grade 7), and late adolescents (grade 11). Only tests bearing on the multidimensional structure of SC, as it relates to grade 7 children, are relevant in the present chapter. This study followed from earlier work in which the same four-factor structure of SC was tested for adolescents (see Byrne & Shavelson, 1986) and was part of a larger study that focused on the structure of social SC (Byrne & Shavelson, 1996). For a more extensive discussion of the substantive issues and the related findings, readers should refer to the original Byrne and Worth Gavin article.

The Hypothesized Model

In this first application, the inquiry focuses on the plausibility of a multidimensional SC structure for early adolescents. Although such dimensionality of the construct has been supported by numerous studies for grade 7 children, others have counterargued that SC is less differentiated for children in their pre- and early adolescent years (e.g., Harter, 1990). Thus, the argument could be made for a two-factor structure comprising only GSC and ASC. Still others postulate that SC is a unidimensional structure, with all SC facets embodied within a single SC construct (GSC).

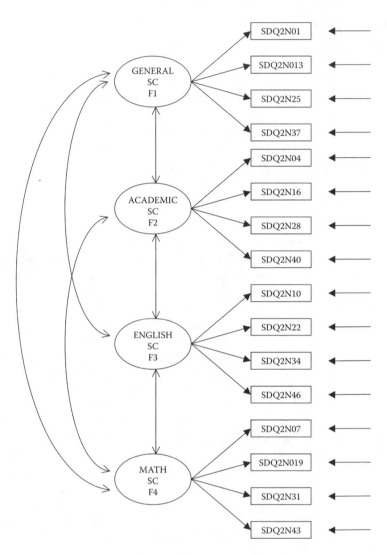

Figure 3.1. Hypothesized four-factor CFA model of self-concept.

(For a review of the literature related to these issues, see Byrne, 1996.) The task presented to us here, then, is to test the original hypothesis that SC is a four-factor structure comprising a general component (GSC), an academic component (ASC), and two subject-specific components (ESC and MSC), against two alternative hypotheses: (a) that SC is a two-factor structure comprising GSC and ASC, and (b) that SC is a one-factor structure in which there is no distinction between general and academic SCs.

We turn now to an examination and testing of each of these hypotheses.

Hypothesis 1: Self-Concept Is a Four-Factor Structure

The model to be tested in Hypothesis 1 postulates a priori that SC is a four-factor structure composed of General SC (GSC), Academic SC (ASC), English SC (ESC), and Math SC (MSC); it is presented schematically in Figure 3.1.

Before any discussion of how we might go about testing this model, let's take a few minutes first to dissect the model and list its component parts as follows:

- There are four SC factors, as indicated by the four ovals labeled General SC, Academic SC, English SC, and Math SC.
- The four factors are correlated, as indicated by the two-headed arrows.
- There are 16 observed variables, as indicated by the 16 rectangles (*SDQ2N01* through *SDQ2N43*); they represent item pairs[1] from the General, Academic, Verbal, and Math SC subscales of the Self-Description Questionnaire II (SDQ2; Marsh, 1992).
- The observed variables load on the factors in the following pattern: *SDQ2N01* to *SDQ2N37* load on Factor 1, *SDQ3N04* to *SDQ2N40* load on Factor 2, *SDQ2N10* to *SDQ2N46* load on Factor 3, and *SDQ2N07* to *SDQ2N42* load on Factor 4.
- Each observed variable loads on one and only one factor.
- Residuals associated with each observed variable are uncorrelated.

Summarizing these observations, we can now present a more formal description of our hypothesized model. As such, we state that the CFA model presented in Figure 3.1 hypothesizes a priori that

1. SC responses can be explained by four factors: General SC, Academic SC, English SC, and Math SC;
2. each item-pair measure has a nonzero loading on the SC factor that it was designed to measure (termed a *target loading*) and a zero loading on all other factors (termed *nontarget loadings*);
3. the four SC factors, consistent with the theory, are correlated; and
4. residual errors associated with each measure are uncorrelated.

Another way of conceptualizing the hypothesized model in Figure 3.1 is within a matrix framework as presented in Table 3.1. Thinking about the model components in this format can be very helpful because it is consistent with the manner by which the results from structural equation modeling (SEM) analyses are commonly reported in program output files. The tabular representation of our model in Table 3.1 shows the pattern of parameters to be estimated within the framework of three matrices:

Table 3.1 Pattern of Estimated Parameters for Hypothesized Four-Factor Model

Factor-Loading Matrix

Observed Variables	Factors			
	GSC (F1)	ASC (F2)	ESC (F3)	MSC (F4)
SDQ2N01	1.0[a]	0.0	0.0	0.0
SDQ2N13	#[b]	0.0	0.0	0.0
SDQ2N25	#	0.0	0.0	0.0
SDQ2N37	#	0.0	0.0	0.0
SDQ2N04	0.0[c]	1.0	0.0	0.0
SDQ2N16	0.0	#	0.0	0.0
SDQ2N28	0.0	#	0.0	0.0
SDQ2N40	0.0	#	0.0	0.0
SDQ2N10	0.0	0.0	1.0	0.0
SDQ2N22	0.0	0.0	#	0.0
SDQ2N34	0.0	0.0	#	0.0
SDQ2N46	0.0	0.0	#	0.0
SDQ2N07	0.0	0.0	0.0	1.0
SDQ2N19	0.0	0.0	0.0	#
SDQ2N31	0.0	0.0	0.0	#
SDQ2N43	0.0	0.0	0.0	#

Factor Variance–Covariance Matrix

GSC	#			
ASC	#	#		
ESC	#	#	#	
MSC	#	#	#	#

Error Variance–Covariance Matrix

SDQ2N01 (y25)	#															
SDQ2N13 (y26)	0.0	#														
SDQ2N25 (y27)	0.0	0.0	#													
SDQ2N37 (y28)	0.0	0.0	0.0	#												
SDQ2N04 (y29)	0.0	0.0	0.0	0.0	#											
SDQ2N16 (y30)	0.0	0.0	0.0	0.0	0.0	#										
SDQ2N28 (y31)	0.0	0.0	0.0	0.0	0.0	0.0	#									
SDQ2N40 (y32)	0.0	0.0	0.0	0.0	0.0	0.0	0.0	#								
SDQ2N10 (y33)	0.0	0.0	0.0	0.0	0.0	0.0	0.0	0.0	#							
SDQ2N22 (y34)	0.0	0.0	0.0	0.0	0.0	0.0	0.0	0.0	0.0	#						
SDQ2N34 (y35)	0.0	0.0	0.0	0.0	0.0	0.0	0.0	0.0	0.0	0.0	#					
SDQ2N46 (y36)	0.0	0.0	0.0	0.0	0.0	0.0	0.0	0.0	0.0	0.0	0.0	#				
SDQ2N07 (y37)	0.0	0.0	0.0	0.0	0.0	0.0	0.0	0.0	0.0	0.0	0.0	0.0	#			
SDQ2N19 (y38)	0.0	0.0	0.0	0.0	0.0	0.0	0.0	0.0	0.0	0.0	0.0	0.0	0.0	#		
SDQ2N31 (y39)	0.0	0.0	0.0	0.0	0.0	0.0	0.0	0.0	0.0	0.0	0.0	0.0	0.0	0.0	#	
SDQ2N43 (y40)	0.0	0.0	0.0	0.0	0.0	0.0	0.0	0.0	0.0	0.0	0.0	0.0	0.0	0.0	0.0	#

[a] Parameter fixed to 1.0.
[b] Parameter to be estimated.
[c] Parameter fixed to 0.0.

the factor-loading matrix, the factor variance–covariance matrix, and the residual variance–covariance matrix. In statistical language, these parameter arrays are termed the *lambda*, *psi*, and *theta* matrices, respectively. We will revisit these matrices later in the chapter in discussion of the TECH1 Output option.

For purposes of model identification and latent variable scaling (see Chapter 2), you will note that the first of each congeneric set (see Chapter 2, note 2) of SC measures in the factor-loading matrix is set to 1.0, which you may recall is default in M*plus*; all other parameters are freely estimated (as represented by the pound sign: #). Likewise, as indicated in the factor variance–covariance matrix, all parameters are freely estimated. Finally, in the residual variance–covariance matrix, only the residual variances are estimated; all residual covariances are presumed to be zero.

Provided with these two views of this hypothesized four-factor model, let's now move on to the testing of this model. We begin, of course, by structuring an input file that fully describes the model to M*plus*.

Mplus Input File Specification and Output File Results

Input File Specification

In Chapter 2, I advised you of the M*plus* language generator and provided a brief description of its function and limitations, together with an illustration of how this facility can be accessed. In this first application, I now wish to illustrate how to use this valuable feature by walking you through the steps involved in structuring the input file related to Figure 3.1. Following from the language generator menu shown in Figure 2.2, we begin by clicking on the SEM option as illustrated in Figure 3.2.

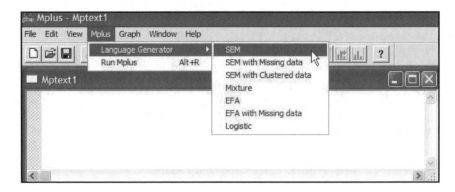

Figure 3.2. M*plus* language generator: Selecting category of analytic model.

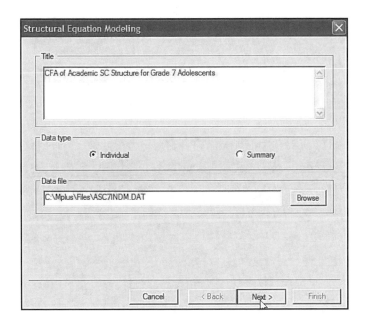

Figure 3.3. M*plus* language generator: Specification of title and location of data.

Once you click on the SEM option, you will be presented with the dialog box shown in Figure 3.3. Here I have entered a title for the model to be tested (see Figure 3.1), indicated that the data represent individual scores, and provided the location of the data file on my computer. The Browse button simplifies this task.

The next dialog box presented to you (see Figure 3.4) requests information related to the data: (a) whether they are in free or fixed format and, if the latter, specifics of the Fortran statement format state; and (b) if there are any missing data. The data to be used in this application (ascindm.dat) are in fixed format as noted, and the format statement is 40F1.0, X, 6F2.0. This expression tells the program to read 40 single-digit numbers, to skip one column, and then to read six double-digit numbers. The first 40 columns represent item scores on the Self-Perception Profile for Children (SPPC; not used in the present study) and the SDQ2; the remaining six scores represent scores for the *MASTENG1* through *SMAT1* variables (not used in the present study). Finally, we note that there are no missing data.

The next three dialog boxes (Figures 3.5, 3.6, and 3.7) focus on the variable names. The first dialog box, shown in Figure 3.5, requests the names of all variables in the entire data set. Here you can see that they are first entered and then added to the list one at a time. In the dialog box shown in Figure 3.6, you are asked to specify which variables will actually be used in the analyses. Shown on the left side of this dialog box, you can see that I have

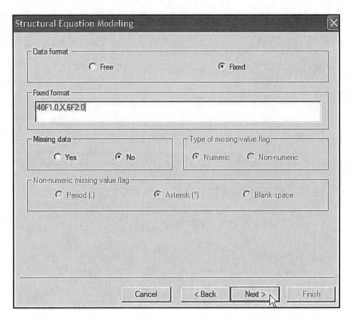

Figure 3.4. M*plus* language generator: Specification of fixed format for data.

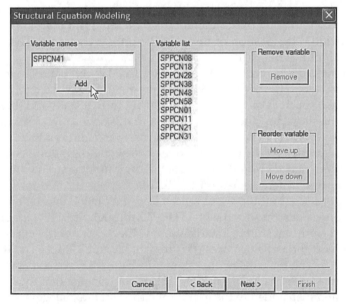

Figure 3.5. M*plus* language generator: Specification and adding all observed variables in the data to the variable list.

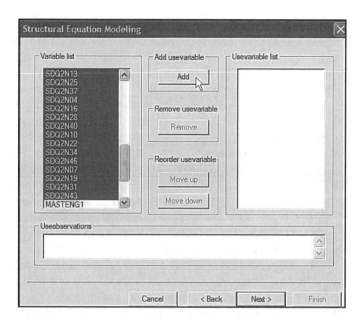

Figure 3.6. M*plus* language generator: Selected observed variables to be used in the analyses.

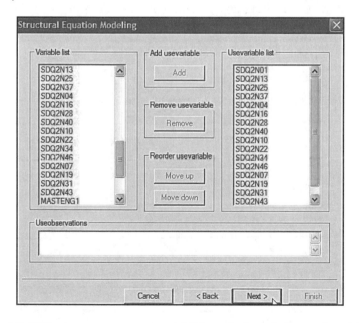

Figure 3.7. M*plus* language generator: Addition of selected observed variables to the usevariable list.

blocked this specific set of variables, which is now ready for transfer over to the Usevariable List. Finally, Figure 3.7 shows the completion of this process.

The next two dialog boxes, in the present instance, do not require any additional input information; nonetheless, it is important that I show them to you in the interest of your own work in the future. The dialog box shown in Figure 3.8 provides the opportunity of specifying (a) a grouping variable, which is not applicable to the present analyses; (b) a weight variable, which is not applicable; and (c) existing categorical variables; all variables in the present data set are of continuous scale. The dialog box shown in Figure 3.9 allows for analyses based on Mean Structures or of a summative nature, as provided by the Basic option. However, it is important to note that, beginning with Mplus 5, MEANSTRUCTURE is default and the option is now NOMEANSTRUCTURE. Our analyses are categorized as the General type, which, as noted in Chapter 2, is default. Models that can be estimated in this category include regression analysis, path analysis, CFA, SEM, latent growth curve modeling, discrete-time survival analysis, and continuous-time survival analysis. Review of the middle section of this dialog box indicates that the estimator to be used in testing our hypothesized model is that of maximum likelihood (ML), which, again, is the default. Finally, the criteria for termination are automatically entered by the program, again by default.

The dialog box shown in Figure 3.10 shows the output options available to you when the language generator is used. For purposes of this first

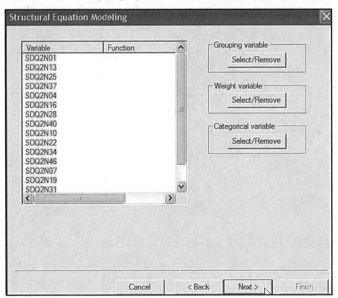

Figure 3.8. Mplus language generator: Dialog box showing additional options if needed.

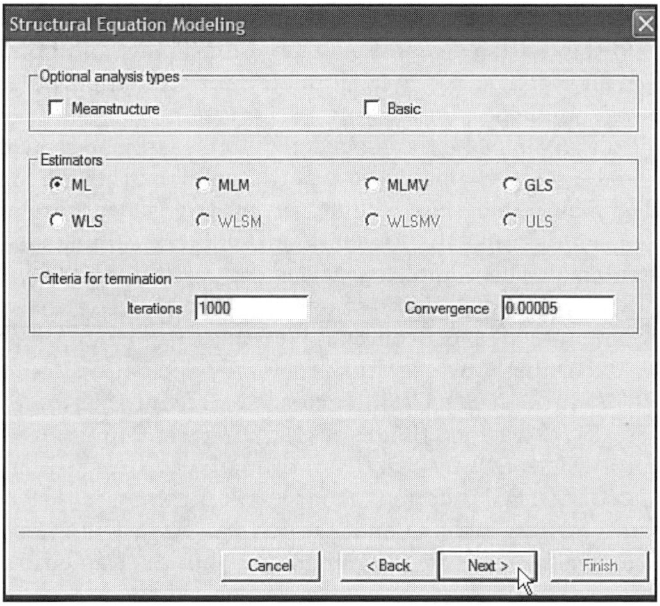

Figure 3.9. M*plus* language generator: Dialog box showing default ML estimator.

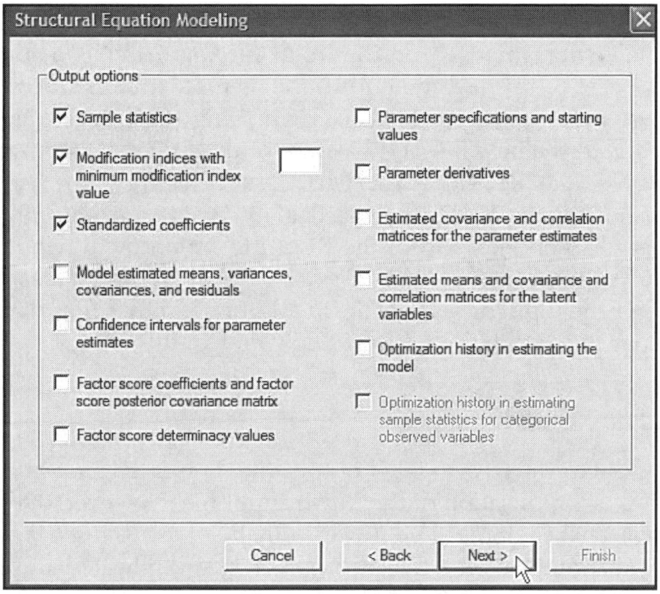

Figure 3.10. M*plus* language generator: Dialog box showing selected output options.

application, I have selected only three: sample statistics, modifications indices, and standardized coefficients. Of course, other additional output options can always be added to the input file after the language-generated file has been completed.

The next two dialog boxes associated with the language generator display the final input file, albeit only a portion of it is visible in Figure 3.11 because the main dialog box includes an overlay dialog box cautioning that statements defining the MODEL and DEFINE commands must be added separately. The completed M*plus* input file describing the CFA model shown in Figure 3.1 is presented in Figure 3.12. As you will note, I have added the MODEL command to the final language-generated input file. Accordingly, we see that Factor 1 (General SC) is measured by *SDQ2N01* through *SDQ2N37*, Factor 2 (Academic SC) by *SDQ2N04* through *SDQ2N40*, Factor 3 (English SC) by *SDQ2N10* through *SDQ2N46*, and Factor 4 (Math SC) by *SDQ2N07* through *SDQ2N43*. In addition, I have included the TECH1 option to the OUTPUT command as it replicates the pattern shown in Table 3.1 and, as such, can be instructive in helping you to visualize the estimated parameters within the framework of their matrices.

Now that we have finalized the input file, we are ready to execute the job and have M*plus* perform the analysis. Figure 3.13 illustrates how easy this process is. Simply click on the M*plus* tab, which will release the drop-down menu; then click on Run M*plus*. Once the analysis is completed (typically in only a few seconds), the file is saved as an output file and is immediately superimposed on the input file; the latter is automatically saved as mptext1.inp, and the output file as mptext1.out. Of course, you can change these labels to suit your own filing preferences. Figure 3.14 illustrates both the labeling and location of these files. As you will see, I have relabeled the file as CFA.asc7F4i. As such, the input file has an ".inp extension," whereas the output file has an ".out extension." To retrieve these files, click on File, and in the resulting drop-down menu, click on Open. By clicking on the arrow associated with types of files, you can select either the input or output file, in addition to other files that may be listed under this particular folder (titled Chp 3 in the present case).

Output File Results

We turn now to the CFA.asc7F4i output file. Presented first in all M*plus* output files is a replication of the M*plus* input file. However, due to space restrictions, I have not repeated this information here (but see Figure 3.12). Initially, you might query the purpose of this duplicated information. However, this feature can be a valuable one in the event that you are presented with an error message related to your analysis, as it enables you to

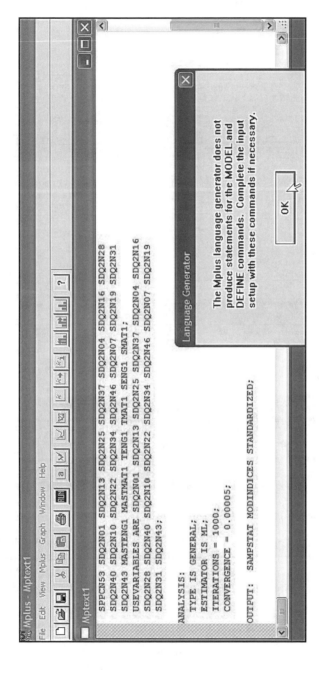

Figure 3.11. *Mplus* language generator: Partially completed input file showing pop-up caveat regarding MODEL and DEFINE commands.

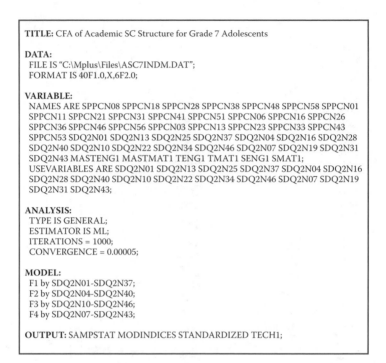

TITLE: CFA of Academic SC Structure for Grade 7 Adolescents

DATA:
FILE IS "C:\Mplus\Files\ASC7INDM.DAT";
FORMAT IS 40F1.0,X,6F2.0;

VARIABLE:
NAMES ARE SPPCN08 SPPCN18 SPPCN28 SPPCN38 SPPCN48 SPPCN58 SPPCN01
SPPCN11 SPPCN21 SPPCN31 SPPCN41 SPPCN51 SPPCN06 SPPCN16 SPPCN26
SPPCN36 SPPCN46 SPPCN56 SPPCN03 SPPCN13 SPPCN23 SPPCN33 SPPCN43
SPPCN53 SDQ2N01 SDQ2N13 SDQ2N25 SDQ2N37 SDQ2N04 SDQ2N16 SDQ2N28
SDQ2N40 SDQ2N10 SDQ2N22 SDQ2N34 SDQ2N46 SDQ2N07 SDQ2N19 SDQ2N31
SDQ2N43 MASTENG1 MASTMAT1 TENG1 TMAT1 SENG1 SMAT1;
USEVARIABLES ARE SDQ2N01 SDQ2N13 SDQ2N25 SDQ2N37 SDQ2N04 SDQ2N16
SDQ2N28 SDQ2N40 SDQ2N10 SDQ2N22 SDQ2N34 SDQ2N46 SDQ2N07 SDQ2N19
SDQ2N31 SDQ2N43;

ANALYSIS:
TYPE IS GENERAL;
ESTIMATOR IS ML;
ITERATIONS = 1000;
CONVERGENCE = 0.00005;

MODEL:
F1 by SDQ2N01-SDQ2N37;
F2 by SDQ2N04-SDQ2N40;
F3 by SDQ2N10-SDQ2N46;
F4 by SDQ2N07-SDQ2N43;

OUTPUT: SAMPSTAT MODINDICES STANDARDIZED TECH1;

Figure 3.12. M*plus* language generator: Completed input file for hypothesized four-factor model.

Figure 3.13. Executing the M*plus* input file for analysis.

quickly check your specification of a model without having to switch to the original input file. I now present the remaining output material within the context of three blocks of information: "Summary of Model and Analysis Specifications," "Model Assessment," and "Model Misspecification."

Summary of Model and Analysis Specifications

In Table 3.2, you will see a summary of model specifications related to Figure 3.1. Essentially, with exception of the first vector NU, Table 3.2 is

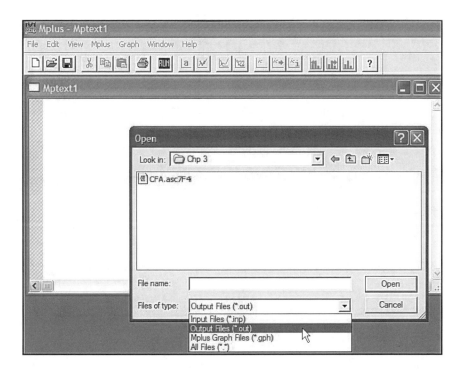

Figure 3.14. Dialog box showing selection and opening of the M*plus* output file.

analogous to Table 3.1 in that it details the pattern of fixed versus estimated parameters in the model. This information results from inclusion
of the TECH1 option in the OUTPUT command. Accordingly, this option
displays, in matrix format, all freely estimated parameters with the assignment of a numeral to each. Although this option also yields start values
for each of these parameters, they are not included here in the interest
of space restrictions. It is important for you to know that, under normal
circumstances, the location of these TECH1 results in the output file will
follow those for the modification indices. However, for my purposes in
helping you to understand both the concepts of SEM and the M*plus* program, I prefer to show you these arrays first as I believe they can serve
importantly in helping you to formulate a mental picture of each parameter housed within its own particular matrix.

There are at least two important aspects of these TECH1 results that I
wish to highlight for you. First, associated with each matrix and/or vector,
you will observe a label bearing a Greek matrix label. These matrices and
vectors are grounded in SEM theory and thus are consistently recognized
across all SEM software programs. To the best of my knowledge, however,
only the LISREL and M*plus* programs explicitly display these parameter

Table 3.2 M*plus* Output: Summary of Model Specifications

	Technical 1 Output: Parameter Specification			
			NU		
	SDQ2N01	SDQ2N13	SDQ2N25	SDQ2N37	SDQ2N04
1	1	2	3	4	5

			NU		
	SDQ2N16	SDQ2N28	SDQ2N40	SDQ2N10	SDQ2N22
1	6	7	8	9	10

			NU		
	SDQ2N34	SDQ2N46	SDQ2N07	SDQ2N19	SDQ2N31
1	11	12	13	14	15

			NU	
	SDQ2N43			
1	16			

			LAMBDA	
	F1	F2	F3	F4
SDQ2N01	0	0	0	0
SDQ2N13	17	0	0	0
SDQ2N25	18	0	0	0
SDQ2N37	19	0	0	0
SDQ2N04	0	0	0	0
SDQ2N16	0	20	0	0
SDQ2N28	0	21	0	0
SDQ2N40	0	22	0	0
SDQ2N10	0	0	0	0
SDQ2N22	0	0	23	0
SDQ2N34	0	0	24	0
SDQ2N46	0	0	25	0
SDQ2N07	0	0	0	0
SDQ2N19	0	0	0	26
SDQ2N31	0	0	0	27
SDQ2N43	0	0	0	28

Table 3.2 M*plus* Output: Summary of Model Specifications (*continued*)

	THETA				
	SDQ2N01	SDQ2N13	SDQ2N25	SDQ2N37	SDQ2N04
DQ2N01	29				
SDQ2N13	0	30			
SDQ2N25	0	0	31		
SDQ2N37	0	0	0	32	
SDQ2N04	0	0	0	0	33
SDQ2N16	0	0	0	0	0
SDQ2N28	0	0	0	0	0
SDQ2N40	0	0	0	0	0
SDQ2N10	0	0	0	0	0
SDQ2N22	0	0	0	0	0
SDQ2N34	0	0	0	0	0
SDQ2N46	0	0	0	0	0
SDQ2N07	0	0	0	0	0
SDQ2N19	0	0	0	0	0
SDQ2N31	0	0	0	0	0
SDQ2N43	0	0	0	0	0

	THETA				
	SDQ2N16	SDQ2N28	SDQ2N40	SDQ2N10	SDQ2N22
SDQ2N16	34				
SDQ2N28	0	35			
SDQ2N40	0	0	36		
SDQ2N10	0	0	0	37	
SDQ2N22	0	0	0	0	38
SDQ2N34	0	0	0	0	0
SDQ2N46	0	0	0	0	0
SDQ2N07	0	0	0	0	0
SDQ2N19	0	0	0	0	0
SDQ2N31	0	0	0	0	0
SDQ2N43	0	0	0	0	0

Table 3.2 Mplus Output: Summary of Model Specifications (*continued*)

	THETA				
	SDQ2N34	SDQ2N46	SDQ2N07	SDQ2N19	SDQ2N31
SDQ2N34	39				
SDQ2N46	0	40			
SDQ2N07	0	0	41		
SDQ2N19	0	0	0	42	
SDQ2N31	0	0	0	0	43
SDQ2N43	0	0	0	0	0

	THETA
	SDQ2N43
SDQ2N43	44

	PSI			
	F1	F2	F3	F4
F1	45			
F2	46	47		
F3	48	49	50	
F4	51	52	53	54

arrays in this manner. Indeed, knowledge of these matrices is critical in using LISREL, as its syntax is matrix based.[2] In Table 3.2, only one vector (NU) and three matrices (LAMBDA, THETA, and PSI) are shown as only these are relevant to the model under test in this chapter. Parameters in the NU vector represent the intercepts of continuous observed variables (in the present case, the item pair scores). The LAMBDA matrix reflects the pattern of factor loadings and, as such, is consistent with the first matrix shown in Table 3.1. In this regard, note in Table 3.2 that the first parameter of each congeneric set of observed indicator variables (e.g., *SDQ2N01, SDQ2N04, SDQ2N10,* and *SDQ2N07*) has an assigned 0 rather than a numeral, thereby indicating that it is a fixed parameter and thus is not estimated. The THETA matrix represents the residuals. As in Table 3.1, these estimated parameters appear on the outside diagonal as only estimates for the variances of these parameters are of interest; no residual covariances are specified, thus these parameters remain fixed to zero. Finally, the PSI matrix represents the variances and covariances of the continuous latent variables, in other words, the factor variances and covariances as specified in Figure 3.1.

Second, the number assigned to each of the parameters shown in Table 3.2 serves three important purposes: (a) to identify, in error messages, the parameter likely to be the source of difficulty with issues related to nonidentification and other such problems; (b) to enable you to determine if all estimated parameters were specified correctly and, if not, to identify in which matrix the error occurred; and (c) to provide you with easy access to the number of parameters to be estimated. With respect to this latter point, I need to alert you to one very important aspect of the numbered parameters shown in Table 3.2. Specifically, you will note that the total number of parameters to be estimated is shown to be 54 (see the PSI matrix). However, in reviewing Figure 3.1, we see that the number of parameters to be estimated is 12 factor loadings, 16 observed variable residual variances, 4 factor variances, and 6 factor covariances, which equals 38 and *not* 54. Why this discrepancy? The answer lies in the fact that, by default, as discussed in Chapter 2, M*plus* always includes observed variable intercepts in the model. However, if there is no structure on these parameters (i.e., they are not specified in the model), the program ignores these parameters.

Let's move on now to the next two sets of information provided in the output file. The first of these (see Table 3.3) provides a summary of the analysis specifications, and the second (see Table 3.4) reports the sample statistics as requested in the OUTPUT command, in addition to portions of both the sample covariance and correlation matrices. Turning first to Table 3.3, we see that the input file was properly structured, and, as a result, the program encountered no difficulties in reading the model specifications and other related input information. The summary information here reports the number of groups to be one and the number of cases to be 265. With respect to the model, we are advised that there are 16 dependent variables (the observed item pair scores) and 4 continuous latent variables (i.e., the factors), all of which are subsequently identified below. Finally, we note that (a) maximum likelihood was used to estimate the parameters, and (b) the name of the data file and its related input data format. The importance of this summary information is that it assures you that the program has interpreted the input instructions and read the data appropriately.

The sample statistics are reported in Table 3.4. Unfortunately, however, M*plus* reports only the observed variable means (i.e., the intercepts), and not the full range of univariate and multivariate descriptive statistics when this option is requested. These values are for information only, given that these parameters are not of interest with respect to this application. Included in this table also, although in substantially abbreviated form, is a portion of the sample covariance and correlation matrices. I include this material solely to familiarize you with the structure of the M*plus* output file.

Table 3.3 M*plus* Output: Summary of Analysis Specifications

Input Reading Terminated Normally

CFA of Academic Self-Concept structure—Grade 7
"ASC7F4I"

Summary of Analysis	
Number of groups	1
Number of observations	265
Number of dependent variables	16
Number of independent variables	0
Number of continuous latent variables	4

Observed Dependent Variables

Continuous

SDQ2N01	SDQ2N13	SDQ2N25	SDQ2N37	SDQ2N04	SDQ2N16
SDQ2N28	SDQ2N40	SDQ2N10	SDQ2N22	SDQ2N34	SDQ2N46
SDQ2N07	SDQ2N19	SDQ2N31	SDQ2N43		

Continuous Latent Variables

F1	F2	F3	F4

Estimator	ML
Information matrix	OBSERVED
Maximum number of iterations	1000
Convergence criterion	0.500D-04
Maximum number of steepest descent iterations	20

Input data file(s)
C:\Mplus\Files\Books\Chap3\ASC7INDM.DAT
Input data format
(40F1.0,X,6F2.0)

Table 3.4 M*plus* Output: Sample Statistics

Sample Statistics				
Means				
SDQ2N01	SDQ2N13	SDQ2N25	SDQ2N37	SDQ2N04
4.408	5.004	5.098	4.826	4.521
Means				
SDQ2N16	SDQ2N28	SDQ2N40	SDQ2N10	SDQ2N22
4.649	4.691	4.977	4.623	5.377

Table 3.4 M*plus* Output: Sample Statistics (*continued*)

Means				
SDQ2N34	SDQ2N46	SDQ2N07	SDQ2N19	SDQ2N31
3.891	5.268	4.321	4.543	4.740

Means
SDQ2N43
4.977

Covariances					
	SDQ2N01	SDQ2N13	SDQ2N25	SDQ2N37	SDQ2N04
SDQ2N01	1.811				
SDQ2N13	0.681	1.838			
SDQ2N25	0.749	0.502	1.500		
SDQ2N37	0.475	0.653	0.428	1.306	
SDQ2N04	0.418	0.662	0.300	0.468	1.955
SDQ2N16	0.464	0.552	0.393	0.577	0.749
SDQ2N28	0.375	0.477	0.347	0.539	0.689
SDQ2N40	0.451	0.540	0.432	0.660	0.514
SDQ2N10	0.350	0.409	0.252	0.323	0.593

⋮

Covariances	
	SDQ2N43
SDQ2N43	1.954

Correlations					
	SDQ2N01	SDQ2N13	SDQ2N25	SDQ2N37	SDQ2N04
SDQ2N01	1.000				
SDQ2N13	0.374	1.000			
SDQ2N25	0.454	0.302	1.000		
SDQ2N37	0.309	0.422	0.306	1.000	
SDQ2N04	0.222	0.349	0.175	0.293	1.000
SDQ2N16	0.278	0.329	0.259	0.408	0.432
SDQ2N28	0.210	0.264	0.213	0.355	0.371
SDQ2N40	0.247	0.293	0.260	0.426	0.271
SDQ2N10	0.226	0.262	0.179	0.246	0.369

⋮

Correlations	
	SDQ2N43
SDQ2N43	1.000

Assessment of Model as a Whole

Of primary interest in SEM is the extent to which a hypothesized model "fits," or, in other words, adequately describes the sample data. Given findings of inadequate goodness-of-fit, the next logical step is to detect the source of misfit in the model. Ideally, evaluation of model fit should be based on several criteria that can assess model fit from a diversity of perspectives. In particular, these focus on the adequacy of (a) the model as a whole, and (b) the individual parameter estimates.

Before examining this section of the *Mplus* output, however, I consider it instructive to review four important aspects of fitting hypothesized models; these are (a) the rationale upon which the model-fitting process is based, (b) the issue of statistical significance, (c) the estimation process, and (d) the goodness-of-fit statistics.

The Model-Fitting Process

In Chapter 1, I presented a general description of this process and noted that the primary task is to determine the goodness-of-fit between the hypothesized model and the sample data. In other words, the researcher specifies a model and then uses the sample data to test the model.

With a view to helping you gain a better understanding of the material to be presented next in the output file, let's take a few moments to recast this model-fitting process within a more formalized framework. As such, let S represent the sample covariance matrix (of observed variable scores), Σ (sigma) to represent the population covariance matrix, and θ (theta) to represent a vector that comprises the model parameters. As such, $\Sigma(\theta)$ represents the restricted covariance matrix implied by the model (i.e., the specified structure of the hypothesized model). In SEM, the null hypothesis (H_0) being tested is that the postulated model holds in the population [i.e., $\Sigma = \Sigma(\theta)$]. In contrast to traditional statistical procedures, however, the researcher hopes *not* to reject H_0 (but see MacCallum, Browne, & Sugawara, 1996, for proposed changes to this hypothesis-testing strategy).

The Issue of Statistical Significance

As you are no doubt aware, the rationale underlying the practice of statistical significance testing has generated a plethora of criticism over, at least, the past 4 decades. Indeed, Cohen (1994) has noted that, despite Rozeboom's (1960) admonition more than 50 years ago that "the statistical folkways of a more primitive past continue to dominate the local scene" (p. 417), this dubious practice still persists. (For an array of supportive as well as opposing views with respect to this article, see the *American Psychologist* [1995], *50*, 1098–1103.) In light of this historical bank of criticism, together with the pressure by methodologists to cease this traditional ritual (see, e.g., Cohen, 1994; Kirk, 1996; Schmidt, 1996; Thompson, 1996), the Board of Scientific Affairs for the American Psychological Association (APA) appointed a task force to study the feasibility of possibly phasing out the use of null hypothesis significance (NHST) procedures, as typically described in course texts and reported in journal articles. As a consequence of findings reported and conclusions drawn by this task force (see Wilkinson and the Task Force on Statistical Inference, 1999), the APA (2010) now stresses that "NHST is but a starting point and that additional reporting elements such as effect sizes, confidence intervals, and extensive description are needed to convey the most complete meaning of results" (p. 33). (For additional perspectives on this topic, see Harlow, Mulaik, & Steiger, 1997; Jones & Tukey, 2000; Kline, 2004.)

It can be argued that NHST, with respect to the analysis of covariance structures, is somewhat different in that it is driven by degrees of freedom involving the number of elements in the sample covariance matrix and the number of parameters to be estimated. Nonetheless, it is interesting to note that many of the issues raised with respect to the traditional statistical methods (e.g., practical significance, importance of confidence intervals, and importance of replication) have long been addressed in SEM applications. Indeed, it was this very issue of practical "nonsignificance" in model testing that led Bentler and Bonett (1980) to develop one of the first subjective indices of fit (the Normed Fit Index [NFI]). Indeed, their work subsequently spawned the development of numerous additional practical indices of fit, some of which are included in the M*plus* output shown in Table 3.5. Likewise, the early work of Steiger (1990; Steiger & Lind, 1980) precipitated the call for use of confidence intervals in the reporting of SEM findings (see, e.g., MacCallum et al., 1996). More recently, Rodgers (2010) has referred to this movement for change "a quiet methodological revolution." For a comprehensive and intriguing historical review of NHST and modeling, their relation to one another, and their implications for current methodological practice, I urge you to read Rodger's very informative article, which I'm sure will become a classic in the field!

The Estimation Process
The primary focus of the estimation process, in SEM, is to yield parameter values such that the discrepancy (i.e., residual) between the sample covariance matrix S and the population covariance matrix implied by the model $[\Sigma(\theta)]$ is minimal. This objective is achieved by minimizing a discrepancy function, $F[S, \Sigma(\theta)]$, such that its minimal value (F_{min}) reflects the point in the estimation process where the discrepancy between S and $\Sigma(\theta)$ is least $[S - \Sigma(\theta) = \text{minimum}]$. Taken together, then, F_{min} serves as a measure of the extent to which S differs from $\Sigma(\theta)$; any discrepancy between the two is captured by the residual covariance matrix.

Table 3.5 Mplus Output: Goodness-of-Fit Statistics

The Model Estimation Terminated Normally: Tests of Model Fit	

Chi-Square Test of Model Fit

Value	159.112
Degrees of freedom	98
p-value	0.0001

Chi-Square Test of Model Fit for the Baseline Model

Value	1703.155
Degrees of freedom	120
p-value	0.0000

CFI/TLI

CFI	0.961
TLI	0.953

Loglikelihood

H_0 value	−6562.678
H_1 value	−6483.122

Information Criteria

Number of free parameters	54
Akaike (AIC)	13233.356
Bayesian (BIC)	13426.661
Sample-size adjusted BIC (n* = (n + 2)/24)	13255.453

Root Mean Square Error of Approximation (RMSEA)

Estimate	0.049
90% confidence interval (CI)	0.034 0.062
Probability RMSEA <= .05	0.556

Standardized Root Mean Square Residual (SRMR)

Value	0.045

The Goodness-of-Fit Statistics

Let's turn now to the model fit statistics, which are presented in Table 3.5. Here we find several goodness-of-fit values, all of which relate to the model as a whole. The first of these values represents the Chi-Square Test of Model Fit. The value of 159.112 represents the discrepancy between the unrestricted sample covariance matrix S and the restricted covariance matrix $\Sigma(\theta)$ and, in essence, represents the Likelihood Ratio Test statistic, most commonly expressed as a chi-square (χ^2) statistic. Although this statistic is typically calculated as $(N-1)F_{min}$ (sample size minus 1, multiplied by the minimum fit function), M*plus* uses only a value of N, rather than $N-1$ (Brown, 2006). In general, H_0 $\Sigma = \Sigma(\theta)$ is equivalent to the hypothesis that $\Sigma - \Sigma(\theta) = 0$; the χ^2 test, then, simultaneously tests the extent to which all residuals in $\Sigma - \Sigma(\theta)$ are zero (Bollen, 1989). Framed a little differently, the null hypothesis (H_0) postulates that specification of the factor loadings, factor variances and covariances, and residual (i.e., measurement error) variances for the model under study are valid; the likelihood ratio test statistic (χ^2), then, simultaneously tests the extent to which this specification is true. The probability value associated with χ^2 represents the likelihood of obtaining a χ^2 value that exceeds the χ^2 value when H_0 is true. Thus, the higher the probability associated with χ^2, the closer the fit between the hypothesized model (under H_0) and the perfect fit (Bollen, 1989).

The test of our H_0—that SC is a four-factor structure, as depicted in Figure 3.1—yielded a χ^2 value of 159.112, with 98 degrees of freedom and a probability of less than .0001 ($p < .0001$), thereby suggesting that the fit of the data to the hypothesized model is not entirely adequate. Interpreted literally, this test statistic indicates that, given the present data, the hypothesis bearing on SC relations, as summarized in the model, represents an unlikely event (occurring less than one time in a thousand under the null hypothesis) and should be rejected. The sensitivity of the χ^2 likelihood ratio test to sample size, however, is well known and is addressed shortly.

The next fit statistic reported in the M*plus* output is the Chi-Square Test of Model Fit for the Baseline Model, which is shown to have a χ^2 value of 1703.155 with 120 degrees of freedom ($p < .000$). Although the baseline model in most SEM computer programs represents what is commonly termed the *independence* (or *null*) model,[3] the baseline model in M*plus* is structured somewhat differently. Common to both baseline models is the assumption of zero covariation among the observed indicator variables. However, whereas the only parameters in the independence model related to a CFA model (such as the one in this chapter) are the observed variable variances (given that no estimated means are of interest), those in the M*plus* baseline model comprise both the variances and means (i.e., intercepts) of the observed variables. As discussed earlier in this chapter in relation to Table 3.2, M*plus* always estimates the observed variable intercepts even though they may not actually be part of the structured model, which is the case with the present application.

Because both baseline models assume zero covariation among the observed variables, it is not surprising that the χ^2 value of these models is typically always substantially larger than that of the structured hypothesized model. Indeed, this is precisely the situation here, where we find the χ^2 value of the hypothesized model to be 159.112 with 98 degrees of freedom versus the M*plus* baseline model χ^2 value of 1703.155 with 120 degrees of freedom. The relevance of this comparison between the baseline and hypothesized models plays out in assessing the extent to which the hypothesized model fits the data, compared with the baseline model. To the extent that the χ^2 value of the hypothesized model is less than that of the baseline model, the hypothesized model is considered to exhibit an improvement of fit over the baseline model. In other words, the structured model is superior to the unstructured model.

Given the prominence of the likelihood ratio statistic (χ^2) in the SEM literature, I believe it will be helpful to you if we take a slight digression before moving on to examine the remaining model fit results. As such, I hope to provide you with a framework within which to comprehend the link between the χ^2 statistic and other goodness-of-fit statistics reported in the SEM literature, a few of which are included in the M*plus* output and discussed shortly. Specifically, I wish to alert you not only to the many problematic features of the χ^2 statistic but also to its more valuable uses within the model-fitting process. We turn first to the widely known difficulties associated with this statistic.

Perhaps the most challenging and frustrating aspect of the likelihood ratio test statistic is its sensitivity to sample size. Because the χ^2 statistic equals $(N-1)F_{min}$ or $(N)F_{min}$, this value tends to be substantial when the model does *not* hold and the sample size is large (Jöreskog & Sörbom, 1993). The conundrum here, however, is that the analysis of covariance structures is grounded in large sample theory. As such, large samples are critical to obtaining precise parameter estimates, as well as to the tenability of asymptotic distributional approximations (MacCallum et al., 1996). Thus, findings of well-fitting hypothesized models, where the χ^2 value approximates the degrees of freedom, have proven to be unrealistic in most SEM empirical research. That is, despite relatively negligible difference between a sample covariance matrix (S) and its associated restricted covariance matrix (Σ), it is not unusual that a model would be rejected given a large sample size. Most common to SEM research, then, are findings of a large χ^2 relative to degrees of freedom, thereby indicating a need to modify the model in order to better fit the data (Jöreskog & Sörbom, 1993). Thus, results related to the test of our hypothesized model are not unexpected. Indeed, given this problematic aspect of the Likelihood Ratio Test and the fact that postulated models (no matter how good) can only ever fit real-world data *approximately* and *never exactly*, MacCallum et al. (1996) proposed changes to the traditional hypothesis-testing approach in covariance structure modeling. (For an extended discussion of these changes, see MacCallum et al., 1996.)

At least two additional problematic features of the χ^2 statistic are also well known. The first of these relates to conditions of small sample size and/or data that are nonnormally distributed. In such instances, the underlying distribution is not χ^2 distributed, thereby distorting the statistical significance of the model test (Brown, 2006). The second troublesome aspect of the χ^2 statistic is that it is based on the excessively stringent hypothesis that the sample covariance matrix (S) is equal to the restricted covariance matrix (Σ).

Having cautioned you about the negative aspects of the χ^2 statistic, allow me now to offset those rather bad features by describing two of its more notably positive ones. The first of these is the fact that the χ^2 statistic is used in the computation of many alternative model fit indices, most of which, if not all, were developed for the purposes of addressing particular weaknesses in the likelihood ratio test statistic as an index of model fit. (The likelihood ratio χ^2 statistic holds the honor of being the first index developed and used in the assessment of model fit in SEM.) Four of these alternate indices of fit are included in the M*plus* output (see Table 3.5; the Comparative Fit Index [CFI], Tucker-Lewis Fit Index [TLI], Akaike's Information Criterion [AIC], and Bayes Information Criterion [BIC]) and are described shortly. The second important use of the χ^2 statistic is in the comparison of nested models,[4] a mechanism used in testing for evidence of measurement and structural equivalence (i.e., invariance) across groups. These comparisons are illustrated in applications addressed in Chapters 7, 8, and 9.

Now that you are aware of both the good and not-so-good aspects of the χ^2 statistic, let's move on to review the remaining model fit statistics in the M*plus* output in Table 3.5. As a result of the problematic features just noted regarding this statistic, you can now appreciate why researchers have been motivated to address these limitations via the development of alternative goodness-of-fit indices that take a more pragmatic approach to the evaluation process. To this end, the past 2 decades have witnessed a plethora of newly developed fit indices as well as unique approaches to the model-fitting process (for reviews, see, e.g., Gerbing & Anderson, 1993; Hu & Bentler, 1995; Marsh, Balla, & McDonald, 1988; Tanaka, 1993). In overcoming the problematic nature of the χ^2 statistic, a fit index quantifies the degree of model fit along a continuum (Hu & Bentler, 1999). These criteria, commonly referred to as *subjective*, *practical*, or *ad hoc* indices of fit, are now commonly used as adjuncts to the χ^2 statistic given that the latter is rarely, if ever, used as the sole index of model fit. Although the χ^2 statistic, by convention, is always reported, decisions regarding adequacy of model fit are typically based on alternate indices of fit, four of which we review now in Table 3.5.

In general, model fit indices fall into one of two categories: *incremental* (Hu & Bentler, 1995, 1999), also termed *comparative* (Browne, MacCallum, Kim, Andersen, & Glaser, 2002), and *absolute*, with incremental indices seemingly being the most widely used in SEM. Whereas incremental indices of fit measure the proportionate improvement in fit of a hypothesized model compared with a more restricted, albeit nested, baseline model (Hu & Bentler, 1999), absolute indices of fit assess the extent to which an a priori model reproduces the sample data. That is, in contrast to incremental fit indices, no reference model is used in determining the amount of improvement in model fit. Nonetheless, either an implicit or explicit comparison may be made to a saturated model[5] that exactly reproduces the sample covariance matrix (Hu & Bentler, 1999).

More recently, there has been a tendency to consider a third category of fit indices sometimes referred to as *predictive* indices of fit (e.g., Kline, 2011) and other times as *parsimony-corrective* indices of fit (e.g., Brown, 2006). This third category, however, is much less clearly defined than the two primary fit index categories, as a review of the SEM literature reveals not only an overlapping of these characteristics (predictability and parsimony correction) but also the tendency on the part of some authors to categorize them as either incremental or absolute indices of fit. Thus, in describing the goodness-of-fit statistics reported in the M*plus* output reported in Table 3.5, I include this third category but refer to it as the *predictive* or *parsimony-corrected* category. Characteristics of this rather tenuous category are presented later in conjunction with details of its two related fit indices, the AIC and BIC. We turn now to a description of all model indices of fit.

Two of the most commonly used incremental indices of fit in SEM are the CFI (Bentler, 1990) and the TLI (Tucker & Lewis, 1973). Both measure the proportionate improvement in model fit by comparing the hypothesized model in which structure is imposed with the less restricted nested baseline model. Values for the CFI are normed in the sense that they range from zero to 1.00, with values close to 1.00 being indicative of a well-fitting model. Although a value > .90 was originally considered representative of a well-fitting model (see Bentler, 1992), a revised cutoff value close to .95 has more recently been advised (Hu & Bentler, 1999). Computation of the CFI is as follows:

$$\text{CFI} = 1 - [(\chi^2_H - df_H)/(\chi^2_B - df_B)]$$

where H = the hypothesized model, and B = the baseline model.

Based on the results reported in Table 3.5, this equation translates into

$$\text{CFI} = 1 - [(159.112 - 98)/1703.155 - 120)]$$

$$= 1 - 61.112/1583.155$$

$$= 1 - .039$$

$$= 0.961$$

This value, of course, is consistent with the CFI value of 0.961 reported in Table 3.5 and assures us that the hypothesized four-factor model displayed in Figure 3.1 fits our sample of Grade 7 adolescents very well.

In contrast to the CFI, the TLI is a nonnormed index, which means that its values can extend outside the range of 0.0 to 1.0. This condition explains why some computer programs refer to the TLI as the *nonnormed index*. This feature of the TLI notwithstanding, it is customary to interpret its values in the same way as for the CFI, with values close to 1.0 being indicative of a well-fitting model. A second differentiating aspect of the TLI, compared with the CFI, is its inclusion of a penalty function for models that are overly complex. What I mean by this statement is that when a model under study includes parameters that contribute minimally to improvement in model fit, this fact is taken into account in the computation of the TLI value. Computation of the TLI is as follows:

$$\text{TLI} = [(\chi_B^2/df_B) - (\chi_H^2/df_H)] - [(\chi_B^2/df_B) - 1]$$

$$= [(1703.155/120) - (159.112/98)] - [(1703.155/120) - 1]$$

$$= [(14.193) - 1.624)] - [(14.193) - 1]$$

$$= 12.569 - 13.193$$

$$= 0.953$$

As reported in Table 3.5, we see that this value replicates the reported TLI value of 0.953, and is consistent with that of the CFI in advising that our hypothesized four-factor SC model is very well-fitting, thereby describing the sample data extremely well.

Turning again to the M*plus* output in Table 3.5, I draw your attention now to the next two sets of information provided. The first set, listed under the heading *Loglikelihood*, reports two loglikelihood values—one for the hypothesized model (H_0 value) and one for the baseline model (H_1 value). These values are used in computation of the two model fit indices listed under the second heading, "Information Criteria."

We turn now to the second heading and these two model fit indices, the AIC (Akaike, 1987) and BIC (Raftery, 1993; Schwartz, 1978), both of which are considered candidates for the predictive and parsimony-corrected category of fit indices. In contrast to the CFI and TLI, both of which focus on comparison of *nested* models, the AIC and BIC are used in the comparison of two or more *nonnested* models, with the smallest value overall representing the best fit of the hypothesized model. Both the AIC and BIC take into account model fit (as per the χ^2 value) as well as the complexity of the model (as per model degrees of freedom or number of estimated parameters). The BIC, however, assigns a greater penalty in this regard and, thus, is more apt to select parsimonious models (Arbuckle, 2007).

Of these two indices, the AIC is the more commonly used in SEM. This is particularly so with respect to the situation where a researcher proposes a series of plausible models and wishes to determine which one in the series yields the best fit (Raykov & Marcoulides, 2000), as well as reflects the extent to which parameter estimates from an original sample will cross-validate in future samples (Bandalos, 1993). In this latter sense, the AIC is akin to the Expected Cross-Validation Index (ECVI; Browne & Cudeck, 1989), another popular index included in most computer SEM packages, although not in the M*plus* program. Given the similar application of the AIC and BIC, albeit the more common usage of the former, an example calculation of only the AIC is presented here.

Interestingly, at least three versions of computation exist with respect to the AIC with the result that these versions vary across SEM computer software (Brown, 2006). These differences notwithstanding, they have been shown to be equivalent (see Kaplan, 2000). Computation of the AIC pertinent to the M*plus* program is as follows:

$$AIC = -2 \text{ (loglikelihood)} + 2a$$

where *loglikelihood* refers to the H_0 value and *a* is the number of estimated parameters. Recall that M*plus* always computes estimates for the observed variable intercepts, regardless of whether or not they are structured in the model. Thus, although the actual number of estimated parameters in our hypothesized four-factor model is 38, M*plus* considers the number of estimated parameters here to be 54 (38 + 16 intercepts).

$$AIC = -2 \ (-6562.678) + 2 \ (54)$$

$$= 13{,}125.356 + 108$$

$$= 13233.356$$

The last two model fit indices listed in Table 3.5, the Root Mean Square Error of Approximation (RMSEA; Steiger & Lind, 1980) and the Standardized Root Mean Square Residual (SRMR), belong to the category of *absolute* indices of fit. However, Browne and colleagues (2002) have termed them, more specifically, as "absolute *misfit* indices" (p. 405). In contrast to incremental fit indices, as noted earlier, absolute fit indices do not rely on comparison with a reference model in determining the extent of model improvement; rather, they depend only on determining how well the hypothesized model fits the sample data. Thus, whereas incremental fit indices *increase* as goodness-of-fit improves, absolute fit indices *decrease* as goodness-of-fit improves, thereby attaining their lower-bound values of zero when the model fits perfectly (Browne et al., 2002).

The RMSEA and the conceptual framework within which it is embedded were first proposed by Steiger and Lind in 1980, yet failed to gain recognition until approximately 1 decade later, as one of the most informative criteria in covariance structure modeling. The RMSEA takes into account the error of approximation in the population and asks the question "How well would the model, with unknown but optimally chosen parameter values, fit the population covariance matrix if it were available?" (Browne & Cudeck, 1993, pp. 137–138). This discrepancy, as measured by the RMSEA, is expressed per degree of freedom, thus making it sensitive to the number of estimated parameters in the model (i.e., the complexity of the model); values less than .05 indicate good fit, and values as high as .08 represent reasonable errors of approximation in the population (Browne & Cudeck, 1993). MacCallum et al. (1996), in elaborating on these cutpoints, noted that RMSEA values ranging from .08 to .10 indicate mediocre fit, and those greater than .10 indicate poor fit. Although Hu and Bentler (1999) have suggested a value of .06 to be indicative of good fit between the hypothesized model and the observed data, they cautioned that when the sample size is small, the RMSEA tends to overreject true population models. Noting that these criteria are based solely on subjective judgment, and therefore cannot be regarded as infallible or correct, Browne and Cudeck (1993) and MacCallum et al. (1996) nonetheless argued that they would appear to be more realistic than a requirement of exact fit, where RMSEA = 0.0. (For a generalization of the RMSEA to multiple independent samples, see Steiger, 1998.)

Overall, MacCallum and Austin (2000) have strongly recommended routine use of the RMSEA for at least three reasons: (a) It would appear to be adequately sensitive to model misspecification (Hu & Bentler, 1998), (b) commonly used interpretative guidelines would appear to yield appropriate conclusions regarding model quality (Hu & Bentler, 1998, 1999), and (c) it is possible to build confidence intervals around RMSEA values.

Now, let's examine computation of the RMSEA, which involves a two-step process. This index approximates a *noncentral* χ^2 distribution, which does not require a true null hypothesis; that is to say, it assumes that the hypothesized model is somewhat imperfect. In contrast to the usual χ^2 distribution, the noncentral χ^2 distribution has an additional parameter termed the *noncentrality parameter* (NCP), which is typically assigned the lowercase Greek symbol of delta (δ). The function of δ is to measure the extent to which the specified model (i.e., the null hypothesis) is false. Thus, as the hypothesized model becomes increasingly false, the value of δ becomes greater.

In essence, then, δ can be considered a gauge of the extent to which the hypothesized model is misspecified in one of two ways: (a) Its estimated value (δ_H) represents the difference between the hypothesized model (χ^2_H) and its related number of degrees of freedom (df_H), or (b) its difference from zero in the event that the value for δ_H is negative (which is not permissible). Measuring discrepancy in fit (represented by δ) per each degree of freedom in the model therefore makes it possible for the RMSEA to compensate for the effect of model complexity. In summary, the greater the model complexity, the larger the δ value and, ultimately, the larger the RMSEA value. Expressed in equation form, the estimation of δ_H is as follows:

$$\delta_H = \max\ (\chi^2_H - df_H,\ 0)$$

where *max* represents either ($\chi^2_H - df_H$) or zero, whichever is greater.

In contrast to χ^2, which measures the extent to which a hypothesized model fits *exactly* in the population, the RMSEA assesses the extent to which it fits *reasonably well* in the population. For this reason, then, it is considered an "error of approximation" index (Brown, 2006). In computation of the RMSEA, this distinction between the central and noncentral χ^2 values is taken into account, and the δ_H value is generally rescaled as follows:

$$\delta_H = (\chi^2_H - df_H)/(N = 1)$$

Importantly, however, this rescaling process can vary slightly across SEM computer programs. M*plus*, for example, adjusts the equation as follows:

$$\delta_H = (\chi^2_H - df_H)/N$$

The resulting computation of the RMSEA, based on the M*plus* δ_H formula, is as follows:

$$\sqrt{\frac{\delta_H}{df_H}}$$

Applying the two-step RMSEA formula to our own model tested in this application yields the following result:

$$\delta_H = (\chi_H^2 - df_H)/N = (159.112 - 98)/265$$

$$= 61.112/265 = 0.231$$

$$= \sqrt{\frac{0.231}{98}}$$

$$= \sqrt{0.0023571}$$

$$= 0.0485499 \ (0.049)$$

As you can see, this result is consistent with the value as shown in Table 3.5 in reflecting that our hypothesized CFA model is sufficiently parsimonious and well fitting.

Addressing Steiger's (1990) call for the use of confidence intervals to assess the precision of RMSEA estimates, M*plus* reports a 90% interval around the RMSEA value. In contrast to point estimates of model fit (which do not reflect the imprecision of the estimate), confidence intervals can yield this information, thereby providing the researcher with more assistance in the evaluation of model fit. Thus, MacCallum et al. (1996) strongly urged the use of confidence intervals in practice. Presented with a small RMSEA, albeit a wide confidence interval, a researcher would conclude that the estimated discrepancy value is quite imprecise, thereby negating any possibility to determine accurately the degree of fit in the population. In contrast, a very narrow confidence interval would argue for good precision of the RMSEA value in reflecting model fit in the population (MacCallum et al., 1996).

Turning to Table 3.5, we see that our RMSEA value of .049 has a 90% confidence interval ranging from .034 to .062. Interpretation of the confidence interval indicates that we can be 90% confident that the true RMSEA value in the population will fall within the bounds of .034 and .062, which represents a good degree of precision. Given that (a) the RMSEA point estimate is < .05 (.049), and (b) the upper bound of the 90% interval is .062, which is less than the value suggested by Browne and Cudeck (1993), albeit equal to the cutoff value proposed by Hu and Bentler (1999), we can conclude that the initially hypothesized model fits the data well enough.

Before leaving this discussion of the RMSEA, it is important to note that confidence intervals can be influenced seriously by sample size as well as model complexity (MacCallum et al., 1996). For example, if sample size is small and the number of estimated parameters large, the confidence interval will be wide. Given a complex model (i.e., a large number of estimated parameters), a very large sample size would be required in order to obtain a reasonably narrow confidence interval. On the other hand, if the number of parameters is small, then the probability of obtaining a narrow confidence interval is high, even for samples of rather moderate size (MacCallum et al., 1996).

The Root Mean Square Residual (RMR) represents the average residual value derived from the fitting of the variance–covariance matrix for the hypothesized model $\Sigma(\theta)$ to the variance–covariance matrix of the sample data (S). However, because these residuals are relative to the sizes of the observed variances and covariances, they are difficult to interpret. Thus, they are best interpreted in the metric of the correlation matrix (Hu & Bentler, 1995; Jöreskog & Sörbom, 1989), which is represented by its standardized value (the SRMR). The SRMR represents the average value across all standardized residuals, and ranges from zero to 1.00; in a well-fitting model, this value will be small (say, .05 or less). In reviewing the output in Table 3.5, we see that the SRMR value is .045. Given that the SRMR represents the average discrepancy between the observed sample and hypothesized correlation matrices, we can interpret this value as meaning that the model explains the correlations to within an average error of .045.

Having worked your way through these goodness-of-fit measures and their computation, you may be wondering what you do with all this information. Although you certainly don't need to report the entire set of fit indices as reported in Table 3.5, such information, nonetheless, can give you a good sense of how well your model fits the sample data. But, how does one choose which indices are appropriate in the assessment of model fit? Unfortunately, this choice is not a simple one, largely because particular indices have been shown to operate somewhat differently given the sample size, estimation procedure, model complexity, and/or violation of the underlying assumptions of multivariate normality and variable independence (Fan & Sivo, 2007; Saris, Satorra, & van der Veld, 2009). Thus, in choosing which goodness-of-fit indices to use in the assessment of model fit, careful consideration of these critical factors is essential, and the use of multiple, albeit complementary, indices is highly recommended (Fan & Sivo, 2005; Hu & Bentler, 1995). In reporting results for the remaining applications in this volume, goodness-of-fit indices will be limited to the CFI, TLI, RMSEA, and SRMR, along with the related χ^2 value and RMSEA 90% confidence interval. Readers interested in acquiring further elaboration on the above goodness-of-fit statistics, in addition to many other indices of fit, their formulae and functions, and/or the extent to which they are affected by sample size, estimation procedures, misspecification, and/or violations of assumptions, are referred to Bandalos (1993); Bentler and Yuan (1999); Bollen (1989); Browne and Cudeck (1993); Curran, West, and Finch (1996); Fan, Thompson, and Wang (1999); Finch, West, and

MacKinnon (1997); Gerbing and Anderson (1993); Hu and Bentler (1995, 1998, 1999); Hu, Bentler, and Kano (1992); Jöreskog and Sörbom (1993); La Du and Tanaka (1989); Marsh et al. (1988); Mulaik et al. (1989); Raykov and Widaman (1995); Sugawara and MacCallum (1993); Tomarken and Waller (2005); Weng and Cheng (1997); West, Finch, and Curran (1995); Wheaton (1987); and Williams and Holahan (1994); for an annotated bibliography, see Austin and Calderón (1996).

In finalizing this section on model assessment, I wish to leave you with this important reminder—that global fit indices alone cannot possibly envelop all that needs to be known about a model in order to judge the adequacy of its fit to the sample data. As Sobel and Bohrnstedt (1985) so cogently stated over 2 decades ago, "Scientific progress could be impeded if fit coefficients (even appropriate ones) are used as the primary criterion for judging the adequacy of a model" (p. 158). They further posited that, despite the problematic nature of the χ^2 statistic, exclusive reliance on goodness-of-fit indices is unacceptable and, indeed, provides no guarantee whatsoever that a model is useful. In fact, it is entirely possible for a model to fit well and yet still be incorrectly specified (Wheaton, 1987). (For an excellent review of ways by which such a seemingly dichotomous event can happen, readers are referred to Bentler and Chou, 1987.) Fit indices yield information bearing only on the model's *lack of fit*. More importantly, they can in no way reflect the extent to which the model is plausible; *this judgement rests squarely on the shoulders of the researcher*. Indeed, Saris et al. (2009) have recently questioned the validity of goodness-of-fit indices in the evaluation of model fit given that they are incapable of providing any indication of the "size" of a model's misspecification. Thus, assessment of model adequacy must be based on multiple criteria that take into account theoretical, statistical, and practical considerations.

Assessment of Individual Parameter Estimates

Thus far in our discussion of model fit assessment, we have concentrated on the model as a whole. Now, we turn our attention to the fit of individual parameters in the model. There are two aspects of concern here: (a) the appropriateness of the estimates, and (b) their statistical significance.

Feasibility of Parameter Estimates

The initial step in assessing the fit of individual parameters in a model is to determine the viability of their estimated values. In particular, parameter estimates should exhibit the correct sign and size, and be consistent with the underlying theory. Any estimates falling outside the admissible range signal a clear indication that either the model is wrong or the input matrix lacks sufficient information. Parameter estimates taken from covariance or correlation matrices that are not positive definite, as well as estimates exhibiting out-of-range values such as correlations > 1.00 and negative variances (known as *Heywood cases*), exemplify unacceptable estimated values.

Appropriateness of Standard Errors

Another indicator of poor model fit is the presence of standard errors that are excessively large or small. For example, if a standard error approaches zero, the test statistic for its related parameter cannot be defined (Bentler, 2005). Likewise, standard errors that are extremely large indicate parameters that cannot be determined (Jöreskog & Sörbom, 1989). Because standard errors are influenced by the units of measurement in observed and/ or latent variables, as well as the magnitude of the parameter estimate itself, no definitive criteria of "small" and "large" have been established (see Jöreskog & Sörbom, 1989).

Statistical Significance of Parameter Estimates

The test statistic here represents the parameter estimate divided by its standard error; as such, it operates as a z-statistic in testing that the estimate is statistically different from zero. Based on an α level of .05, then, the test statistic needs to be > ±1.96 before the hypothesis (that the estimate = 0.0) can be rejected. Nonsignificant parameters, with the exception of error variances, can be considered unimportant to the model; in the interest of scientific parsimony, albeit given an adequate sample size, they should be deleted from the model. On the other hand, it is important to note that nonsignificant parameters can be indicative of a sample size that is too small (K. G. Jöreskog, personal communication, January 1997).

Let's turn now to this part of the Mplus output, as presented in Table 3.6. Scanning the output, you will see five columns of information, with the first column on the left listing the names of the parameters, grouped according to their model function. The initial four blocks of parameters headed with the word BY (e.g., F1------BY) represent the factor loadings. The next three blocks, headed with the word WITH (F2 WITH F1), represent the factor covariances. Finally, the last three blocks of parameters represent, respectively, the observed variable intercepts, the factor variances, and the residual variances associated with the observed variables. All estimate information is presented in the remaining four columns, with unstandardized parameter estimates presented in Column 2, standard errors in Column 3, z-scores (i.e., an estimate divided by its standard error) in Column 4, and the two-tailed probability associated with these parameter estimates appearing in Column 5.

Table 3.6 M*plus* Output: Unstandardized Parameter Estimates

	Model Results			
	Estimate	Standard Error (*SE*)	Estimate/*SE*	Two-Tailed *p*-Value
F1 BY				
SDQ2N01	1.000	0.000	999.000	999.000
SDQ2N13	1.083	0.156	6.939	0.000
SDQ2N25	0.851	0.125	6.806	0.000
SDQ2N37	0.934	0.141	6.607	0.000
F2 BY				
SDQ2N04	1.000	0.000	999.000	999.000
SDQ2N16	1.279	0.151	8.489	0.000
SDQ2N28	1.247	0.155	8.022	0.000
SDQ2N40	1.259	0.159	7.913	0.000
F3 BY				
SDQ2N10	1.000	0.000	999.000	999.000
SDQ2N22	0.889	0.104	8.561	0.000
SDQ2N34	0.670	0.148	4.541	0.000
SDQ2N46	0.843	0.118	7.160	0.000
F4 BY				
SDQ2N07	1.000	0.000	999.000	999.000
SDQ2N19	0.841	0.058	14.447	0.000
SDQ2N31	0.952	0.048	19.905	0.000
SDQ2N43	0.655	0.050	13.182	0.000
F2 WITH				
F1	0.415	0.078	5.325	0.000
F3 WITH				
F1	0.355	0.072	4.928	0.000
F2	0.464	0.080	5.825	0.000
F4 WITH				
F1	0.635	0.117	5.437	0.000
F2	0.873	0.134	6.507	0.000
F3	0.331	0.100	3.309	0.001

Table 3.6 M*plus* Output: Unstandardized Parameter Estimates (*continued*)

	Estimate	Standard Error (*SE*)	Estimate/*SE*	Two-Tailed *p*-Value
Model Results				
Intercepts				
SDQ2N01	4.408	0.083	53.312	0.000
SDQ2N13	5.004	0.083	60.087	0.000
SDQ2N25	5.098	0.075	67.766	0.000
SDQ2N37	4.826	0.070	68.758	0.000
SDQ2N04	4.521	0.086	52.630	0.000
SDQ2N16	4.649	0.076	61.116	0.000
SDQ2N28	4.691	0.082	57.419	0.000
SDQ2N40	4.977	0.083	59.717	0.000
SDQ2N10	4.623	0.071	65.454	0.000
SDQ2N22	5.377	0.067	80.384	0.000
SDQ2N34	3.891	0.104	37.256	0.000
SDQ2N46	5.268	0.080	66.253	0.000
SDQ2N07	4.321	0.109	39.560	0.000
SDQ2N19	4.543	0.104	43.738	0.000
SDQ2N31	4.740	0.096	49.225	0.000
SDQ2N43	4.977	0.086	57.961	0.000
Variances				
F1	0.613	0.141	4.342	0.000
F2	0.561	0.126	4.449	0.000
F3	0.668	0.116	5.744	0.000
F4	2.307	0.272	8.483	0.000
Residual Variances				
SDQ2N01	1.198	0.130	9.228	0.000
SDQ2N13	1.119	0.124	9.000	0.000
SDQ2N25	1.056	0.109	9.675	0.000
SDQ2N37	0.771	0.089	8.621	0.000
SDQ2N04	1.394	0.128	10.890	0.000
SDQ2N16	0.616	0.070	8.856	0.000
SDQ2N28	0.896	0.092	9.739	0.000
SDQ2N40	0.952	0.095	10.061	0.000
SDQ2N10	0.653	0.082	7.926	0.000
SDQ2N22	0.657	0.076	8.703	0.000
SDQ2N34	2.590	0.233	11.093	0.000

Table 3.6 Mplus Output: Unstandardized Parameter Estimates (*continued*)

	Estimate	Standard Error (*SE*)	Estimate/*SE*	Two-Tailed *p*-Value
		Model Results		
SDQ2N46	1.201	0.118	10.164	0.000
SDQ2N07	0.854	0.098	8.729	0.000
SDQ2N19	1.228	0.125	9.808	0.000
SDQ2N31	0.365	0.065	5.581	0.000
SDQ2N43	0.964	0.093	10.410	0.000

Turning to the unstandardized estimates reported in Table 3.6, let's look first at only the factor loadings. Here we note that for variables *SDQ2N01*, *SDQ2N04*, *SDQ2N10*, and *SDQ2N07*, the estimates all have a value of 1.00; their standard errors, a value of 0.00; and their z-values and probabilities, a value of 999.00. These values, of course, were fixed to 1.00 for purposes of identification and, thus, not freely estimated. All remaining factor-loading parameters, however, were freely estimated. A review of this information reveals all estimates to be reasonable (Column 2), as well as statistically significant as indicated by values > 1.96 (Column 4), and all standard errors (Column 3) to be in good order.

In contrast to other SEM programs, Mplus does not provide standardized estimates by default. Thus, if these estimates are of interest, the STANDARDIZED option must be added to the OUTPUT command statement. Once added, three types of standardization are provided by default, together with R-SQUARED values for both the observed and latent dependent variables in the model. Note, however, that users can opt for results based on only one of these three types of standardization as follows:

- STDYX: Standardization is based on background and outcome variables.
- SDY: Standardization is based on variances of continuous latent variables (i.e., factors), as well as variances of background and outcome variables.
- STD is based on variances of the continuous latent variables (i.e., factors).

Now that you are aware of the three types of standardization available in Mplus, no doubt you are wondering (as I did) which one is the correct one to use. However, it is not a matter of one being correct and the others not. It's just that there are many ways of conceptualizing standardization

(L. Muthén, personal communication, February 20, 2010). As a result, SEM programs can vary in the manner by which they standardize estimates. For example, whereas the EQS program (Bentler, 2005) uses all variables in the linear structural equation system, including measurement and residual (i.e., disturbance) variances (Bentler, 2005), the LISREL program (Jöreskog & Sörbom, 1996) uses neither the measured variables nor their error and residual terms in the standardization process (see Byrne, 2006, p. 108, note 12). In contrast, Mplus provides users with the opportunity to choose their method of choice.

In the current application, estimates were based on the STDYX standardization; they are reported in Table 3.7. In reviewing these estimates, you will want to verify that particular parameter values are consistent with the literature. For example, within the context of the present application, it is of interest to inspect correlations among the SC factors in seeking evidence of their consistency with previously reported values; in the present example, these estimates met this criterion.

In addition, there are two other aspects of standardized estimates that are worthy of mention. First, note that parameters reported as 1.0 in the unstandardized solution (*SDQ2N01, SDQ2N04, SDQ2N10,* and *SDQ2N07*) take on new values in the standardized solution. Second, note also that all factor variances are reported as 1.00 with the consequence that no other information is reported for these parameters. These values remain the same regardless of which standardization is used, as in standardized solutions all variables are rescaled to have a variance of 1.00.

In closing out this section on standardized estimates, we return to the R^2 values mentioned earlier. Whenever the standardized estimates are requested in the OUTPUT command, an R^2 value and its standard error are reported for each observed and latent dependent variable in the model. Each R^2 value reported in Table 3.8 represents the proportion of variance in each observed variable accounted for by its related factor; it is computed by subtracting the square of the residual (i.e., measurement error) term from 1.0. (In factor analytic terms, these R^2 values are termed *communalities.*) In reviewing these values in Table 3.8, we can see that the observed variable, *SDQ2N34* measuring English SC (see Figure 3.1) and having an R^2 of .104, appears to be the weakest of the indicator variables.

Model Misspecification

Determination of misspecified parameters is accomplished in Mplus by means of the Modification Index (MI) proposed by Sörbom (1989) for the case where all *y* variables are continuous and multivariate normal.[6] Essentially, the function of the MI is to identify parameter constraints that

Table 3.7 Mplus Output: Standardized Parameter Estimates

	Estimate	Standard Error (*SE*)	Estimate/*SE*	Two-Tailed *p*-Value
Standardized Model Results: STDYX Standardization				
F1 BY				
SDQ2N01	0.582	0.055	10.613	0.000
SDQ2N13	0.626	0.050	12.426	0.000
SDQ2N25	0.544	0.056	9.644	0.000
SDQ2N37	0.640	0.051	12.608	0.000
F2 BY				
SDQ2N04	0.536	0.048	11.143	0.000
SDQ2N16	0.774	0.031	24.983	0.000
SDQ2N28	0.703	0.037	19.071	0.000
SDQ2N40	0.695	0.036	19.043	0.000
F3 BY				
SDQ2N10	0.711	0.044	16.167	0.000
SDQ2N22	0.668	0.046	14.447	0.000
SDQ2N34	0.322	0.064	5.002	0.000
SDQ2N46	0.532	0.054	9.873	0.000
F4 BY				
SDQ2N07	0.854	0.020	41.953	0.000
SDQ2N19	0.755	0.030	24.825	0.000
SDQ2N31	0.923	0.016	59.292	0.000
SDQ2N43	0.712	0.033	21.287	0.000
F2 WITH				
F1	0.707	0.057	12.421	0.000
F3 WITH				
F1	0.555	0.072	7.733	0.000
F2	0.758	0.052	14.652	0.000
F4 WITH				
F1	0.534	0.061	8.756	0.000
F2	0.767	0.038	20.291	0.000
F3	0.266	0.073	3.652	0.000

Table 3.7 M*plus* Output: Standardized Parameter Estimates (*continued*)

		Standard		Two-Tailed
	Estimate	Error (*SE*)	Estimate/*SE*	*p*-Value
Intercepts				
SDQ2N01	3.275	0.155	21.135	0.000
SDQ2N13	3.691	0.172	21.498	0.000
SDQ2N25	4.163	0.191	21.798	0.000
SDQ2N37	4.224	0.193	21.831	0.000
SDQ2N04	3.233	0.153	21.092	0.000
SDQ2N16	3.754	0.174	21.544	0.000
SDQ2N28	3.527	0.165	21.368	0.000
SDQ2N40	3.668	0.171	21.481	0.000
SDQ2N10	4.021	0.185	21.718	0.000
SDQ2N22	4.938	0.223	22.132	0.000
SDQ2N34	2.289	0.117	19.584	0.000
SDQ2N46	4.070	0.187	21.746	0.000
SDQ2N07	2.430	0.122	19.898	0.000
SDQ2N19	2.687	0.132	20.372	0.000
SDQ2N31	3.024	0.145	20.854	0.000
SDQ2N43	3.561	0.166	21.396	0.000
Variances				
F1	1.000	0.000	999.000	999.000
F2	1.000	0.000	999.000	999.000
F3	1.000	0.000	999.000	999.000
F4	1.000	0.000	999.000	999.000
Residual Variances				
SDQ2N01	0.661	0.064	10.366	0.000
SDQ2N13	0.609	0.063	9.665	0.000
SDQ2N25	0.704	0.061	11.467	0.000
SDQ2N37	0.591	0.065	9.096	0.000
SDQ2N04	0.713	0.051	13.847	0.000
SDQ2N16	0.402	0.048	8.381	0.000
SDQ2N28	0.506	0.052	9.784	0.000
SDQ2N40	0.517	0.051	10.195	0.000
SDQ2N10	0.494	0.063	7.905	0.000
SDQ2N22	0.554	0.062	8.987	0.000

Standardized Model Results: STDYX Standardization

Table 3.7 M*plus* Output: Standardized Parameter Estimates (*continued*)

Standardized Model Results: STDYX Standardization			
	Estimate	Standard Error (*SE*)	Estimate/*SE*	Two-Tailed *p*-Value
SDQ2N34	0.896	0.042	21.583	0.000
SDQ2N46	0.717	0.057	12.493	0.000
SDQ2N07	0.270	0.035	7.763	0.000
SDQ2N19	0.429	0.046	9.341	0.000
SDQ2N31	0.148	0.029	5.170	0.000
SDQ2N43	0.493	0.048	10.351	0.000

Table 3.8 M*plus* Output: R-SQUARE Values for Observed Variables

R^2				
Observed Variable	Estimate	Standard Error (*SE*)	Estimate/*SE*	Two-Tailed *p*-Value
SDQ2N01	0.339	0.064	5.307	0.000
SDQ2N13	0.391	0.063	6.213	0.000
SDQ2N25	0.296	0.061	4.822	0.000
SDQ2N37	0.409	0.065	6.304	0.000
SDQ2N04	0.287	0.051	5.572	0.000
SDQ2N16	0.598	0.048	12.492	0.000
SDQ2N28	0.494	0.052	9.535	0.000
SDQ2N40	0.483	0.051	9.522	0.000
SDQ2N10	0.506	0.063	8.083	0.000
SDQ2N22	0.446	0.062	7.224	0.000
SDQ2N34	**0.104**	**0.042**	**2.501**	**0.012**
SDQ2N46	0.283	0.057	4.936	0.000
SDQ2N07	0.730	0.035	20.976	0.000
SDQ2N19	0.571	0.046	12.412	0.000
SDQ2N31	0.852	0.029	29.646	0.000
SDQ2N43	0.507	0.048	10.643	0.000

Table 3.9 M*plus* Output: Modification Indices (MIs)

Model Modification Indices

	MI	Expected Parameter Change (EPC)	Standard EPC	StdYX EPC
BY Statements				
F2 BY SDQ2N07	11.251	−0.563	−0.422	−0.237
WITH Statements				
SDQ2N25 WITH SDQ2N01	17.054	0.359	0.359	0.319
SDQ2N31 WITH SDQ2N07	10.696	0.305	0.305	0.546
SDQ2N31 WITH SDQ2N19	17.819	−0.331	−0.331	−0.495

Note: Modification indices for direct effects of observed dependent variables regressed on covariates may not be included. To include these, request MODINDICES (ALL). Minimum MI value for printing the modification index 10.000.

are badly chosen. As such, all fixed parameters (i.e., those fixed to a value of 0.00) and/or those constrained to the value of another parameter (not the case in the present application) are assessed to identify which parameters, if freely estimated, would contribute to a significant drop in the χ^2 statistic. Results for our hypothesized model are presented in Table 3.9.

In reviewing these results, you will note that they appear in five columns, with the names of the variables appearing in the first column on the left, followed by their related analytic information in the remaining four columns. The MI value appears in Column 2 and represents the approximate amount by which the χ^2 value would decrease if the cited parameter were to be specified and freely estimated in a subsequent model. Presented in Column 3 are results for the expected parameter change (EPC) statistic (Saris, Satorra, & Sörbom, 1987). This statistic represents the predicted estimated change in either a positive or negative direction for each fixed parameter in the model should it be estimated in a subsequent test of the model. Finally, the last two columns represent two standardized versions of the EPC statistics; the STD EPC and the STDYX EPC.

Reviewing the results in Table 3.9, we see only four variables identified by M*plus* as representing possibly misfitting parameters in the model. In other words, this information suggests that if these parameters were freely estimated, their specification would lead to a better fitting model. By default, as noted in the output file, M*plus* reports only those parameters having an MI value equal to or greater than 10.00.[7] Given this default, we see only four parameters specified in Table 3.9—one factor loading, as is evident from the BY statement (F2 BY SDQ2N07), and three covariances, as indicated by the WITH statements.

Let's now inspect these four parameters a little more closely. We turn first to the factor loading (F2 BY SDQ2N07). This MI represents a secondary factor loading (also termed a *cross-loading*), suggesting that if the observed variable SDQ2N07 (designed to measure Math SC; Factor 4) were to load additionally onto Factor 2 (Academic SC), the overall model χ^2 value would decrease by approximately 11.251 and this parameter's unstandardized estimate would be approximately −0.563. Although the EPC can be helpful in determining whether a parameter identified by the MI is justified as a candidate for respecification as a freely estimated parameter, Bentler (2005) has cautioned that these EPC statistics are sensitive to the way by which variables and factors are scaled or identified. Thus, their absolute values can sometimes be difficult. In the present case, from a substantive perspective, I would definitely be concerned that the EPC value is negative (−0.563), as any relation between *SDQ2N07* and Academic SC should be positive.

Turning to information related to the three remaining MIs, we see that they all represent covariances between specified observed variables. However, given that (a) the observed variables in a CFA model are always dependent variables in the model, and (b) in SEM neither variances nor covariances of dependent variables are eligible for estimation, these MIs must necessarily represent observed variable residual covariances. Accordingly, these MI results suggest that if we were to estimate, for example, a covariance between the residuals associated with *SDQ2N25* and *SDQ2N01*, the approximate value of this estimated residual covariance would be 0.359.

Overall, both the MIs and their related EPCs, although admittedly > 10.00, are very small and not worthy of inclusion in a subsequently specified model. Of prime importance in determining whether or not to include additional parameters in the model is the extent to which (a) they are substantively meaningful, (b) the existing model exhibits adequate fit, and (c) the EPC value is substantial. Superimposed on this decision is the ever constant need for scientific parsimony. Because model respecification is commonly conducted in SEM in general, as well as in several applications highlighted in this book, I consider it important to provide you with a brief overview of the various issues related to these post hoc analyses.

Post Hoc Analyses

In the application of SEM in testing for the validity of hypothesized models, the researcher will be faced, at some point, with the decision of whether or not to respecify and reestimate the model. If he or she elects to follow this route, it is important to realize that analyses will then be framed within an *exploratory* rather than a *confirmatory* mode. In other words, once a hypothesized CFA model has been rejected, this spells the end of the confirmatory factor analytic approach in its truest sense. Although CFA procedures continue to be used in any respecification and reestimation of the model, these analyses are exploratory in the sense that they focus on the detection of misfitting parameters in the originally hypothesized model. Such post hoc analyses are conventionally termed *specification searches* (see MacCallum, 1986). (The issue of post hoc model fitting is addressed further in Chapter 9 in the section dealing with cross-validation.)

The ultimate decision underscoring whether or not to proceed with a specification search is threefold, and focuses on substantive as well as statistical aspects of the MI results. First, the researcher must determine whether the estimation of the targeted parameter is substantively meaningful. If, indeed, it makes no sound substantive sense to free up the parameter exhibiting the MI value, one may wish to consider the parameter having the next largest value (Jöreskog, 1993). Second, both the MI and EPC values should be substantially large. Third, one needs to consider whether or not the respecified model would lead to an overfitted model. The issue here is tied to the idea of knowing when to stop fitting the model, or, as Wheaton (1987) phrased the problem, "knowing … how much fit is enough without being too much fit" (p. 123). In general, overfitting a model involves the specification of additional parameters in the model after having determined a criterion that reflects a minimally adequate fit. For example, an *overfitted model* can result from the inclusion of additional parameters that (a) are "fragile" in the sense of representing weak effects that are not likely replicable; (b) lead to a significant inflation of standard errors; and (c) influence primary parameters in the model, even though their own substantive meaningfulness is somewhat equivocal (Wheaton, 1987). Although residual covariances often fall into this latter category,[8] there are many situations, particularly with respect to social psychological research, where these parameters can make strong substantive sense and therefore should be included in the model (Cole, Ciesla, & Steiger, 2007; Jöreskog & Sörbom, 1993).

Having laboriously worked our way through the process involved in testing for the validity of this initial postulated model, what can we conclude regarding the CFA model under scrutiny in this chapter? In answering this question, we must necessarily pool all the information gleaned from our study of the Mplus output. Taking into account (a) the feasibility and statistical significance of all parameter estimates; (b) the substantially good fit of the model, with particular reference to the CFI (.961) and RMSEA (.049) values; and (c) the lack of any substantial evidence of model misfit, I conclude that any further incorporation of parameters into the model would result in an overfitted model. Indeed,

MacCallum, Roznowski, and Necowitz (1992) have cautioned that "when an initial model fits well, it is probably unwise to modify it to achieve even better fit because modifications may simply be fitting small idiosyncratic characteristics of the sample" (p. 501). Adhering to this caveat, I conclude that the four-factor model schematically portrayed in Figure 3.1 represents an adequate description of self-concept structure for Grade 7 adolescents.

In keeping with the goals of the original study (Byrne & Worth Gavin, 1996), we turn next to the first alternative hypothesis—that SC for Grade 7 adolescents is a two-factor model consisting of only the constructs of General SC and Academic SC.

Hypothesis 2: Self-Concept Is a Two-Factor Structure

The model to be tested here postulates a priori that SC is a two-factor structure consisting of GSC and ASC. As such, it argues against the viability of subject-specific academic SC factors. As with the four-factor model, the four GSC measures load onto the GSC factor; in contrast, all other measures load onto the ASC factor. This hypothesized model is represented schematically in Figure 3.15, and the M*plus* input file is shown in Figure 3.16.

Mplus Input File Specification and Output File Results

Input File

In reviewing these graphical and equation model specifications, three points relative to the modification of the input file are of interest. First, although the pattern of factor loadings remains the same for the GSC and ASC measures, it changes for both the ESC and MSC measures in allowing them to load onto the ASC factor. Second, because only one of these 12 ASC factor loadings needs to be fixed to 1.0, the two previously constrained parameters (*SDQ2N10* and *SDQ2N07*) are now freely estimated. Finally, given that the observed variables specified in this analysis are sequentially listed in the data file, we need to enter only two rows of specifications under the MODEL command in the M*plus* input file.

Output File

Because only the goodness-of-fit statistics are relevant to the present application, these sole results are presented in Table 3.10. In reviewing this

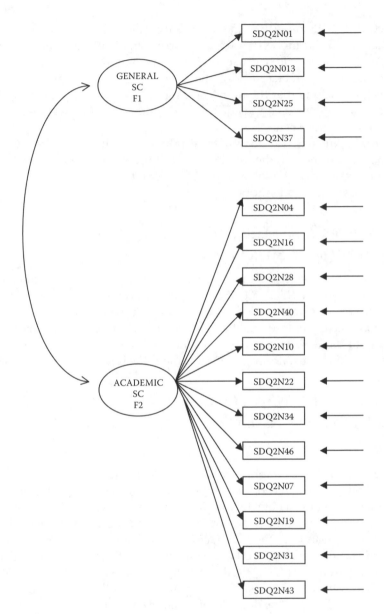

Figure 3.15. Hypothesized two-factor CFA model of self-concept.

output file, I limit our examination to only the χ^2 statistic and the CFI, TLI, and RMSEA indices, which are shown as framed within the rectangular boxes. As indicated here, the $\chi^2_{(103)}$ value of 457.653 clearly represents a poor fit to the data, and certainly a substantial decrement from the overall

```
TITLE: CFA of Academic SC Structure for Grade 7 Adolescents
       2-Factor Model

DATA:
  FILE IS "C:\Mplus\Files\ASC7INDM.DAT";
  FORMAT IS 40F1.0,X,6F2.0;

VARIABLE:
  NAMES ARE SPPCN08 SPPCN18 SPPCN28 SPPCN38 SPPCN48 SPPCN58 SPPCN01
  SPPCN11 SPPCN21 SPPCN31 SPPCN41 SPPCN51 SPPCN06 SPPCN16 SPPCN26
  SPPCN36 SPPCN46 SPPCN56 SPPCN03 SPPCN13 SPPCN23 SPPCN33 SPPCN43
  SPPCN53 SDQ2N01 SDQ2N13 SDQ2N25 SDQ2N37 SDQ2N04 SDQ2N16 SDQ2N28
  SDQ2N40 SDQ2N10 SDQ2N22 SDQ2N34 SDQ2N46 SDQ2N07 SDQ2N19 SDQ2N31
  SDQ2N43 MASTENG1 MASTMAT1 TENG1 TMAT1 SENG1 SMAT1;
  USEVARIABLES ARE SDQ2N01 SDQ2N13 SDQ2N25 SDQ2N37 SDQ2N04 SDQ2N16
  SDQ2N28 SDQ2N40 SDQ2N10 SDQ2N22 SDQ2N34 SDQ2N46 SDQ2N07 SDQ2N19
  SDQ2N31 SDQ2N43;

MODEL:
  F1 by SDQ2N01-SDQ2N37;
  F2 by SDQ2N04-SDQ2N43;
```

Figure 3.16. M*plus* language generator: Input file for hypothesized two-factor model.

fit of the four-factor model ($\chi^2_{[98]} = 159.112$). The gain of five degrees of freedom can be explained by the estimation of two fewer factor variances and five fewer factor covariances, albeit the estimation of two additional factor loadings (formerly *SDQ2N10* and *SDQ2N07*). As expected, all other indices of fit reflect the fact that SC structure is not well represented by the hypothesized two-factor model. In particular, the CFI value of .776, TLI value of .739, and RMSEA value of .114 are strongly indicative of inferior goodness-of-fit between the hypothesized two-factor model and the sample data.

Finally, we turn to our third and last alternative model, which postulates that adolescent SC is a unidimensional, rather than a multidimensional, construct.

Hypothesis 3: Self-Concept Is a One-Factor Structure

Although it now seems obvious that a multidimensional model best represents the structure of SC for Grade 7 adolescents, there are still researchers who contend that self-concept is a unidimensional construct. Thus, for purposes of completeness, and to address the issue of unidimensionality, Byrne and Worth Gavin (1996) proceeded in testing the above hypothesis. However, because the one-factor model represents a restricted version of the two-factor model, and thus cannot possibly represent a better fitting model, in the interest of space, these analyses are not presented here.

Structural Equation Modeling With Mplus

Table 3.10 Mplus Output: Goodness-of-Fit Statistics for Two-Factor Model

The Model Estimation Terminated Normally:
Tests of Model Fit

Chi-Square Test of Model Fit	
Value	457.653
Degrees of freedom	103
p-value	0.0000

Chi-Square Test of Model Fit for the Baseline Model

Value	1703.155
Degrees of freedom	120
p-value	0.0000

CFI/TLI	
CFI	0.776
TLI	0.739

Loglikelihood

H_0 value	−6711.949
H_1 value	−6483.122

Information Criteria

Number of free parameters	49
Akaike (AIC)	13521.897
Bayesian (BIC)	13697.304
Sample-size adjusted BIC ($n^* = (n + 2)/24$)	13541.948

Root Mean Square Error of Approximation (RMSEA)

Estimate	0.114
90% confidence interval (Percent CI)	0.103 0.125
Probability RMSEA <= .05	0.000

Standardized Root Mean Square Residual (SRMR)	0.095

In summary, it is evident from these analyses that both the two-factor and one-factor models of SC represent a misspecification of factorial structure for early adolescents. Based on these findings, then, Byrne and Worth Gavin (1996) concluded that SC is a multidimensional construct, which in their study comprised the four facets of general, academic, English, and mathematics SCs.

Notes

1. The use of item pairs is consistent with other construct validity research based on the Self-Description Questionnaire (SDQ) instruments conducted by Marsh and colleagues (see Byrne, 1996; Marsh, 1992).
2. LISREL (see Jöreskog & van Thillo, 1972) is considered to be the first SEM computer program produced. Although Wolfle (2003) noted that for all practical purposes, this 1972 article described LISREL I, in actuality the first commercially produced LISREL program was marketed as LISREL III (see Byrne, in press; Sörbom, 2001).
3. The independence (or null) model is so named as it represents complete independence of all variables in the model (i.e., all variables in the model are mutually uncorrelated). Beginning with the work of Tucker and Lewis (1973), the independence baseline model appears to be the one most widely used (Rigdon, 1996).
4. Nested models are hierarchically related to one another in the sense that their parameter sets are subsets of one another (i.e., particular parameters are freely estimated in one model but fixed to zero in a second model) (Bentler & Chou, 1987; Bollen, 1989).
5. A saturated model is one in which the number of estimated parameters equals the number of data points (i.e., variances and covariances of the observed variables), as in the case of the just-identified model discussed in Chapter 2. In contrast to the baseline (or independence) model, which is the most restrictive SEM model, the saturated model is the least restricted SEM model. Conceptualized within the framework of a continuum, the saturated (i.e., least restricted) model would represent one extreme endpoint, whereas the independence (the most restricted) model would represent the other; a hypothesized model will always represent a point somewhere between the two.
6. For details regarding the formulation of the MI, readers are referred to the M*plus* Technical Appendices, which can be accessed through the M*plus* website, http://www.statmodel.com.
7. This default can be overridden by stating "MODINDICES (3.84)" in the OUTPUT command; this value, of course, represents the cutpoint of $p = .05$ for χ^2 distribution with one degree of freedom.
8. Typically, the misuse in this instance arises from the incorporation of residual covariances into the model purely on the basis of statistical fit, with no consideration of substantive meaningfulness, in order to achieve a better fitting model.

chapter 4

Testing the Factorial Validity of Scores From a Measuring Instrument
First-Order Confirmatory Factor Analysis Model

For our second application, we once again examine a first-order confirmatory factor analysis (CFA) model. However, this time we test hypotheses bearing on a single measuring instrument, the Maslach Burnout Inventory (MBI; Maslach & Jackson, 1981, 1986), designed to measure three dimensions of burnout, which the authors labeled Emotional Exhaustion (EE), Depersonalization (DP), and Reduced Personal Accomplishment (PA). The term *burnout* denotes the inability to function effectively in one's job as a consequence of prolonged and extensive job-related stress: "Emotional exhaustion represents feelings of fatigue that develop as one's energies become drained"; "depersonalization," the development of negative and uncaring attitudes toward others; and "reduced personal accomplishment," a deterioration of self-confidence and dissatisfaction in one's achievements.

Purposes of the original study (Byrne, 1994a), from which this example is taken, were to test for the validity and invariance of factorial structure within and across gender for elementary and secondary teachers. For the purposes of this chapter, however, only analyses bearing on the factorial validity of the MBI for a calibration sample of elementary male teachers ($n = 372$) are of interest.

CFA of a measuring instrument is most appropriately applied to measures that have been fully developed, and their factor structures validated. The legitimacy of CFA application, of course, is tied to its conceptual rationale as a hypothesis-testing approach to data analysis. That is to say, based on theory, empirical research, or a combination of both, the researcher postulates a model and then tests for its validity given the sample data. Thus, the application of CFA procedures to assessment instruments that are still in the initial stages of development represents a serious misuse of this analytic strategy. In testing for the validity of factorial structure for an assessment measure, the researcher seeks to determine the extent to which items designed to measure a particular factor (i.e., latent construct) actually do so. In general, subscales of a measuring instrument are considered to represent the factors; all items comprising a particular subscale are therefore expected to load onto their related factor.

Given that the MBI has been commercially marketed since 1981, is the most widely used measure of occupational burnout, and has undergone substantial testing of its psychometric properties over the years (see, e.g., Byrne, 1991, 1993, 1994b), it most certainly qualifies as a candidate for CFA research. Interestingly, until my 1991 study of the MBI, virtually all previous factor analytic work had been based on only exploratory procedures. We turn now to a description of this assessment instrument.

The Measuring Instrument Under Study

The MBI is a 22-item instrument structured on a 7-point Likert-type scale that ranges from 0 (*feeling has never been experienced*) to 6 (*feeling experienced daily*). It is composed of three subscales, each measuring one facet of burnout: The EE subscale comprises nine items, the DP subscale five, and the PA subscale eight. The original version of the MBI (Maslach & Jackson, 1981) was constructed from data based on samples of workers from a wide range of human service organizations. Subsequently, however, Maslach and Jackson (1986), in collaboration with Schwab, developed the Educators' Survey (MBI Form Ed), a version of the instrument specifically designed for use with teachers. The MBI Form Ed parallels the original version of the MBI except for the modified wording of certain items to make them more appropriate to a teacher's work environment.

The Hypothesized Model

The CFA model of MBI structure hypothesizes a priori that (a) responses to the MBI can be explained by three factors: EE, DP, and PA; (b) each item has a nonzero loading on the burnout factor it was designed to measure, and zero loadings on all other factors; (c) the three factors are correlated; and (d) the residuals associated with each indicator item variable are uncorrelated. A schematic representation of this model is shown in Figure 4.1.[1]

An important aspect of the data to be used this chapter is that they are somewhat nonnormally distributed. That is to say, certain item scores on the MBI scale tend to exhibit kurtosis values that may be regarded as moderately high. Thus, before examining the M*plus* input file related to the hypothesized model shown in Figure 4.1, I wish first to address the

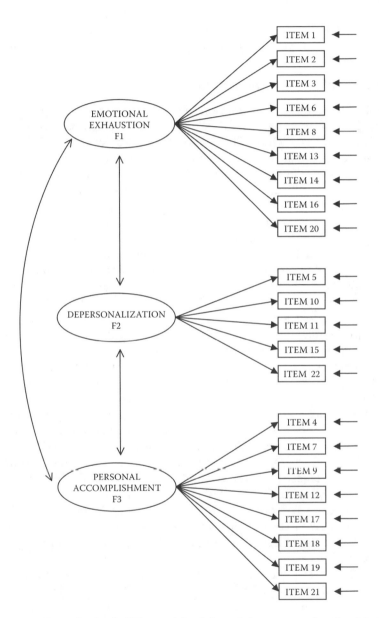

Figure 4.1. Hypothesized CFA model of factorial structure for the Maslach Burnout Inventory (MBI).

issue of nonnormality in structural equation modeling (SEM) and then outline how this problem can be addressed using M*plus*. I begin with a brief overview of the nonnormality issue in SEM, followed by an overview of the MBI item scores with respect to evidence of nonnormality. Finally, I outline the approach taken by M*plus* in the analyses of nonnormal data.

The Issue of Nonnormality in SEM

A critically important assumption in the conduct of SEM analyses is that the data are multivariate normal. This requirement is rooted in large sample theory from which the SEM methodology was spawned. Thus, before any analyses of data are undertaken, it is always important to check that this criterion has been met. Particularly problematic to SEM analyses are data that are multivariate kurtotic, the situation where the multivariate distribution of the observed variables has both tails and peaks that differ from those characteristic of a multivariate normal distribution (see Raykov & Marcoulides, 2000). More specifically, in the case of multivariate *positive* kurtosis, the distributions will exhibit peakedness together with heavy (or thick) tails; conversely, multivariate *negative* kurtosis will yield flat distributions with light tails (DeCarlo, 1997). To exemplify the most commonly found condition of multivariate kurtosis in SEM, let's take the case of a Likert-scaled questionnaire, for which responses to certain items result in the majority of respondents selecting the same scale point. For each of these items, the score distribution would be extremely peaked (i.e., leptokurtic); considered jointly, these particular items would reflect a multivariately positive kurtotic distribution. (For an elaboration of both univariate and multivariate kurtosis, readers are referred to DeCarlo, 1997.)

Prerequisite to the assessment of multivariate normality is the need to check for univariate normality, as the latter is a necessary, although not sufficient, condition for multivariate normality (DeCarlo, 1997). Research has shown that whereas skewness tends to impact tests of means, kurtosis severely affects tests of variances and covariances (DeCarlo, 1997). Given that SEM is based on the analysis of covariance structures, evidence of kurtosis is always of concern, in particular evidence of multivariate kurtosis as it is known to be exceptionally detrimental in SEM analyses.

M*plus*, in contrast to other SEM programs (e.g., AMOS and EQS), does not provide a single measure of multivariate kurtosis. However, it does enable the provision of actual univariate skewness and kurtosis values. That M*plus* does not yield a coefficient of multivariate kurtosis is moot and in no way detracts from its capacity or approach in dealing with the presence of such nonnormality in the data. Rather, the omission of this coefficient is simply in keeping with Muthén and Muthén's (2007–2010) contention that such representation based on a single number is both unnecessary and somewhat meaningless given the current availability of robust estimators today; as such, they recommend a comparison of both the scaled and unscaled χ^2 statistics, as well as the parameter standard errors (M*plus* Product Support, March 4, 2010).

Although it is possible to obtain values of skewness and kurtosis using M*plus*, the process requires a greater understanding of the program notation than can be expected for my readers at this early stage of the book. To avoid much unnecessary confusion, then, I do not include these details here. However, for readers who may have an interest in knowing how to obtain observed variable skewness and kurtosis values using M*plus*, I present this information via a walkthrough of the process in the addendum at the end of this chapter.

Based on other construct validity research bearing on the MBI (Byrne, 1991, 1993, 1994a), and as will be shown in Figure 4.8 in the addendum, it is evident that the data used in this application certainly exhibit evidence of kurtosis, an issue that must be addressed in our current analyses of MBI factorial structure.

In judging the extent to which kurtosis values may be indicative of nonnormality, we must first know the range of values expected in a normal distribution. Accordingly, when scores are normally distributed, the Standardized Kurtosis Index has a value of 3.00, with larger values representing positive kurtosis and lesser values representing negative kurtosis. However, computer programs typically rescale this value such that zero serves as the indicator of a normal distribution and its sign serves as the indicator of positive or negative kurtosis (DeCarlo, 1997; Kline, 2011; West, Finch, & Curran, 1995).

At this point, no doubt you are wondering how far a kurtosis value must deviate from zero before it can be regarded as problematic. Unfortunately, to date, there appears to be no clear consensus regarding this question (Kline, 2011) as absolute kurtosis values ranging from ± 2.0 (Boomsma & Hoogland, 2001; Muthén & Kaplan, 1985) to ± 7.0 (West et al., 1995) and higher (DeCarlo, 1997) have been proposed as possible early departure points of nonnormality. Thus, although kurtosis values may appear not to be excessive, they may nonetheless be sufficiently nonnormal to make interpretations based on the usual χ^2 statistic, as well as the Comparative Fit Index (CFI), Tucker-Lewis Fit Index (TLI), and Root Mean Square Error of Approximation (RMSEA) indices, problematic. Thus, it is always best to err on the side of caution by taking this information into account.

In contrast to the lack of consensus regarding the point at which the onset of nonnormality can be considered to begin, there is strong consensus that when variables demonstrate substantial nonzero univariate kurtosis, they most certainly will not be multivariately normally distributed.

As such, the presence of kurtotic variables may be sufficient enough to render the distribution as multivariate nonnormal, thereby violating the underlying assumption of normality associated with the ML method of estimation. Violation of this assumption can seriously invalidate statistical hypothesis testing with the result that the normal theory test statistic (χ^2) may not reflect an adequate evaluation of the model under study (Hu, Bentler, & Kano, 1992). (For an elaboration of other problems arising from the presence of nonnormal variables, readers are referred to Bentler, 2005; Curran, West, & Finch, 1996; West et al., 1995.) Although alternative estimation methods have been developed for use when the normality assumption does not hold (e.g., asymptotic distribution-free [ADF], elliptical, and heterogeneous kurtotic), Chou, Bentler, and Satorra (1991) and Hu et al. (1992) contended that it may be more appropriate to correct the test statistic, rather than use a different mode of estimation.

Indeed, Satorra and Bentler (1988) developed such a statistic that incorporates a scaling correction for the χ^2 statistic (subsequently termed the Satorra-Bentler χ^2, or S-Bχ^2) when distributional assumptions are violated; its computation takes into account the model, the estimation method, and the sample kurtosis values. In this regard, the S-Bχ^2 has been shown to be the most reliable test statistic for evaluating mean and covariance structure models under various distributions and sample sizes (Curran, West, & Finch, 1996; Hu et al., 1992). The S-Bχ^2 statistic is available in M*plus* when the MLM estimator is specified. As such, it is described as being capable of estimating ML parameter estimates with standard errors and a mean-adjusted χ^2 test statistic that are robust to nonnormality (Muthén & Muthén, 2007–2010).[2] In addition, robust versions of the CFI, TLI, and RMSEA are also computed. That these statistics are *robust* means that their computed values are valid, despite violations of the normality assumption underlying the estimation method.

Over and above the existence of nonnormal variables that lead ultimately to the presence of multivariate nonnormality, it is now known that the converse is not necessarily true. That is, regardless of whether the distribution of observed variables is univariate normal, the multivariate distribution can still be multivariate nonnormal (West et al., 1995). Thus, from a purely practical perspective, it seems clearly reasonable always to base model analyses on the robust estimator if and when it is appropriate to do so, that is to say, as long as all conditions associated with the estimation process are met within the framework of a particular program. For example, both the ML and MLM estimators noted in this chapter are appropriate for data that are continuous, and the type of analyses (within the framework of M*plus*) can be categorized as *General*. On the other hand, in the event that the data are in any way incomplete, then the MLM estimator cannot be used. (For detailed descriptions of additional robust estimators in M*plus*, readers are referred to Muthén & Muthén, 2007–2010.)

In summary, a critically important assumption associated with applications of SEM is that the data are multivariate normal. Given that conditions associated with the MLM estimator (as well as other robust estimators) can be met, it seems perfectly reasonable to base analyses on this estimator, rather than on the ML estimator. Although the latter is considered to be fairly robust to minor evidence of nonnormality, it will certainly be less effective in dealing with data that may suffer from stronger levels of nonnormality. One very simple way of assessing the extent to which data might be nonnormally distributed is to test the model of interest on the basis of both estimators; that is, test it once using the ML estimator, and then test a second time using the MLM estimator. If the data are multivariate normal, there will be virtually no, or at least very little, difference between the two χ^2 values. If, on the other hand, there is a large discrepancy in these values, then it is clear that the data are multivariate nonnormal, and thus use of the MLM estimator is the most appropriate approach to the analyses.

With this information on nonnormality in hand, let's now move on to a review of analyses related to tests for the validity of hypothesized MBI structure as portrayed in Figure 4.1. The M*plus* input file related to this initial test of the model is shown in Figure 4.2. However, because I wish to illustrate the extent to which the χ^2 statistic can vary when the data are nonnormally distributed—and even minimally so—I present you with two M*plus* input files: the upper one specifying analyses based on the ML estimator (which is default and thus not included here), and the lower one based on the MLM estimator.

Mplus Input File Specification and Output File Results

Input File 1

Turning first to the DATA command, we see that the name of the data file is elemm1.dat, with the format statement showing that there are 22 variables, each of which occupies one column. From the VARIABLE command, we learn that these observed measures are labeled *ITEM 1* through *ITEM 22*, and all 22 will be used in the analyses. The only difference between these two files is that, because ML estimation is default, there is no need to include the ANALYSIS command in the ML input file. In contrast, this command is included for the MLM file as the request for MLM estimation must be explicitly stated. The OUTPUT command for both files is the same and requests that Modification Indices (MIs) be reported in the output file.

```
TITLE: CFA of MBI for Male Elementary Teachers (Calibration Group)
       Initial Model - ML Estimation

DATA:
  FILE IS "C:\Mplus\Files\elemm1.dat";
  FORMAT IS 22F1.0;

VARIABLE:
  NAMES ARE ITEM1 - ITEM22;
  USEVARIABLES ARE ITEM1 - ITEM22;

MODEL:
  F1 by ITEM1 - ITEM3 ITEM6 ITEM8 ITEM13 ITEM14 ITEM16 ITEM20;
  F2 by ITEM5 ITEM10 ITEM11 ITEM15 ITEM22;
  F3 by ITEM4 ITEM7 ITEM9 ITEM12 ITEM17 - ITEM19 ITEM21;

OUTPUT: MODINDICES;
```

```
TITLE: CFA of MBI for Male Elementary Teachers (Calibration Group)
       Initial Model - MLM Estimation

DATA:
  FILE IS "C:\Mplus\Files\elemm1.dat";
  FORMAT IS 22F1.0;

VARIABLE:
  NAMES ARE ITEM1 - ITEM22;
  USEVARIABLES ARE ITEM1 - ITEM22;

ANALYSIS:
  ESTIMATOR = MLM;

MODEL:
  F1 by ITEM1 - ITEM3 ITEM6 ITEM8 ITEM13 ITEM14 ITEM16 ITEM20;
  F2 by ITEM5 ITEM10 ITEM11 ITEM15 ITEM22;
  F3 by ITEM4 ITEM7 ITEM9 ITEM12 ITEM17 - ITEM19 ITEM21;

OUTPUT: MODINDICES;
```

Figure 4.2. M*plus* input files based on the maximum likelihood (ML) estimator (upper file) and robust maximum likelihood (MLM) estimator (lower file).

Comparison of ML and MLM Output

Model Assessment

In Figure 4.3, you will see goodness-of-fit statistics for the hypothesized model as they relate to the ML and MLM estimations (see file outputs on the left and right sides of the table, respectively). My major focus here is in highlighting differences between the two with respect to the χ^2 statistic, as well as the CFI, TLI, and RMSEA indices. As you will readily observe,

TESTS OF MODEL FIT – ML ESTIMATION

Chi-Square Test of Model Fit

Value   695.719
Degrees of Freedom   206
P-value

CFI/TLI

CFI   0.848
TLI   0.830

RMSEA (Root Mean Square Error Of Approximation)

Estimate   0.080
90 Percent C.I.   0.073 0.087
Probability RMSEA <= .05   0.000

SRMR (Standardized Root Mean Square Residual)

Value   0.070

TESTS OF MODEL FIT – MLM ESTIMATION

Chi-Square Test of Model Fit

Value   588.869*
Degrees of Freedom   206
P-Value   0.0000
Scaling Correction Factor   1.181
for MLM

CFI/TLI

CFI   0.858
TLI   0.841

RMSEA (Root Mean Square Error Of Approximation)

Estimate   0.071

SRMR (Standardized Root Mean Square Residual)

Value   0.070

Figure 4.3. M*plus* output files showing goodness-of-fit statistics based on ML estimation (on the left) and on MLM estimation (on the right).

there is a fairly large χ^2 discrepancy resulting from ML estimation (695.719) compared with that from MLM estimation (588.869). Pertinent to the latter, as noted earlier, the value has been corrected to take into account the non-normality of the data. Under the MLM estimation results, note that M*plus* has reported the scaling correction factor as being 1.181. Accordingly, this value multiplied by the MLM χ^2 value should approximate the uncorrected ML χ^2 value, which, indeed, it does (588.869 * 1.181 = 695.454). Given that values > 1.00 are indicative of distributions that deviate more than would be expected according to normal theory, we can interpret the value of 1.181 as signifying a slight elevation in the presence of scores that are nonnormally distributed (see Bentler, 2005).

In addition to the discrepancy in χ^2 values, note also that the scaling factor made a difference to both the CFI and TLI values, which are very slightly higher for the MLM, than for the ML estimator; likewise, the RMSEA value is lower. Although M*plus* reports a 90% confidence interval for the ML estimate, no interval accompanies the robust RMSEA value.

Given that estimation of the hypothesized model based on the robust MLM estimator yielded results that appropriately represented the moderate nonnormality of the data, all subsequent discussion related to results of this initial test of the model will be based on the MLM output. Accordingly, let's turn once again to tests of model fit presented in Figure 4.3, albeit with specific attention to results for the MLM model. Although both the Standardized Root Mean Square Residual (SRMR; 0.070) and RMSEA (0.071) values are barely within the scope of adequate model fit, those for the CFI (0.858) and TLI (0.841) are clearly indicative of an ill-fitting model. To assist us in pinpointing possible areas of misfit, we examine the MIs. Of course, as noted in Chapter 3, it is important to realize that once we have determined that the hypothesized model represents a poor fit to the data (i.e., the null hypothesis has been rejected) and subsequently embark upon post hoc model fitting to identify areas of misfit in the model, we cease to operate in a confirmatory mode of analysis. All model specification and estimation henceforth represent exploratory analyses. We turn now to the issue of misspecification with respect to our hypothesized model.

Model Misspecification

Recall from Chapter 3 that the targets of model modification are only those parameters specified as constrained either to zero or to some non-zero value, or as equal to some other estimated parameter. In this chapter, only parameters constrained to zero are of interest, with the primary focus being the factor loadings and observed variable residual covariances. As such, the zero factor loadings represent the loading of an item on a nontarget factor (i.e., a factor the item was not designed to measure). Zero values for the residual covariances, of course, simply represent the fact that none

Table 4.1 M*plus* Output: Modification Indices (MIs) for Hypothesized Model

	MI	Expected Parameter Change (EPC)	Standard EPC	StdYX EPC
Model Modification Indices				
BY Statements				
→F1 BY ITEM12	**35.141**	**−0.313**	**−0.400**	**−0.335**
F2 BY ITEM12	11.992	−0.329	−0.276	−0.232
F3 BY ITEM1	24.320	0.872	0.383	0.231
F3 BY ITEM2	10.741	0.565	0.248	0.161
F3 BY ITEM13	10.712	−0.583	−0.256	−0.152
WITH Statements				
→ITEM2 WITH ITEM1	**69.786**	**0.613**	**0.613**	**0.549**
ITEM6 WITH ITEM5	14.552	0.354	0.354	0.232
ITEM7 WITH ITEM4	28.298	0.209	0.209	0.324
ITEM11 WITH ITEM10	32.234	0.580	0.580	0.525
ITEM12 WITH ITEM3	13.129	−0.255	−0.255	−0.225
ITEM15 WITH ITEM5	13.190	0.313	0.313	0.243
→**ITEM16 WITH ITEM6**	**77.264**	**0.733**	**0.733**	**0.529**
ITEM18 WITH ITEM7	10.000	−0.145	−0.145	−0.211
ITEM19 WITH ITEM18	15.749	0.250	0.250	0.285
ITEM20 WITH ITEM8	12.029	0.230	0.230	0.240
ITEM20 WITH ITEM13	11.059	0.237	0.237	0.214
ITEM21 WITH ITEM4	11.090	0.201	0.201	0.201
ITEM21 WITH ITEM7	28.380	0.263	0.263	0.326

of the item residual variances are correlated with one another. In reviewing misspecification results for the factor loadings (listed under the BY statements), large MI values argue for the presence of factor cross-loadings (i.e., a loading on more than one factor), whereas large MIs appearing under the WITH statements represent the presence of residual covariances. Let's turn now to Table 4.1, where the MIs resulting from this initial test of the hypothesized model are reported.

Although a review of the MIs presented here reveals a few very large values, two in particular stand apart from the rest (MI = 77.264; MI = 69.786). Both MIs signify residual covariances, with the larger of the two representing a residual covariance between Item 16 and Item 6, and the next largest representing a covariance between Item 1 and Item 2; both are flagged with boldface type. As you will recall from my extensive explanation of this topic in Chapter 3, the MI value of 77.264, for example, indicates that if this parameter were to be freely estimated, the overall χ^2 statistic could decrease by approximately that amount.

Other important additional information is the expected parameter change (EPC) values, which, as you may recall from Chapter 3, represent the approximate value that a parameter is expected to attain should it be subsequently estimated. In the case of both residual covariances here, the EPC values can be considered to be extremely high (Items 16/6 = 0.733; Items 2/1 = 0.613) and argue strongly for their model specification.

These measurement residual covariances represent systematic rather than random measurement error in item responses, and they may derive from characteristics specific either to the items or to the respondents (Aish & Jöreskog, 1990). For example, if these parameters reflect item characteristics, they may represent a small omitted factor. If, on the other hand, they represent respondent characteristics, they may reflect bias such as yeasaying or naysaying, social desirability, and the like (Aish & Jöreskog, 1990). Another type of method effect that can trigger residual covariances is a high degree of overlap in item content. Such redundancy occurs when an item, although worded differently, essentially asks the same question. I believe the latter situation to be the case here. For example, Item 16 asks whether working with people directly puts too much stress on the respondent, whereas Item 6 asks whether working with people all day puts a real strain on him or her.[3]

Although a review of the MIs related to the factor loadings reveals five parameters representative of cross-loadings, I draw your attention to the one with the highest value (MI = 35.141). This parameter, which represents the cross-loading of Item 12 on the EE factor, stands apart from the other three possible cross-loading misspecifications. Such misspecification, for example, could mean that Item 12, in addition to measuring personal accomplishment, also measures emotional exhaustion; alternatively, it could indicate that, although Item 12 was postulated to load on the PA factor, it may load more appropriately on the EE factor.

Post Hoc Analyses

Provided with information related both to model fit and to possible areas of model misspecification, a researcher may wish to consider respecifying an originally hypothesized model. As emphasized in Chapter 3 and noted earlier in this chapter, should this be the case, it is critically important to be cognizant of both the exploratory nature of and the dangers associated with the process of post hoc model fitting. Having determined (a) inadequate fit of the hypothesized model to the sample data, and (b) at least two substantially misspecified parameters in the model (e.g., the two residual covariances were originally specified as zero), it seems both reasonable and logical that we now move into exploratory mode and attempt to modify this model in a sound and responsible manner. Thus, for didactic purposes in illustrating the various aspects of post hoc model fitting, we'll proceed to respecify the initially hypothesized model of MBI structure taking this information into account.

Model respecification that includes correlated residuals, as with other parameters, must be supported by a strong substantive and/or empirical rationale (Jöreskog, 1993), and I believe that this condition exists here. In light of (a) apparent item content overlap, (b) the replication of these same residual covariances in previous MBI research (e.g., Byrne, 1991, 1993), and (c) Bentler and Chou's (1987) admonition that forcing large error terms to be uncorrelated is rarely appropriate with real data, I consider respecification of this initial model to be justified. Testing of this respecified model (Model 2) now falls within the framework of post hoc analyses. We turn now to this modification process.

Testing the Validity of Model 2

Respecification of the hypothesized model of MBI structure involves the addition of freely estimated parameters to the model. However, because the estimation of MIs in M*plus* is based on a univariate approach (cf. EQS and a multivariate approach), it is critical that we add only one parameter at a time to the model as the MI values can change substantially from one tested parameterization to another. (An excellent example of such fluctuation is evidenced in Chapter 6 of this volume.) Thus, in building Model 2, it seems most reasonable to proceed first in adding to the model the residual covariance having the largest MI. Recall from Table 4.1 that this parameter represents the residual covariance between Items 6 and 16 and, according to the EPC statistic, should result in a parameter estimated value of approximately 0.733. The M*plus* input file for Model 2 is shown in Figure 4.4.

Input File 2

In reviewing this revised input file, note the newly specified parameter representing a residual covariance between Item 6 and Item 16. The only other change to the original input file is the title, which indicates that the model under study is Model 2.

Output File 2

Selected results pertinent to the testing of Model 2 are reported in Table 4.2. Included here are the key model goodness-of-fit statistics, as well as the estimated value of the specified residual covariance between Items 6 and 16.

```
TITLE: CFA of MBI for Male Elementary Teachers (Calibration Group)
       MLM Estimation

DATA:
  FILE IS "C:\Mplus\Files\elemm1.dat";
  FORMAT IS 22F1.0;

VARIABLE:
  NAMES ARE ITEM1 - ITEM22;
  USEVARIABLES ARE ITEM1 - ITEM22;

ANALYSIS:
  ESTIMATOR = MLM;

MODEL:
  F1 by ITEM1 - ITEM3 ITEM6 ITEM8 ITEM13 ITEM14 ITEM16 ITEM20;
  F2 by ITEM5 ITEM10 ITEM11 ITEM15 ITEM22;
  F3 by ITEM4 ITEM7 ITEM9 ITEM12 ITEM17 - ITEM19 ITEM21;     ┌─────────────────┐
                                                              │ Newly specified  │
  ITEM6 WITH ITEM16; ─────────────────────────────────────── │ residual covariance │
                                                              └─────────────────┘
OUTPUT: MODINDICES;
```

Figure 4.4. M*plus* input file showing specification of the addition of a residual covariance between Items 6 and 16.

Turning first to the test of model fit, we find a substantial drop in the MLM χ^2 from 588.869 to 507.188. It is important at this time for me to explain that when analyses are based on ML estimation, it has become customary to determine if the difference in fit between the two models is statistically significant. As such, the researcher examines the difference in χ^2 ($\Delta\chi^2$) values between the two models. Doing so, however, presumes that the two models are nested.[4] This difference between the models is itself χ^2 distributed, with degrees of freedom equal to the difference in degrees of freedom (Δdf); it can thus be tested statistically, with a significant $\Delta\chi^2$ indicating substantial improvement in model fit. However, as the asterisk in Table 4.2 serves to remind us, when model comparisons are based on MLM estimation, it is inappropriate to calculate the difference between the two scaled χ^2 values as they are not distributed as χ^2. Although a formula is available for computing this differential (see the "Technical Appendices" on the M*plus* website, http://www.statmodel.com; Bentler, 2005), there is no particular need to determine this information here. (A detailed example of how this differential value is computed will be illustrated in Chapter 6.) Suffice it to say that the inclusion of this one residual covariance to the model made a very influential difference to the model fit, which is also reflected in increased values for both the CFI (from 0.858 to 0.888) and TLI (from 0.841 to 0.874), albeit slightly lower values for the RMSEA (from 0.071 to 0.063) and SRMR (from 0.070 to 0.069).

Turning now to the model results in Table 4.2, we can see that the estimated value for the residual covariance is 0.733, exactly in tune with

Table 4.2 M*plus* Output for Model 2:
Selected Goodness-of-Fit Statistics and Model Results

Tests of Model Fit	
Chi-Square Test of Model Fit	
Value	507.188*
Degrees of freedom	205
p-value	0.0000
Scaling Correction Factor for MLM	1.179
CFI/TLI	
CFI	0.888
TLI	0.874
Root Mean Square Error of Approximation (RMSEA)	
Estimate	0.063
Standardized Root Mean Square Residual (SRMR)	
Value	0.069

Model Results				
	Estimate	Standard Error (*SE*)	Estimate/*SE*	Two-Tailed *p*-Value
ITEM6 WITH ITEM16	0.733	0.108	6.772	0.000

* The chi-square value for MLM, MLMV, MLR, ULSMV, WLSM, and WLSMV cannot be used for chi-square difference testing in the regular way. MLM, MLR, and WLSM chi-square difference testing is described on the M*plus* website. MLMV, WLSMV, and ULSMV difference testing is done using the DIFFTEST option.

the predicted EPC value. With a standard error of 0.108, the *z*-value of this parameter is 6.772 (0.733/0.108), which is highly significant. Results from both the fit statistics and the estimated value for the residual covariance between Items 6 and 16 provide sound justification for the inclusion of this parameter in the model.

Let's now review the resulting MIs for Model 2, which are shown in Table 4.3. Here we observe that the residual covariance related to Items 1 and 2 remains a strongly misspecified parameter (MI = 66.418) in the model, with the EPC statistic suggesting that if this parameter were incorporated into the model, it would result in an estimated value of approximately 0.591, which, again, is exceptionally high. As with the residual covariance between Items 6 and 16, the one between Items 1 and 2 suggests redundancy due to content overlap. Item 1 asks if the respondent feels emotionally drained from his or her work, whereas Item 2 asks if the respondent feels used up at the end of the workday. Clearly, there appears to be an overlap of content between these two items.

Table 4.3 M*plus* Output for Model 2: Modification Indices (MIs)

Model Modification Indices				
	MI	Expected Parameter Change (EPC)	Standard EPC	StdYX EPC
BY Statements				
F1 BY ITEM12	35.584	−0.310	−0.400	−0.336
F2 BY ITEM12	12.038	−0.331	−0.276	−0.232
F3 BY ITEM1	23.917	0.851	0.374	0.225
F3 BY ITEM2	10.252	0.543	0.239	0.155
F3 BY ITEM13	12.415	−0.628	−0.276	−0.164
WITH Statements				
→ITEM2 WITH ITEM1	**66.418**	**0.591**	**0.591**	**0.545**
ITEM7 WITH ITEM4	28.329	0.209	0.209	0.323
ITEM11 WITH ITEM10	31.691	0.578	0.578	0.526
ITEM12 WITH ITEM3	12.977	−0.253	−0.253	−0.225
ITEM13 WITH ITEM1	10.521	−0.249	−0.249	−0.221
ITEM13 WITH ITEM2	10.269	−0.237	−0.237	−0.213
ITEM15 WITH ITEM5	13.633	0.318	0.318	0.246
ITEM18 WITH ITEM7	10.080	−0.146	−0.146	−0.211
ITEM19 WITH ITEM18	15.797	0.250	0.250	0.285
ITEM20 WITH ITEM2	10.069	−0.216	−0.216	−0.202
ITEM20 WITH ITEM8	11.592	0.227	0.227	0.239
ITEM20 WITH ITEM13	11.369	0.242	0.242	0.218
ITEM21 WITH ITEM4	11.086	0.200	0.200	0.200
ITEM21 WITH ITEM7	28.423	0.263	0.263	0.326

Given the strength of both the MI and EPC values for this residual covariance, together with the obvious overlap of item content, I recommend that this residual covariance parameter also be included in the respecified model, which we'll call Model 3. Let's move on, then, to the testing of this second respecified model.

Testing the Validity of Model 3

Specification of Model 3 is simply a matter of modifying the Model 2 input file (see Figure 4.4) such that it includes the additional WITH statement "ITEM 1 WITH ITEM 2." Model fit statistics for this model, together with the resulting estimate for the residual covariance between Items 1 and 2, are shown in Table 4.4.

Table 4.4 M*plus* Output for Model 3:
Selected Goodness-of-Fit Statistics and Model Results

Tests of Model Fit	
Chi-Square Test of Model Fit	
Value	441.687
Degrees of freedom	204
p-value	0.0000
Scaling Correction Factor for MLM	1.178
CFI/TLI	
CFI	0.912
TLI	0.900
Root Mean Square Error of Approximation (RMSEA)	
Estimate	0.056
Standardized Root Mean Square Residual (SRMR)	
Value	0.066

Model Results			
	Estimate	Standard Error (*SE*)	Estimate/*SE*	Two-Tailed *p*-Value
ITEM1 WITH ITEM2	0.596	0.070	8.573	0.000

In reviewing goodness-of-fit statistics related to Model 3, we again observe a substantially large improvement in fit over that of Model 2 (MLM $\chi^2_{[204]}$ = 441.687 versus MLM $\chi^2_{[205]}$ = 507.188; CFI = 0.912 versus CFI = 0.888; TLI = 0.900 versus TLI = 0.874; and RMSEA = 0.056 versus RMSEA = 0.063).

Likewise, examination of the model results reveals the estimated value of the residual covariance between Items 1 and 2 to approximate its EPC value (see Table 4.4) and to be statistically significant (Estimate [Est]/ standard error [*SE*] = 8.573).

Turning to the MIs, presented in Table 4.5, we see that there is still at least one residual covariance with a fairly large MI (Item 11 with Item 10). Item 11 asks the teacher respondent if it is a concern that the job may be hardening him or her emotionally, whereas Item 10 asks if the teacher believes she or he has become more callous since taking the job.

In addition to this residual covariance, however, it is important to note results related to the misspecified factor loading (Item 12) noted earlier, as indicated by an MI value of 34.815, which is slightly higher than the MI value of 31.563 for the residual covariance. In the initially hypothesized

Table 4.5 M*plus* Output for Model 3: Modification Indices (MIs)

	MI	Expected Parameter Change (EPC)	Standard EPC	StdYX EPC
Model Modification Indices				
BY Statements				
→F1 BY ITEM12	**34.815**	**−0.332**	**−0.404**	**−0.339**
F2 BY ITEM12	11.882	−0.329	−0.274	−0.230
F3 BY ITEM1 12.254	0.560	0.246	0.148	
WITH Statements				
ITEM3 WITH ITEM1	11.815	0.248	0.248	0.192
ITEM7 WITH ITEM4	28.448	0.210	0.210	0.324
→ITEM11 WITH ITEM10	**31.563**	**0.575**	**0.575**	**0.523**
ITEM12 WITH ITEM3	13.944	−0.265	−0.265	−0.233
ITEM15 WITH ITEM5	13.518	0.316	0.316	0.245
ITEM19 WITH ITEM18	15.777	0.250	0.250	0.285
ITEM21 WITH ITEM4	11.161	0.201	0.201	0.201
ITEM21 WITH ITEM7	28.544	0.264	0.264	0.327

model, this item was specified as loading on Factor 3 (Reduced Personal Accomplishment), yet the MI is telling us that it should additionally load on Factor 1 (Emotional Exhaustion). In trying to understand why this cross-loading might be occurring, let's take a look at the essence of the item content, which asks for a level of agreement or disagreement with the statement that the respondent feels very energetic. Although this item was deemed by Maslach and Jackson (1981, 1986) to measure a sense of personal accomplishment, it seems both evident and logical that it also taps one's feelings of emotional exhaustion. Ideally, items on a measuring instrument should clearly target only one of its underlying constructs (or factors).[5] The question related to our analysis of the MBI, however, is whether or not to include this parameter in a third respecified model. Provided with some justification for the double-loading effect, together with evidence from the literature that this same cross-loading has been noted in other research, I consider it appropriate to respecify Model 4 with this parameter freely estimated.

Given (a) the presence of these two clearly misspecified parameters (residual covariance between Items 10 and 11, and cross-loading of Item 12 on Factor 3), (b) the close proximity of their MI values, (c) the logical and substantively viable rationales for both respecifications, and (d) the need to keep a close eye on model parsimony, we face the question of how to proceed from here. Do we respecify the model to include the residual covariance, or do we respecify it to include a factor cross-loading? Presented with such results, it is prudent to also compare their EPC values. In this instance, we find that if the cross-loading were specified, the expected estimated value would be −0.332; in contrast, the expected estimate for the residual covariance would be 0.575. That the projected estimate for the residual covariance is the stronger of the two argues in favor of its selection over the cross-loading for inclusion in the model (see, e.g., Kaplan, 1989). Thus, with the residual covariance between Items 10 and 11 added to the (Model 3) input file, we now move on to test this newly respecified model, labeled here as Model 4. Goodness-of-fit results, together with the estimated value of this new parameter, are presented in Table 4.6.

In reviewing these results, we see that once again, there has been a substantial drop in the overall MLM χ^2 (MLM $\chi^2_{[203]}$ = 413.639), as well as an increase in the CFI (0.922) and TLI (0.911), and a slight reduction in the RMSEA (0.053). Likewise, we observe that the estimated value of 0.519, although lower than the predicted value, is still highly significant as evidenced from its z-value of 5.030. Nonetheless, we are still presented with

Table 4.6 *Mplus* Output for Model 4:
Selected Goodness-of-Fit Statistics and Model Results

Tests of Model Fit	
Chi-Square Test of Model Fit	
Value	413.639
Degrees of freedom	203
p-value	0.0000
Scaling Correction Factor for MLM	1.180
CFI/TLI	
CFI	0.922
TLI	0.911
Root Mean Square Error of Approximation (RMSEA)	
Estimate	0.053
Standardized Root Mean Square Residual (SRMR)	
Value	0.065

Model Results				
	Estimate	Standard Error (*SE*)	Estimate/*SE*	Two-Tailed *p*-Value
ITEM10 WITH ITEM11	0.519	0.103	5.030	0.000

Table 4.7 Mplus Output for Model 4: Modification Indices

		Expected Parameter Change (EPC)	Standard EPC	StdYX EPC
	MI			
BY Statements				
→**F1 BY ITEM12**	**34.439**	**−0.331**	**−0.402**	**−0.337**
F2 BY ITEM12	12.098	−0.324	−0.290	−0.243
F3 BY ITEM1	12.277	0.561	0.246	0.148
WITH Statements				
ITEM3 WITH ITEM1	11.848	0.249	0.249	0.192
ITEM7 WITH ITEM4	28.247	0.209	0.209	0.323
ITEM12 WITH ITEM3	14.200	−0.268	−0.268	−0.236
ITEM18 WITH ITEM7	10.221	−0.147	−0.147	−0.213
ITEM19 WITH ITEM18	15.599	0.248	0.248	0.284
ITEM21 WITH ITEM4	11.183	0.201	0.201	0.201
ITEM21 WITH ITEM7	28.320	0.262	0.262	0.326

a model fit that is not completely adequate. Although still fully cognizant of the parsimony issue, yet aware of the two similarly sized MIs related to Model 3, I believe that we are fully justified in checking out the MIs on Model 4; these results are reported in Table 4.7.

As expected, the cross-loading of Item 12 onto Factor 1 is still very strong, and its MI remains the highest value reported. Given that specification of this cross-loading can be logically and substantively supported, as noted earlier, we can proceed in testing a further model (Model 5) in which this parameter is included.

Although you will observe several remaining misspecified parameters, I consider it inappropriate to continue fitting the model beyond this point for at least three important reasons. First, given that we will have already added four parameters, despite the strong substantive justification for doing so, the issue of scientific parsimony must be taken into account. Second, of the nine remaining suggested misspecified parameters, seven represent residual covariances. Finally, in addition to having weaker MIs than the four previously acknowledged misspecified parameters, these remaining parameters are difficult to justify in terms of substantive meaningfulness. Model 5, then, represents our final model of MBI structure.

The Mplus input file for this final model is shown in Figure 4.5, and the resulting goodness-of-fit statistics are reported in Table 4.8. Turning first to the Mplus input file (Figure 4.5) and comparing it with the initial

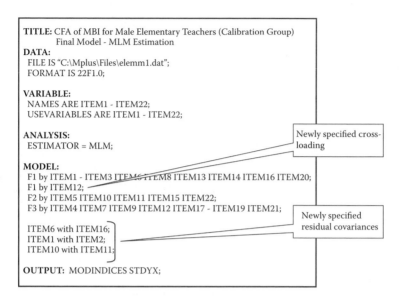

Figure 4.5. M*plus* input file for a final model of MBI structure.

input file, I draw your attention to the four additionally specified parameters as derived from examination of the MIs related to post hoc analyses of the initially hypothesized model. As noted in the callouts, the first newly specified parameter represents the cross-loading of Item 12 on F1. The three additionally specified parameters appear below the factor loadings and represent residual covariances. Finally, the OUTPUT command has been revised to include only the STDYX standardized estimates.

Let's turn now to the goodness-of-fit statistics presented in Table 4.8 and, in particular, to the CFI, TLI, RMSEA, and SRMR results. Both the CFI and TLI results represent a fairly well-fitting model, albeit one not quite reaching the recommended criterion of 0.95 (see Hu & Bentler, 1999). Nonetheless, both the RMSEA value of 0.048 and the SRMR value of 0.054 are indicative of good fit. Thus, these findings, in combination with the three important considerations noted earlier, stand in favor of allowing this fifth model to serve as the final model of MBI structure. Selected parameter estimates for this final model are reported in Table 4.9.

Both unstandardized and standardized parameter estimates are presented here as they appear in the M*plus* output. In the interest of space, however, only the unstandardized estimates for the first and last four residual variances are included. All specified parameters were found to be statistically significant.

In reviewing these results, two sets of estimates are of primary import: (a) those related to the four post hoc–added parameters, and (b) the factor

Table 4.8 Mplus Output for Final Model: Selected Goodness-of-Fit Statistics

Tests of Model Fit	
Chi-Square Test of Model Fit	
Value	378.656
Degrees of freedom	202
p-value	0.0000
Scaling Correction Factor for MLM	1.179
CFI/TLI	
CFI	0.934
TLI	0.925
Root Mean Square Error of Approximation (RMSEA)	
Estimate	0.048
Standardized Root Mean Square Residual (SRMR)	
Value	0.054

correlations. Turning first to the four additionally specified parameters, you will note that I have highlighted both the cross-loading and the residual covariances within rectangles with respect to both the unstandardized and standardized solutions. Let's examine the cross-loading of Item 12 on Factors 1 and 3 first. Recall that the originally intended loading of Item 12 was on Factor 3; the post hoc analyses, however, revealed a very strong misspecification indicating that this item should also load on Factor 1. As shown in Table 4.9 for the unstandardized estimates, both parameterizations were found to be highly significant. That the estimated loading on Factor 1 had a negative value is perfectly reasonable as the item states that the respondent feels very energetic, albeit Factor 1 represents the construct of Emotional Exhaustion. Turning to the standardized solution, it is not surprising to find that Item 12 has very similar and moderately high loadings on both factors (Factor 1 = −0.323; Factor 3 = 0.424). This finding attests to the fact that Item 12 is in definite need of modification such that it more appropriately loads cleanly on only one of these two factors.

In reviewing the three residual covariances, we see that not only are they highly significant parameters in the model, but also they represent extremely high correlated residuals, ranging from 0.368 to 0.488. Such results are highly suggestive of excessively redundant item content.

Our second important focus concerned the latent factor correlations. Of critical import here is the extent to which these values are consistent with the theory. Based on previous construct validity research on the MBI,

Table 4.9 M*plus* Output for Final Model: Parameter Estimates

		Standard		Two-Tailed
	Estimate	Error (*SE*)	Estimate/*SE*	*p*-Value
F1 BY				
ITEM1	1.000	0.000	999.000	999.000
ITEM2	0.878	0.040	21.834	0.000
ITEM3	1.073	0.056	19.094	0.000
ITEM6	0.764	0.075	10.162	0.000
ITEM8	1.215	0.064	18.892	0.000
ITEM13	1.072	0.067	16.094	0.000
ITEM14	0.880	0.063	13.903	0.000
ITEM16	0.727	0.072	10.161	0.000
ITEM20	0.806	0.066	12.196	0.000
ITEM12	−0.316	0.052	−6.107	0.000
F2 BY				
ITEM5	1.000	0.000	999.000	999.000
ITEM10	0.889	0.120	7.394	0.000
ITEM11	1.105	0.133	8.334	0.000
ITEM15	0.921	0.121	7.637	0.000
ITEM22	0.776	0.119	6.531	0.000
F3 BY				
ITEM4	1.000	0.000	999.000	999.000
ITEM7	0.973	0.118	8.232	0.000
ITEM9	1.763	0.309	5.705	0.000
ITEM12	1.131	0.170	6.651	0.000
ITEM17	1.327	0.177	7.508	0.000
ITEM18	1.890	0.263	7.191	0.000
ITEM19	1.695	0.261	6.503	0.000
ITEM21	1.342	0.211	6.366	0.000
F2 WITH				
F1	0.747	0.106	7.057	0.000
F3 WITH				
F1	−0.167	0.038	−4.426	0.000
F2	−0.181	0.036	−5.055	0.000

Table 4.9 M*plus* Output for Final Model: Parameter Estimates (*continued*)

Model Results			
	Estimate	Standard Error (*SE*)	Estimate/*SE*	Two-Tailed *p*-Value
ITEM6 WITH				
ITEM16	0.706	0.108	6.543	0.000
ITEM1 WITH				
ITEM2	0.588	0.069	8.509	0.000
ITEM10 WITH				
ITEM11	0.517	0.102	5.062	0.000
Variances				
F1	1.486	0.149	9.972	0.000
F2	0.800	0.168	4.774	0.000
F3	0.199	0.048	4.165	0.000
Residual Variances				
ITEM1	1.268	0.088	14.447	0.000
ITEM2	1.238	0.090	13.727	0.000
•				
•				
•				
ITEM21	1.240	0.123	10.123	0.000
ITEM22	2.008	0.169	11.859	0.000

Standardized Model Results: STDYX Standardization			
	Estimate	Standard Error (*SE*)	Estimate/*SE*	Two-Tailed *p*-Value
F1 BY				
ITEM1	0.735	0.025	29.720	0.000
ITEM2	0.693	0.027	25.487	0.000
ITEM3	0.756	0.023	32.227	0.000
ITEM6	0.589	0.042	14.054	0.000
ITEM8	0.859	0.015	57.049	0.000
ITEM13	0.778	0.024	31.926	0.000
ITEM14	0.622	0.034	18.362	0.000
ITEM16	0.616	0.041	15.102	0.000
ITEM20	0.696	0.040	17.595	0.000
ITEM12	−0.323	0.048	−6.755	0.000

Table 4.9 M*plus* Output for Final Model: Parameter Estimates (*continued*)

	Estimate	Standard Error (*SE*)	Estimate/*SE*	Two-Tailed *p*-Value
F2 BY				
ITEM5	0.602	0.054	11.049	0.000
ITEM10	0.551	0.049	11.296	0.000
ITEM11	0.647	0.043	15.141	0.000
ITEM15	0.635	0.045	14.145	0.000
ITEM22	0.440	0.049	8.895	0.000
F3 BY				
ITEM4	0.448	0.048	9.333	0.000
ITEM7	0.518	0.042	12.203	0.000
ITEM9	0.599	0.049	12.179	0.000
ITEM12	0.424	0.050	8.503	0.000
ITEM17	0.696	0.036	19.080	0.000
ITEM18	0.663	0.046	14.331	0.000
ITEM19	0.637	0.041	15.490	0.000
ITEM21	0.474	0.049	9.759	0.000
F2 WITH				
F1	0.685	0.046	14.952	0.000
F3 WITH				
F1	−0.306	0.057	−5.371	0.000
F2	−0.453	0.062	−7.278	0.000
ITEM6 WITH				
ITEM16	0.488	0.055	8.821	0.000
ITEM1 WITH				
ITEM2	0.469	0.042	11.123	0.000
ITEM10 WITH				
ITEM11	0.368	0.059	6.221	0.000

Standardized Model Results: STDYX Standardization

the correlational values of 0.685, −0.306, and −0.453 for Factor 1 (Emotional Exhaustion) with Factor 2 (Depersonalization), Factor 1 with Factor 3 (Personal Accomplishment), and Factor 2 with Factor 3, respectively, are strongly supported in the literature.

In closing out this chapter, albeit prior to the inclusion of the addendum, I wish to address the issue of post hoc model fitting, as, historically, one of the major concerns in this regard has been the potential for capitalization on chance factors in the respecification of alternate models. Indeed,

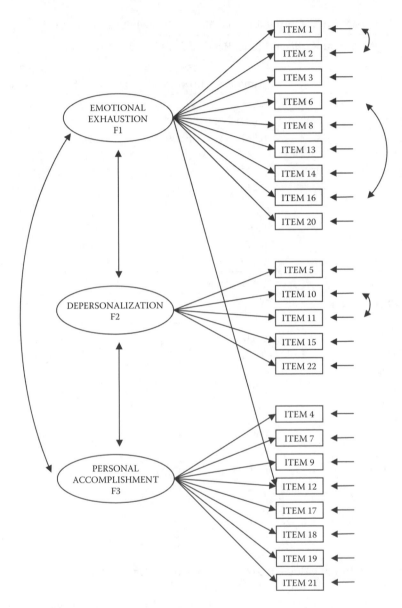

Figure 4.6. Final model of MBI structure.

there has been some attempt to address this issue. In 1999, Hancock introduced a Scheffé-type adjustment procedure that is now implemented in
the EQS program (Bentler, 2005). However, this approach to controlling
for Type I error is very conservative, leading Bentler (2005) to caution that,

in practice, this criterion will likely be helpful only in situations where there are huge misspecifications in a model (χ^2/df = or > 5.0).

Taking a different approach to the problem of Type I errors in post hoc model fitting, Green and colleagues (Green & Babyak, 1997; Green, Thompson, & Poirier, 2001) proposed a Bonferroni-type correction to the number of parameters added to a respecified model during post hoc analyses. Although a third approach to controlling for Type I errors was originally informally suggested by Chou and Bentler (1990), it was later regenerated and presented in a more formal manner by Green, Thompson, and Poirier (1999). This strategy is based on a two-step process in which parameters are first added to the model in the process of optimizing model fit, and then subsequently tested and deleted from the model if they cease to contribute importantly to model fit. Finally, a fourth approach to the problem of chance factors is to cross-validate the final model in a second independent new or split sample. Indeed, my own work with the MBI has provided me with the opportunity to test for the replication of the four misspecified parameters found in this chapter across split and independent samples. Results have revealed consistent problems with the seven MBI items cited in the present application across calibration and validation samples, as well as across elementary, intermediate, secondary, and postsecondary educators (see Byrne, 1991, 1993, 1994b); total replication of the residual covariances has been found across elementary and secondary teachers, as well as across gender (see Byrne 1994a). I address the issue of cross-validation more fully in Chapter 9.

In this chapter, we have tested for the validity of scores derived from the MBI for a sample of male elementary school teachers. Based on sound statistical and theoretical rationales, we can feel confident that the modified model of MBI structure, as determined through post hoc model-fitting procedures based on both the Modification Index results and determined substantive meaningfulness of the targeted misspecified parameters, most appropriately represents the data. A schematic summary of this final well-fitting model is presented in Figure 4.6.

Notes

1. As was the case in Chapter 3, the first of each congeneric set of items was constrained to 1.00 by default by the program.
2. M*plus* also provides for use of the MLMV estimator. Although the MLM and MLMV yield the same estimates (equivalent to ML) and standard errors (robust to nonnormality), their χ^2 values differ and are corrected in both cases. Whereas the MLM χ^2 is based on mean correction, the MLMV χ^2 is based on mean and variance correction. As a consequence, one should expect p-values of the MLMV-corrected χ^2 to be more accurate than for the MLM-corrected χ^2, albeit at the expense of a greater number of computations. This computational difference between MLM and MLMV estimations is most apparent in the analysis of models that include a large number of variables.

3. Unfortunately, refusal of copyright permission by the MBI test publisher prevents me from presenting the actual item statements for your perusal.
4. As noted earlier in this book, nested models are hierarchically related to one another in the sense that their parameter sets are subsets of one another (i.e., particular parameters are freely estimated in one model but fixed to zero in a second model) (Bentler & Chou, 1987; Bollen, 1989).
5. Prior to specifying the cross-loading here, I would suggest loading the aberrant item onto the alternate factor in lieu of its originally targeted factor. However, in the case of Item 12, past experience has shown this item to present the same misspecification results regardless of which factor it is specified to load on.

Addendum

The purpose of this addendum is to illustrate steps to follow in acquiring univariate skewness and kurtosis statistics pertinent to one's data using *Mplus*. As such, we now examine both the input file and output file results based on the present data. We turn first to the related input file, which is presented in Figure 4.7.

Of initial note with this input file is the ANALYSIS command, which states that TYPE = MIXTURE. The rationale behind this specification is related to the fact that, in order to obtain values of univariate skewness and kurtosis in *Mplus*, it is necessary to specify a mixture model. However, whereas the latent variables in mixture models are categorical (Brown, 2006), those in all models tested in this book are continuous.

```
TITLE: CFA of MBI for Male Elementary Teachers (Calibration Group)
       Univariate Skewness and Kurtosis Values

DATA:
  FILE IS "C:\Mplus\Files\elemm1.dat";
  FORMAT IS 22F1.0;

VARIABLE:
  NAMES ARE ITEM1 - ITEM22;
  USEVARIABLES ARE ITEM1 - ITEM22;
  CLASSES = C(1);

ANALYSIS:
  TYPE = MIXTURE;

MODEL:
  %OVERALL%
  F1 by ITEM1 - ITEM3 ITEM6 ITEM8 ITEM13 ITEM14 ITEM16 ITEM20;
  F2 by ITEM5 ITEM10 ITEM11 ITEM15 ITEM22;
  F3 by ITEM4 ITEM7 ITEM9 ITEM12 ITEM17 - ITEM19 ITEM21;

OUTPUT: TECH12;
```

Figure 4.7. *Mplus* input file for obtaining skewness and kurtosis values of observed variables.

Given that our model does *not* represent a mixture model and is pertinent to only one group (or class), the procedure here requires that two important specification statements be included in the input file: (a) CLASSES = c (1), as shown under the VARIABLE command; and (b) %OVERALL%, as shown on the first line of the MODEL command. The first statement (in the VARIABLE command) indicates that the model is of a regular nonmixture type pertinent to only one class. The second statement (in the MODEL command) indicates that the model describes the overall part of a specified nonmixture model. The remainder of the MODEL command, consistent with Figure 4.1, specifies that Factor 1 is measured by Items 1, 2, 3, 6, 8, 13, 14, 16, and 20; Factor 2 by Items 5, 10, 11, 15, and 22; and Factor 3 by Items 4, 7, 9, 12, 17, 18, 19, and 21. Finally, the OUTPUT command requests the TECH12 option, which yields information related to univariate skewness and kurtosis.

Let's now review the results of the TECH12 output, which are presented in Figure 4.8. As noted earlier, given that kurtosis remains the

Observed Variable	Skewness	Kurtosis
ITEM 1	−0.115	−1.166
ITEM 2	−0.505	−0.705
ITEM 3	0.316	−1.110
ITEM 4	−1.804	3.631
ITEM 5	1.323	0.909
ITEM 6	0.920	−0.009
ITEM 7	−1.642	3.766
ITEM 8	0.738	−0.610
ITEM 9	−1.536	1.843
ITEM 10	1.198	0.563
ITEM 11	1.268	0.795
ITEM 12	−1.314	1.841
ITEM 13	0.346	−0.792
ITEM 14	0.031	−0.936
ITEM 15	2.088	4.240
ITEM 16	0.968	0.156
ITEM 17	−1.970	5.057
ITEM 18	−1.226	1.341
ITEM 19	−1.478	2.213
ITEM 20	1.295	1.170
ITEM 21	−1.295	1.160
ITEM 22	1.062	0.181

Figure 4.8. M*plus* output results for univariate skewness and kurtosis values.

primary concern in analyses of covariance structures (the present case), we focus only on these values. As such, a review of these kurtosis values reveals that, in general, most are quite acceptable as they deviate minimally from zero. Nonetheless, there are four observed variables that may be of concern: Items 4, 7, 15, and 17, each of which is shown as circled in Figure 4.8.

Although the four aberrant items noted here are clearly not excessively kurtotic, they may nonetheless be sufficiently nonnormal to make interpretations based on the ML χ^2 statistic, as well as the CFI, TLI, and RMSEA indices, problematic. Thus, it is always best to err on the side of caution by taking this information into account, which is exactly what we did in our analyses of the MBI data in this chapter.

chapter 5

Testing the Factorial Validity of Scores From a Measuring Instrument

Second-Order Confirmatory Factor Analysis Model

The application to be illustrated in this chapter differs from those of the previous chapters in two ways. First, it focuses on a confirmatory factor analysis (CFA) model that comprises a second-order factor structure. Second, whereas analyses in Chapters 3 and 4 were based on continuous data, analyses in the present application are based on categorical data. As such, the ordinality of the item data is taken into account. Specifically, in this chapter, we test hypothesized factorial structure related to the Chinese version (Chinese Behavioral Sciences Society, 2000) of the Beck Depression Inventory-II (BDI-II; Beck, Steer, & Brown, 1996) as it bears on a community sample of adolescents. The example is taken from a study by Byrne, Stewart, and Lee (2004). Although this particular study was based on an updated version of the original BDI (Beck, Ward, Mendelson, Mock, & Erbaugh, 1961), it nonetheless follows from a series of studies that have tested for the validity of second-order BDI factorial structure for high school adolescents in Canada (Byrne & Baron, 1993, 1994; Byrne, Baron, & Campbell, 1993, 1994), Sweden (Byrne, Baron, Larsson, & Melin, 1995, 1996), and Bulgaria (Byrne, Baron, & Balev, 1996, 1998). The purposes of the original Byrne et al. (2004) study were to test for construct validity of the structure of the Chinese version of the BDI-II (C-BDI-II) based on three independent groups of students drawn from 11 Hong Kong high schools. In this example, we focus only on the Group 2 data ($N = 486$), which served as the calibration sample in testing for the factorial validity of the C-BDI-II. (For further details regarding the sample, analyses, and results, readers are referred to the original article.)

The C-BDI-II is a 21-item scale that measures symptoms related to cognitive, behavioral, affective, and somatic components of depression. Specific to the Byrne et al. (2004) study, only 20 of the 21 C-BDI-II items were used in tapping depressive symptoms for high school adolescents. Item 21, designed to assess changes in sexual interest, was considered to be objectionable by several school principals, and the item was subsequently deleted from the inventory. For each item, respondents are presented with four statements rated from 0 to 3 in terms of intensity, and they are asked to select the one that most accurately describes their own feelings; higher scores represent a more severe level of reported depression. As noted in Chapter 4, the CFA of a measuring instrument is most appropriately conducted with fully developed assessment measures that have demonstrated satisfactory factorial validity. Justification for CFA procedures in the present instance is based on evidence provided by Tanaka and Huba (1984), and replicated studies by Byrne and associates (Byrne & Baron, 1993, 1994; Byrne, Baron, & Campbell, 1993, 1994; Byrne, Baron, Larsson, & Melin, 1995, 1996; Byrne, Baron, & Balev, 1996, 1998), that BDI score data are most adequately represented by a hierarchical factorial structure. That is to say, the first-order factors are explained by some higher order structure that, in the case of the C-BDI-II, is a single second-order factor of general depression.

Let's turn now to a description of the postulated structure of the C-BDI-II.

The Hypothesized Model

The CFA model tested in the present application hypothesizes a priori that (a) responses to the C-BDI-II can be explained by three first-order factors (Negative Attitude, Performance Difficulty, and Somatic Elements) and one second-order factor (General Depression); (b) each item has a nonzero loading on the first-order factor it was designed to measure, and zero loadings on the other two first-order factors; (c) residuals associated with each item are uncorrelated; and (d) covariation among the three first-order factors is explained fully by their regression on the second-order factor. A diagrammatic representation of this model is presented in Figure 5.1.

One additionally important point I need to make concerning this model is that, in contrast to the CFA models examined in Chapters 3 and 4, the first factor loading of each congeneric set of indicator variables is *not* fixed to 1.0 for purposes of model identification and latent variable scaling. Rather, these fixed values are specified for the factor loadings associated with *CBDI2_3* for Factor 1, *CBDI2_12* for Factor 2, and *CBDI2_16* for Factor 3, as indicated in Figure 5.1.[1]

Analysis of Categorical Data

Thus far in the book, analyses have been based on maximum likelihood (ML) estimation (Chapter 3) and robust ML (MLM) estimation (Chapter 4).

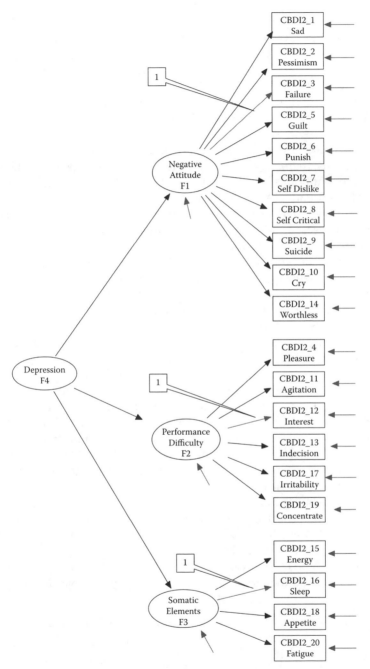

Figure 5.1. Hypothesized second-order model of factorial structure for the Chinese version of the Beck Depression Inventory II.

An important assumption underlying both of these estimation procedures is that the scale of the observed variables is continuous. Although, admittedly, the data analyzed in Chapter 4 involved Likert-scaled items that, technically speaking, represented categorical data, they were treated as if they were continuous on the basis of the relatively large number of scale points upon which the instrument items were based. (This issue is addressed shortly.) In contrast, the C-BDI-II data used in the present application comprise items having four scale points, and it is appropriate for analyses to take this categorical nature of the data into account.

For many years, researchers have tended to treat categorical data as if they were continuous. This trend applies to traditional statistical techniques (e.g., ANOVA and MANOVA) as well as to structural equation modeling (SEM) analyses. The primary reason this practice occurred with respect to SEM analyses, in particular, was because there were no well-developed strategies for addressing the categorical nature of the data. Despite the seminal work of Muthén (1978, 1983, 1984, 1993) in advancing the need to address the categorical nature of data with appropriate analytic methods, accompanied by his development of LISCOMP (Muthén, 1987), a computer program (and forerunner of M*plus*) capable of meeting this challenge, it has really been only in the last decade or so that SEM researchers have begun to act upon these earlier caveats. Clearly, methodological advancements both in the development of estimators capable of analyzing categorical data and in their incorporation into the major SEM computer software packages have played a major role not only in heightening researchers' awareness to the importance of addressing the categorical nature of data but also in enabling them to apply these appropriate analytic procedures.

This changing trend among SEM researchers notwithstanding, it would be reasonable for you to query (a) how serious it is to treat categorical data as if they are continuous, and (b) if there are instances where it makes little difference whether the data are treated as categorical or as continuous. Thus, before discussing the basic framework underlying the analysis of categorical variables, I believe a brief review of the literature that has addressed these issues may be of substantial help in providing you with a broader perspective of the two analytic strategies. We turn first to the case where categorical variables are treated as if they are continuous variables, and then to their treatment as categorical variables.

Categorical Variables Analyzed as Continuous Variables

From a review of Monte Carlo studies that have addressed this issue (see, e.g., Babakus, Ferguson, & Jöreskog, 1987; Boomsma, 1982; Muthén & Kaplan, 1985), West, Finch, and Curran (1995) reported several important findings. First, Pearson correlation coefficients appear to be higher when computed between two continuous variables than when computed between the same two variables restructured with an ordered categorical scale. However, the greatest attenuation occurs with variables having less than five categories and those exhibiting a high degree of skewness, the latter condition being made worse by variables that are skewed in opposite directions (i.e., one variable positively skewed, and the other negatively skewed; see Bollen & Barb, 1981). Second, when categorical variables approximate a normal distribution:

1. The number of categories has little effect on the χ^2 likelihood ratio test of model fit. Nonetheless, increasing skewness, and particularly differential skewness (variables skewed in opposite directions), leads to increasingly inflated χ^2 values.
2. Factor loadings and factor correlations are only modestly underestimated. However, underestimation becomes more critical when there are fewer than three categories, skewness is greater than 1.0, and differential skewness occurs across variables.
3. Residual variance estimates, more so than other parameters, appear to be most sensitive to the categorical and skewness issues noted in Item 2.
4. Standard error estimates for all parameters tend to be too low, with this result being more so when the distributions are highly and differentially skewed (see also Finch, West, & MacKinnon, 1997).

In summary, the literature to date would appear to support the notion that when the number of categories is large and the data approximate a normal distribution, failure to address the ordinality of the data is likely negligible (Atkinson, 1988; Babakus et al., 1987; Muthén & Kaplan, 1985). Indeed, Bentler and Chou (1987) argued that, given normally distributed categorical variables, "continuous methods can be used with little worry when a variable has four or more categories" (p. 88). More recent findings support these earlier contentions and have further shown that (a) the χ^2 statistic is influenced most by the two-category response format and becomes less so as the number of categories increases (Green, Akey, Fleming, Hershberger, & Marquis, 1997), (b) attenuation of parameter estimates may be heightened in the presence of floor and ceiling effects (Brown, 2006), and (c) there is a risk of yielding "pseudo-factors" that may be artifacts of item difficulty and extremeness (Brown, 2006).

Categorical Variables Analyzed as Categorical Variables

The Theory

In addressing the categorical nature of observed variables, the researcher automatically assumes that each has an underlying continuous scale. As such, the categories can be regarded as only crude measurements of an unobserved variable that, in truth, has a continuous scale (Jöreskog & Sörbom, 1993), with each pair of thresholds (or initial scale points) representing a portion of the continuous scale. The crudeness of these measurements arises from the splitting of the continuous scale of the construct into a fixed number of ordered categories (DiStefano, 2002). Indeed, this categorization process led O'Brien (1985) to argue that the analysis of Likert-scaled data actually contributes to two types of error: (a) categorization error resulting from the splitting of the continuous scale into the categorical scale, and (b) transformation error resulting from categories of unequal widths.

For purposes of illustration, let's consider the measuring instrument under study in this current chapter, in which each item is structured on a 4-point scale, thereby representing polytomous categorical variables. I draw from the work of Jöreskog and Sörbom (1993) in describing the decomposition of these categorical variables, albeit I replace the original use of the letter z with the letter y for consistency with the work of Muthén (1983, 1984) and Muthén and Muthén (2007–2010). Accordingly, let y represent the categorical variable (i.e., the item, the dependent indicator variable in the CFA model), and y^* the unobserved and underlying continuous variable. The threshold values can then be conceptualized as follows:

If $y^* \leq \tau_1$, y is scored 1.

If $\tau_1 < y^* \leq \tau_2$, y is scored 2.

If $\tau_2 < y^* \leq \tau_3$, y is scored 3.

If $\tau_3 < y^*$, y is scored 4.

where τ represents *tau* (a vector containing threshold information), and $\tau_1 < \tau_2 < \tau_3$ represents threshold values for y^*. The number of thresholds will always be one less than the number of categories.[2]

In testing SEM models with categorical data, analyses are no longer based on the sample variance–covariance matrix (S) as is the case for continuous data. Rather, they must be based on the correct correlation matrix. Where the correlated variables are both of an ordinal scale, the resulting matrix will comprise polychoric correlations; where one variable is of an ordinal scale, and the other of a continuous scale, the resulting matrix will comprise polyserial correlations. If two variables are dichotomous, this special case of a polychoric correlation is called a *tetrachoric correlation*. If a polyserial correlation involves a dichotomous rather than a more general ordinal variable, the polyserial correlation is also called a *biserial correlation*.

Underlying Assumptions

Applications involving the use of categorical data are based on three critically important assumptions: (a) Underlying each categorical observed variable is an unobserved latent counterpart, the scale of which is both continuous and normally distributed; (b) sample size is sufficiently large to enable reliable estimation of the related correlation matrix; and (c) the number of observed variables is kept to a minimum. However, Bentler (2005) noted that it is this very set of assumptions that essentially epitomizes the primary weakness in this methodology. Let's now take a brief look at why this should be so.

That each categorical variable has an underlying continuous and normally distributed scale is undoubtedly a difficult criterion to meet and, in fact, may be totally unrealistic. For example, in the present chapter, we examine scores tapping aspects of depression for nonclinical adolescents. Clearly, we would expect such item scores for normal adolescents to be low, thereby reflecting no incidence of depressive symptoms. As a consequence, we can expect to find evidence of kurtosis, and possibly skewness, related to these variables, with this pattern being reflected in their presumed underlying continuous distribution. Consequently, in the event that the model under test is deemed to be less than adequate, it may well be that the normality assumption is unreasonable in this instance.

The rationale underlying the latter two assumptions stems from the fact that, in working with categorical variables, analyses must proceed *from* a frequency table comprising the number of thresholds, multiplied by the number of observed variables, *to* estimation of the correlation matrix. The problem here lies with the occurrence of cells having zero or near-zero cases, which can subsequently lead to estimation difficulties (Bentler, 2005). This problem can arise because (a) sample size is small relative to the number of response categories (i.e., specific category scores across all categorical variables), (b) the number of variables is excessively large, and/or (c) the number of thresholds is large. Taken in combination, then, the larger the number of observed variables and/or number of thresholds for these variables, and the smaller the sample size, the greater the chance of having cells comprising zero to near-zero cases.

General Analytic Strategies

Until approximately a decade or so ago, two primary approaches to the analysis of categorical data (Jöreskog, 1990, 1994; Muthén, 1984) have dominated this area of research. Both methodologies use standard estimates of polychoric and polyserial correlations, followed by modified implementation of the asymptotic distribution-free (ADF) estimator originally proposed by Browne (1982, 1984a); it is also known as the *weighted least squares* (WLS) estimator and is more commonly referred to as such today. Unfortunately, the positive aspects of these original categorical variable methodologies have been offset by the ultrarestrictive assumptions noted earlier that, for most practitioners, are both impractical and difficult to meet. Of particular note is the requirement of an exceptionally large sample size in order to yield stable estimates. For example, Jöreskog and Sörbom (1996) proposed, as a minimal sample size, $(k + 1)$ $(k + 2)$ / 2, where k represents the number of indicators in the model to be tested; alternatively, Raykov and Marcoulides (2000) recommended that sample size be greater than 10 times the number of estimated model parameters. (For an excellent recapitulation of this issue, readers are referred to Flora & Curran, 2004.)

Although attempts to resolve these difficulties over the past few years have resulted in the development of several different approaches to the modeling and testing of categorical data (see, e.g., Bentler, 2005; Coenders, Satorra, & Saris, 1997; Moustaki, 2001; Muthén & Muthén, 2007–2010), there appear to be only three primary estimators: unweighted least squares (ULS), WLS, and diagonally weighted least squares (DWLS). Corrections to the estimated means and/or means and variances based on only ULS and DWLS estimation yield their related robust versions as follows: correction to means and variances of ULS estimates (ULSMV), correction to means of DWLS estimates (WLSM), and correction to means and variances of DWLS estimates (WLSMV).[3] (Admittedly, the interweaving of the WLS and DWLS labeling is unnecessarily confusing.) Of these, Brown (2006) contended that the WLSMV estimator performs best in the CFA modeling of categorical data.

The WLSMV estimator was developed by Muthén, du Toit, and Spisic (1997) based on earlier robustness research reported by Satorra and Bentler (1986, 1988, 1990) and designed specifically for use with small and moderate sample sizes (at least in comparison with those needed for use with the WLS estimator). The parameter estimates derive from use of a diagonal weight matrix (W), robust standard errors, and a robust mean- and variance-adjusted χ^2 statistic (Brown, 2006). Thus, the robust goodness-of-fit test of model fit can be considered analogous to the Satorra-Bentler-scaled χ^2 statistic that was the basis of our work in Chapter 4. Subsequent simulation research related to the WLSMV estimator has shown it to yield accurate test statistics, parameter estimates, and standard errors under both normal and nonnormal latent response distributions[4] across sample sizes ranging from 100 to 1,000, as well as across four different CFA models (one-factor models with 5 and 10 indicators, and two-factor models with 5 and 10 indicators; see Flora & Curran, 2004). More recently, Beauducel and Herzberg (2006) also reported satisfactory results for the WLSMV estimator, albeit findings of superior model fit and more precise factor loadings when the number of categories is low (e.g., two or three categories, compared with four, five, or six). M*plus* currently offers seven estimators (see Muthén & Muthén, 2007–2010) for use with data comprising at least one binary or ordered categorical indicator variable; the WLSMV estimator is default. As this book goes to press, the WLSMV estimator is available only in M*plus*.

Now that you have some idea of the issues involved in the analysis of categorical variables, let's move on to our task at hand, which is to test a second-order CFA model based on the C-BDI-II data described at the beginning of this chapter.

Mplus Input File Specification and Output File Results

Input File

Four features of the present application differ from the previous two and, thus, are of interest here with respect to composition of the M*plus* input file: (a) The CFA model is hierarchically structured, (b) the data upon which the analysis is based are ordinally scaled, (c) the factor-loading paths fixed to 1.0 for purposes of identification and scaling differ from the M*plus* defaulted paths, and (d) one equality constraint has been specified with respect to the higher order structure. Presented here are two versions of this input file. The input file shown first in Figure 5.2 (Input file a), with the exception of the alternative fixed factor loadings, represents what would be considered the usual default version of the model shown in Figure 5.1. Given that WLSMV is the default estimator for analyses of categorical variables in M*plus*, it need not be specified. In addition, the first factor-loading path for each congeneric set of parameters would automatically be constrained to 1.0 and, thus, requires no specification. Finally, no equality constraints would be placed at the second-order level of the model.

The input file presented in Figure 5.3 (Input file b) represents the alternative specification to be used in our analyses here. For clarification, I have included the ANALYSIS command and specified the WLSMV estimator, although this is not necessary (as noted above). Turning next to the MODEL command, we focus first on the first-order factors, the specifications for which are shown in the first three lines of this input information. Of import here is the inclusion of asterisks assigned to variables *CBDI2_1*, *CBDI2_4*, and *CBDI2_15*. A review of the CFA model in Figure 5.1 reveals these three parameters (in contrast to the usual defaulted constraints of 1.0) to be freely estimated. Alternatively, the parameters *CBDI2_3*, *CBDI2_12*, and *CBDI2_16* are constrained to a value of 1.0 and hence now serve as the reference indicator variables in the model. Accordingly, in Figure 5.3, you will observe that each of these latter parameters is specified

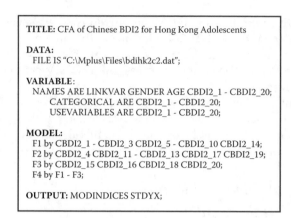

Figure 5.2. M*plus* input file based on usual program defaults.

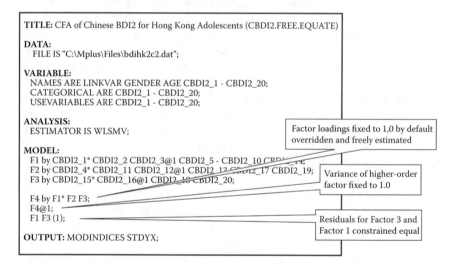

Figure 5.3. M*plus* input file with alternative specification and no program defaults.

as the appropriately fixed parameter through the addition of "@1" (e.g., CBDI2_3@1).

Let's turn now to the last three lines of the MODEL input, which contains specifications related to the second-order factor structure. Within this set of specifications, the first two lines again refer to a modification of the reference indicator variables, albeit this time with respect to the higher order factor loadings. That is, by default, M*plus* would automatically constrain the first second-order factor-loading path (F4 → F1) to 1.0. However, because in specifying a higher order model, researchers are

---

ESTIMATION TERMINATED NORMALLY

THE STANDARD ERRORS OF THE MODEL PARAMETER ESTIMATES COULD NOT
BE COMPUTED. THE MODEL MAY NOT BE IDENTIFIED. CHECK YOUR MODEL.
PROBLEM INVOLVING PARAMETER 84.

THE CONDITION NUMBER IS   -0.806D-16.

Figure 5.4. M*plus* error message regarding higher order factor specifications.

		PSI		
	F1	F2	F3	F4
F1	81			
F2	0	82		
F3	0	0	83	
F4	0	0	0	84

Figure 5.5. M*plus* TECH1 output for factor covariance matrix (PSI).

particularly interested in the estimation of the higher order factor loadings, there is some preference for freely estimating each of these parameters. An important corollary in SEM states that either a regression path or
a variance can be estimated, but not both. The underlying rationale of this
corollary is linked to the issue of model identification. Thus, if we wish to
freely estimate all second-order factor loadings, we will need to constrain
the variance of the second-order factor (F4, Depression) to a value of 1.0;
otherwise, it would automatically be freely estimated by default. Because
it can be instructive to see what happens if this corollary is not adhered
to, I executed this file without fixing the F4 variance to 1.00. Accordingly,
shown in Figure 5.4 is the error message generated by M*plus* resulting
from the estimation of this model wherein all second-order factor loadings were freely estimated, as well as the variance of Factor 4.

Note in Figure 5.4 that M*plus* identifies Parameter 84 as the source of
the problem. In checking the related output file, as shown in Figure 5.5,
we see that this parameter is none other than the higher order Factor 4,
which needs to be constrained to 1.0 in order that the model is identified.
In addressing this identification corollary, then, note on the second line of
the higher order factor specification (see Figure 5.3) that Factor 4 has been
assigned a fixed value of 1.0 (F4@1;).

The final specification of note lies on line 3 of this higher order set of
specifications, where you will see the "F1 F3 (1);" statement. This specification indicates that the residual variances associated with Factors 1 and

3 are to be constrained equal. Technically speaking, the estimate for F3 will be constrained equal to the estimate for F1. The parenthesized value of 1 indicates that only one constraint has been specified, and it pertains to both F1 and F3. In M*plus*, each specified constraint must appear on a separate line. Thus, for example, if the higher order model were to comprise six factors (in lieu of the present three), and if we wanted to equate two additional residual variances (say, F5 and F6, also with F1 and F3), the related constraint specification would appear on a separate line but still be accompanied by a bracketted value of 1 ("F1 F3 F5 F6 [1]"). If, on the other hand, we were to equate the estimate of F6 to that of F5, then this would represent an entirely different constraint and, thus, would be accompanied by the number 2 in brackets ("F5 F6 [2]").

What is the rationale for such specification? Recall that in Chapters 2 and 3, I emphasized the importance of computing the degrees of freedom associated with hypothesized models in order to ascertain their status with respect to statistical identification. I further noted that, with hierarchical models, it is additionally critical to check the identification status of the higher order portion of the model. For example, in the case of a second-order factor model, the first-order factors replace the observed variables in serving as the data upon which second-order model identification is based. In the present case, given the specification of only three first-order factors, the higher order structure will be just-identified unless a constraint is placed on at least one parameter in this upper level of the model (see, e.g., Bentler, 2005; Rindskopf & Rose, 1988). More specifically, with three first-order factors, we have six ([4 × 3] / 2) pieces of information; the number of estimable parameters is also six (three factor loadings and three residual variances), thereby resulting in a just-identified model. Although acceptable in general terms, should we wish to resolve this condition of just identification, equality constraints can be placed on particular parameters known to yield estimates that are approximately equal. From earlier work in validating the C-BDI-II (Byrne et al., 2004), an initial test of the hypothesized model shown in Figure 5.1 revealed the estimates for the residual variances associated with F1 and F3 to be very close. Accordingly, these two parameters were constrained equal, thereby providing one degree of freedom at the higher order level of the model.

Output File

Table 5.1 presents the summary information appearing first in the M*plus* output file. Here we see that the sample size is 486 and the number of dependent variables is 20, independent variables 0, and continuous latent variables 4. The dependent variables, as usual, represent the 20 observed

Table 5.1 Mplus Output for Hypothesized Model: Selected Summary Information

Summary of Analysis	
Number of groups	1
Number of observations	486
Number of dependent variables	20
Number of independent variables	0
Number of continuous latent variables	4

Observed Dependent Variables

Binary and Ordered Categorical (Ordinal)

CBDI2_1	CBDI2_2	CBDI2_3	CBDI2_4	CBDI2_5	CBDI2_6
CBDI2_7	CBDI2_8	CBDI2_9	CBDI2_10	CBDI2_11	CBDI2_12
CBDI2_13	CBDI2_14	CBDI2_15	CBDI2_16	CBDI2_17	CBDI2_18
CBDI2_19	CBDI2_20				

Continuous Latent Variables

F1	F2	F3	F4

Estimator	WLSMV

indicator variables (in this case, the C-BDI-II item scores), whereas the latent variables represent the three first-order and one second-order factors. Finally, the analyses are based on the WLSMV estimator.

Presented next in Table 5.2 are the proportions of sample respondents who endorsed each of the four categories. For one example of how to interpret these results, let's examine the reported numbers as they relate to Item 1 (*CBDI2_1*). This item elicits a response to the statement "I feel sad," which resulted in 51% (0.508) of the sample indicating the absence of sad feelings. A review of this proportion information for all 20 items reveals that for 16 out of 20 items, most respondents opted for Category 1, thereby reflecting no evidence of depressive symptoms. In other words, proportion results pertinent to Category 1 exceeded those for Categories 2 through 4 for 16 out of the 20 C-BDI-II items.[5] As such, it is apparent that these data reflect a leptokurtic pattern and are thus nonnormally distributed. However, given that the data represent a community sample of high school adolescents and, thus, no presence of depressive symptoms is expected, this finding is certainly not unexpected. Indeed, it actually represents the usual finding when the C-BDI-II as well as the BDI-I are used with normal adolescents.

Let's turn next to Table 5.3, in which the goodness-of-fit statistics are reported. The WLSMV robust $\chi^2_{(82)}$ of 200.504 represents a scaled (i.e., corrected) version of the usual chi-square statistic for which both the categorical and nonnormal natures of the data have been taken into account.

Table 5.2 M*plus* Output for Hypothesized Model:
Summary of Categorical Proportions

CBDI2_1		CBDI2_8		CBDI2_15	
Category 1	0.508	Category 1	0.630	Category 1	0.430
Category 2	0.247	Category 2	0.278	Category 2	0.397
Category 3	0.222	Category 3	0.053	Category 3	0.142
Category 4	0.023	Category 4	0.039	Category 4	0.031
CBDI2_2		CBDI2_9		CBDI2_16	
Category 1	0.607	Category 1	0.790	Category 1	0.276
Category 2	0.313	Category 2	0.167	Category 2	0.481
Category 3	0.060	Category 3	0.039	Category 3	0.218
Category 4	0.021	Category 4	0.004	Category 4	0.025
CBDI2_3		CBDI2_10		CBDI2_17	
Category 1	0.465	Category 1	0.739	Category 1	0.516
Category 2	0.261	Category 2	0.140	Category 2	0.342
Category 3	0.255	Category 3	0.049	Category 3	0.130
Category 4	0.019	Category 4	0.072	Category 4	0.012
CBDI2_4		CBDI2_11		CBDI2_18	
Category 1	0.603	Category 1	0.352	Category 1	0.558
Category 2	0.323	Category 2	0.438	Category 2	0.311
Category 3	0.051	Category 3	0.169	Category 3	0.088
Category 4	0.023	Category 4	0.041	Category 4	0.043
CBDI2_5		CBDI2_12		CBDI2_19	
Category 1	0.644	Category 1	0.582	Category 1	0.346
Category 2	0.267	Category 2	0.321	Category 2	0.424
Category 3	0.051	Category 3	0.078	Category 3	0.189
Category 4	0.037	Category 4	0.019	Category 4	0.041
CBDI2_6		CBDI2_13		CBDI2_20	
Category 1	0.632	Category 1	0.527	Category 1	0.267
Category 2	0.210	Category 2	0.377	Category 2	0.556
Category 3	0.068	Category 3	0.076	Category 3	0.154
Category 4	0.091	Category 4	0.021	Category 4	0.023
CBDI2_7		CBDI2_14			
Category 1	0.628	Category 1	0.630		
Category 2	0.247	Category 2	0.235		
Category 3	0.086	Category 3	0.117		
Category 4	0.039	Category 4	0.019		

Table 5.3 Mplus Output for Hypothesized Model: Selected Goodness-of-Fit Statistics

Tests of Model Fit	
Chi-Square Test of Model Fit	
Value	200.504*
Degrees of freedom	82**
p-value	0.0000
CFI/TLI	
CFI	0.958
TLI	0.987
Number of free parameters	82
Root Mean Square Error of Approximation (RMSEA)	
Estimate	0.055
Weighted Root Mean Square Residual (WRMR)	
Value	0.947

* The chi-square value for MLM, MLMV, MLR, ULSMV, WLSM, and WLSMV cannot be used for chi-square difference tests. MLM, MLR, and WLSM chi-square difference testing is described in the M*plus* "Technical Appendices" at the M*plus* website, http://www.statmodel.com. See "chi-square difference testing" in the index of the Mplus *User's Guide* (Muthén & Muthén, 2007–2010).

** The degrees of freedom for MLMV, ULSMV, and WLSMV are estimated according to a formula given in the M*plus* "Technical Appendices" at http://www.statmodel.com. See "degrees of freedom" in the index of the Mplus *User's Guide* (Muthén & Muthén, 2007–2010).

Accompanying this information are two asterisked notations. The first of these advises that, consistent with the MLM estimator (as noted in Chapter 4), no direct chi-square difference tests are permitted involving the WLSMV estimator, as this between-model value is not distributed as chi-square. Nonetheless, these tests are made possible via additional model testing, which is described and exemplified in Muthén and Muthén (2007–2010) as well as on the M*plus* website (http://www.statmodel.com), and will be detailed in a walkthrough of this procedure relevant to the MLM estimator in Chapter 6. The second notation serves as a caveat that when the WLSMV estimator is used, calculation of degrees of freedom necessarily differs from the usual CFA procedure used with normally distributed continuous data as outlined earlier in this book. Interested readers can find details related to this computation from the M*plus* website as noted in the output file.

A review of the remaining model fit statistics (CFI = 0.958; TLI = .987; RMSEA = 0.055) reveals the hypothesized model to exhibit a good fit to the data. Finally, given that the Weighted Root Mean Square Residual

(WRMR) has been found to perform better than the Standardized Root Mean Square Residual (SRMR) with categorical data (Yu, 2002), only the WRMR value of 0.947 is repeated in the output. Indeed, Yu (2002) determined that a cutoff criterion of 0.95 can be regarded as indicative of good model fit with continuous as well as categorical data. As this book goes to press, the WLSMV estimator is still considered to be an experimental statistic (M*plus* Product Support, April 23, 2010) and, thus, awaits further testing of its properties.

We turn next to the unstandardized parameter estimates, which are presented in Table 5.4. Note first that items *CBDI2_3*, *CBDI2_12*, and *CBDI2_16* each has a value of 1.00 as they were the reference variables assigned to each congeneric set of factor loadings for Factors 1, 2, and 3, respectively. A review of both the first-order and second-order factor loadings reveals all to be statistically significant.

Table 5.4 M*plus* Output for Hypothesized Model: Parameter Estimates

		Model Results		
	Estimate	Standard Error (*SE*)	Estimate/*SE*	Two-Tailed *p*-Value
F1 BY				
CBDI2_1	1.173	0.063	18.607	0.000
CBDI2_2	1.178	0.064	18.438	0.000
CBDI2_3	1.000	0.000	999.000	999.000
CBDI2_5	0.976	0.070	13.928	0.000
CBDI2_6	0.874	0.068	12.825	0.000
CBDI2_7	1.233	0.068	18.188	0.000
CBDI2_8	1.034	0.064	16.208	0.000
CBDI2_9	0.959	0.075	12.750	0.000
CBDI2_10	0.831	0.079	10.519	0.000
CBDI2_14	1.233	0.068	18.115	0.000
F2 BY				
CBDI2_4	0.884	0.042	20.828	0.000
CBDI2_11	0.939	0.041	23.129	0.000
CBDI2_12	1.000	0.000	999.000	999.000
CBDI2_13	0.931	0.043	21.882	0.000
CBDI2_17	0.936	0.044	21.104	0.000
CBDI2_19	0.807	0.045	18.094	0.000

Table 5.4 Mplus Output for Hypothesized Model: Parameter Estimates (*continued*)

	Estimate	Standard Error (*SE*)	Estimate/*SE*	Two-Tailed *p*-Value
Model Results				
F3 BY				
CBDI2_15	1.481	0.107	13.784	0.000
CBDI2_16	1.000	0.000	999.000	999.000
CBDI2_18	0.799	0.103	7.791	0.000
CBDI2_20	1.388	0.108	12.873	0.000
F4 BY				
F1	0.599	0.033	18.276	0.000
F2	0.784	0.028	27.693	0.000
F3	0.502	0.039	12.783	0.000
Thresholds				
CBDI2_1$1	0.021	0.057	0.363	0.717
CBDI2_1$2	0.691	0.062	11.130	0.000
CBDI2_1$3	2.002	0.126	15.953	0.000
CBDI2_2$1	0.271	0.058	4.712	0.000
CBDI2_2$2	1.403	0.083	16.970	0.000
CBDI2_2$3	2.042	0.130	15.728	0.000
•				
•				
•				
•				
•				
CBDI2_20$1	−0.620	0.061	−10.169	0.000
CBDI2_20$2	0.927	0.067	13.902	0.000
CBDI2_20$3	2.002	0.126	15.953	0.000
Variances				
F4	1.000	0.000	999.000	999.000
Residual Variances				
F1	0.077	0.012	6.128	0.000
F2	0.033	0.021	1.565	0.118
F3	0.077	0.012	6.128	0.000

Appearing next in Table 5.4 are the thresholds specific to each C-BDI-II item. When observed indicator variables represent categorical item content, as noted earlier, there will be as many thresholds as there are categories less one. Thus, for each of the 20 items, we can expect to see three thresholds. In M*plus*, these parameters are denoted by the assignment of a dollar sign ($) following the variable name. For example, the three thresholds for the first item, *CBDI2_1*, are *CBDI2_1$1*, *CBDI2_1$2*, and *CBDI2_1$3*. Due to constraints of space, only a subset of item threshold parameters is presented here.

The final two sets of parameters appearing here are (a) the variance for the higher order factor (Factor 4), which you will recall was fixed to 1.00; and (b) the residual variances associated with each of the first-order factor loadings. Recall that because these factors are themselves dependent latent variables in this CFA model (i.e., they have a single-headed arrow pointing at them) and therefore cannot have their variances estimated, the variances of their residuals are computed instead; their estimation is default in M*plus*. Recall also that we constrained the estimated residual variance for Factor 3 to be equal to that for Factor 1. Thus, these two parameters have the same value (0.077), which is statistically significant (Estimate [Est]/standard error [*SE*] = 6.128). In contrast, the residual variance for Factor 2 is shown not to be significant (Est/*SE* = 1.565).

Notably missing in this output are residual variances for the observed categorical variables. Recall, however, that when SEM models involve categorical rather than continuous variables, analyses must be based on the appropriate sample correlation matrix (*S*),[6] rather than on the sample covariance matrix. Because this correlation matrix represents the underlying continuous variable *y**, the residual variances of categorical variables are not identified and therefore not estimated (Brown, 2006).

Given that the estimates in Tables 5.5 and 5.6 are linked statistically and, as such, bear importantly on their combined interpretation, I have chosen to present them as a pair. Table 5.5 presents the standardized estimates for each of the parameters listed in Table 5.4, whereas Table 5.6 reports the reliability estimates for each of the categorical variables (i.e., the items), in addition to the three first-order latent factors.

In the analysis of CFA models in which the observed variables are categorical (likewise for the measurement portion of full SEM path analytic models), the *y** variances of these variables are standardized to 1.0. Thus, the parameter estimates should be interpreted accordingly (Brown, 2006). This caveat signifies that we should focus on the standardized, rather than on the unstandardized, estimates in our interpretation of the findings. For example, whereas factor-loading estimates for continuous variables are interpreted as the proportion of variance in the *observed* variables explained by the underlying factor,

Table 5.5 M*plus* Output for Hypothesized Model:
Standardized Parameter Estimates

	Standardized Model Results: STDYX Standardization			
	Estimate	Standard Error (*SE*)	Estimate/*SE*	Two-Tailed *p*-Value
F1 BY				
CBDI2_1	0.774	0.027	28.514	0.000
CBDI2_2	0.778	0.029	27.046	0.000
CBDI2_3	0.660	0.031	21.145	0.000
CBDI2_5	0.644	0.037	17.281	0.000
CBDI2_6	0.577	0.042	13.878	0.000
CBDI2_7	0.814	0.024	33.656	0.000
CBDI2_8	0.682	0.034	20.071	0.000
CBDI2_9	0.633	0.043	14.817	0.000
CBDI2_10	0.548	0.045	12.061	0.000
CBDI2_14	0.813	0.024	34.219	0.000
F2 BY				
CBDI2_4	0.712	0.032	22.522	0.000
CBDI2_11	0.756	0.026	29.583	0.000
CBDI2_12	0.805	0.025	31.949	0.000
CBDI2_13	0.749	0.029	25.905	0.000
CBDI2_17	0.753	0.028	26.917	0.000
CBDI2_19	0.649	0.033	19.818	0.000
F3 BY				
CBDI2_15	0.849	0.026	32.972	0.000
CBDI2_16	0.573	0.038	15.241	0.000
CBDI2_18	0.458	0.050	9.150	0.000
CBDI2_20	0.796	0.028	28.331	0.000
F4 BY				
F1	0.908	0.016	57.837	0.000
F2	0.974	0.017	57.942	0.000
F3	0.876	0.021	41.206	0.000
Thresholds				
CBDI2_1$1	0.021	0.057	0.363	0.717
CBDI2_1$2	0.691	0.062	11.130	0.000
CBDI2_1$3	2.002	0.126	15.953	0.000
CBDI2_2$1	0.271	0.058	4.712	0.000

Table 5.5 Mplus Output for Hypothesized Model:
Standardized Parameter Estimates (*continued*)

	Estimate	Standard Error (*SE*)	Estimate/*SE*	Two-Tailed p-Value
		Standardized Model Results: STDYX Standardization		
CBDI2_2$2	1.403	0.083	16.970	0.000
CBDI2_2$3	2.042	0.130	15.728	0.000
•				
•				
•				
•				
•				
CBDI2_20$1	−0.620	0.061	−10.169	0.000
CBDI2_20$2	0.927	0.067	13.902	0.000
CBDI2_20$3	2.002	0.126	15.953	0.000
Variances				
F4	1.000	0.000	999.000	999.000
Residual Variances				
F1	0.176	0.029	6.169	0.000
F2	0.051	0.033	1.569	0.117
F3	0.233	0.037	6.256	0.000

interpretation of factor-loading estimates for categorical variables is based on the squared standardized factor loadings. To see how this plays out, let's look at the standardized loading for *CBDI2_1* (see Table 5.5), which is 0.774. Squaring this loading yields a value of 0.599, thereby representing the R^2 estimate reported in Table 5.6 for the same variable (*CBDI2_1*). We interpret this value as representing the proportion of the variance in the underlying continuous and latent aspect (y^*) of *CBDI2_1* that can be explained by Factor 1 of the hypothesized model. In other words, results for the first *CBDI2* item (*CBDI2_1*) suggest that 60% of its variance (as represented by the latent continuous aspect of this categorical item) can be explained by the construct of Negative Attitude to which it is linked.

Likewise, residual variances express the proportion of y^* variances that are *not* explained by the associated latent factor (Brown, 2006). Accordingly, keeping our focus on *CBDI2_1*, if we subtract the squared standardized loading (0.599) from 1.00, we obtain a value of 0.401, which you will note is reported as the residual variance for *CBDI2_1* in Table 5.6.

Table 5.6 M*plus* Output for Hypothesized Model:
Reliability Estimates and Modification Indices

			R^2		
Observed Variable	Estimate	Standard Error (*SE*)	Estimate/*SE*	Two-Tailed *p*-Value	Residual Variance
CBDI2_1	0.599	0.042	14.257	0.000	0.401
CBDI2_2	0.605	0.045	13.523	0.000	0.395
CBDI2_3	0.436	0.041	10.573	0.000	0.564
CBDI2_4	0.506	0.045	11.261	0.000	0.494
CBDI2_5	0.415	0.048	8.640	0.000	0.585
CBDI2_6	0.332	0.048	6.939	0.000	0.668
CBDI2_7	0.662	0.039	16.828	0.000	0.338
CBDI2_8	0.466	0.046	10.036	0.000	0.534
CBDI2_9	0.400	0.054	7.408	0.000	0.600
CBDI2_10	0.301	0.050	6.031	0.000	0.699
CBDI2_11	0.571	0.039	14.791	0.000	0.429
CBDI2_12	0.647	0.041	15.975	0.000	0.353
CBDI2_13	0.561	0.043	12.953	0.000	0.439
CBDI2_14	0.662	0.039	17.109	0.000	0.338
CBDI2_15	0.721	0.044	16.486	0.000	0.279
CBDI2_16	0.329	0.043	7.621	0.000	0.671
CBDI2_17	0.568	0.042	13.458	0.000	0.432
CBDI2_18	0.210	0.046	4.575	0.000	0.790
CBDI2_19	0.421	0.043	9.909	0.000	0.579
CBDI2_20	0.634	0.045	14.166	0.000	0.366
Latent Variable					
F1	0.824	0.029	28.919	0.000	
F2	0.949	0.033	28.971	0.000	
F3	0.767	0.037	20.603	0.000	

Model Modification Indices (MIs)[a]

Modification Index	Expected parameter change (EPC)	Standard EPC	StdYX EPC	StdYX EPC

[a] Modification indices for direct effects of observed dependent variables regressed on covariates and residual covariances among observed dependent variables may not be included. To include these, request MODINDICES (ALL). Minimum MI value for printing the modification index: 10.000. No MIs above the minimum value.

Finally, results for the three latent factors operate in the same manner. For example, squaring the standardized estimate for the first higher order factor loading (F4 by F1; 0.908) yields a value of 0.824 that, again, is reported as the R^2 estimate presented in Table 5.6. The residual variance for this parameter $(1.00 - 0.824 = 0.176)$, however, is reported in the output file under the standardized results (see Table 5.5) rather than under the R^2 results (Table 5.6).

In closing out this chapter, I can report that analyses resulted in the presence of no MIs, as shown in the lower section of Table 5.6. Although the possibility to request MIs for the direct effects of observed dependent variables regressed on covariates and residual covariances among observed dependent variables is noted in the M*plus* output, these parameters are considered to be inappropriate here. Thus, on the basis of a model that has been shown to fit the data extremely well, together with the absence of any suggested misspecifications in the model, we can feel confident that the hypothesized second-order factor structure of the C-BDI-II shown in Figure 5.1 is appropriate for use with Hong Kong adolescents.

Notes

1. Due to space restrictions, labeling of the C-BDI-II items was necessarily reduced to *CBDI2_*.
2. M*plus* places a limit of 10 on the number of ordered categories (Muthén & Muthén, 2007–2010).
3. I am grateful to Albert Maydeu-Olivares for his detailed clarification of these estimates.
4. The term "latent variable distribution" was coined by Muthén (1983, 1984) and refers to the *observed* ordinal distribution as generated from the *unobserved* continuous distribution of y^* noted earlier.
5. The four divergent items were *CBDI2_11*, *CBDI2_16*, *CBDI2_19*, and *CBDI2*.
6. In the present application, a polychoric correlation matrix represents the sample data.

chapter 6

Testing the Validity
of a Causal Structure
Full Structural Equation Model

In this chapter, we take our first look at a *full* structural equation model
(SEM). The hypothesis to be tested relates to the pattern of causal structure
linking several stressor variables considered to contribute to the presence
of burnout. Of primary interest here, however, was identification of the
key determinants of teacher burnout. The original study from which this
application is taken (Byrne, 1994b), tested and cross-validated the impact
of organizational and personality variables on three dimensions of burnout for elementary, intermediate, and secondary teachers. For purposes of
illustration here, however, the application is limited to secondary teachers
only (*N* = 1430).

Consistent with the confirmatory factor analysis (CFA) applications
illustrated in Chapters 3 through 5, those structured as full structural
equation models are presumed to be of a confirmatory nature. That is to
say, postulated causal relations among all variables in the hypothesized
model are supported in theory and/or empirical research. Typically, the
hypothesis under test argues for the validity of specified causal linkages
among the variables of interest. Let's turn now to a comprehensive examination of the hypothesized model under study in this chapter.

The Hypothesized Model

Postulated structure of the model to be tested here is presented schematically in Figure 6.1. Formulation of this model derived from a consensus of
findings based on a review of the burnout literature pertinent to the teaching profession. As no SEM research bearing on aspects of teacher burnout
existed at the time of this original work (Byrne, 1994b), these findings were
based solely on the more traditional analytic approaches, which mostly
included multiple regression. (Readers wishing a more detailed summary
of this research are referred to Byrne, 1994b, 1999.) In reviewing this model,
you will note that burnout, represented by the broken-line oval, is a multidimensional construct postulated to encompass three conceptually distinct

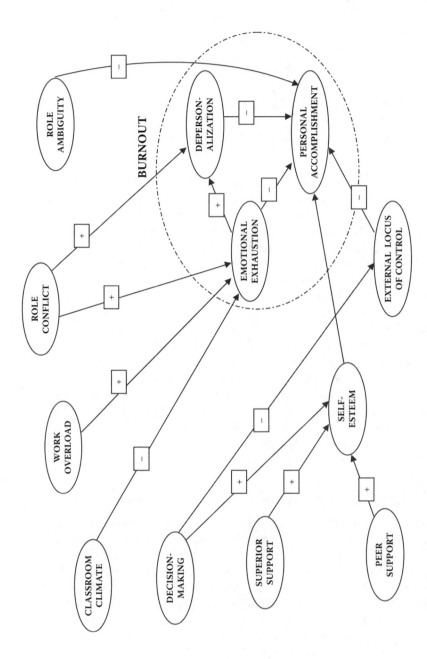

Figure 6.1. Proposed structural model of teacher burnout.

factors: Emotional Exhaustion (EE), Depersonalization (DP), and Personal Accomplishment (PA).[1] This part of the model is based on the work of Leiter (1991) in conceptualizing burnout as a cognitive-emotional reaction to chronic stress. The paradigm argues that EE holds the central position because it is considered to be the most responsive of the three facets to various stressors in the teacher's work environment. DP and PA, on the other hand, represent the cognitive aspects of burnout in that they are indicative of the extent to which teachers' perceptions of their students, their colleagues, and themselves become diminished. As indicated by the signs associated with each path in the model, EE is hypothesized to impact positively on DP but negatively on PA; DP is hypothesized to impact negatively on PA.

The paths (and their associated signs) leading from the organizational (role ambiguity, role conflict, work overload, classroom climate, decision making, superior support, and peer support) and personality (self-esteem and external locus of control) constructs to the three dimensions of burnout reflect findings in the literature.[2] For example, high levels of role conflict are expected to cause high levels of emotional exhaustion; in contrast, high (i.e., good) levels of classroom climate are expected to generate low levels of emotional exhaustion.

In viewing the model shown in Figure 6.1, we can see that it represents only the structural portion of the full SEM. Thus, before being able to test this model, we need to determine the manner by which each of the constructs in this model is to be measured. In other words, we now need to specify the measurement portion of the model (see Chapter 1). In contrast to the CFA models studied previously, the task involved in developing the measurement model of a full SEM is twofold: (a) to decide on the number of indicators to use in measuring each latent construct, and (b) to identify how the items will be packaged in formulating each indicator variable.

Formulation of Indicator Variables

In the applications examined in Chapters 3 through 5, the formulation of measurement indicators has been relatively straightforward; all examples have involved CFA models and, as such, comprised only measurement models. In the measurement of multidimensional facets of self-concept (see Chapter 3), each indicator variable represented a pairing of the items comprising each subscale designed to measure a particular self-concept facet. In Chapters 4 and 5, our interest focused on the factorial validity of a measuring instrument. As such, we were concerned with the extent to which the individual items loaded onto their targeted factor. Adequate assessment of this specification demanded that each item be included in the model. Thus, each indicator variable represented one item in the measuring instrument under study.

In contrast to these previous examples, formulation of the indicator variables in the present application is slightly more complex. Specifically, multiple indicators of each construct were formulated through the judicious combination of particular items in comprising item parcels. As such, items were carefully grouped according to content in order to equalize the measurement weighting across the set of indicators measuring the same construct (see, e.g., Hagtvet & Nasser, 2004). For example, the Classroom Environment Scale (Bacharach, Bauer, & Conley, 1986), used to measure Classroom Climate, consists of items that tap classroom size, the ability and interest of students, and various types of abuse by students. Indicators of this construct were formed such that each item in the composite measured a different aspect of classroom climate. In the measurement of classroom climate, self-esteem, and external locus of control, all parcels consisted of items from single unidimensional scales; all remaining item parcels derived from subscales of multidimensional scales. (For an extensive description of the measuring instruments, see Byrne, 1994b.) In total, 32 item parcel indicator variables were used to measure the hypothesized structural model, and all were unidimensional in structure. This issue of parcel unidimensionality is an important one as it substantiates our use of parceling in this full SEM application (see Bandalos, 2002, 2008; Sass & Smith, 2006). Figure 6.2 presents this hypothesized full SEM model of burnout.

In the time since the present study was conducted, there has been a growing interest in the question of item parceling. Research has focused on such issues as method of parceling (Bandalos, 2008; Bandalos & Finney, 2001; Hagtvet & Nasser, 2004; Kim & Hagtvet, 2003; Kishton & Widaman, 1994; Little, Cunningham, Shahar, & Widaman, 2002; Rogers & Schmitt, 2004), the number of indicators per factor (Marsh, Hau, Balla, & Grayson, 1998; Nasser-Abu & Wisenbaker, 2006), the extent to which item parcels affect model fit (Bandalos, 2002; Nasser-Abu & Wisenbaker, 2006; Sass & Smith, 2006), the effects of item parcel use with both sample size (Hau & Marsh, 2004; Nasser-Abu & Wisenbaker, 2006) and nonnormal data (Bandalos, 2008; Hau & Marsh, 2004), and, more generally, whether or not researchers should even engage in item parceling at all (Little et al., 2002; Little, Lindenberger, & Nesselroade, 1999). For an excellent summary of the pros and cons of item parceling, see Little et al. (1999); and for a thorough review of issues related to item parceling, see Bandalos and Finney (2001). (For details related to each of these aspects of item parceling, readers are advised to consult these references directly.)

Confirmatory Factor Analyses

Because (a) the structural portion of a full SEM involves relations among only latent variables, and (b) the primary concern in working with a full

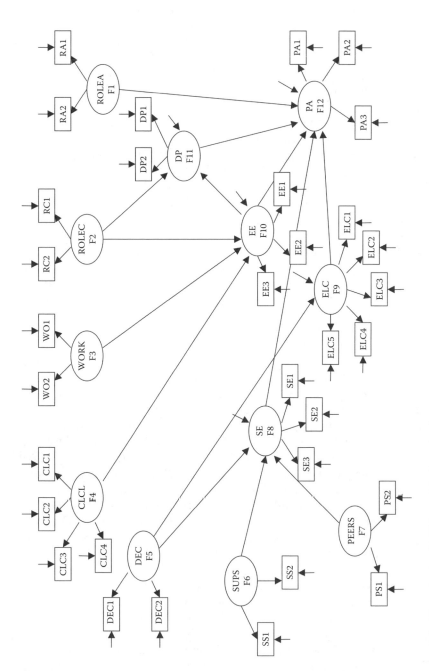

Figure 6.2. Hypothesized SEM model of teacher burnout.

SEM model is to assess the extent to which these relations are valid, it is critical that the measurement of each latent variable be psychometrically sound. Thus, an important preliminary step in the analysis of full latent variable models is to test first for the validity of the measurement model before making any attempt to evaluate the structural model. Accordingly, CFA procedures are used in testing the validity of the indicator variables. Once it is known that the measurement model is operating adequately, one can then have more confidence in findings related to assessment of the hypothesized structural model.

In the present case, CFAs were conducted for indicator variables derived from each of the two multidimensional scales—the Teacher Stress Scale (TSS; Pettegrew & Wolf, 1982) and the Maslach Burnout Inventory (MBI; Maslach & Jackson, 1981, 1986). The TSS comprises six subscales, with items designed to measure Role Ambiguity, Role Conflict, Work Overload, Decision Making, Superior Support, and Peer Support. The MBI, as you know from our work in Chapter 4, comprises three subscales, with items designed to measure three facets of burnout—Emotional Exhaustion, Depersonalization, and (reduced) Personal Accomplishment.

As preanalysis of these data revealed evidence of some nonnormality, all subsequent analyses to be conducted in this chapter are based on robust maximum likelihood (MLM) estimation. CFA results for both the TSS (MLM $\chi^2_{[39]}$ = 328.470; Comparative Fit Index [CFI] = .959; Root Mean Square Error of Approximation [RMSEA] = .072; Standardized Root Mean Square Residual [SRMR] = .041) and MBI (MLM $\chi^2_{[17]}$ = 148.601; CFI = .970; RMSEA = .074; SRMR = .039) were found to exhibit exceptionally good fit to the data. Nonetheless, examination of the Modification Indices (MIs) for the TSS revealed the freely estimated indicator variable of Decision Making (DEC2) to cross-load significantly onto both Factor 1 (Role Ambiguity) and Factor 5 (Superior Support). Given that these subscales are components of the same measuring instrument, it is not surprising that there may be some overlap of item content across subscales; the CFA model for the TSS was respecified to include these two additional parameters. Results of this analysis yielded a statistically and substantially better fitting model (MLM $\chi^2_{[37]}$ = 153.285; CFI = .983; RMSEA = .047; SRMR = .020).

Models of both the revised TSS and the MBI are schematically portrayed in Figure 6.3. It is important that I draw your attention to the numbered labeling of the TSS factors, which you will note are designated as F1, F2, F3, and F5, F6, F7, rather than as F1–F6. My reasoning here was simply to retain consistency with the labeling of these factors in the full SEM model (see Figure 6.2). The TSS retained this revised specification throughout all analyses of the full causal model.

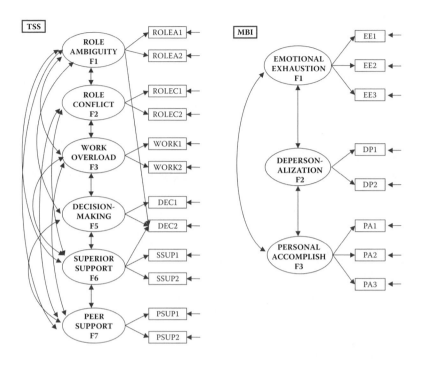

Figure 6.3. Final CFA models of the Teacher Stress Scale (TSS; Pettegrew & Wolf, 1982) and the Maslach Burnout Inventory (MBI; Maslach & Jackson, 1981, 1986).

Mplus Input File Specification and Output File Results

Input File 1

Now that we have established the best fitting and substantively appropriate measurement model, allow me to highlight particular aspects of the input file for the initially hypothesized model as shown in Figure 6.4.

Turning first to the VARIABLE command, we see that all observed variables listed are consistent with those modeled in Figure 6.2. That is, there are no other variables in the model other than the 32 indicator variables listed in the input file. Second, note that an ANALYSIS command is included. The reason for this specification derives from the fact that analyses will not be based on defaulted ML estimation but, rather, on robust MLM estimation in order to address the known nonnormality in the data. Third, consistent with Figure 6.2, the MODEL command comprises two sets of specifications—one set detailing the measurement model (lines 1 to 12), and the other detailing the structural model (lines 13

```
TITLE: Full SEM Model of Burnout for Secondary Teachers
       Hypothesized Model

DATA:
  FILE IS "C:\Mplus\Files\allsecondary.DAT";

VARIABLE:
  NAMES ARE ROLEA1 ROLEA2 ROLEC1 ROLEC2 WORK1 WORK2 CCLIM1 CCLIM2
  CCLIM3 CCLIM4 DEC1 DEC2 SSUP1 SSUP2 PSUP1 PSUP2 SELF1 SELF2 SELF3
  ELC1 ELC2 ELC3 ELC4 ELC5 EE1 EE2 EE3 DP1 DP2 PA1 PA2 PA3;
  USEVARIABLES ARE ROLEA1-PA3;

ANALYSIS:
  ESTIMATOR IS MLM;

MODEL:
  F1 by ROLEA1-ROLEA2 (DEC2;)
  F2 by ROLEC1-ROLEC2;
  F3 by WORK1-WORK2;
  F4 by CCLIM1-CCLIM4;
  F5 by DEC1-DEC2;
  F6 by SSUP1-SSUP2 (DEC2;)
  F7 by PSUP1-PSUP2;
  F8 by SELF1-SELF3;
  F9 by ELC1-ELC5;
  F10 by EE1-EE3;
  F11 by DP1-DP2;
  F12 by PA1-PA3;

  F8 ON F5 F6 F7;
  F9 ON F5;
  F10 ON F2 F3 F4;
  F11 ON F2 F10;
  F12 ON F1 F8 F9 F10 F11;

OUTPUT: MODINDICES TECH1;
```

Figure 6.4. M*plus* input file for hypothesized model of teacher burnout.

to 17). Although you likely will have no difficulty in following the specification of most indicator variables, I wish to draw your attention to one in particular, that of DEC2. Recall that, in testing for the validity of factor structure for the TSS in which this variable represents a subscale, we determined that DEC2 exhibited large and statistically significant cross-loadings on Factor 1 (Role Ambiguity) and on Factor 6 (Superior Support). Thus, in addition to its intended loading onto Factor 5 (Decision Making), the indicator variable of DEC2 is shown also to load onto Factors 1 and 6 (circled in Figure 6.4). Fourth, we turn now to specifications related to the structural model. In working through this section, I believe you will find it very helpful if you check each specification against the model itself as shown in Figure 6.2 The first thing you will note with this section of the specifications is use of the word ON, which has not appeared in any of the three previous applications. Nonetheless, in Chapter 2, I explained that the ON statement is short for "regressed on." Thus, for example, the first structural command specifies that Factor 8 (Self-Esteem) is regressed onto three factors: Factor 5 (Decision Making), Factor 6 (Superior Support), and Factor 7 (Peer Support). In reviewing the model in Figure 6.2, you will readily discern these specified structural paths. Finally, the OUTPUT command requests the reporting of both the MIs and the TECH1 option (for details related to this option, see Chapter 3). My rationale for including the TECH1 option here is that it provides for a check on the extent to which the reported number of degrees of freedom is correct and consistent with our hypothesized model. More specifically, the TECH1 option requests that all freely estimated parameters be presented in array form. Given that these parameters are assigned a number,[3] it can assist in determining the expected number of degrees of freedom. Nonetheless, this process is not exactly straightforward in M*plus* and will be detailed shortly.

Undoubtedly, you may wonder why I have not requested the standardized solution on the OUTPUT command. In testing for the validity of full SEM models, I prefer to work through all analyses first so that I can establish the final best fitting, albeit most parsimonious, model. Once I have determined this final model, I then request results bearing on the standardized solution.

It is important to mention that although you do not see specifications related to variances of the independent (i.e., exogenous) latent variables in the model (Factors 1 through 7), residuals associated with the observed variables, and residuals with the dependent (i.e., endogenous) latent variables in the model (Factors 8 through 12), these parameters are automatically estimated by default in M*plus* (see Muthén & Muthén, 2007–2010). Likewise, covariances among the independent latent variables in the model (Factors 1 through 7) are also estimated by default.

Output File 1

In reviewing this initial output file, results are reported separately for each selected section.

Summary Information

Appearing first in the output is a section detailing the Summary of Analysis; shown in Table 6.1 is a listing of the number of groups (1), observations ($N = 1430$), all observed and latent variables in the model, as well as other information related to estimation of the model.

Given the complexity of specification related to this application, compared with previous applications thus far, I consider it worthwhile to more fully detail the categorization of all variables in the model to ensure that you fully comprehend the status of each. From my own perspective, I find it easiest to conceptualize all variables in the model (regardless of

Table 6.1 M*plus* Output for Hypothesized Model:
Summary Information

Summary of Analysis	
Number of groups	1
Number of observations	1430
Number of dependent variables	32
Number of independent variables	0
Number of continuous latent variables	12

Observed Dependent Variables

Continuous

ROLEA1   ROLEA2   ROLEC1   ROLEC2   WORK1   WORK2   CCLIM1
CCLIM2 CCLIM3 CCLIM4 DEC1 DEC2 SSUP1 SSUP2 PSUP1 PSUP2
SELF1 SELF2 SELF3 ELC1 ELC2 ELC3 ELC4 ELC5 EE1 EE2 EE3
DP1 DP2 PA1 PA2 PA3

Continuous Latent Variables

F1	F2	F3	F4	F5	F6
F7	F8	F9	F10	F11	F12

Estimator	MLM
Information matrix	EXPECTED
Maximum number of iterations	1000
Convergence criterion	0.500D-04
Maximum number of steepest descent iterations	20

whether observed or latent) as either *dependent* or *independent* variables
in the model. As noted previously, independent variables in a model are
also termed *exogenous* variables, whereas dependent variables in a model
are termed *endogenous* variables. Although these latter terms are typically used with respect to latent variables (i.e., factors), they can, of course,
also pertain to observed variables. Simplistically, the key defining feature
associated with any dependent variable within a causal modeling framework is that it will have one or more single-headed arrows *leading to* it
from other variables in the model; in contrast, all arrows will *lead away*
from independent variables.

With this simple rule in hand, let's now review the remaining M*plus*
summary output in Table 6.1. Listed here, we see reported 32 dependent
variables and 12 continuous latent variables, followed by their labels.
However, because it can be helpful in understanding why certain parameters are not estimated, I prefer to expand on this information in showing
that, in fact, the number of variables in the model is as follows:

- 37 dependent variables:
  - 32 observed indicators (ROLEA1 to PA3)
  - 5 factors (F8–F12)

- 7 independent variables:
  - 7 factors (F1–F7)

Appearing next in the output is the warning message shown in Figure 6.5 regarding the latent variable covariance (PSI) matrix.

THE MODEL ESTIMATION TERMINATED NORMALLY

WARNING: THE LATENT VARIABLE COVARIANCE MATRIX (PSI) IS NOT POSITIVE DEFINITE. THIS COULD INDICATE A NEGATIVE VARIANCE/RESIDUAL VARIANCE FOR A LATENT VARIABLE, A CORRELATION GREATER OR EQUAL TO ONE BETWEEN TWO LATENT VARIABLES, OR A LINEAR DEPENDENCY AMONG MORE THAN TWO LATENT VARIABLES. CHECK THE TECH4 OUTPUT FOR MORE INFORMATION. PROBLEM INVOLVING VARIABLE F10.

Figure 6.5. M*plus* error message concerning input data.

Recall from Chapter 3 that the PSI matrix represents the variance–covariance matrix for the latent factors. Here, it is suggested that the problem may lie with Factor 10 (Emotional Exhaustion). Indeed, not uncommon to full SEM models is the finding of a negative variance related to one of the factors, and this is the case here, as we shall see shortly when we examine the parameter estimates.

Model Assessment

Preceding the reporting of parameter estimates in the M*plus* output is a summary of the tests for model fit; these values are reported in Table 6.2. Here we see that the rescaled χ^2 value (i.e., the MLM χ^2) is 1554.942 with 427 degrees of freedom. The reported scaling correction value for the MLM estimator indicates that if the MLM χ^2 were multiplied by 1.117, it would approximate the uncorrected ML χ^2 value (1736.870). Indeed, reanalysis of the hypothesized model based on ML estimation certainly approximated this value in yielding a χ^2 value of 1737.090.

Further on this topic, as noted in both Chapters 4 and 5, whenever robust parameter estimation is used, chi-square difference tests between nested models are inappropriate because the chi-square-difference values are not distributed as chi-square. These tests, however, can still be conducted, albeit using the correction formula reported in a paper by Satorra and Bentler (2001) that is also available on the M*plus* website (http://www.statmodel. com/chidiff.shtml). Accordingly, results based on robust estimation are always accompanied by a caveat in the M*plus* output as shown in Table 6.2.

Table 6.2 Mplus Output for Hypothesized Model:
Selected Goodness-of-Fit Statistics

Tests of Model Fit	
Chi-Square Test of Model Fit	
Value	1554.942*
Degrees of freedom	427
p-value	0.0000
Scaling Correction Factor for MLM	1.117
CFI/TLI	
CFI	0.945
TLI	0.936
Number of free parameters	133
Root Mean Square Error of Approximation (RMSEA)	
Estimate	0.043
Standardized Root Mean Square Residual (SRMR)	
Value	0.051

* The chi-square value for MLM, MLMV, MLR, ULSMV, WLSM, and WLSMV cannot be used for chi-square difference testing in the regular way. MLM, MLR, and WLSM chi-square difference testing is described on the Mplus website (http://www.statmodel.com). MLMV, WLSMV, and ULSMV difference testing is done using the DIFFTEST option.

As indicated by the CFI and Tucker-Lewis Fit Index (TLI) values of 0.945 and 0.936, respectively, the hypothesized model exhibits a relatively good fit to the data. Reported values of both the RMSEA (0.043) and SRMR (0.051) provide additional support in this regard. Nonetheless, examination of the MIs will enable us to refine this initial model assessment.

Earlier in this chapter, in my review of the Mplus input file, I noted that inclusion of the TECH1 option in the OUTPUT command can be helpful in determining if the number of reported estimated parameters and, ultimately, the number of degrees of freedom are correct as this information can alert you to whether or not the model is correctly specified. Thus, prior to moving on to an examination of the parameter estimates, I wish first to digress slightly in order to review several related important points. To aid us in this process, we turn to the selected portions of the TECH1 output reported in Figure 6.6.

Although results pertinent to only the BETA and PSI matrices are included here, the information provided is sufficient for our immediate purposes. First, I noted earlier that the TECH1 option presents matrix-formatted arrays of all freely estimated parameters in the model; accordingly, each parameter is assigned a number. In the BETA matrix, for example, you will note that the numbers range from 87 through 100. The

14 numbers assigned to parameters in this matrix represent the 14 structural paths to be estimated in the model. In the F1 column, for example, the number 96 is the number assigned to the parameter representing the path leading from Factor 1 to Factor 12.

Second, turning next to the PSI matrix, we find estimated parameters on both its diagonal and a portion of its off-diagonals. As noted in the callouts in this table, the bolded numbers on the diagonal represent the variances of Factors 1 through 7, whereas the italicized numbers on the lower section of the diagonal represent the residuals associated with Factors 8 through 12. Why the difference between the two sets of factors? Recall from Chapter 2 that one important tenet of SEM is that the estimation of variances and covariances is pertinent to only the independent variables in a model. Thus, only the variances of Factors 1 through 7 are estimated. In contrast, the variances for Factors 8 through 12 actually represent their residuals as these latter parameters, technically speaking, are independent parameters in the model. Likewise, the 21 factor covariances estimated represent those among Factors 1 through 7.

Third, note that the variance of the residual associated with Factor 12 represents the final parameter to be estimated, and note also that it is assigned the number 133. Thus, according to the M*plus* TECH1 output, there are 133 parameters to be estimated for the hypothesized model. (See also the number of free parameters noted in the section of the output file reported in Table 6.2.) Recall that by default, M*plus* always estimates the intercepts for the observed variables, and, therefore, this number is correctly reported in Table 6.2. However, given that we are working within the framework of covariance, rather than mean structure modeling, the observed variable means (i.e., intercepts) are of no interest, and, thus, the program automatically fixes these values to 0.0. As a consequence, the *actual* number of estimated parameters is 101 (133 − 32), and not 133, given that there are 32 observed variables and, hence, 32 intercepts.

Finally, recall that in Chapter 2, I explained how to calculate the number of degrees of freedom associated with a specified model. At that time, I introduced you to the formula $p\,(p + 1)/2$, where p represents the number of observed variables in a specified model. I also noted at that time that, because M*plus* estimates the observed variable intercepts by default, additional pieces of information must necessarily include the observed variable means. Thus, the complete formula is $p\,(p + 1)/2 + p$ means. Calculations based on this formula yield the number of elements (or moments; i.e., pieces of information) upon which analyses will be based; this resulting number minus the number of estimated parameters equals the number of degrees of freedom. However, as noted previously, when SEM analyses are based on covariance rather than on mean structures, the factor mean estimates are fixed to zero by default and the number of

Mplus Output for Hypothesized Model:
Selected Parameter Arrays from TECH1

PARAMETER SPECIFICATION

BETA

	F1	F2	F3	F4	F5
F1	0	0	0	0	0
F2	0	0	0	0	0
F3	0	0	0	0	0
F4	0	0	0	0	0
F5	0	0	0	0	0
F6	0	0	0	0	0
F7	0	0	0	0	0
F8	0	0	0	0	87
F9	0	0	0	0	90
F10	0	91	92	93	0
F11	0	94	0	0	0
F12	96	0	0	0	0

BETA

	F6	F7	F8	F9	F10
F1	0	0	0	0	0
F2	0	0	0	0	0
F3	0	0	0	0	0
F4	0	0	0	0	0
F5	0	0	0	0	0
F6	0	0	0	0	0
F7	0	0	0	0	0
F8	88	89	0	0	0
F9	0	0	0	0	0
F10	0	0	0	0	0
F11	0	0	0	0	95
F12	0	0	97	98	99

BETA

	F11	F12
F1	0	0
F2	0	0
F3	0	0
F4	0	0
F5	0	0
F6	0	0
F7	0	0
F8	0	0
F9	0	0
F10	0	0
F11	0	0
F12	100	0

Figure 6.6. Mplus parameter arrays resulting from TECH1 specification in OUTPUT command.

observed variable intercepts is not included in calculations of degrees of freedom. With this information in hand, then, let's now review the number of estimated parameters in our hypothesized model and then calculate the number of expected degrees of freedom.

PSI

	F1	F2	F3	F4	F5
F1	**101**				
F2	102	**103**			
F3	104	105	**106**		
F4	107	108	109	**110**	
F5	111	112	113	114	**115**
F6	116	117	118	119	120
F7	122	123	124	125	126
F8	0	0	0	0	0
F9	0	0	0	0	0
F10	0	0	0	0	0
F11	0	0	0	0	0
F12	0	0	0	0	0

Bolded diagonal values represent factor variances

PSI

	F6	F7	F8	F9	F10
F6	**121**				
F7	127	**128**			
F8	0	0	*129*		
F9	0	0	0	*130*	
F10	0	0	0	0	*131*
F11	0	0	0	0	0
F12	0	0	0	0	0

Italicized diagonal values represent factor residual variances

PSI

	F11	F12
F11	*132*	
F12	0	*133*

Figure 6.6 (continued).

- 101 estimated parameters:
  22 factor loadings (20 original and 2 additional)
  44 variances (7 factors, 32 error residuals, and 5 factor residuals)
  21 factor covariances (Factors 1–7)
  14 structural regression paths

- 528 pieces of information:
  Number of observed variables = 32
  $p\,(p + 1)/2$
  $= 32\,(32 + 1)/2$
  $= 32\,(33)/2$
  $= 1056/2 = 528$

- 427 degrees of freedom $(528 - 101)$

MODEL RESULTS

		Estimate	S.E.	Two-Tailed Est./S.E.	P-Value
F8	**ON**				
	F5	0.475	0.050	9.462	0.000
	F6	−0.155	0.025	−6.194	0.000
	F7	−0.066	0.029	−2.307	0.021
F9	**ON**				
	F5	−0.288	0.021	−13.784	0.000
F10	**ON**				
	F2	−8.707	6.309	−1.380	0.168
	F3	8.082	5.321	1.519	0.129
	F4	−0.930	0.658	−1.415	0.157
F11	**ON**				
	F2	0.258	0.048	5.356	0.000
	F10	0.373	0.033	11.377	0.000
F12	**ON**				
	F1	−0.071	0.046	−1.548	0.122
	F8	0.472	0.085	5.562	0.000
	F9	−0.208	0.049	−4.264	0.000
	F10	−0.064	0.025	−2.564	0.010
	F11	−0.218	0.031	−7.115	0.000

Residual Variances

	Estimate	S.E.	Est./S.E.	P-Value
F8	0.079	0.007	10.672	0.000
F9	0.143	0.011	13.432	0.000
F10	−0.432	0.770	−0.562	0.574
F11	0.605	0.047	12.880	0.000
F12	0.383	0.023	16.815	0.000

Figure 6.7. Mplus output showing structural regression path and residual variance estimates.

A quick comparison with the results reported in Table 6.2 reveals this number of degrees of freedom to be correct.

Model Parameter Estimation

Given the large number of parameters estimated in this model, the reported results are understandably lengthy. Thus, in the interest of space, I report findings pertinent to only the structural parameters, as well as a few residual variances. These results are presented in Figure 6.7.

Examination of estimated parameters in the model revealed all to be statistically significant except for five as reported in Figure 6.7. Four of these nonsignificant parameters are shown within ovals and represent the following structural regression paths: (a) F10 on F2 (Role Conflict → Emotional Exhaustion), F10 on F3 (Work Overload → Emotional Exhaustion), F10 on F4 (Classroom Climate → Emotional Exhaustion), and (b) F12 on F1 (Role Ambiguity → Personal Accomplishment). In my writings, I have stressed that final models in SEM should represent the best fitting, albeit most parsimonious, model of any set of tested models. As such, all parameters in the model must be statistically significant. However, at this point in our testing of the hypothesized model, it is not yet known whether we will need to conduct post hoc analyses in order to further refine the model. Thus, because MI values can fluctuate widely during the process of these post hoc analyses, it is more appropriate to first determine the best fitting model. Once this final model is established, then we can conduct a final model in which any nonsignificant parameters in the model are deleted. Thus, these nonsignificant structural parameters will remain in the model until we have determined our final model.

Let's turn now to estimates of the factor residual variances, also included in Figure 6.7. Pertinent to the warning message noted earlier regarding the nonpositive status of the PSI matrix, we can now see the source of the problem as being a negative variance for the residual associated with Factor 10. It seems likely that this variance is close to zero and, as a boundary parameter, can just as easily be a negative as a positive value. Interpreted literally, this finding implies that the combination of Role Conflict (F2), Work Overload (F3), and Classroom Climate (F4) is perfect in its prediction of Emotional Exhaustion (F10), thereby resulting in no residual variance. However, in the testing of full structural equation models such as the one in this chapter, post hoc model fitting often results in a solution in which the negative variance disappears, which, as you will see later in this chapter, turns out to be the case in the present application.

Model Misspecification
Over and above the fit of our hypothesized model as a whole, which we noted to be relatively good (CFI = .945; TLI= .936), a review of the MIs reveals some evidence of misfit in the model. Because we are interested solely in the causal paths of the model at this point, only MIs related to these parameters are included in Table 6.3.[4] The M*plus* output reports these results in the form of ON/BY, rather than as just ON statements; for each pair, the ON statement, of course, represents the opposite of the BY statement. For example, turning to the first result in Table 6.3, we can recognize that F2 *on* F8 is the reverse of F8 *by* F2. Thus, whereas *F2 on F8* conveys the notion that F2 is regressed on F8 (i.e., follow the point of the single-headed arrow [at F2] backward to its source [F8]), the statement *F8 by F2* signals that F2 is influenced by F8 (i.e., the arrow points *from* F8 *to* F2). Accompanying the reported MI estimate associated with each ON/BY statement is the expected parameter change (EPC) statistic, along with its standardized values. We turn now to these results in Table 6.3.

Table 6.3 Mplus Output for Hypothesized Model:
Selected Modification Indices (MIs)

		Model Modification Indices			
ON/BY Statements		MI	Expected Parameter Change (EPC)	Standard EPC	StdYX EPC
F2	ON F8 /				
F8	BY F2	35.930	0.109	0.049	0.049
F2	ON F11 /				
F11	BY F2	23.636	0.058	0.074	0.074
F3	ON F8 /				
F8	BY F3	36.336	−0.133	−0.051	−0.051
F3	ON F10 /				
F10	BY F3	18.323	2.682	3.428	3.428
F3	ON F11 /				
F11	BY F3	37.804	−0.079	−0.085	−0.085
F4	ON F10 /				
F10	BY F4	19.564	−3.187	−10.884	−10.884
F4	ON F11 /				
F11	BY F4	81.295	−0.141	−0.404	−0.404
F4	ON F12 /				
F12	BY F4	40.224	0.114	0.252	0.252
F5	ON F10 /				
F10	BY F5	12.842	1.657	2.663	2.663
F6	ON F8 /				
F8	BY F6	23.002	2.295	0.728	0.728
F6	ON F9 /				
F9	BY F6	43.709	0.530	0.212	0.212
F6	ON F12 /				
F12	BY F6	13.758	0.164	0.113	0.113
F7	ON F8 /				
F8	BY F7	14.891	2.235	0.986	0.986
F8	ON F1 /				
F1	BY F8	25.964	0.244	0.461	0.461
F8	ON F2 /				
F2	BY F8	17.305	0.161	0.357	0.357
F8	ON F9 /				
F9	BY F8	22.229	−0.136	−0.171	−0.171
F8	ON F10 /				
F10	BY F8	29.728	−0.117	−0.391	−0.391

Table 6.3 M*plus* Output for Hypothesized Model: Selected Modification Indices (MIs) (*continued*)

		Model Modification Indices			
ON/BY Statements		MI	Expected Parameter Change (EPC)	Standard EPC	StdYX EPC
F8	ON F11 /				
F11	BY F8	25.604	−0.066	−0.187	−0.187
F8	ON F12 /				
F12	BY F8	44.745	0.329	0.719	0.719
F9	ON F1 /				
F1	BY F9	19.280	0.193	0.288	0.288
F9	ON F2 /				
F2	BY F9	37.370	0.199	0.350	0.350
F9	ON F3 /				
F3	BY F9	31.173	0.157	0.326	0.326
F9	ON F6 /				
F6	BY F9	28.365	0.127	0.317	0.317
F9	ON F8 /				
F8	BY F9	38.038	−0.295	−0.234	−0.234
F10	ON F1 /				
F1	BY F10	11.974	2.303	1.297	1.297
F10	ON F5 /				
F5	BY F10	16.369	−2.238	−1.393	−1.393
F10	ON F6 /				
F6	BY F10	10.882	−0.772	−0.725	−0.725
F10	ON F8 /				
F8	BY F10	39.661	−1.047	−0.312	−0.312
F10	ON F11 /				
F11	BY F10	17.616	−0.388	−0.326	−0.326
F11	ON F3 /				
F3	BY F11	76.378	−4.799	−4.467	−4.467
F11	**ON F4 /**				
F4	BY F11	**100.790**	**−0.974**	**−0.339**	**−0.339**
F11	ON F5 /				
F5	BY F11	21.850	−0.326	−0.241	−0.241
F11	ON F6 /				
F6	BY F11	15.985	−0.122	−0.137	−0.137
F11	ON F8 /				
F8	BY F11	21.333	−0.436	−0.155	−0.155

Table 6.3 M*plus* Output for Hypothesized Model:
Selected Modification Indices (MIs) (*continued*)

			Expected Parameter Change (EPC)	Standard EPC	StdYX EPC
		Model Modification Indices			
ON/BY Statements		MI			
F11	ON F12 /				
F12	BY F11	36.433	−0.882	−0.683	−0.683
F12	ON F2 /				
F2	BY F12	13.723	0.233	0.237	0.237
F12	ON F3 /				
F3	BY F12	19.370	0.272	0.327	0.327
F12	ON F4 /				
F4	BY F12	21.923	0.355	0.160	0.160
F12	ON F5 /				
F5	BY F12	43.159	0.486	0.465	0.465
F12	ON F6 /				
F6	BY F12	35.982	0.155	0.223	0.223
F12	ON F7 /				
F7	BY F12	16.148	0.138	0.143	0.143

Given that the primary research focus bearing on the current model is to identify determinants of teacher burnout, only paths leading from the independent factors in the model (F1 through F7) to the dependent factors (F8 through F12) qualify as candidates for inclusion in subsequent models. Thus, although we may find MIs related to paths leading from dependent to independent factors or the presence of reciprocal paths, these parameters are not considered with respect to the current research and model. The dotted line shown in Table 6.3 serves to separate most (but not all) MIs related to paths flowing in the desired direction (independent to dependent) from those flowing from dependent to independent factors.

In reviewing the ON/BY statements below the dotted line, you will note that two are encased within a rectangle. Focusing on these captured values, we see that the maximum MI (bolded text) is associated with the regression of F11 on F4 (Depersonalization on Classroom Climate). The value of 100.790 indicates that, if this parameter were to be freely estimated in a subsequently specified model, the overall χ^2 value would drop by at least this amount. The EPC statistic related to this parameter is shown to be −0.974; this value represents the approximate value that the newly estimated parameter would assume. The negative sign associated with this value is substantively correct and as expected, given that items from the Classroom

Environment Scale were reflected such that low scores were indicative of a poor classroom milieu, and high scores of a good classroom milieu.

The other ON/BY statement (F11 on F3) within the rectangle is included here as it provides me with an opportunity to stress the importance of selecting potentially additional model parameters only on the basis of their substantive meaningfulness. Given the noticeably high MI associated with this structural path and its exceptionally high EPC value, a researcher might consider the selection of this parameter over the previous one. Indeed, there has been some suggestion in the literature that the selection of post hoc parameters on the basis of their EPCs may be more appropriate than on the basis of their MIs (see, e.g., Kaplan, 1989; but see Bentler's [2005] caveat that these values can be affected by both the scaling and identification of factors and variables). However, let's take a closer look at this parameter representing the regression path leading from F3 (Work Overload) to F11 (Depersonalization). That the EPC value is negative is a clear indication that this parameter is inappropriate as this would be interpreted to mean that high Work Overload would lead a teacher to exhibit low levels of Depersonalization, which clearly runs counter to both burnout theory and practical sense.

From a substantive perspective, it would seem perfectly reasonable that secondary teachers whose responses yielded low scores for Classroom Climate should concomitantly display high levels of Depersonalization. Given the meaningfulness of this influential flow, we now proceed within a post hoc modeling framework to reestimate the model, with the path from Classroom Climate to Depersonalization (F11 on F4) specified as a freely estimated parameter; this model is subsequently labeled as Model 2. Results derived from this respecified model are subsequently discussed within the framework of post hoc analyses. I wish once again to stress two important caveats with respect to the post hoc model-fitting process: (a) Once the hypothesized model has been rejected, as we have done here, we are no longer working within a confirmatory framework, and from now on these analyses are of an exploratory nature; and (b) when identification of misspecified parameters is based on the MI, it is critical that any respecification of the model include the addition of only one parameter at a time.

In the post hoc model fitting of full structural equation models in general, and the application included here in particular, the process can be very tedious and time-consuming. Thus, I am certain that you will find this to be the case in this chapter. However, I consider it important to walk you through each and every step in determining the various post hoc models as this, in essence, is really the only way to fully appreciate what is involved in the selection of the various additional parameters to be included in the model.

Post Hoc Analyses

Output File 2

In the interest of space, only portions of the MI results pertinent to each respecified model will be presented in table form; other relevant results are presented and discussed in the text.

Model Assessment

The estimation of Model 2 yielded an overall MLM $\chi^2_{(426)}$ value of 1450.985 (scaling correction factor = 1.117); CFI and TLI values of 0.950 and 0.941, respectively; a RMSEA value of 0.041; and a SRMR value of 0.046. It is important to note that throughout the post hoc analyses, assessment and reporting of the extent to which reestimated models improved model fit were determined from chi-square-difference values (MLM$\Delta\chi^2$) that were, in turn, recalculated on the basis of the correction formula provided in the M*plus* website (http://www.statmodel.com) for use with robust estimation. Although improvement in model fit for Model 2, compared with the originally hypothesized model, would appear to be somewhat minimal on the basis of the CFI, TLI, RMSEA, and SRMR values, this decision was ultimately based on the corrected chi-square difference test, which in this case was found to be statistically significant (MLM$\Delta\chi^2_{[1]}$ = 104.445). To provide you with a clear understanding of how this value was derived, I consider it important to walk you through the most relevant stages of this three-step process, as presented in the M*plus* website; these comprise the following:

- Computation of the scaling correction factors
- Computation of scaling correction associated with the difference test
- Computation of the MLM χ^2–difference test

Given that the scaling correction factors are provided by the M*plus* program, there is no need to work through the first step. Thus, for this first comparison model, I illustrate only Steps 2 and 3 as follows:

Step 2.   cd = (d0 * c0) – (d1 * c1)/(d0 – d1)

where d0 = degrees of freedom for the nested (i.e., more restricted) model;
      d1 = degrees of freedom for the comparison (i.e., less restricted) model;
      c0 = scaling correction factor for the nested model (see Table 6.2);
      c1 = scaling correction factor for the comparison model (see text);

      cd = (427 * 1.117) – (426 * 1.117)/(427 – 426)
         = (476.959 – 475.842)/1
         = 1.117

That the scaling correction factor for the difference test is 1.117, of course, is not unexpected, given that this value was reported to be the same for both the hypothesized model (Model 1) and Model 2.

Step 3.   TRd = (T0 – T1)/cd

where TRd = MLM χ^2-difference test;
      T0 = ML χ^2 for the nested model;[5]
      T1 = ML χ^2 for the comparison model;
    TRd = (1737.090 – 1620.425)/1.117
         = 116.665/1.117
         = 104.445

Given a reasonably good fit of the model to the data, and the fact that respecification of Model 2 yielded little difference in fit indices from those of the hypothesized model, you may wonder at this point (and rightly so) why we should continue in the search for a better fitting model via specification of additional parameters to the model. The answer to this query is tied to the fact that we are working toward the validation of a full SEM model where the key parameters represent causal structure among several latent constructs. Clearly, our overall aim is to determine the best fitting, albeit most parsimonious, model in representing the determinants of burnout for secondary teachers. Thus, the thrust of these post hoc analyses is to fine-tune our hypothesized structure such that it includes all viable and statistically significant structural paths (which it is here: ΔMLM $\chi^2_{[1]}$ = 104.445), and, at the same time, eliminates all nonsignificant paths. Consequently, as long as the $\Delta\chi^2$-difference test is statistically significant, and the newly added parameters are substantively meaningful, I consider the post hoc analyses to be appropriate.

Model Parameter Estimation

Importantly, the estimated value of the path from Classroom Climate to Depersonalization was found to be both statistically significant (–9.643) and exceptionally close to the one predicted by the EPC statistic (–0.969 versus –0.974). Of substantial import is the fact that (a) the warning message noted and described earlier regarding Factor 10 (Emotional Exhaustion) and its negative residual variance remained in the output for Model 2, and (b) the estimated structural regression paths for the three factors hypothesized to influence Factor 10 (Factors 2, 3, and 4) remained statistically nonsignificant.

Modification Indices

All MIs related *only* to the structural regression parameters for Model 2 are shown in Table 6.4. Consistent with Table 6.3, all ON/BY statements

Table 6.4 M*plus* Output for Model 2:
Selected Modification Indices (MIs)

| | Model Modification Indices | | | |
| | | | | |

ON/BY Statements		MI	Expected Parameter Change (EPC)	Standard EPC	StdYX EPC
F2 F8	ON F8 / BY F2	34.766	0.110	0.050	0.050
F3 F8	ON F8 / BY F3	34.891	−0.134	−0.051	−0.051
F3 F10	ON F10 / BY F3	17.670	2.936	3.749	3.749
F4 F10	ON F10 / BY F4	18.689	−3.195	−10.959	−10.959
F4 F12	ON F12 / BY F4	11.687	0.070	0.155	0.155
F5 F10	ON F10 / BY F5	13.292	1.865	3.003	3.003
F6 F8	ONF8 / BY F6	21.084	2.191	0.695	0.695
F6 F9	ON F9 / BY F6	43.782	0.530	0.213	0.213
F6 F12	ON F12 / BY F6	13.014	0.160	0.111	0.111
F7 F8	ON F8 / BY F7	14.951	2.238	0.987	0.987
F8 F1	ON F1 / BY F8	26.110	0.245	0.462	0.462
F8 F2	ON F2 / BY F8	17.785	0.161	0.358	0.358
F8 F9	ON F9 / BY F8	22.165	−0.135	−0.171	−0.171
F8 F10	ON F10 / BY F8	29.240	−0.115	−0.385	−0.385
F8 F11	ON F11 / BY F8	26.918	−0.070	−0.200	−0.200
F8 F12	ON F12 / BY F8	44.643	0.330	0.720	0.720

Table 6.4 M*plus* Output for Model 2:
Selected Modification Indices (MIs) (*continued*)

	Model Modification Indices			
ON/BY Statements		MI	Expected Parameter Change (EPC)	Standard EPC	StdYX EPC
F9 F1	ON F1 / BY F9	19.160	0.192	0.287	0.287
F9 F2	ON F2 / BY F9	35.751	0.193	0.339	0.339
F9 F3	ON F3 / BY F9	30.622	0.155	0.321	0.321
F9 F6	ON F6 / BY F9	28.522	0.127	0.317	0.317
F9 F8	ON F8 / BY F9	38.013	−0.295	−0.234	−0.234
F10 F1	ON F1 / BY F10	11.621	2.201	1.237	1.237
F10 F5	ON F5 / BY F10	15.505	−2.111	−1.311	−1.311
F10 F6	ON F6 / BY F10	10.204	−0.725	−0.680	−0.680
F10 F8	ON F8 / BY F10	38.297	−1.029	−0.306	−0.306
F11 F8	ON F8 / BY F11	19.497	−0.402	−0.142	−0.142
F12 F2	ON F2 / BY F12	14.555	0.235	0.240	0.240
F12 F3	ON F3 / BY F12	17.767	0.255	0.308	0.308
F12 F4	ON F4 / BY F12	18.509	0.364	0.163	0.163
F12 F5	ON F5 / BY F12	42.163	0.480	0.458	0.458
F12 F6	ON F6 / BY F12	34.604	0.152	0.219	0.219
F12 F7	ON F7 / BY F12	16.004	0.137	0.142	0.142

appearing above the broken line represent structural regression paths that run counter to expected direction and therefore are not of interest here. Again, although some inappropriate directional paths appear below this line, most are eligible for consideration in our search for improvement to model fit. In a review of the eligible MIs, I determined the one appearing in the solid rectangle to be most appropriate both substantively and statistically. In addition to having the largest MI (based on appropriate causal direction), it also has a substantial EPC value. This parameter represents the regression of Factor 12 (Personal Accomplishment) on F5 (Decision Making) and suggests that the greater the opportunity for secondary teachers to participate in decision making with respect to their work environment, the stronger will be their sense of personal accomplishment. On the basis of this rationale, I consider it acceptable to once again respecify the model with this new structural path included (Model 3).

Before leaving these MI results for Model 2, however, I direct your attention to the MI results appearing within the broken rectangle. Given that the MI value is larger than the one I selected, some readers may wonder why I didn't choose the parameter represented here. The explanation relates to the causal direction associated with this parameter as it represents the regression of Factor 8 (Self-Esteem) on F12 (Personal Accomplishment). Although, admittedly, a flow of causal direction from Personal Accomplishment to Self-Esteem is logically possible, it runs counter to the focus of the present intended research in identifying determinants of teacher burnout. On this basis, then, it does not qualify here for considered addition to the model.

Output File 3

Model Assessment

Model 3 yielded an overall MLM $\chi^2_{(425)}$ value of 1406.517 (scaling correction factor = 1.117), with CFI = 0.952, TLI = 0.944, RMSEA = 0.040, and SRMR = 0.044. Again, the MLM χ^2 difference between Models 2 and 3 is statistically significant (ΔMLM $\chi^2_{[1]}$ = 44.277), albeit differences in the other fit indices across Models 2 and 3 were once again minimal.

Model Parameter Estimation

As expected, the estimate for the newly incorporated path from Decision Making to Personal Accomplishment (F5 $\rightarrow$ F12) was found to be statistically significant. Also of interest is the finding that only two of the three previous paths leading to F10 (F2 and F4) are nonsignificant. Furthermore, the structural path leading from F1 (Role Ambiguity) to F12 (Personal Accomplishment) is now statistically significant, albeit the path from F10 to F12 is not so. These dramatic shifts in the parameter estimate results represent a good example of why it is important to include only one respecified parameter at a time when working with univariate MIs in post hoc analyses.[6] Finally, once again the negative variance associated with the F10 residual was retained, hence the related warning message.

Modification Indices

MIs related to Model 3 are presented in Table 6.5. Because the first reasonable MI to be considered is once again F8 on F1, I have chosen to delete all MIs between this one and the first one reported in the output file. Following a review of all remaining MIs, the one considered most appropriate for inclusion in a subsequent model is the structural path flowing from F2 (Role Conflict) to F9 (External Locus of Control). Thus, information related to the MI representing this parameter is shown within the rectangle.

Again, I believe it is worthwhile to note why two alternate MI values, close in value to the one chosen here, are considered to be inappropriate. I refer to results related to the structural paths of F10 on F8 (MI = 38.868) and of F9 on F8 (MI = 35.670). In both cases, the flow of causal direction is incorrect. In contrast, the structural path noted earlier (F9 on F2) is viable both statistically and substantively in that high levels of role conflict can be expected to generate high levels of external locus of control, thereby yielding a positive EPC statistic value, which is the case here (EPC = 0.191). Thus, Model 4 was subsequently specified with the path leading from Role Conflict to External Locus of Control (F9 on F2) freely estimated.

Output File 4

Model Assessment

The estimation of Model 4 yielded a MLM χ^2 value of 1366.129 (scaling correction factor = 1.118) with 424 degrees of freedom. Values related to the CFI, TLI, RMSEA, and SRMR were .954, .946, 0.039, and 0.041, respectively. Again, the difference in fit between this model (Model 4) and its predecessor (Model 3) was statistically significant (MLM$\Delta\chi^2_{[1]}$ = 63.782).

Model Parameter Estimation

As expected, the newly specified parameter (F9 on F2) was found to be statistically significant (Estimate = 0.189; Estimate [Est]/standard error [SE] = 7.157). However, once again the three paths leading from F2, F3, and F4 to F10 were all found to be nonsignificant, in addition to yet another different path leading to F12—that of F12 on F10 (Emotional Exhaustion → Personal Accomplishment). Finally, once again, the warning message regarding the negative residual associated with Factor 10 appeared in the output file.

Table 6.5 M*plus* Output for Model 3:
Selected Modification Indices (MIs)

			Model Modification Indices			
ON/BY Statements			MI	Expected Parameter Change (EPC)	Standard EPC	StdYX EPC
F2	ON F8	/	31.379	0.134	0.060	0.060
F8	BY F2					
•						
•						
•						
F8	ON F1	/	26.548	0.248	0.467	0.467
F1	BY F8					
F8	ON F9	/	20.217	−0.128	−0.162	−0.162
F9	BY F8					
F8	ON F10	/	31.309	−0.116	−0.389	−0.389
F10	BY F8					
F8	ON F11	/	26.731	−0.069	−0.197	−0.197
F11	BY F8					
F8	ON F12	/	35.425	0.295	0.647	0.647
F12	BY F8					
F9	ON F1	/	20.770	0.204	0.303	0.303
F1	BY F9					
F9	ON F2	/	37.015	0.191	0.336	0.336
F2	BY F9					
F9	ON F3	/	32.286	0.154	0.321	0.321
F3	BY F9					
F9	ON F6	/	30.219	0.130	0.323	0.323
F6	BY F9					
F9	ON F8	/	35.670	−0.284	−0.225	−0.225
F8	BY F9					
F10	ON F1	/	12.330	1.816	1.016	1.016
F1	BY F10					
F10	ON F5	/	16.046	−1.647	−1.025	−1.025
F5	BY F10					
F10	ON F8	/	38.868	−1.021	−0.304	−0.304
F8	BY F10					
F10	ON F12	/	10.236	−0.345	−0.226	−0.226
F12	BY F10					
F11	ON F8	/	19.309	−0.398	−0.140	−0.140
F8	BY F11					

Table 6.5 M*plus* Output for Model 3:
Selected Modification Indices (MIs) (*continued*)

| | | | Model Modification Indices | | |
ON/BY Statements			MI	Expected Parameter Change (EPC)	Standard EPC	StdYX EPC
F12	ON F2	/	15.947	0.272	0.275	0.275
F2	BY F12					
F12	ON F3	/	17.959	0.283	0.340	0.340
F3	BY F12					

Modification Indices

MIs related to the estimation of Model 4 are presented in Table 6.6. Once again, I have deleted all ineligible MI values appearing between the first *appropriate* result (F8 on F1) and the first MI result specified in the output (F2 on F8). As usual, the parameter that I consider most appropriate for inclusion in the model is encased within a rectangle; in the case of Model 4, it represents the structural regression path from Factor 8 (Self-Esteem) to Factor 9 (External Locus of Control). This parameter represents the largest by far of all MI estimates that qualify for inclusion in a subsequent model; and, again, it is substantively meaningful because, clearly, the lower a teacher's sense of self-esteem, the more he or she is going to feel under the control of others. Thus, we move on to Model 5, in which this parameter has been included in the model.

Output File 5

Model Assessment

The estimation of Model 5 yielded a MLM $\chi^2_{(423)}$ value of 1331.636 (scaling correction factor = 1.117), with other fit indices as follows: CFI = 0.955, TLI = 0.948, RMSEA = 0.039, and SRMR = 0.039. Again, the difference in fit between this model (Model 5) and its predecessor (Model 4) was found to be statistically significant (S-B$\Delta\chi^2_{[1]}$ = 25.410).

Model Parameter Estimation

Once again, the newly specified parameter (F9 on F8) was found to be statistically significant and accompanied by the correct sign (Estimate = 0.257; Est/*SE* = 5.337). However, as with Model 3, again two of the three paths leading to F10 (F2 → F10; F4 → F10) remained statistically nonsignificant,

Table 6.6 M*plus* Output for Model 4:
Selected Modification Indices (MIs)

			Model Modification Indices		
ON/BY Statements			MI	Expected Parameter Change (EPC)	Standard EPC	StdYX EPC
F2	ON F8	/	19.160	0.095	0.043	0.043
F8	BY F2					
•						
•						
•						
F8	ON F1	/	21.079	0.241	0.453	0.453
F1	BY F8					
F8	ON F9	/	24.852	−0.139	−0.175	−0.175
F9	BY F8					
F8	ON F10	/	21.163	−0.122	−0.408	−0.408
F10	BY F8					
F8	ON F11	/	23.427	−0.066	−0.189	−0.189
F11	BY F8					
F8	ON F12	/	33.473	0.302	0.662	0.662
F12	BY F8					
F9	ON F6	/	12.980	0.090	0.226	0.226
F6	BY F9					
F9	ON F8	/	34.615	−0.261	−0.208	−0.208
F8	BY F9					
F9	ON F12	/	27.194	−0.265	−0.464	−0.464
F12	BY F9					
F10	ON F1	/	13.858	2.586	1.449	1.449
F1	BY F10					
F10	ON F5	/	13.676	−1.882	−1.166	−1.166
F5	BY F10					
F10	ON F8	/	26.604	−1.048	−0.312	−0.312
F8	BY F10					
F11	ON F8	/	18.905	−0.396	−0.139	−0.139
F8	BY F11					
F12	ON F2	/	15.073	0.267	0.271	0.271
F2	BY F12					
F12	ON F3	/	18.238	0.291	0.348	0.348
F3	BY F12					
F12	ON F4	/	10.262	0.283	0.126	0.126
F4	BY F12					

albeit the third previously nonsignificant path now yielded a significant estimated value. Finally, the path leading from F10 (Emotional Exhaustion) to F12 (Personal Accomplishment) remained statistically nonsignificant, and the warning message regarding the negative residual associated with Factor 10 remained unchanged.

Modification Indices

MIs related to the estimation of Model 5 are presented in Table 6.7. This output file reveals the structural path leading from Self-Esteem to Emotional Exhaustion (F8 → F10) as having the largest MI value. Because Factor 10 has been problematic regarding the estimation of its residual in yielding a negative variance, it would seem likely that if this parameter were to be included in the model, this undesirable result may finally be resolved. Thus, given that the related EPC statistic related to this parameter exhibits the correct sign, together with the fact that it seems reasonable that teachers who exhibit high levels of self-esteem may, concomitantly, exhibit low levels of emotional exhaustion, the model was reestimated once again, with this path freely estimated (Model 6).

Selected Mplus Output: Model 6

Model Assessment

The estimation of Model 6 yielded a MLM $\chi^2_{(422)}$ value of 1297.489 (scaling correction factor = 1.116), with the remaining fit indices as follows: CFI = 0.957, TLI = 0.949, RMSEA = 0.038, and SRMR = 0.039. As might be expected given the newly specified path involving Factor 10, the difference in fit between this model (Model 6) and its predecessor (Model 5) was found to be statistically significant (MLM$\Delta\chi^2_{[1]}$ = 39.973).

Model Parameter Estimation

Perhaps the most interesting finding here is that the warning message concerning Factor 10 no longer appeared in the output file as the negative residual variance associated with this factor had now been eliminated. As expected, the estimated value for the newly specified path (F10 on F8) was statistically significant (Estimate = −0.884; Est/SE = −8.116). Interestingly, the previously determined nonsignificant paths loading onto F10 (F2, F3, F4), were all statistically significant. Nonetheless, the regression path leading from F10 to F12, which has been consistently nonsignificant, remained so. In addition, however, the parameter, F8 on F7 (Peer Support → Self-Esteem), was found to be statistically nonsignificant.

Table 6.7 M*plus* Output for Model 5:
Selected Modification Indices (MIs)

	Model Modification Indices				
ON/BY Statements		MI	Expected Parameter Change (EPC)	Standard EPC	StdYX EPC
F2 F8	ON F8 / BY F2	19.063	0.129	0.058	0.058
• • •					
F8 F1	ON F1 / BY F8	22.803	0.261	0.491	0.491
F8 F10	ON F10 / BY F8	18.589	−0.121	−0.406	−0.406
F8 F11	ON F11 / BY F8	22.979	−0.066	−0.188	−0.188
F8 F12	ON F12 / BY F8	18.652	0.239	0.526	0.526
F10 F1	ON F1 / BY F10	12.636	1.839	1.030	1.030
F10 F5	ON F5 / BY F10	13.448	−1.368	−0.841	−0.841
F10 F8	ON F8 / BY F10	26.941	−1.068	−0.318	−0.318
F11 F8	ON F8 / BY F11	19.676	−0.404	−0.142	−0.142
F12 F2	ON F2 / BY F12	14.653	0.261	0.265	0.265
F12 F3	ON F3 / BY F12	17.470	0.282	0.338	0.338
F12 F4	ON F4 / BY F12	10.359	0.284	0.127	0.127

Modification Indices

Of the two highest MIs reported in Table 6.8 (F11 on F8; F12 on F2), only the latter one makes sense substantively; this parameter is highlighted within the rectangle. More specifically, the first parameter represents a causal

Table 6.8 M*plus* Output for Model 6:
Selected Modification Indices (MIs)

			Expected Parameter Change	Standard	StdYX
ON/BY Statements		MI	(EPC)	EPC	EPC
F1	ON F12 /	13.204	−0.172	−0.202	−0.202
F12	BY F1				
•					
•					
•					
F11	ON F3 /	19.196	−0.938	−0.911	−0.911
F3	BY F11				
F11	ON F8 /	20.357	−0.409	−0.144	−0.144
F8	BY F11				
F12	ON F2 /	20.428	0.339	0.345	0.345
F2	BY F12				
F12	ON F3 /	19.589	0.259	0.325	0.325
F3	BY F12				

path flowing from F8 (Self-Esteem) to F11 (Depersonalization). However, the fact that the EPC statistic has a negative sign makes interpretation of this path illogical as it conveys the notion that high self-esteem leads to low levels of depersonalization; more appropriately, the path should have a positive sign. In contrast, the positive sign associated with the path leading from Role Conflict to Personal Accomplishment does make sense as this construct actually represents a sense of reduced personal accomplishment. Thus, I consider it worthwhile to specify one more model (Model 7) that incorporates this parameter (F12 on F2).

Output File 7

Model Assessment

The estimation of Model 7 yielded a MLM $\chi^2_{(421)}$ value of 1277.061 (scaling correction factor = 1.115), with the remaining fit indices as follows: CFI = 0.958, TLI = 0.950, RMSEA = 0.038, and SRMR = 0.038. Again, the difference in fit between this model (Model 7) and its predecessor (Model 6) was found to be statistically significant (MLM$\Delta\chi^2_{[1]}$ = 15.149).

Model Parameter Estimation

Here again, the new parameter added to the model (F12 on F2) was found to be statistically significant (Estimate = 0.332; Est/SE = 4.736). However, the structural regression paths F8 (Self-Esteem) on F7 (Peer Support), and F12 (Personal Accomplishment) on F1 (Role Ambiguity), remained the only two statistically nonsignificant parameters in the model.

At this point, I believe that we have exhausted the search for a better fitting model that best represents the data for secondary teachers. Thus, I do not include a section dealing with the MIs. Rather, I suggest that we move on to the establishment of an appropriate final model. Up to this point in the post hoc modeling process, we have focused on only the addition of parameters to the model, all of which were found to be justified from both a statistical and a practical perspective. Now we need to look at the flip side of the coin in identifying all paths that were originally specified in the hypothesized model but remain statistically non-significant as per the results for Model 7; these parameters need to be deleted from the model. Accordingly, Model 8 is now specified in which the two nonsignificant parameters noted above (F7 → F8; F1 → F12) are not included. This model will represent our final best fitting and most parsimonious model of burnout for secondary teachers. Because standardized estimates are typically of interest in presenting results from structural equation models, I have included this requested information on the OUTPUT command. The input file for this final model is shown in Figure 6.8.

Output File 8 (Final Model)

As Model 8 represents the final model, key components of the output files are presented in tabled form. We begin, as usual, with the goodness-of-fit results.

Model Assessment

As shown in Table 6.9, estimation of this final model (Model 8) yielded an overall MLM $\chi^2_{(423)}$ value of 1277.333 (scaling correction factor = 1.116). Of course, the reason for the additional two degrees of freedom, compared with the previously tested model (Model 7), derives from the deletion of the two structural regression paths. As you can readily determine from the CFI value of 0.958, this final model represents a very good fit to the data for secondary teachers. The remaining TLI, RMSEA, and SRMR values further substantiate these results. In contrast to all previous models

---

TITLE: Full SEM Model of Burnout for Secondary Teachers
       Final Model
       Deleted NS Paths (F8 on F7) (F12 on F1)

DATA:
  FILE IS "C:\Mplus\Files\allsecondary.DAT";

VARIABLE:
  NAMES ARE ROLEA1 ROLEA2 ROLEC1 ROLEC2 WORK1 WORK2 CCLIM1 CCLIM2
  CCLIM3 CCLIM4 DEC1 DEC2 SSUP1 SSUP2 PSUP1 PSUP2 SELF1 SELF2 SELF3
  ELC1 ELC2 ELC3 ELC4 ELC5 EE1 EE2 EE3 DP1 DP2 PA1 PA2 PA3;
  USEVARIABLES ARE ROLEA1-PA3;

ANALYSIS:
  ESTIMATOR IS MLM;

MODEL:
  F1 by ROLEA1-ROLEA2 DEC2;
  F2 by ROLEC1-ROLEC2;
  F3 by WORK1-WORK2;
  F4 by CCLIM1-CCLIM4;
  F5 by DEC1-DEC2;
  F6 by SSUP1-SSUP2 DEC2;
  F7 by PSUP1-PSUP2;
  F8 by SELF1-SELF3;
  F9 by ELC1-ELC5;
  F10 by EE1-EE3;
  F11 by DP1-DP2;
  F12 by PA1-PA3;

  F8 ON F5 F6;
  F9 ON F5 F2 F8;
  F10 ON F2 F3 F4 F8;
  F11 ON F2 F10 F4;
  F12 ON F8 F9 F10 F11 F5 F2;

OUTPUT: STDYX;

Figure 6.8. M*plus* input file for final model of teacher burnout for secondary teachers.

tested here, we can expect the corrected chi-square difference between the present model and Model 7 to be statistically nonsignificant given that the two parameters deleted in this model were already found to be statistically nonsignificant in Model 7. Indeed, this was the case as the corrected $\Delta\chi^2_{(2)}$ value was found to be 3.371.

Table 6.9 M*plus* Output for Model 8 (Final Model):
Selected Goodness-of-Fit Statistics

Tests of Model Fit	
Chi-Square Test of Model Fit	
Value	1277.333*
Degrees of freedom	423
p-value	0.0000
Scaling Correction Factor for MLM	1.116
CFI/TLI	
CFI	0.958
TLI	0.951
Root Mean Square Error of Approximation (RMSEA)	
Estimate	0.038
Standardized Root Mean Square Residual (SRMR)	
Value	0.038

Model Parameter Estimation

Although all estimated parameters were statistically significant, space restrictions prevent me from presenting them all in the table. Thus, reported in Table 6.10 are the unstandardized estimates pertinent to only the structural regression paths and the factor covariances. The standardized estimates are presented in Table 6.11.

In a review of the standardized estimates, I draw your attention to the WITH statements and subsequently to one disturbingly high correlation of 0.926 between F3 (Work Overload) and F2 (Role Conflict). That both constructs represent subscales from the same measuring instrument (TSS), however, is not surprising and suggests that the items in one or both scales contain content that may not be clearly specific to its targeted underlying construct. A subsequent respecification of this burnout model might benefit from the inclusion of only one of these two constructs, albeit using all four indicators in its measurement (see, e.g., Chapter 9). A schematic representation of this final model is shown in Figure 6.9.

In working with structural equation models, it is very important to know when to stop fitting a model. Although there are no firm rules or regulations to guide this decision, the researcher's best yardsticks include (a) a thorough knowledge of the substantive theory, (b) an adequate assessment of statistical criteria based on information pooled from various indices of fit, and (c) a watchful eye on parsimony. In this regard, the

Table 6.10 M*plus* Output:
Selected Model Unstandardized Parameter Estimates

		Model Results		
	Estimate	Standard Error (*SE*)	Estimate/*SE*	Two-Tailed *p*-Value
F8 ON				
F5	0.347	0.039	8.836	0.000
F6	−0.118	0.024	−4.875	0.000
F9 ON				
F5	−0.081	0.033	−2.482	0.013
F2	0.165	0.029	5.630	0.000
F8	−0.252	0.048	−5.296	0.000
F10 ON				
F2	−0.860	0.295	−2.921	0.003
F3	1.298	0.249	5.203	0.000
F4	−0.539	0.115	−4.672	0.000
F8	−0.902	0.104	−8.647	0.000
F11 ON				
F2	0.176	0.047	3.719	0.000
F10	0.303	0.032	9.378	0.000
F4	−0.942	0.099	−9.515	0.000
F12 ON				
F8	0.382	0.085	4.496	0.000
F9	−0.212	0.057	−3.698	0.000
F10	−0.085	0.027	−3.103	0.002
F11	−0.213	0.031	−6.852	0.000
F5	0.458	0.060	7.615	0.000
F2	0.372	0.064	5.835	0.000
F2 WITH				
F1	0.384	0.024	15.737	0.000
F3 WITH				
F1	0.403	0.027	14.988	0.000
F2	0.678	0.033	20.278	0.000
F4 WITH				
F1	−0.065	0.008	−8.253	0.000
F2	−0.081	0.010	−8.092	0.000
F3	−0.097	0.012	−7.766	0.000
F3	−0.097	0.012	−7.766	0.000

Table 6.10 M*plus* Output:
Selected Model Unstandardized Parameter Estimates (*continued*)

	Estimate	Standard Error (*SE*)	Estimate/*SE*	Two-Tailed *p*-Value
Model Results				
F5 WITH				
F1	−0.387	0.025	−15.767	0.000
F2	−0.430	0.028	−15.557	0.000
F3	−0.496	0.030	−16.787	0.000
F4	0.104	0.011	9.803	0.000
F6 WITH				
F1	−0.383	0.028	−13.487	0.000
F2	−0.443	0.031	−14.441	0.000
F3	−0.485	0.034	−14.144	0.000
F4	0.121	0.013	9.262	0.000
F5	0.640	0.036	17.833	0.000
F7 WITH				
F1	−0.242	0.021	−11.690	0.000
F2	−0.247	0.022	−11.042	0.000
F3	−0.270	0.025	−10.593	0.000
F4	0.056	0.009	6.272	0.000
F5	0.377	0.026	14.553	0.000
F6	0.393	0.030	13.123	0.000

SEM researcher must walk a fine line between incorporating a sufficient number of parameters to yield a model that adequately represents the data, and falling prey to the temptation of incorporating too many parameters in a zealous attempt to attain the statistically best fitting model. Two major problems with the latter tack are that (a) the model can comprise parameters that actually contribute only trivially to its structure, and (b) the more parameters a model contains, the more difficult it is to replicate its structure should future validation research be conducted.

In bringing this chapter to a close, it may be instructive to summarize and review findings from the various models tested in this full SEM application. A visual summary of both the original and post hoc–added structural paths is presented in Figure 6.10. First, of the 14 structural regression paths specified in the hypothesized model (see Figure 6.2), 10 were found to be statistically significant for secondary teachers. These paths reflected the impact of (a) decision making, superior support, and peer support on

Table 6.11 M*plus* Output:
Selected Standardized Parameter Estimates

Standardized Model Results: STDYX Standardization

	Estimate	Standard Error (*SE*)	Estimate/*SE*	Two-Tailed *p*-Value
F8 ON				
F5	0.748	0.066	11.340	0.000
F6	−0.371	0.071	−5.236	0.000
F9 ON				
F5	−0.139	0.055	−2.512	0.012
F2	0.299	0.052	5.796	0.000
F8	−0.201	0.035	−5.801	0.000
F10 ON				
F2	−0.581	0.198	−2.935	0.003
F3	1.085	0.198	5.473	0.000
F4	−0.158	0.033	−4.762	0.000
F8	−0.270	0.028	−9.695	0.000
F11 ON				
F2	0.140	0.038	3.711	0.000
F10	0.356	0.036	9.771	0.000
F4	−0.325	0.028	−11.426	0.000
F12 ON				
F8	0.174	0.037	4.668	0.000
F9	−0.120	0.033	−3.702	0.000
F10	−0.129	0.041	−3.123	0.002
F11	−0.275	0.038	−7.318	0.000
F5	0.448	0.058	7.757	0.000
F2	0.382	0.064	5.939	0.000
F2 WITH				
F1	0.776	0.023	33.546	0.000
F3 WITH				
F1	0.657	0.028	23.379	0.000
F2	0.926	0.018	51.456	0.000
F4 WITH				
F1	−0.302	0.031	−9.811	0.000
F2	−0.317	0.032	−9.783	0.000
F3	−0.304	0.033	−9.257	0.000

Table 6.11 Mplus Output:
Selected Standardized Parameter Estimates (*continued*)

Standardized Model Results: STDYX Standardization

	Estimate	Standard Error (*SE*)	Estimate/*SE*	Two-Tailed *p*-Value
F5 WITH				
F1	−0.819	0.023	−36.040	0.000
F2	−0.762	0.025	−30.587	0.000
F3	−0.710	0.027	−26.623	0.000
F4	0.425	0.033	12.723	0.000
F6 WITH				
F1	−0.555	0.027	−20.478	0.000
F2	−0.537	0.025	−21.499	0.000
F3	−0.474	0.026	−17.910	0.000
F4	0.337	0.029	11.697	0.000
F5	0.814	0.023	34.733	0.000
F7 WITH				
F1	−0.488	0.030	−16.188	0.000
F2	−0.417	0.029	−14.239	0.000
F3	−0.368	0.029	−12.494	0.000
F4	0.216	0.031	7.006	0.000
F5	0.667	0.026	25.726	0.000
F6	0.475	0.029	16.594	0.000

self-esteem; (b) decision making on external locus of control; (c) role conflict and emotional exhaustion on depersonalization; and (d) self-esteem, external locus of control, emotional exhaustion, and depersonalization on reduced personal accomplishment. Second, six structural paths, not specified a priori, proved to be essential components of the causal structure and therefore were added to the model. These paths were (a) Role Conflict → Personal Accomplishment, (b) Role Conflict → External Locus of Control, (c) Classroom Climate → Depersonalization, (d) Decision Making → Personal Accomplishment, (e) Self-Esteem → Emotional Exhaustion, and (f) Self-Esteem → External Locus of Control. Finally, two originally hypothesized paths (Role Ambiguity → Personal Accomplishment; Peer Support → Self-Esteem) were found not to be statistically significant and were therefore deleted from the model. As a consequence of these deletions, the constructs of Role Ambiguity and Peer Support became redundant and were also removed from the model.[7]

In conclusion, based on our analyses of this full SEM application, it seems evident that role conflict, work overload, classroom climate, (the

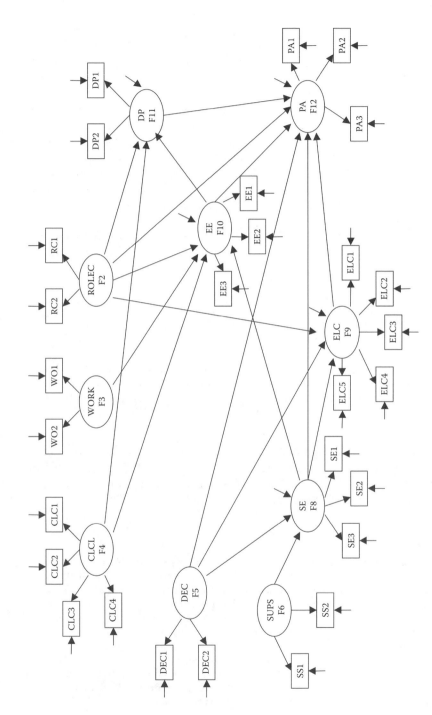

Figure 6.9. Final model of burnout for secondary teachers.

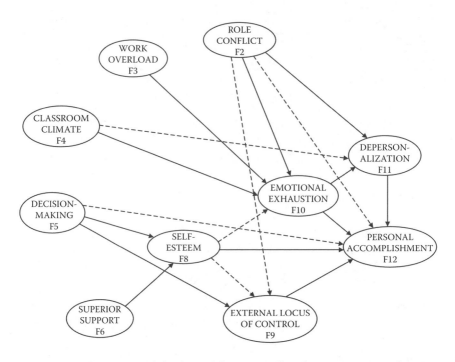

Figure 6.10. Summary of final model structural paths representing determinants of burnout for secondary teachers. *Note*: Solid arrows represent originally hypothesized regression paths; broken arrows represent regression paths added to model following tests of its validity.

opportunity to participate in) decision making, and the support of one's superiors are potent organizational determinants of burnout for high school teachers. However, the process appears to be tempered by one's general sense of self-esteem and locus of control.

Notes

1. More correctly, the PA factor actually represents *reduced* PA.
2. To facilitate interpretation, particular items were reflected such that high scores on role ambiguity, role conflict, work overload, EE, DP, and external locus of control represented negative perceptions, and high scores on the remaining constructs represented positive perceptions.
3. The assignment of numbers is primarily for purposes of parameter identification in error messages pertinent to model nonidentification and other uses.
4. The reasoning here is because in working with full structural equation models, any misfit to components of the measurement model should be addressed when that portion of the model is tested for its validity. Indeed, this approach is consistent with our earlier work in this chapter.

5. The ML χ^2 values are obtained from separate analyses of the two models based on ML estimation.
6. In contrast, for example, the Lagrange Multiplier Test used in the EQS program utilizes a multivariate approach to testing for evidence of misspecification.
7. Although not included here, but illustrated in Chapter 9, in order to portray this final model more appropriately, it should be restructured with the assignment of factor numerals revised accordingly.

section III

Multiple-Group Analyses

Confirmatory Factor Analytic Models

The Full Latent Variable Model

chapter 7

Testing the Factorial Equivalence of a Measuring Instrument
Analysis of Covariance Structures

Up to this point, all applications have illustrated analyses based on single samples. In this section, however, we focus on applications involving more than one sample where the central concern is whether or not components of the measurement model and/or the structural model are invariant (i.e., equivalent) across particular groups of interest. Throughout this chapter and others involving multigroup applications, the terms *invariance* and *equivalence* are used synonymously (and, likewise, the adjectives *invariant* and *equivalent*); use of either term is merely a matter of preference.

In seeking evidence of multigroup invariance, researchers are typically interested in finding the answer to one of five questions. First, do the items comprising a particular measuring instrument operate equivalently across different populations (e.g., gender, age, ability, culture)? In other words, is the measurement model group-invariant? Second, is the factorial structure of a single instrument or of a theoretical construct equivalent across populations as measured either by items of a single assessment measure or by subscale scores from multiple instruments? Typically, this approach exemplifies a construct validity focus. In such instances, equivalence of both the measurement and structural models is of interest. Third, are certain paths in a specified causal structure equivalent across populations? Fourth, are the latent means of particular constructs in a model different across populations? Finally, does the factorial structure of a measuring instrument replicate across independent samples drawn from the same population? This latter question, of course, addresses the issue of cross-validation. Applications presented in this chapter, as well as the next two chapters, provide you with specific examples of how each of these questions can be answered using structural equation modeling (SEM) based on the M*plus* program. The applications illustrated in Chapters 7 and 9 are based on the analysis of covariance structures (COVS), whereas the application in Chapter 8 is based on the analysis of mean and covariance structures (MACS). When analyses are based on COVS, only the sample variances and covariances are of interest; all single-group applications illustrated thus far in the book have been based on the analysis of COVS. In contrast, when analyses are based on MACS, the modeled data include the sample means, as well as the sample variances and covariances. Details related to the MACS approach to invariance are addressed in Chapter 8.

In this first multigroup application, we test hypotheses related to the invariance of a single measuring instrument across two different panels of teachers. Specifically, we test for equivalency of the factorial measurement (i.e., scale items) of the Maslach Burnout Inventory (MBI; Maslach & Jackson, 1986)[1] and its underlying latent structure (i.e., relations among dimensions of burnout) across elementary and secondary teachers. Purposes of the original study, from which this example is taken (Byrne, 1993), were (a) to test for the factorial validity of the MBI separately for each of three teacher groups; (b) given findings of inadequate fit, to propose and test an alternative factorial structure; (c) to cross-validate this structure over independent samples within each teacher group; and (d) to test for the equivalence of item measurements and theoretical structure across the three teaching panels. Only analyses bearing on tests for invariance across calibration samples of elementary ($n = 580$) and secondary ($n = 692$) teachers are of interest in the present chapter.[2] Before reviewing the model under scrutiny, however, I wish first to provide you with a brief overview of the general procedure involved in testing for invariance across groups.

Testing Multigroup Invariance: The General Notion

Development of a procedure capable of testing for multigroup invariance derives from the seminal work of Jöreskog (1971b). Accordingly, Jöreskog recommended that all tests for equivalence begin with a global test of the equality of covariance structures across the groups of interest. Expressed more formally, this initial step tests the null hypothesis (H_0), $\Sigma_1 = \Sigma_2 = \ldots$ Σ_G, where Σ is the population variance–covariance matrix, and G is the number of groups. Rejection of the null hypothesis then argues for the nonequivalence of the groups and, thus, for the subsequent testing of increasingly restrictive hypotheses in order to identify the source of nonequivalence. On the other hand, if H_0 cannot be rejected, the groups are considered to have equivalent covariance structures, and, thus, tests for invariance are not needed. Presented with such findings, Jöreskog recommended that group data should be pooled and all subsequent investigative work based on single-group analyses.

Although this omnibus test appears to be reasonable and fairly straightforward, it often leads to contradictory findings with respect to equivalencies across groups. For example, sometimes the null hypothesis is found to be tenable, yet subsequent tests of hypotheses related to the equivalence of particular measurement or structural parameters must be rejected (see, e.g., Jöreskog, 1971b). Alternatively, the global null hypothesis may be rejected, yet tests for the equivalence of measurement and structural invariance hold (see, e.g., Byrne, 1988a). Such inconsistencies in the global test for equivalence stem from the fact that there is no baseline model for the test of invariant variance–covariance matrices, thereby making it substantially more restrictive than is the case for tests of invariance related to sets of model parameters. Indeed, any number of inequalities may possibly exist across the groups under study. Realistically, then, testing for the equality of specific sets of model parameters would appear to be the more informative and interesting approach to multigroup invariance. Thus, tests for invariance typically begin with a model termed the *configural model* (to be discussed shortly).

In testing for invariance across groups, sets of parameters are put to the test in a logically ordered and increasingly restrictive fashion. Depending on the model and hypotheses to be tested, the following sets of parameters are most commonly of interest in answering questions related to multigroup invariance: (a) factor loadings, (b) factor covariances, (c) structural regression paths, and (d) latent factor means. Historically, the Jöreskog tradition of invariance testing held that the equality of residual variances and their covariances should also be tested. However, it is now widely accepted that this test for equivalence not only is of least interest and importance (Bentler, 2005; Widaman & Reise, 1997) but also may be considered somewhat unreasonable (Little, Card, Slegers, & Ledford, 2007) and indeed not recommended (see Selig, Card, & Little, 2008). Two important exceptions to this widespread consensus, however, are in testing for multigroup equivalence related to item reliability (see, e.g., Byrne, 1988a) as well as for commonly specified residual (i.e., error) covariances.

The Testing Strategy

Testing for factorial equivalence encompasses a series of steps that build upon one another and begins with the determination of a separate baseline model for each group. This model represents one that best fits the data from the perspectives of both parsimony and substantive meaningfulness. Addressing this somewhat tricky combination of model fit and model parsimony, it ideally represents one for which fit to the data and minimal parameter specification are optimal. Following completion of this preliminary task, tests for the equivalence of parameters are conducted across groups at each of several increasingly stringent levels.

Once the group-specific baseline models have been established, testing for invariance entails a hierarchical set of steps that typically begins with the determination of a well-fitting multigroup baseline model for which sets of parameters are put to the test of equality in a logically ordered and increasingly restrictive fashion. In technical terms, this model is commonly termed the *configural model* and is the first and least restrictive one to be tested (Horn & McArdle, 1992). With this initial multigroup model, only the extent to which the same pattern (or configuration) of fixed and freely estimated parameters holds across groups is of interest, and thus no equality constraints are imposed. In contrast to the configural model, all remaining tests for equivalence involve the specification of cross-group equality constraints for particular parameters. In general terms, the first set of steps in testing for invariance focuses on the measurement model (Jöreskog, 1971b). As such, all parameters associated with the observed variables and their linkage to the latent factors in a model are targeted; these include the factor loadings, observed variable intercepts, and residual variances. Because each of these three tests for invariance represents an increased level of restrictiveness, Meredith (1993) categorized them as weak, strong, and strict tests of equivalence, respectively.

Once it is known which measures are group-invariant, these parameters are constrained equal while subsequent tests of the structural parameters (factor variances/covariances, regression paths, and latent means) are conducted. As each new set of parameters is tested, those known to be group-invariant are cumulatively constrained equal across groups. Thus, the process of determining the group-invariant measurement and structural parameters involves the testing of a series of increasingly restrictive hypotheses.

It is important to note that, although I have listed all parameters that can be considered eligible for tests of invariance, the inclusion of all in the process is not always necessary or reasonable. For example, although some researchers contend that tests for invariant observed variable intercepts should always be conducted (e.g., Little, 1997; Little et al., 2007; Meredith, 1993; Selig et al., 2008), others argue that tests related only to the factor loadings, variances, and covariances may be the most appropriate approach to take in addressing the issues and interests of a particular study (see, e.g., Cooke, Kosson, & Michie, 2001; Marsh, 1994, 2007; Marsh, Hau, Artelt, Baumert, & Peschar, 2006). Construct validity studies pertinent to a particular assessment scale, such as the one under study in the current application (Byrne, 1993), or to a theoretical construct (e.g., Byrne & Shavelson, 1986) exemplify such research. For additional articles addressing practical issues related to tests for invariance, readers are referred to Byrne (2008) and Byrne and van de Vijver (2010). We turn now to the invariance tests of interest in the present chapter.

As noted earlier, this multigroup application is based solely on the analysis of COVS. I consider this approach to the topic less complex (compared with that of MACS) and more appropriate at this time for at least three important reasons. First, this application represents your first overview of, and experience with, multigroup analyses; thus, I prefer to keep things as simple as possible. Second, the current application represents a construct validity study related to a measuring instrument, the major focus being the extent to which its factorial structure is invariant across groups; of primary interest are the factor loadings, variances, and covariances. Finally, group differences in the latent means are of no particular interest in the construct validity study, and, thus, tests for invariant intercepts are not relevant in this application.

Testing Multigroup Invariance Across Independent Samples

Our focus here is to test for equivalence of the MBI across elementary and secondary teachers. Given that details regarding the structure of this measuring instrument, together with a schematic portrayal of its hypothesized model structure, were presented in Chapter 4, this material is not repeated here. As noted earlier, a necessary requisite in testing for multigroup invariance is the establishment of a well-fitting baseline model structure for each group. Once these models are established, they (if two different baseline models are ascertained) represent the hypothesized multigroup model under test. We turn now to these initial analyses of MBI structure as they relate to elementary and secondary teachers.

The Hypothesized Model

As noted previously, the model under test in this initial multigroup application is the same postulated three-factor structure of the MBI that was tested in Chapter 4 for male elementary teachers. Thus, the same model of hypothesized structure shown in Figure 4.1 holds here. As such, it serves as the initial model tested in the establishment of baseline models for the two groups of teachers.

Establishing Baseline Models: The General Notion

Because the estimation of baseline models involves no between-group constraints, the data can be analyzed separately for each group. However, in testing for invariance, equality constraints are imposed on particular parameters, and, thus, the data for all groups must be analyzed simultaneously to obtain efficient estimates (Bentler, 2005; Jöreskog & Sörbom, 1996); the pattern of fixed and free parameters nonetheless remains consistent with the baseline model specification for each group. However, it is important to note that measuring instruments are often group specific in the way they operate, and, thus, it is possible that baseline models may not be completely identical across groups (see Bentler, 2005; Byrne, Shavelson, & Muthén, 1989). For example, it may be that the best-fitting model for one group includes a residual covariance (see, e.g., Bentler, 2005) or a cross-loading (see, e.g., Byrne, 1988b, 2004; Reise, Widaman, & Pugh, 1993), whereas these parameters may not be specified for the other group. Presented with such findings, Byrne et al. (1989) showed that by implementing a condition of *partial measurement invariance*, multigroup analyses can still continue. As such, some but not all measurement parameters are constrained equal across groups in the testing for structural equivalence (or latent factor mean differences, if applicable). It is important to note, however, that over the intervening years, the concept of partial measurement equivalence has sparked a modest debate in the technical literature (see Millsap & Kwok, 2004; Widaman & Reise, 1997). Nonetheless, its application remains a popular strategy in testing for multigroup equivalence and is especially so in the area of cross-cultural research. The perspective taken in this book is consistent with that of Muthén and Muthén (2007–2010) in the specification of partial measurement invariance where appropriate in the application of invariance-testing procedures.

Establishing Baseline Models: Elementary and Secondary Teachers

In testing for the validity of the three-factor structure of the MBI (see Figure 4.1), findings were consistent in revealing goodness-of-fit statistics for this initial model that were less than optimal for both elementary (MLM $\chi^2_{[206]}$ = 826.573; CFI = 0.857; RMSEA = 0.072 ; SRMR = 0.068) and secondary (MLM $\chi^2_{[206]}$ = 999.359; CFI = 0.836; RMSEA = 0.075; SRMR = 0.077) levels. Consistent with findings for male elementary teachers (see Chapter 4), three exceptionally large residual covariances and one cross-loading contributed to the misfit of the model for both teacher panels. The residual covariances involved Items 1 and 2, Items 6 and 16, and Items 10 and 11; the cross-loading involved the loading of Item 12 on Factor 1 (Emotional Exhaustion) in addition to its targeted Factor 3 (Personal Accomplishment). (For discussion related to possible reasons for these misfitting parameters, readers are referred to Chapter 4.)[3] To observe the extent to which these four parameters eroded fit of the originally hypothesized model to data for elementary and secondary teachers, we turn to Table 7.1, where the Modification Index (MI) results pertinent to the BY

Table 7.1 M*plus* Output for Initially Hypothesized Model:
Selected Modification Indices (MIs)

	MI	Expected Parameter Change (EPC)	Standard EPC	StdYX EPC
Elementary Teachers				
BY Statements				
F1 BY ITEM10	10.590	−0.221	−0.285	−0.193
→**F1 BY ITEM12**	**66.376**	**−0.400**	**−0.515**	**−0.400**
F1 BY ITEM19	10.921	0.141	0.181	0.160
F2 BY ITEM2	14.500	−0.350	−0.297	−0.189
F2 BY ITEM6	10.759	0.362	0.308	0.186
F2 BY ITEM16	20.938	0.459	0.390	0.257
F3 BY ITEM1	14.707	0.624	0.260	0.157
F3 BY ITEM2	12.148	0.554	0.231	0.147
F3 BY ITEM14	18.728	0.891	0.372	0.204
WITH Statements				
→**ITEM2 WITH ITEM1**	**84.217**	**0.534**	**0.534**	**0.494**
ITEM6 WITH ITEM5	19.388	0.337	0.337	0.217
ITEM7 WITH ITEM4	34.962	0.184	0.184	0.294
ITEM11 WITH ITEM5	16.546	−0.304	−0.304	−0.274
→**ITEM11 WITH ITEM10**	**55.292**	**0.687**	**0.687**	**0.832**
ITEM12 WITH ITEM3	23.007	−0.287	−0.287	−0.245
ITEM13 WITH ITEM12	10.160	0.189	0.189	0.164
ITEM14 WITH ITEM2	11.423	0.246	0.246	0.173
ITEM14 WITH ITEM13	11.154	0.266	0.266	0.171
ITEM15 WITH ITEM5	21.072	0.273	0.273	0.234
ITEM16 WITH ITEM1	13.108	−0.228	−0.228	−0.186
ITEM16 WITH ITEM2	14.397	−0.233	−0.233	−0.193
ITEM16 WITH ITEM5	15.047	0.270	0.270	0.191
→**ITEM16 WITH ITEM6**	**147.167**	**0.893**	**0.893**	**0.595**
ITEM19 WITH ITEM18	35.644	0.279	0.279	0.340
ITEM20 WITH ITEM1	12.323	−0.191	−0.191	−0.187
ITEM20 WITH ITEM2	14.508	−0.202	−0.202	−0.200
ITEM20 WITH ITEM8	11.628	0.182	0.182	0.198
ITEM20 WITH ITEM13	13.110	0.210	0.210	0.190

Structural Equation Modeling With Mplus

Table 7.1 M*plus* Output for Initially Hypothesized Model:
Selected Modification Indices (MIs) (*continued*)

	Secondary Teachers			
	MI	Expected Parameter Change (EPC)	Standard EPC	StdYX EPC
BY Statements				
F1 BY ITEM10	35.534	−0.394	−0.473	−0.302
→**F1 BY ITEM12**	**92.031**	**−0.468**	**−0.561**	**−0.419**
F1 BY ITEM22	17.727	0.304	0.364	0.227
F2 BY ITEM1	17.029	−0.423	−0.281	−0.177
F2 BY ITEM2	23.824	−0.494	−0.329	−0.215
F2 BY ITEM12	21.021	−0.434	−0.288	−0.215
F2 BY ITEM14	11.748	−0.446	−0.297	−0.167
F2 BY ITEM16	19.322	0.482	0.320	0.221
F2 BY ITEM20	15.579	0.379	0.252	0.180
F3 BY ITEM1	14.569	0.603	0.226	0.142
F3 BY ITEM5	10.375	−0.633	−0.237	−0.162
F3 BY ITEM6	10.082	−0.597	−0.224	−0.136
F3 BY ITEM10	14.779	0.704	0.264	0.169
F3 BY ITEM14	12.279	0.704	0.264	0.149
F3 BY ITEM15	11.768	−0.647	−0.242	−0.171
F3 BY ITEM16	13.648	−0.625	−0.234	−0.162
WITH Statements				
→**ITEM2 WITH ITEM1**	**133.695**	**0.627**	**0.627**	**0.583**
ITEM3 WITH ITEM2	10.190	0.192	0.192	0.158
ITEM11 WITH ITEM5	37.618	−0.446	−0.446	−0.369
→**ITEM11 WITH ITEM10**	**105.818**	**1.181**	**1.181**	**1.426**
ITEM12 WITH ITEM3	14.280	−0.229	−0.229	−0.179
ITEM14 WITH ITEM2	14.960	0.263	0.263	0.185
ITEM15 WITH ITEM5	60.143	0.580	0.580	0.355
ITEM15 WITH ITEM1	47.472	−0.485	−0.485	−0.420
ITEM16 WITH ITEM1	15.475	−0.228	−0.228	−0.189
ITEM16 WITH ITEM2	14.861	−0.220	−0.220	−0.183
ITEM16 WITH ITEM3	11.253	−0.217	−0.217	−0.158
→**ITEM16 WITH ITEM6**	**99.508**	**0.686**	**0.686**	**0.458**

Table 7.1 Mplus Output for Initially Hypothesized Model:
Selected Modification Indices (MIs) (*continued*)

		Secondary Teachers		
		MI	Expected Parameter Change (EPC)	Standard EPC	StdYX EPC
ITEM18	WITH ITEM7	10.165	−0.134	−0.134	−0.168
ITEM18	WITH ITEM17	17.740	0.150	0.150	0.222
ITEM19	WITH ITEM9	36.309	0.360	0.360	0.358
ITEM19	WITH ITEM17	13.565	−0.145	−0.145	−0.196
ITEM20	WITH ITEM1	23.369	−0.247	−0.247	−0.240
ITEM20	WITH ITEM2	41.300	−0.324	−0.324	−0.316
ITEM20	WITH ITEM8	22.545	0.238	0.238	0.255
ITEM20	WITH ITEM16	14.212	0.204	0.204	0.177
ITEM21	WITH ITEM7	18.612	0.262	0.262	0.200
ITEM22	WITH ITEM5	14.223	0.322	0.322	0.172
ITEM22	WITH ITEM10	12.709	−0.282	−0.282	−0.220

and WITH statements are shown. In reviewing both the MIs and expected parameter change (EPC) statistics for elementary teachers, it is clear that all four parameters are contributing substantially to model misfit, with the residual covariance between Item 6 and Item 16 exhibiting the most profound effect.

Turning to these results, as they relate to secondary teachers, we see precisely the same pattern, albeit the effect would appear to be even more pronounced than it was for elementary teachers. However, note one slight difference between the two groups of teachers regarding the impact of these four parameters on model misfit. Whereas the residual covariance between Items 6 and 16 was found to be the most seriously misfitting parameter for elementary teachers, the residual covariance between Items 1 and 2 held this dubious honor for secondary teachers.

As noted in Chapter 4, presented with MI results indicative of several possibly misspecified parameters, it is strongly recommended that only one new parameter at a time be included in any respecification of the model. In the present case, however, given our present knowledge of these four misfitting parameters in terms of both their performance and justified specification for male elementary teachers (see Chapter 4), I consider it appropriate to include all four in a post hoc model, labeled as Model 2. Estimation of this respecified model, for each teacher group, yielded model fit statistics that were significantly improved from those for the initially hypothesized model (elementary: ΔMLM $\chi^2_{[4]} = 1012.654$, $p < .001$; secondary: ΔMLM $\chi^2_{[4]} = 1283.053$, $p < .001$);[4] all newly specified parameters were statistically significant. Model goodness-of-fit statistics for each teacher group were as follows:

Elementary teachers: MLM $\chi^2_{(202)} = 477.666$; CFI = 0.936; RMSEA = 0.049; SRMR = 0.050

Secondary teachers: MLM $\chi^2_{(202)} = 587.538$; CFI = 0.920; RMSEA = 0.053; SRMR = 0.05

Let's turn now to Table 7.2, where the MI results pertinent to Model 2 are presented. In reviewing this information for elementary teachers, we observe two MIs under the WITH statements that are substantially larger than all other MIs (ITEM7 with ITEM4; ITEM19 with ITEM18); both represent residual covariances. Of the two, only the residual covariance between Items 7 and 4 is substantively viable in that there is a clear overlapping of item content. In contrast, the content of Items 19 and 18 exhibits no such redundancy, and, thus, there is no reasonable justification for including this parameter in a succeeding Model 3.

Table 7.2 M*plus* Output for Model 2: Selected Modification Indices (MIs)

Elementary Teachers				
	MI	Expected Parameter Change (EPC)	Standard EPC	StdYX EPC
BY Statements				
F1 BY ITEM11	12.045	0.250	0.311	0.205
F2 BY ITEM16	12.849	0.310	0.299	0.197
F2 BY ITEM17	10.444	−0.173	−0.166	−0.188
F3 BY ITEM14	19.957	0.864	0.373	0.205
WITH Statements				
→ITEM7 WITH ITEM4	**31.795**	**0.174**	**0.174**	**0.284**
ITEM12 WITH ITEM3	19.583	−0.250	−0.250	−0.227
ITEM13 WITH ITEM12	16.737	0.231	0.231	0.211
ITEM14 WITH ITEM2	13.428	0.245	0.245	0.163
ITEM14 WITH ITEM13	12.119	0.281	0.281	0.180
→ITEM19 WITH ITEM18	**31.643**	**0.266**	**0.266**	**0.333**

Table 7.2 M*plus* Output for Model 2:
Selected Modification Indices (MIs) (*continued*)

	Secondary Teachers			
	MI	Expected Parameter Change (EPC)	Standard EPC	StdYX EPC
BY Statements				
F1　BY ITEM5	13.781	−0.306	−0.345	−0.235
F1　BY ITEM10	11.592	−0.221	−0.249	−0.159
→F1　**BY ITEM11**	**52.558**	**0.472**	**0.532**	**0.339**
F1　BY ITEM15	12.532	−0.283	−0.319	−0.225
F2　BY ITEM13	12.575	0.339	0.294	0.176
F2　BY ITEM14	17.329	−0.490	−0.424	−0.239
F2　BY ITEM16	14.020	0.330	0.286	0.198
F3　BY ITEM14	12.912	0.693	0.266	0.150
WITH Statements				
ITEM11　WITH ITEM5	14.332	−0.244	−0.244	−0.162
ITEM13　WITH ITEM3	10.714	−0.212	−0.212	−0.169
ITEM14　WITH ITEM2	14.998	0.234	0.234	0.153
ITEM15　WITH ITEM5	27.843	0.416	0.416	0.310
ITEM15　WITH ITEM10	13.305	0.227	0.227	0.162
ITEM15　WITH ITEM11	22.708	−0.297	−0.297	−0.206
ITEM15　WITH ITEM12	12.013	0.191	0.191	0.168
ITEM18　WITH ITEM7	14.456	−0.160	−0.160	−0.203
ITEM18　WITH ITEM17	16.888	0.147	0.147	0.219
→ITEM19　**WITH ITEM9**	**34.189**	**0.355**	**0.355**	**0.357**
ITEM19　WITH ITEM17	16.230	−0.159	−0.159	−0.217
ITEM20　WITH ITEM2	15.666	−0.171	−0.171	−0.162
ITEM20　WITH ITEM6	10.441	−0.173	−0.173	−0.137
ITEM20　WITH ITEM16	22.614	0.227	0.227	0.201
ITEM21　WITH ITEM7	16.722	0.247	0.247	0.191

In reviewing the results for secondary teachers, on the other hand, it appears that more work is needed in establishing an appropriate baseline model. I make this statement based on two considerations: (a) The model does not yet reflect a satisfactorily good fit to the data (CFI = 0.920); and (b) in reviewing the MIs in Table 7.2, we observe one very large misspecified parameter representing the loading of Item 11 on Factor 1 (F1 by ITEM11), as well as another substantially large MI representing a residual covariance between Items 19 and 9, both of which can be substantiated as substantively meaningful parameters. Following my previous caveat, we proceed in specifying only one of these parameters at this time. Given the substantially large MI representing the cross-loading of Item 11 on Factor 1, only this parameter is included in our next post hoc model (Model 3 for secondary teachers). MI results derived from this analysis of Model 3 will then determine if further respecification is needed. Findings are reported in Table 7.3.

Results from the estimation of Model 3 for elementary teachers yielded goodness-of-fit statistics that represented a satisfactorily good fit to the data (MLM $\chi^2_{[201]}$ = 451.060; CFI = 0.942; RMSEA = 0.046; SRMR = 0.049) and a corrected difference from the previous model (Model 2) that was statistically significant (ΔMLM $\chi^2_{[1]}$ = 9.664, $p < .005$). Although a review of Table 7.3 reveals several additional moderately large MIs, it is important always to base final model decisions on goodness-of-fit in combination with model parsimony. With these caveats in mind, I consider Model 3 to best serve as the baseline model for elementary teachers.

Results from the estimation of Model 3 for secondary teachers, on the other hand, further substantiated the residual covariance between Items 19 and 9 as representing an acutely misspecified parameter in the model. Thus, for secondary teachers only, Model 4 was put to the test with this

Table 7.3 Mplus Output for Model 3: Selected Modification Indices (MIs)

Elementary Teachers				
	MI	Expected Parameter Change (EPC)	Standard EPC	StdYX EPC
BY Statements				
F1 BY ITEM11	12.212	0.251	0.312	0.206
F2 BY ITEM16	12.970	0.310	0.299	0.197
F2 BY ITEM17	11.420	−0.181	−0.174	−0.197
F3 BY ITEM14	20.992	0.977	0.383	0.210
WITH Statements				
ITEM12 WITH ITEM3	19.547	−0.248	−0.248	−0.226
ITEM13 WITH ITEM12	17.224	0.232	0.232	0.213
ITEM14 WITH ITEM2	13.599	0.245	0.245	0.163
ITEM14 WITH ITEM13	12.266	0.282	0.282	0.180
ITEM17 WITH ITEM4	11.706	0.096	0.096	0.174
ITEM19 WITH ITEM18	26.859	0.247	0.247	0.319

Table 7.3 M*plus* Output for Model 3: Selected Modification Indices (MIs) (*continued*)

Secondary Teachers				
	MI	Expected Parameter Change (EPC)	Standard EPC	StdYX EPC
BY Statements				
F1 BY ITEM22	15.920	0.321	0.360	0.225
F2 BY ITEM13	12.617	0.293	0.270	0.162
F2 BY ITEM14	15.794	−0.404	−0.372	−0.210
F2 BY ITEM16	11.700	0.261	0.240	0.166
F3 BY ITEM14	13.338	0.707	0.271	0.153
WITH Statements				
ITEM13 WITH ITEM3	10.197	−0.206	−0.206	−0.164
ITEM14 WITH ITEM2	15.599	0.239	0.239	0.155
ITEM15 WITH ITEM5	12.889	0.304	0.304	0.245
ITEM15 WITH ITEM12	10.877	0.178	0.178	0.164
ITEM18 WITH ITEM7	14.240	−0.159	−0.159	−0.202
ITEM18 WITH ITEM17	17.212	0.148	0.148	0.221
→ITEM19 WITH ITEM9	**33.467**	**0.351**	**0.351**	**0.355**
ITEM19 WITH ITEM17	16.338	−0.160	−0.160	−0.218
ITEM20 WITH ITEM2	14.476	−0.164	−0.164	−0.155
ITEM20 WITH ITEM6	10.363	−0.171	−0.171	−0.136
ITEM20 WITH ITEM16	22.169	0.223	0.223	0.199
ITEM21 WITH ITEM7	16.938	0.248	0.248	0.192

residual covariance specified as a freely estimated parameter. Results from this analysis are shown in Table 7.4.

Although a review of the MI results in Table 7.4 reveals a few large values, here again, based on a moderately satisfactory goodness-of-fit (MLM $\chi^2_{[200]} = 505.831$; CFI = 0.937; RMSEA = 0.047; SRMR = 0.052) and bearing in mind the importance of model parsimony, I consider Model 4 as the final baseline model for secondary teachers. Comparison of these Model 4 results with those for Model 3 reveals the corrected difference to be statistically significant (ΔMLM $\chi^2_{[1]} = 23.493$, $p < .001$).

Having now established a separate baseline model for both elementary and secondary teachers, we are ready to test hypotheses bearing on the equivalence of the MBI across the two teaching panels. A pictorial representation of these baseline models is shown in Figure 7.1; it provides

Table 7.4 Mplus Output for Model 4: Selected Modification Indices (MIs)

		Secondary Teachers		
	MI	Expected Parameter Change (EPC)	Standard EPC	StdYX EPC
BY Statements				
F1 BY ITEM22	15.715	0.317	0.357	0.223
F2 BY ITEM13	12.497	0.292	0.268	0.161
F2 BY ITEM14	15.839	−0.404	−0.371	−0.209
F2 BY ITEM16	11.933	0.263	0.242	0.167
F3 BY ITEM14	13.689	0.685	0.279	0.157
WITH Statements				
ITEM13 WITH ITEM3	10.245	−0.206	−0.206	−0.164
ITEM14 WITH ITEM2	15.600	0.239	0.239	0.155
ITEM15 WITH ITEM5	12.778	0.301	0.301	0.243
ITEM15 WITH ITEM12	12.395	0.190	0.190	0.176
ITEM18 WITH ITEM7	25.806	−0.227	−0.227	−0.296
ITEM19 WITH ITEM18	13.568	0.168	0.168	0.208
ITEM20 WITH ITEM2	14.511	−0.164	−0.164	−0.155
ITEM20 WITH ITEM6	10.352	−0.171	−0.171	−0.136
ITEM20 WITH ITEM16	22.287	0.224	0.224	0.199
ITEM21 WITH ITEM7	15.752	0.242	0.242	0.189
ITEM21 WITH ITEM18	12.230	−0.208	−0.208	−0.186

the foundation against which we test the series of increasingly stringent hypotheses related to MBI structure.

Testing Invariance: The Configural Model

Once the baseline models are established, the initial step in testing for invariance requires only that the same number of factors and the factor-loading pattern be the same across groups. As such, no equality constraints are imposed on any of the parameters. Thus, the same parameters that were estimated in the baseline model for each group *separately* are again estimated in this multigroup model. In essence, then, you can think of the model tested here as a multigroup representation of the baseline models because it incorporates the baseline models for elementary and secondary teachers within the same file. In the SEM literature, this model is commonly termed the *configural model* (Horn & McArdle, 1992); relatedly, we can think of this step as a test of configural invariance.

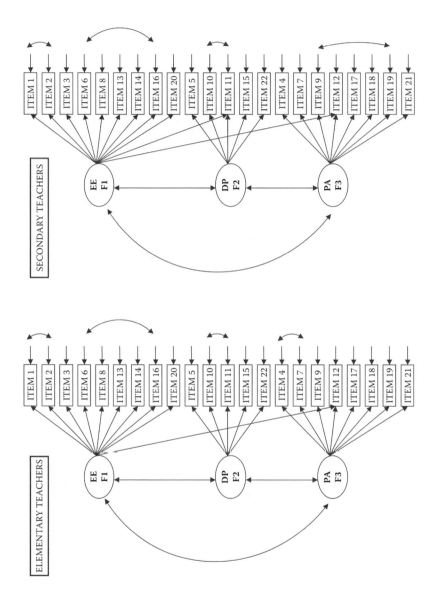

Figure 7.1. Hypothesized multigroup baseline model of MBI structure for elementary and secondary teachers.

From our work in determining the baseline models, and as shown in Figure 7.1, we already know a priori that there are three parameters (two residual covariances [Item 4 with Item 7; Item 9 with Item 19] and one cross-loading [Item 11 on F1]) that were not part of the originally hypothesized model and that differ across the two groups of teachers. However, over and above these group-specific parameters, it is important to stress that, although the originally hypothesized factor structure for each group is similar, it is *not* identical. Because no equality constraints are imposed on any parameters in the model in testing for configural invariance, no determination of group differences can be made. Such claims derive from subsequent tests for invariance to be described shortly.

Given that we have already conducted tests of model structure in the establishment of baseline models, you are no doubt wondering why it is necessary to repeat the process in this testing of the configural model. This multigroup model serves two important functions. First, it allows for invariance tests to be conducted across the two groups *simultaneously*. In other words, parameters are estimated for both groups at the same time. Second, in testing for invariance, the fit of this configural model provides the baseline value against which the first comparison of models (i.e., invariance of factor loadings) is made.[5]

Despite the multigroup structure of the configural and subsequent models, analyses yield only one set of fit statistics in the determination of overall model fit. When maximum likelihood (ML) estimation is used, the χ^2 statistics are summative, and, thus, the overall χ^2 value for the multigroup model should equal the sum of the χ^2 values obtained from separate testing of baseline models. In the present case, ML estimation of the baseline model for elementary teachers yielded a $\chi^2_{(201)}$ value of 545.846 and for secondary teachers a $\chi^2_{(200)}$ value of 643.964, we can expect a ML χ^2 value of 1189.81 with 401 degrees of freedom for the combined multigroup configural model. In contrast, when model estimation is based on the robust statistics, as they were in this application, the MLM χ^2 values are not necessarily summative across the groups.

Mplus Input File Specification and Output File Results

Input File 1

As there are several critically important points to be made in the use of *Mplus* in testing for multigroup invariance in general, as well as with our initial configural model, in particular, I now walk you through this first input file in order that I can elaborate on each of these new and key components of the file. In an effort to minimize confusion related to tests of

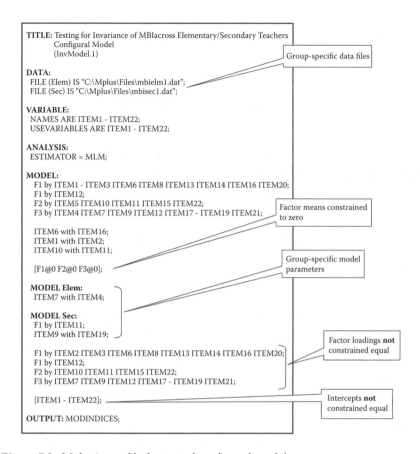

Figure 7.2. M*plus* input file for test of configural model.

invariance for several different models, each is assigned a different label, with this first model being labeled *InvModel.1*. The input file for this configural model is presented in Figure 7.2.

Before addressing the new model commands and specifications, let's first examine those portions of the file with which you are now familiar. As we review this input file, I highly recommend that you work from Figures 7.1 and 7.2 in combination, in order to more fully comprehend this first multigroup file structure.

As indicated in the VARIABLE command, there are 22 observed variables (ITEM1 through ITEM22), all of which are included in the analysis. The factors to which these variables are linked can be evidenced graphically from Figure 7.1. As we know from our work in Chapter 4, the data comprising MBI scores are nonnormally distributed. In light of this information, then, analyses are based on robust ML (MLM) estimation rather than on default ML estimation. Thus, we must specify our esti-mator choice via the ANALYSIS command. Turning next to the MODEL command, we observe only the pattern of factor loadings (lines 1–4) and residual covariances (lines 5–7) that were found to be the same across elementary and secondary teachers. The specification of these parameters represents those that will be tested for their invariance across the two groups. Finally, the OUTPUT command requests that MIs be included in the output file. Because I have not included the parenthesized value of 3.84 (the cutoff value for χ^2 with one degree of freedom at $p = .05$), only MIs with values greater than 10.00 will be reported.

Moving on to new aspects of the file, let's look first at the DATA com-mand, where we find two FILE statements. When the data for each group reside in different files, M*plus* requires a FILE statement specific to each group that provides a relevant label for the group and identifies the loca-tion of its data file. In the present case, as shown in Figure 7.2, we observe two FILE statements, the first one pertinent to elementary teachers and the other to secondary teachers. Note that each has been assigned a label (Elem; Sec), which appears within parentheses and precedes the word *IS*, followed by location of the related data file. It is imperative that each FILE statement include a group label as this information is needed in a later portion of the input file. Finally, M*plus* considers the group associated with the first FILE statement to be Group 1; this designation is relevant when latent means are of interest (not the case here).

In contrast to the present application, but also of relevance, is how the multigroup input file is structured when the data for each group reside in the same file. Accordingly, in lieu of FILE statements, this sit-uation requires use of the GROUPING option for the VARIABLE com-mand. Determination of the group considered to be Group 1 is tied to the values of the grouping variable, with the group assigned the lowest value being Group 1. For example, given data grouping based on gender, with males assigned a grouping value of 0 and females a grouping value of 1, M*plus* would consider males as Group 1. Finally, when analyses are based on summary data, the multigroup M*plus* input file requires use of the NGROUPS option of the DATA command. For more details related to group data residing in a single file, and to summary data, readers are referred to Muthén and Muthén (2007–2010).

Let's move down now to the MODEL command and, in particular, to the specifications appearing within square brackets. Parameter speci-fications in the MODEL command for multigroup analyses, as for single-group analyses, hold for all groups. Thus, in reviewing specifications regarding the factor loadings and residual covariances earlier, I noted that only parameters that were similarly specified across groups were included in this overall model section.

Appearing below these specifications, however, you will see the following: [F1@0 F2@0 F3@0]. In M*plus*, means (i.e., factor means), intercepts (i.e., observed variable means), and thresholds (of categorical observed variables) are indicated by their enclosure within square brackets. Relatedly, then, this specification indicates that the latent means of Factors 1, 2, and 3 are fixed at zero for both groups. The reason for this specification derives from the fact that in multigroup analysis, M*plus*, by default, fixes factor means and intercepts to zero for the first group; these parameters are freely estimated for all remaining groups. This default, however, is relevant only when the estimation of latent factor means is of interest, which of course is not the case here. Thus, in structuring the input file for a configural model, it is necessary to void this default by fixing all factor means to zero, as shown in Figure 7.2.[6]

The next two MODEL commands are termed *model-specific commands* as each enables parameter specification that is unique to a particular group. Importantly, each of these (specific) MODEL commands must be accompanied by the group label used in the related FILE command. Failure to include this label results in an error message and no analysis being performed. Indeed, these two components of the input file are critical in specification of the correct multigroup model as they contain only parameters that differ from the overall MODEL command. Let's now take a closer look at their content, focusing first on parameter specifications contained within the first large bracket. Here, you will quickly recognize the specified residual covariance (Items 7 and 4) for elementary teachers (MODEL Elem:), and the one cross-loading covariance (Item 11 on Factor 1) and one residual covariance (Items 9 and 19) for secondary teachers (MODEL Sec:), as parameter specifications unique to each of their baseline models. As these parameters differ across the two groups, their invariance will not be tested. Thus, our tests for invariance necessarily invoke a condition of partial measurement invariance.

Turning to the next four lines of input appearing within the second bracket, you will recognize the same factor-loading parameters that appeared earlier under the initial overall (versus specific) MODEL command, with one exception—the first variable of each congeneric set is missing. Undoubtedly, you likely now are grappling with two queries concerning these specifications: (a) Why are these factor-loading specifications appearing again in this part of the input file, and (b) why is specification of the first variable for each factor not included?

The answer to the first query lies with the M*plus* approach to specification of constraints in multigroup analyses and, in particular, with its related defaults. In CFA models based on continuous data, all factor loadings and intercepts are constrained equal across groups by default; in contrast, all residual variances are freely estimated by default. The technique for relaxing these defaulted constraints is to specify them under one of the MODEL-specific commands; this accounts for the replicated specification of only the common factor loadings here. Likewise, the same principle holds for the observed variable intercepts. Thus, because these parameters are also constrained equal across groups by default, they too need to be relaxed for the configural model. As noted earlier, means, intercepts, and thresholds are demarcated within square brackets. Accordingly, the specification of [ITEM1–ITEM22] requests that the observed variable intercepts not be constrained equal across groups.

The answer to the second query is tied to the issue of model specification. If you were to include Item 1 (for F1), Item 5 (for F2), and Item 4 (for F3), you would be requesting that these three parameters are free to vary for secondary teachers. The consequence of such specification would mean the model is underidentified.

In summary, the M*plus* input file shown in Figure 7.2 is totally consistent with specification of a configural model in which no equality constraints are imposed. Model fit results derived from execution of this file therefore represent a multigroup version of the combined baseline models for elementary and secondary teachers. Results for this configural model (InvModel.1) were as follows: MLM $\chi^2_{(401)}$ = 958.341, CFI = 0.939, RMSEA = 0.047, and SRMR = 0.051.

Earlier in this chapter, I noted that when analyses are based on ML estimation, χ^2 values are summative in multigroup models. Although analyses here were based on MLM estimation, it may be of interest to observe that this summative information held true when the same analyses were based on ML estimation. Accordingly, results for the configural model yielded an overall $\chi^2_{(401)}$ value of 1189.811, which indeed represents a value equal to the summation of the baseline models for elementary teachers ($\chi^2_{[201]}$ = 545.846) and secondary teachers ($\chi^2_{[200]}$ = 643.964). Recall that the baseline model for secondary teachers comprised an additional cross-loading, which therefore accounts for the loss of one degree of freedom.

Testing Invariance: The Measurement Model

The key measurement model parameters of interest in the present application are the factor loadings and the commonly specified residual covariances. Details related to both the M*plus* input file and analytic results are now presented separately for each.

Factor Loadings

As mentioned previously, in testing for the equivalence of factor loadings across groups, only those that are commonly specified for each group are of interest. Let's take a look now at Figure 7.3, where the input file for this

```
TITLE: Testing for Invariance of MBI across Elementary/Secondary Teachers
       Factor Loadings Invariant
       (InvModel.2)

DATA:
  FILE (Elem) IS "C:\Mplus\Files\mbielm1.dat";
  FILE (Sec) IS "C:\Mplus\Files\mbisec1.dat";

VARIABLE:
  NAMES ARE ITEM1 - ITEM22;
  USEVARIABLES ARE ITEM1 - ITEM22;

ANALYSIS:
  ESTIMATOR = MLM;

MODEL:
  F1 by ITEM1 - ITEM3 ITEM6 ITEM8 ITEM13 ITEM14 ITEM16 ITEM20;
  F1 by ITEM12;
  F2 by ITEM5 ITEM10 ITEM11 ITEM15 ITEM22;
  F3 by ITEM4 ITEM7 ITEM9 ITEM12 ITEM17 - ITEM19 ITEM21;

  ITEM6 with ITEM16;
  ITEM1 with ITEM2;
  ITEM10 with ITEM11;

  [F1@0 F2@0 F3@0];

MODEL Elem:
  ITEM7 with ITEM4;

MODEL Sec:
  F1 by ITEM11;
  ITEM9 with ITEM19;

  [ITEM1 - ITEM22];

OUTPUT: MODINDICES (3.84);
```

Figure 7.3. M*plus* input file for test of invariant factor loadings.

multigroup model is shown, and see how it differs from that of the config-ural model. In reviewing this file, you will readily observe that the major difference between the two files lies with the absence of the additional four lines of factor-loading specifications that were previously listed under the MODEL-specific command for secondary teachers. Deletion of these specifications, which served to relax the equality constraints, thus allows the M*plus* default regarding factor loadings to hold; that is, all fac-tor loadings appearing in the overall MODEL command are constrained equal across the two groups of teachers. One additional change that I made to this input file was the parenthesized value of 3.84 accompanying the request for MIs in the OUTPUT file. As such, this value will be used as the cutpoint, rather than the usual value of 10.00, in the reporting of MI values. We'll label this factor-loading invariant model as *InvModel.2*.

Goodness-of-fit statistics related to InvModel.2 were MLM $\chi^2_{(421)}$ = 1015.228, CFI = 0.935, RMSEA = 0.047, and SRMR = 0.057. Note that the difference in degrees of freedom from the configural model is 20. This gain in the number of degrees of freedom, of course, derives from the fact that 19 factor loadings (excludes the reference variables that were fixed to 1.0) and 1 cross-loading were constrained equal across group. As indicated by the very slightly higher MLM χ^2 value and lower CFI value, compared with the configural model, results suggest that the model does not fit the data quite as well as it did with no factor-loading constraints imposed. Thus, we can expect to find some evidence of noninvariance related to the factor loadings. These results are presented in Table 7.5.

In reviewing results from this analysis, only the MIs related to the factor loadings are of interest, and, thus, only the BY statements are included in Table 7.5. An interesting feature of the M*plus* output is that, in lieu of reporting MI results pertinent to the factor loadings in general, the program provides them for all groups involved in the analysis. In reviewing these MI values, you will quickly note that many of

Table 7.5 M*plus* Output for Initial Test for Invariance of Factor Loadings: Selected Modification Indices (MIs) (InvModel.2)

			Expected Parameter Change (EPC)	Standard EPC	StdYX EPC
		MI			
BY Statements					
F1	BY ITEM11	33.745	0.312	0.380	0.264
F1	BY ITEM15	7.453	−0.142	−0.173	−0.150
F1	BY ITEM17	12.029	−0.108	−0.132	−0.153
F1	BY ITEM19	3.869	0.079	0.096	0.085
F2	BY ITEM5	4.607	0.248	0.224	0.155
→**F2**	**BY ITEM11**	**25.480**	**0.208**	**0.188**	**0.131**
F2	BY ITEM12	7.113	0.196	0.177	0.136
F2	BY ITEM14	5.067	−0.224	−0.202	−0.111
F2	BY ITEM15	9.361	−0.142	−0.129	−0.111
F2	BY ITEM16	11.846	0.244	0.221	0.147
F2	BY ITEM17	15.876	−0.193	−0.174	−0.202
F2	BY ITEM22	5.003	−0.153	−0.138	−0.087
F3	BY ITEM7	7.242	−0.157	−0.061	−0.068
F3	BY ITEM14	17.271	0.840	0.327	0.180
F3	BY ITEM17	4.041	0.151	0.059	0.068

Elementary Teachers

Table 7.5 M*plus* Output for Initial Test for Invariance of Factor Loadings: Selected Modification Indices (MIs) (InvModel.2) (*continued*)

		Secondary Teachers		
	MI	Expected Parameter Change (EPC)	Standard EPC	StdYX EPC
BY Statements				
F1 BY ITEM5	14.231	−0.239	−0.275	−0.184
F1 BY ITEM22	15.918	0.266	0.306	0.195
F2 BY ITEM1	7.001	−0.153	−0.147	−0.092
F2 BY ITEM5	4.607	−0.248	−0.238	−0.159
F2 BY ITEM6	4.033	0.140	0.134	0.082
→**F2 BY ITEM11**	**25.481**	**−0.306**	**−0.294**	**−0.181**
F2 BY ITEM13	12.658	0.243	0.233	0.141
F2 BY ITEM14	12.667	−0.298	−0.286	−0.161
F2 BY ITEM15	9.360	0.156	0.150	0.109
F2 BY ITEM16	6.989	0.165	0.158	0.108
F2 BY ITEM20	7.769	0.166	0.159	0.114
F2 BY ITEM22	5.003	0.116	0.112	0.071
F3 BY ITEM1	6.759	0.295	0.127	0.079
F3 BY ITEM6	4.005	−0.277	−0.119	−0.073
F3 BY ITEM7	7.240	0.257	0.111	0.100
F3 BY ITEM14	12.587	0.585	0.252	0.142
F3 BY ITEM15	4.311	−0.325	−0.140	−0.102
F3 BY ITEM16	5.359	−0.286	−0.123	−0.084
F3 BY ITEM17	4.041	−0.132	−0.057	−0.058

them represent factor-loading parameters that were not specified in the model. However, recall that the MIs bear only on parameters that are either fixed to zero or to some other nonzero value, or are constrained equal to other parameters in the model. In testing for invariance, only the latter are of relevance. In seeking evidence of noninvariance, however, we focus only on the factor loadings that were constrained equal across the groups. Of those falling into this category, we select the parameter exhibiting the largest MI value.[7] As highlighted in Table 7.5, of all the eligible parameters, the factor loading of Item 11 on Factor 2 appears to be the most problematic in terms of its equivalence across elementary and secondary teachers.

Presented with this information, our next step is to modify the input file such that the parameter F2 by ITEM11 is freely estimated. As shown

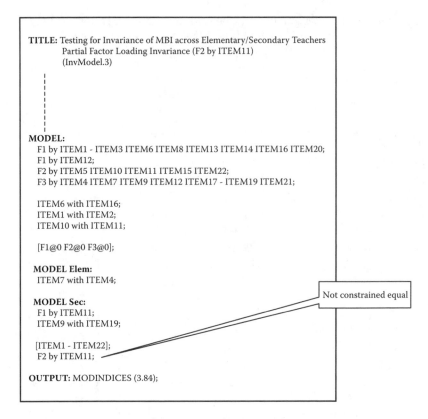

Figure 7.4. M*plus* input file for test of partially invariant factor loadings.

in the InvModel.1 input file, the relaxing of an equality constraint related to this factor loading is accomplished simply by specifying the parameter under one of the MODEL-specific commands. In the present case, I have included it under the MODEL-specific command for secondary teachers as shown in Figure 7.4. Importantly, however, this parameter remains specified under the general MODEL command; otherwise, it would not be estimated at all. This model is labeled *InvModel.3*.

Analysis of this partial invariance model resulted in a MLM χ^2 value of 989.427 with 420 degrees of freedom. (One additional parameter was estimated, thereby accounting for the loss of one degree of freedom.)[8] The other fit indices were CFI = 0.938, RMSEA = 0.046, and SRMR = 0.054. A review of the estimated values of the relaxed parameter, F2 by ITEM11, for the two groups of teachers revealed a fairly substantial discrepancy, with the estimate for elementary teachers being 1.095 and for secondary teachers 0.581.

Of prime interest now is whether difference in model fit between this modified model (InvModel.3), in which the constraint on the loading of ITEM11 on F2 was relaxed, and the configural model (InvModel.1) is or is not statistically significant. To determine this information, given that analyses were based on MLM estimation, requires that we conduct a corrected chi-square difference test. This procedure, as I have noted previously, is available on the M*plus* website (http://www.statmodel.com/chidiff.shtml).

Although I presented a walkthrough of this formula in Chapter 6, application in the case of invariance testing has a slightly different slant in that the second model represents the nested (i.e., more restrictive) model. Thus, I believe it would be helpful to you if I once again walk you through the computation of this difference test as it pertains to our first set of comparative models: that is, between the configural model and the current partially invariant model. For maximum comprehension of this computational work, I strongly suggest that you download the formula from the M*plus* website in order that you can clearly follow all computations. Information you will need in working through this formula is as follows:

Configural model: Scaling correction factor = 1.242

$$ML \ \chi^2_{(401)} = 1189.811$$

Partially invariant model: Scaling correction factor = 1.239

$$ML \ \chi^2_{(420)} = 1225.406$$

$$cd = (420 * 1.239) - (401 * 1.242)/19$$

$$= 520.38 - 498.042/19$$

$$= 22.338/19$$

$$= 1.175$$

$$\Delta \ MLM \ \chi^2_{(19)} = (1225.406 - 1189.811)/1.175$$

$$= 35.595/1.175$$

$$= 30.294 \ p < .02$$

In checking this difference test result in the χ^2 distribution table, you will see that the value of 30.294 is just slightly over the cutpoint of 30.1435 for $p < .05$. Given this finding, we once again review the MIs for this model to peruse evidence of possibly additionally noninvariant factor loadings. These MI values are presented in Table 7.6. Of the four eligible candidates for further testing of invariance (F2 by ITEM5; F2 by ITEM15; F3 by ITEM7; F3 by ITEM17), the largest MI represents the loading of Item 15 on Factor 2.

As a consequence of this result we now return to InvModel.3 and modify it such that it now includes two freely estimated parameters (Items 11 and 15 on Factor 2); this model is labeled as *InvModel.4*. Goodness-of-fit results for this model were MLM $\chi^2_{(419)}$ = 981.189, CFI = 0.939, RMSEA = 0.046, and SRMR = 0.054. Estimates for the factor loading of Item 15 on Factor 2 were 0.683 for elementary teachers and 0.963 for secondary teachers. Finally, comparison of this model with the configural model yielded a corrected ΔMLM $\chi^2_{(18)}$ value of 21.975, which was not statistically significant ($p > .05$).

Table 7.6 M*plus* Output for Test of Invariant Factor Loadings: Selected Modification Indices (MIs) for Partially Invariant Model (InvModel.3)

		Elementary Teachers		
		MI	Expected Parameter Change (EPC)	Standard EPC	StdYX EPC
BY Statements					
F1	BY ITEM11	11.625	0.253	0.308	0.205
F1	BY ITEM15	8.172	−0.149	−0.181	−0.157
F1	BY ITEM17	12.042	−0.108	−0.132	−0.153
F1	BY ITEM19	3.923	0.079	0.096	0.085
F2	BY ITEM5	5.634	0.276	0.241	0.168
F2	BY ITEM12	6.286	0.190	0.167	0.128
F2	BY ITEM14	4.524	−0.220	−0.192	−0.106
→**F2**	**BY ITEM15**	**8.393**	**−0.145**	**−0.127**	**−0.109**
F2	BY ITEM16	11.325	0.248	0.217	0.144
F2	BY ITEM17	14.970	−0.192	−0.168	−0.195
F3	BY ITEM7	7.185	−0.156	−0.061	−0.067
F3	BY ITEM10	4.372	−0.350	−0.136	−0.094
F3	BY ITEM14	17.168	0.838	0.326	0.179
F3	BY ITEM17	3.994	0.150	0.058	0.068

Table 7.6 M*plus* Output for Test of Invariant Factor Loadings:
Selected Modification Indices (MIs) for Partially Invariant Model (InvModel.3)
(*continued*)

		Secondary Teachers		
	MI	Expected Parameter Change (EPC)	Standard EPC	StdYX EPC
BY Statements				
F1 BY ITEM5	14.144	−0.236	−0.271	−0.181
F1 BY ITEM22	16.972	0.274	0.315	0.200
F2 BY ITEM1	7.495	−0.153	−0.151	−0.094
F2 BY ITEM5	5.634	−0.276	−0.272	−0.181
F2 BY ITEM6	4.188	0.138	0.136	0.083
F2 BY ITEM13	11.994	0.228	0.225	0.136
F2 BY ITEM14	12.823	−0.290	−0.285	−0.161
→F2 **BY ITEM15**	**8.393**	**0.139**	**0.137**	**0.100**
F2 BY ITEM16	6.193	0.150	0.148	0.101
F2 BY ITEM20	6.697	0.149	0.146	0.105
F3 BY ITEM1	7.020	0.301	0.130	0.081
F3 BY ITEM6	3.865	−0.272	−0.117	−0.072
F3 BY ITEM7	7.183	0.256	0.110	0.100
F3 BY ITEM10	7.045	0.385	0.166	0.104
F3 BY ITEM11	5.912	−0.350	−0.150	−0.096
F3 BY ITEM14	13.002	0.596	0.256	0.144
F3 BY ITEM15	3.894	−0.308	−0.133	−0.096
F3 BY ITEM16	5.016	−0.277	−0.119	−0.082
F3 BY ITEM17	3.993	−0.132	−0.057	−0.058

Residual Covariances

At this point, we know that all items on the MBI, except for Items 11 and 15, both of which load on Factor 2, are operating equivalently across the two groups of teachers. So now, let's move on to further testing of the invariance of this instrument. Of substantial interest are the three commonly specified residual covariances and the extent to which they may be invariant across the groups. Given that these residual covariances are not constrained equal by default, the process in specifying their invariance necessarily differs from the models analyzed thus far. The input file for this model (InvModel.5) is presented in Figure 7.5.

The only change in this model compared with the previous one is the parenthesized values of 1, 2, and 3, accompanying each of the three specified

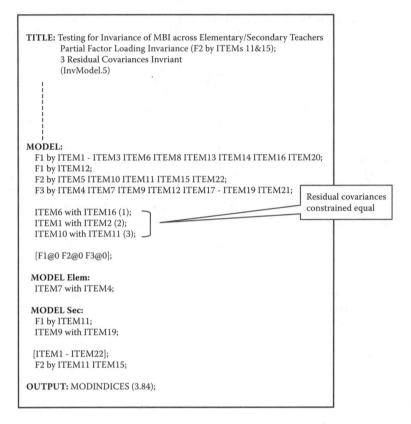

Figure 7.5. M*plus* input file for test of invariant common residual covariances.

residual covariances. The assignment of these parenthesized numbers is indicative of the specification of equality constraints. The placement of each residual covariance and its accompanying parenthesized number (a) within the overall MODEL command and (b) on a separate line, ensures that each of these parameters will be constrained equal across the two groups and not to each other. Thus, an important caveat in specifying equality constraints in M*plus* when the parameters of interest are not constrained equal by default is that only one constraint can be specified per line.

In total, 21 parameters in this model (InvModel.5) were constrained equal across groups: 17 factor loadings, 1 cross-loading, and 3 residual covariances. Model fit results deviated little from InvModel.4 and were as follows: MLM $\chi^2_{(422)}$ = 992.614, CFI = 0.938, RMSEA = 0.046, and SRMR = 0.054. Comparison of this model with the previous one (InvModel.4) representing the final model in the test for invariant factor loadings yielded a corrected ΔMLM $\chi^2_{(3)}$ value of 5.356, which was not statistically significant

(p > .05), thereby indicating that specified residual covariances between Items 6 and 16, Items 1 and 2, and Items 10 and 11 are operating equivalently across elementary and secondary teachers.

Testing Invariance of the Structural Model

Having established invariance related to the measurement model, let's now move on to testing for the invariance of structural parameters in the model; these include only the factor variances and covariances in the present case.[9] The input file for this model (InvModel.6) is presented in Figure 7.6.

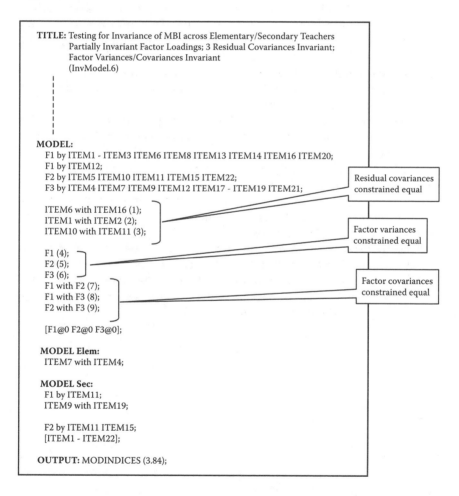

Figure 7.6. M*plus* input file for test of invariant factor variances and covariances.

As you will readily note, consistent with the equality constraints pertinent to the three residual covariances, the factor variances and covariances are also not constrained equal by default and, thus, must be separately noted in the input file. Accordingly, equality constraints across groups for the factor variances are assigned the parenthesized values of 4 to 6, and those for the factor covariances 7 to 9. Note also that the item intercepts remain estimated as indicated by their specification within square brackets appearing under the MODEL-specific section for secondary teachers.∎

Goodness-of-fit results for the testing of InvModel.6 were $\text{MLM}\chi^2_{(428)}$ = 1004.731, CFI = 0.937, RMSEA = 0.046, and SRMR = 0.059. Comparison with InvModel.5 yielded a corrected difference value that was not statistically significant ($\Delta\text{MLM } \chi^2_{(6)}$ = 12.165, $p > 0.05$). This information conveys the notion that, despite the presence of two noninvariant factor loadings, as well as the freely estimated item intercepts, the factor variances and covariances remain equivalent across elementary and secondary teachers. A summary of all *noninvariant* (i.e., freely estimated) unstandardized estimates is presented in Table 7.7.

The primary focus of this first multigroup application was to test for the invariance of a measuring instrument across elementary and secondary teachers. However, because this application represented an initial overview of the invariance-testing process, it was purposely limited to the analysis of COVS only. As such, no tests for invariance of the observed variable intercepts and latent factor means were included. Details related to each step in the process were presented, the related *Mplus* input files reviewed, and relevant portions of the *Mplus* output files discussed. As is typically the case, these analyses resulted in the specification and testing of several different models. Thus, to facilitate your overview of these model results, as well as your understanding of the hierarchical process of invariance testing, a summary of all goodness-fit results, in addition to the $\Delta\text{MLM } \chi^2$ values, are presented in Table 7.8.

Table 7.7 M*plus* Output:
Noninvariant Parameters Across Elementary and Secondary Teachers

		Standard		Two-Tailed
	Estimate	Error (*SE*)	Estimate/*SE*	*p*-Value
Group ELEM				
F2 BY				
ITEM11	0.998	0.074	13.459	0.000
ITEM15	0.684	0.069	9.867	0.000
ITEM7 WITH				
ITEM4	0.169	0.056	3.000	0.003
Intercepts				
ITEM1	3.409	0.069	49.484	0.000
ITEM2	3.976	0.065	60.903	0.000
ITEM3	2.572	0.071	36.229	0.000
ITEM4	5.412	0.039	139.751	0.000
ITEM5	1.053	0.061	17.177	0.000
ITEM6	1.676	0.069	24.353	0.000
ITEM7	5.338	0.036	146.968	0.000
ITEM8	2.184	0.075	29.012	0.000
ITEM9	5.031	0.055	90.946	0.000
ITEM10	1.164	0.061	18.990	0.000
ITEM11	1.122	0.063	17.889	0.000
ITEM12	4.693	0.053	87.789	0.000
ITEM13	2.548	0.072	35.621	0.000
ITEM14	3.122	0.076	41.262	0.000
ITEM15	0.545	0.047	11.713	0.000
ITEM16	1.433	0.063	22.715	0.000
ITEM17	5.416	0.037	147.600	0.000
ITEM18	4.883	0.050	96.794	0.000
ITEM19	5.007	0.047	106.468	0.000
ITEM20	1.281	0.060	21.456	0.000
ITEM21	4.841	0.054	90.467	0.000
ITEM22	1.328	0.064	20.730	0.000

Model Results

Table 7.7 M*plus* Output:
Noninvariant Parameters Across Elementary and Secondary Teachers (*continued*)

	Estimate	Standard Error (*SE*)	Estimate/*SE*	Two-Tailed *p*-Value
Model Results				
Group SEC				
F1 BY				
ITEM11	0.399	0.060	6.691	0.000
F2 BY				
ITEM11	0.588	0.089	6.584	0.000
ITEM15	0.950	0.074	12.812	0.000
ITEM9 WITH				
ITEM19	0.366	0.067	5.433	0.000
Intercepts				
ITEM1	3.371	0.060	55.937	0.000
ITEM2	3.890	0.058	66.973	0.000
ITEM3	2.526	0.065	39.101	0.000
ITEM4	5.168	0.042	123.343	0.000
ITEM5	1.217	0.056	21.817	0.000
ITEM6	1.999	0.063	31.871	0.000
ITEM7	5.014	0.043	116.064	0.000
ITEM8	2.143	0.065	33.039	0.000
ITEM9	4.702	0.057	82.848	0.000
ITEM10	1.275	0.059	21.431	0.000
ITEM11	1.166	0.060	19.550	0.000
ITEM12	4.527	0.051	88.954	0.000
ITEM13	2.653	0.063	41.827	0.000
ITEM14	3.147	0.067	46.680	0.000
ITEM15	1.078	0.054	20.011	0.000
ITEM16	1.548	0.055	28.112	0.000
ITEM17	5.303	0.037	145.039	0.000
ITEM18	4.705	0.045	105.646	0.000
ITEM19	4.600	0.049	93.051	0.000
ITEM20	1.211	0.053	22.713	0.000
ITEM21	4.462	0.057	77.884	0.000
ITEM22	1.790	0.061	29.412	0.000

Table 7.8 Tests for Invariance of MBI Across Elementary and Secondary Teachers: Summary of Model Fit and χ^2-Difference-Test Statistics

Model	MLMχ^2	df	CFI	RMSEA	SRMR	Model Comparison	ΔMLMχ^2 [a]	Δdf	p
Configural Model									
(InvModel.1) No constraints	958.341	401	0.939	0.047	0.051	—	—	—	—
Measurement Parameters									
(InvModel.2) All factor loadings invariant	1015.228	421	0.935	0.047	0.057	2 versus 1	59.052	20	< 0.001
(InvModel.3) All factor loadings except for Item 11 invariant	989.427	420	0.938	0.932	0.054	3 versus 1	30.595	19	< 0.02
(InvModel.4) All factor loadings invariant except for Items 11 and 15	981.189	419	0.939	0.046	0.054	4 versus 1	21.975	18	NS
(InvModel.5) All factor loadings invariant except for Items 11 and 15; 3 common residual covariances invariant	992.614	422	0.938	0.046	0.054	5 versus 4	5.356	3	NS
Structural Parameters									
(InvModel.6) All factor loadings invariant except for Items 11 and 15; 3 common residual covariances invariant; factor variances and covariances invariant	1004.731	428	0.937	0.046	0.059	9 versus 5	12.165	6	NS

[a] Corrected values.

Notes

1. For a detailed description of the MBI, readers are referred to Chapter 4 of the present volume.
2. Middle-school teachers comprised the third group.
3. As noted in Chapter 4, due to refusal of the MBI test publisher to grant copyright permission, I am unable to reprint the items here for your perusal. Nonetheless, a general sense of the item content can be derived from my brief descriptions of them in Chapter 4.
4. All MLM chi-square difference results were based on corrected values calculated from the formula provided on the M*plus* website (http://www.statmodel.com) and as illustrated in Chapter 6.
5. Although it has become the modus operandi for researchers to compare adjacently tested models in computation of the χ^2-difference test, one could also compare each increasingly restrictive model with the configural model, albeit taking into account the relevant increasing number of degrees of freedom.
6. Although M*plus* provides for a model option that negates the estimation of means intercepts, and thresholds (specified under the ANALYSIS command as MODEL = NOMEANSTRUCTURE), this option is not available with MLM (or MLMV, MLF, and MLR) estimation.
7. Other eligible parameters are F2 by ITEM5, F2 by ITEM15, F2 by ITEM22, F3 by ITEM7, and F3 by ITEM17.
8. In testing for invariance of the factor loadings (InvModel.2), the loading of Item 11 on F2 was freely estimated for Group 1 (elementary teachers), albeit constrained equal to this estimated value for Group 2 (secondary teachers). Thus, the loss of one degree of freedom arose from the additional estimation of this factor loading for secondary teachers.
9. As noted earlier, although latent means are also considered to be structural parameters, they are not of interest in the present application.

chapter 8

Testing the Equivalence of Latent Factor Means

Analysis of Mean and Covariance Structures

The multigroup application to be illustrated in this chapter differs from that of Chapter 7 in two major respects. First, analyses are based on mean and covariance structures (MACS), rather than on only covariance structures (COVS). Second, whereas the sample data are complete for one group, they are incomplete for the other. Prior to walking you through procedures related to this chapter's application, I present a brief review of the basic concepts associated with analyses of MACS, followed by the M*plus* approach to analysis of missing data procedures.

Despite Sörbom's (1974) introduction of the MACS strategy in testing for latent mean differences over 30 years ago, a review of the structural equation modeling (SEM) literature reveals only a modicum of studies to have been designed in testing for latent mean differences across groups based on real (as opposed to simulated) data (see, e.g., Aikin, Stein, & Bentler, 1994; Byrne, 1988b; Byrne and Stewart, 2006; Cooke, Kosson, & Michie, 2001; Little, 1997; Marsh & Grayson, 1994; Reise, Widaman, & Pugh, 1993; Widaman & Reise, 1997). The focus in this chapter is to test for the invariance of latent means across two different cultural groups. The present application is taken from a study by Byrne and Watkins (2003) but extends this previous work in two ways: (a) Analyses are based on MACS, rather than on only COVS; and (b) analyses address the issue of missing data with respect to the Nigerian sample, albeit data are complete for the Australian sample.

Testing Latent Mean Structures: The Basic Notion

In the usual univariate or multivariate analyses involving multigroup comparisons, one is typically interested in testing whether the *observed* means representing the various groups are statistically significantly different from each other. Because these values are directly calculable from the raw data, they are considered to be *observed* values. In contrast, the means of latent variables (i.e., latent constructs) are *unobservable*; that is, they are not directly observed. Rather, these latent constructs derive their structure indirectly from their indicator variables, which, in turn, are directly observed and hence measurable. Testing for the invariance of mean structures, then, conveys the notion that we intend to test for the equivalence of means related to each underlying construct or factor. Another way of saying the same thing, of course, is that we intend to test for latent mean differences between or among the groups under study.

For all the examples considered thus far, analyses have been based on COVS rather than on MACS. As such, only parameters representing regression coefficients, variances, and covariances have been of interest. Accordingly, because covariance structure of the observed variables constitutes the crucial parametric information, a hypothesized model can thus be estimated and tested via the sample covariance matrix. One limitation of this level of invariance is that whereas the unit of measurement for the underlying factors (i.e., the factor loading) is identical across groups, the origin of the scales (i.e., the intercepts) is not.[1] As a consequence, comparison of latent factor means is not possible, thereby leading Meredith (1993) to categorize this level of invariance as "weak" factorial invariance. This limitation, notwithstanding evidence of invariant factor loadings, nonetheless permits researchers to move on in testing further for the equivalence of factor variances, factor covariances, and the pattern of these factorial relations, a focus of substantial interest to researchers interested more in construct validity issues than in testing for latent mean differences. These subsequent tests would continue to be based on the analysis of COVS as illustrated in Chapter 7.

In contrast, when analyses are based on MACS, the data to be modeled include both the sample means and the sample covariances. This information is typically contained in a matrix termed a *moment matrix*. The format by which this moment matrix is structured, however, varies across SEM programs.

In the analysis of COVS, it is implicitly assumed that all observed variables are measured as deviations from their means; in other words, their means are equal to zero. As a consequence, the intercept terms generally associated with regression equations are not relevant to the analyses. However, when the observed means take on nonzero values, the intercept parameter must be considered, thereby necessitating a reparameterization of the hypothesized model. Such is the case when one is interested in testing for the invariance of latent *mean structures*. The following example (see Bentler, 2005) may help to clarify both the concept and the term *mean structures*. Consider first the following regression equation:

$$y = \alpha + \beta x + \varepsilon \tag{8.1}$$

where α is an intercept parameter. Although the intercept can assist in defining the mean of y, it does not generally equal the mean. Thus, if we now take expectations of both sides of this equation and assume that the mean of ε is zero, the above expression yields

$$\mu_y = \alpha + \beta\mu_x \tag{8.2}$$

where μ_y is the mean of y, and μ_x is the mean of x. As such, y and its mean can now be expressed in terms of the model parameters α, β, and μ_x. It is this decomposition of the mean of y, the dependent variable, that leads to the term *mean structures*. More specifically, it serves to characterize a model in which the means of the dependent variables can be expressed or "structured" in terms of structural coefficients and the means of the independent variables. The above equation serves to illustrate how the incorporation of a mean structure into a model necessarily includes the new parameters α and μ_x, the intercept and observed mean (of x), respectively. Thus, models with structured means merely extend the basic concepts associated with the analysis of covariance structures.

In summary, any model involving mean structures may include the following parameters:

- Regression coefficients (i.e., the factor loadings)
- Variances and covariances of the independent variables (i.e., the factors and their residuals)
- Intercepts of the dependent variables (i.e., the observed measures)
- Means of the independent variables (i.e., the factors)

Model Parameterization

As with the invariance application presented in Chapter 7, applications based on structured means models involve testing simultaneously across two or more groups. However, in testing for invariance based on the analysis of MACS, testing for latent mean differences across groups is made possible through the implementation of two important strategies—*model identification* and *factor identification*.

Model Identification

Given the necessary estimation of intercepts associated with the observed variables, in addition to those associated with the unobserved latent constructs, it is evident that the attainment of an overidentified model is possible only with the imposition of several specification constraints. Indeed, it is this very issue that complicates, and ultimately renders impossible, the estimation of latent means in single-group analyses. Multigroup analyses, on the other hand, provide the mechanism for imposing severe restrictions on the model such that the estimation of latent means is possible. More specifically, because two (or more) groups under study are tested simultaneously, evaluation of the identification criterion is considered across groups. As a consequence, although the structured means model may not be identified in one group, it can become so when analyzed within the framework of a multigroup model. This outcome occurs as a function of specified equality constraints across groups. More specifically, these equality constraints derive from the underlying assumption that both the observed variable intercepts and the factor loadings are invariant across groups. Nonetheless, partial measurement invariance pertinent to both factor loadings and intercepts can and does occur. Although, in principle, testing for the equivalence of latent mean structures can involve partial measurement invariance related to the factor loadings, the intercepts, or both, this condition can lead to problems of identification, which will be evidenced in the present application.

Factor Identification

This requirement imposes the restriction that the factor intercepts for one group be fixed to zero; this group then operates as a reference group against which latent means for the other group(s) are compared. The reason for this reconceptualization is that when the intercepts of the measured variables are constrained equal across groups, this leads to the latent factor intercepts having no definite origin (i.e., they are undefined in a statistical sense). A standard way of fixing the origin, then, is to set the factor intercepts of one group to zero (see Bentler, 2005; Jöreskog & Sörbom, 1996; Muthén & Muthén, 2007–2010). As a consequence, factor intercepts are interpretable only in a relative sense. That is to say, one can test whether the latent variable means for one group *differ* from those of another, but one *cannot* estimate the mean of each factor in a model for each group. In other words, although it is possible to test for latent mean differences between, say, college men and women, it is not possible to estimate, simultaneously, the mean of each factor for both men and women; the latent means for one group must be constrained to zero.

The Testing Strategy

The approach to testing for differences in latent factor means follows the same pattern that was outlined and illustrated in Chapter 7. That is, we begin by first establishing a well-fitting baseline model for each group separately. This step is followed by a hierarchically ordered series of analyses that test for the invariance of particular sets of parameters across groups.

The primary difference in the tests for invariance in Chapter 7 (based on the analysis of COVS) and those based on the analysis of MACS in this chapter is the additional tests for the equivalence of intercepts and latent factor means across groups. We turn now to the hypothesized model under study and the related tests for invariance of a first-order CFA structure.

The Hypothesized Model

The application examined in this chapter bears on the equivalency of latent mean structures related to four nonacademic self-concept (SC) dimensions—Physical Self-Concept (PSC: Appearance), Physical SC (PSC: Ability), Social SC (SSC: Peers), and Social SC (SSC: Parents)—across Australian and Nigerian adolescents. These constructs comprise the four nonacademic SC components of the Self-Description Questionnaire I (SDQ-I; Marsh, 1992). Although the data for Australian adolescents are complete ($n = 497$), those for Nigerian adolescents ($n = 463$) are incomplete.

Analyses of these data in the Byrne and Watkins (2003) study yielded evidence of substantial multivariate kurtosis.[2] In contrast to use of the robust maximum likelihood (MLM) estimator used with previous analyses of nonnormally distributed data (see Chapters 4, 6, and 7), in this chapter we use the robust maximum likelihood (MLR) estimator, the χ^2 statistic, considered asymptotically equivalent to the Yuan-Bentler (Y-B χ^2; 2000) scaled statistic (Muthén & Muthén, 2007–2010). The Y-B χ^2 is analogous to the S-B χ^2 (i.e., the MLM estimator in M*plus*) when data are both incomplete and nonnormally distributed, which is the case in the present application. Finally, as with the item score data in Chapter 7, SDQ-I responses are analyzed here as continuous data. However, for readers interested in testing for invariance based on ordered-categorical data, I highly recommend the Millsap and Yun-Tein (2004) article in which they addressed the problematic issues of model specification and identification commonly confronted when data are of a categorical nature. Also recommended, albeit more as a guide to these analyses when based on M*plus*, is a web note by Muthén and Asparouov (2002) that is available through the program's website (http://www.statmodel.com).

The originally hypothesized model of SDQ-I factorial structure, tested separately for each group, is presented schematically in Figure 8.1.

Testing Multigroup Invariance

As noted in Chapter 7 and earlier in this chapter, the first step in testing for multigroup invariance is to establish an acceptably well-fitting baseline model for each group of interest. In the present case, we test for the invariance of factor loadings, intercepts, and latent factor means related

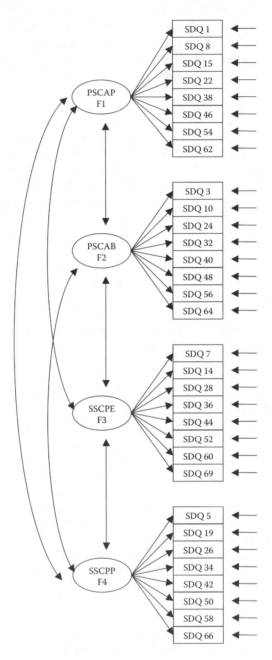

Figure 8.1. Hypothesized model of factorial structure for the Self-Description Questionnaire-I (SDQ-I; Marsh, 1992).

to the four nonacademic SC scales of the SDQ-I across Australian and Nigerian adolescents.

Establishing Baseline Models: Australian and Nigerian Adolescents

Australian Adolescents

Initial testing of the hypothesized model for this group yielded a MLR $\chi^2_{(458)}$ value of 1135.488, with results from the other robust fit indices conveying mixed messages regarding model fit. Whereas the CFI suggested a very poor fit to the data (CFI = 0.882), the RMSEA and SRMR results (0.055 and 0.065, respectively) revealed model fit that could be considered relatively good. A review of the modification indices (MIs) revealed several large values, with the MI for a residual covariance between SDQ40 (I am good at sports) and SDQ24 (I enjoy sports and games) exhibiting the largest value. As discussed in several chapters in this book, such covariance can result from overlapping item content, which appears to be the case here. Thus, Model 2 was specified in which this parameter was freely estimated. Although the (corrected) difference value between the initially hypothesized model (Model 1) and Model 2 was statistically significant, improvement in model fit was minimal ($\chi^2_{[457]}$ = 1067.972; CFI = 0.893; RMSEA = 0.052 ; SRMR = 0.066).

Subsequent testing that included decreasingly restrictive parameter respecifications resulted in a baseline model considered to be the most appropriate in representing the data for Australian adolescents. This final model incorporated three additional parameters: (a) the cross-loading of SDQ38 (Other kids think I am good looking) on Factor 3 (SSC: Peers), (b) a residual covariance between SDQ26 (My parents like me) and SDQ19 (I like my parents), and (c) the cross-loading of SDQ32 (I have good muscles) on Factor 1 (PSC: Appearance). Whereas the underlying rationale in support of the first two respecifications was reasonably clear, the cross-loading of SDQ32 on Factor 1 seemed more tenuous as it suggested possible gender specificity. Nonetheless, two aspects of these results argued in favor of inclusion of this latter parameter: (a) the substantial size of its MI value compared with those of remaining parameters, and (b) misspecification regarding this parameter replicated for Nigerian adolescents. Model fit for this baseline model was as follows: MLR$\chi^2_{(454)}$ = 908.335, CFI = 0.921, RMSEA = 0.045, and SRMR = 0.056.

Admittedly, goodness-of-fit related to this baseline model for Australian adolescents can be considered only moderately acceptable, at best, at least in terms of the CFI. Although MI results suggested several additional parameters that, if included in the model, would improve fit substantially, the rationale and meaningfulness of these potential respecifications were difficult to defend. Coupled with these latter findings is the reality that in multiple-group SEM, the less parsimonious a model (i.e., the more complex it is as a consequence of the inclusion of additional parameters), the more difficult it is to achieve group invariance. As a consequence, the researcher walks a very thin line in establishing a sufficiently well-fitting yet sufficiently parsimonious model. These raisons d'être, then, together with recommendations by some (e.g., Cheung, Leung, & Au, 2006; Rigdon, 1996) that the RMSEA may be a better measure of model fit than the CFI under certain circumstances, stand in support of the baseline model for Australian adolescents presented here.

Nigerian Adolescents

Given the incomplete nature of SDQ-I responses for these adolescents, it was necessary that missingness be addressed in analyses of the data. Although there are many approaches that can be taken in dealing with missing data, the one that has been considered the most efficient and therefore the most highly recommended, for at least the last decade or so, is that of maximum likelihood (ML) estimation (see, e.g., Arbuckle, 1996; Enders & Bandalos, 2001; Gold & Bentler, 2000; Schafer & Graham, 2002). Nonetheless, Bentler (2005) noted that when the amount of missing data is extremely small, there may be some conditions where some of the more commonly used methods such as listwise and pairwise deletion, hot deck, and mean imputation may suffer only marginal loss of accuracy and efficiency compared with the ML method pairwise. (For an abbreviated review of the issues, advantages, and disadvantages of various approaches to handling missing data, readers are referred to Byrne, 2009. For a more extensive and comprehensive treatment of these topics, see Arbuckle, 1996; Enders, 2010; Schafer & Graham, 2002. For a comparison of missing data methods, see Enders & Bandalos, 2001. And for a review of ML methods, see Enders, 2001.)

Mplus provides for many different options regarding the estimation of models with incomplete data. These choices vary in accordance with type of missingness, type of variables (continuous, categorical [ordered and unordered], counts, binary, censored, or any combination thereof), and type of distribution, be it normal or nonnormal (Muthén & Muthén, 2007–2010). In addition, Mplus enables multiple imputation of missing data using Bayesian analyses. (For a general overview of this Bayesian procedure, see Rubin, 1987; Schafer, 1997. For application within the framework of Mplus, see Asparouhov & Muthén, 2010; Muthén, 2010.)

As noted earlier in this chapter, given the presence of incomplete data for Nigerian adolescents, in addition to the fact that data for both groups are known to be nonnormally distributed, all analyses are based on the MLR estimator, which can take both issues into account as it is analogous to the Y-B χ^2 (Yuan & Bentler, 2000). Prior to analyses focused on establishment of the baseline model for these adolescents, I considered it important first to conduct a descriptive analysis of these data in order to determine the percentage and pattern of missing data. This task is easily accomplished either by specifying TYPE=BASIC in the ANALYSIS command, or by requesting the option PATTERNS in the OUTPUT command. The only difference between the two specifications is that whereas the former specification additionally yields information related to the observed variable means and standard deviations, the latter specification does not.

Let's now review the M*plus* output file as it bears on these missing data. Presented in Table 8.1 is the usual summary information pertinent to this analysis. Of particular relevance here is that the number of observations is 463, whereas the number of missing data patterns is 48. A summary of these data patterns is shown in Table 8.2, with the numbered heading of each column identifying one pattern and each *x* representing a data point that is *not* missing. Finally, in Table 8.3, we find a summary of

Table 8.1 M*plus* Output: Selected Summary Information

Summary of Analysis	
Number of groups	1
Number of observations	463
Number of dependent variables	32
Number of independent variables	0
Number of continuous latent variables	4

Observed Dependent Variables

Continuous

SDQ1	SDQ3	SDQ5	SDQ7	SDQ8	SDQ10
SDQ14	SDQ15	SDQ19	SDQ22	SDQ24	SDQ26
SDQ28	SDQ32	SDQ34	SDQ36	SDQ38	SDQ40
SDQ42	SDQ44	SDQ46	SDQ48	SDQ50	SDQ52
SDQ54	SDQ56	SDQ58	SDQ60	SDQ62	SDQ64
SDQ66	SDQ69				

Continuous Latent Variables

F1	F2	F3	F4

Estimator	MLR
Input data file(s)	
C:\Mplus\Files\niger32.DAT	
Input data format	FREE

Summary of Data	
Number of missing data patterns	48

Table 8.2 Mplus Output: Summary of Missing Data Patterns

	Missing Data Patterns (x = Not Missing)																			
	1	2	3	4	5	6	7	8	9	10	11	12	13	14	15	16	17	18	19	20
SDQ1	x	x	x	x	x	x	x	x	x	x	x	x	x	x	x	x	x	x	x	x
SDQ3	x	x	x	x	x	x	x	x	x	x	x	x	x	x	x	x	x	x	x	x
SDQ5	x	x	x	x	x	x	x	x	x	x	x	x	x	x	x	x	x	x	x	x
SDQ7	x	x	x	x	x	x	x	x	x	x	x	x	x	x	x	x	x	x	x	x
SDQ8	x	x	x	x	x	x	x	x	x	x	x	x	x	x	x	x	x	x	x	x
SDQ10	x	x	x	x	x	x	x	x	x	x	x	x	x	x	x	x	x	x	x	x
SDQ14	x	x	x	x	x	x	x	x	x	x	x	x	x	x	x	x	x	x	x	x
SDQ15	x	x	x	x	x	x	x	x	x	x	x	x	x	x	x	x	x	x	x	x
SDQ19	x	x	x	x	x	x	x	x	x	x	x	x	x	x	x	x	x	x	x	x
SDQ22	x	x	x	x	x	x	x	x	x	x	x	x	x	x	x	x	x	x	x	x
SDQ24	x	x	x	x	x	x	x	x	x	x	x	x	x	x	x	x	x	x	x	x
SDQ26	x	x	x	x	x	x	x	x	x	x	x	x	x	x	x	x	x	x	x	x
SDQ28	x	x	x	x	x	x	x	x	x	x	x	x	x	x	x	x	x	x	x	x
SDQ32	x	x	x	x	x	x	x	x	x	x	x	x	x	x	x	x	x	x	x	x
SDQ34	x	x	x	x	x	x	x	x	x	x	x	x	x	x	x	x	x	x	x	x
SDQ36	x	x	x	x	x	x	x	x	x	x	x	x	x	x	x	x	x	x	x	x
SDQ38	x	x	x	x	x	x	x	x	x	x	x	x	x	x	x	x	x	x	x	
SDQ40	x	x	x	x	x	x	x	x	x	x	x	x	x	x	x	x	x	x		x
SDQ42	x	x	x	x	x	x	x	x	x	x	x	x	x	x	x	x	x		x	x
SDQ44	x	x	x	x	x	x	x	x	x	x	x	x	x	x	x	x		x	x	x
SDQ46	x	x	x	x	x	x	x	x	x	x	x	x	x				x	x	x	x
SDQ48	x	x	x	x	x	x	x	x	x	x	x	x		x	x		x	x	x	x
SDQ50	x	x	x	x	x	x	x	x	x	x	x	x	x	x	x		x	x	x	x
SDQ52	x	x	x	x	x	x	x	x	x	x	x	x	x	x			x	x	x	x
SDQ54	x	x	x	x	x	x	x	x	x				x	x	x	x	x	x	x	x
SDQ56	x	x	x	x	x	x	x	x			x		x	x	x	x	x	x	x	x
SDQ58	x	x	x	x	x	x	x		x	x	x		x	x	x	x	x	x	x	x
SDQ60	x	x	x	x	x		x	x	x	x		x	x	x	x	x	x	x	x	x
SDQ62	x	x	x	x			x	x	x	x	x	x	x	x	x	x	x	x	x	x
SDQ64	x	x	x		x		x	x	x	x	x	x	x	x	x	x	x	x	x	x
SDQ66	x	x		x	x	x	x	x	x	x		x	x	x	x	x	x	x	x	x
SDQ69	x		x	x	x	x	x	x			x		x	x	x	x	x	x	x	x

Table 8.2 M*plus* Output: Summary of Missing Data Patterns (*continued*)

	21	22	23	24	25	26	27	28	29	30	31	32	33	34	35	36	37	38	39	40
								Missing Data Patterns (*x* = Not Missing)											
SDQ1	x	x	x	x	x	x	x	x	x	x	x	x	x	x	x	x	x	x	x	x
SDQ3	x	x	x	x	x	x	x	x	x	x	x	x	x	x	x	x	x	x	x	x
SDQ5	x	x	x	x	x	x	x	x	x	x	x	x	x	x	x	x	x	x	x	x
SDQ7	x	x	x	x	x	x	x	x	x	x	x	x	x	x	x	x	x	x	x	x
SDQ8	x	x	x	x	x	x	x	x	x	x	x	x	x	x	x	x	x	x	x	
SDQ10	x	x	x	x	x	x	x	x	x	x	x	x	x	x	x	x	x	x		x
SDQ14	x	x	x	x	x	x	x	x	x	x	x	x	x	x	x	x	x		x	x
SDQ15	x	x	x	x	x	x	x	x	x	x	x	x	x	x	x			x	x	x
SDQ19	x	x	x	x	x	x	x	x	x	x	x	x				x	x	x	x	x
SDQ22	x	x	x	x	x	x	x	x	x	x			x	x	x	x	x	x	x	x
SDQ24	x	x	x	x	x	x	x						x	x	x	x	x	x	x	x
SDQ26	x	x	x	x	x	x		x	x				x	x		x	x	x	x	x
SDQ28	x	x	x				x	x	x	x	x	x	x	x	x	x	x		x	x
SDQ32	x	x		x		x	x	x	x	x	x	x	x	x	x	x	x	x	x	x
SDQ34	x		x	x		x	x	x	x	x	x	x	x	x	x	x	x	x	x	x
SDQ36		x	x	x	x		x	x	x	x	x	x	x	x	x	x	x	x	x	x
SDQ38	x	x	x	x	x		x	x	x	x	x	x	x	x	x	x	x		x	x
SDQ40	x	x	x	x	x		x	x	x	x	x	x	x	x	x	x	x	x	x	x
SDQ42	x	x	x	x	x		x	x	x	x	x	x	x	x	x	x	x	x	x	x
SDQ44	x	x	x	x	x		x	x	x	x	x	x	x	x	x	x	x	x	x	x
SDQ46	x	x	x	x	x		x	x	x	x	x	x	x	x	x	x	x	x	x	x
SDQ48	x	x	x	x			x	x	x	x	x	x	x	x	x	x	x	x	x	x
SDQ50	x	x	x	x	x		x	x	x	x	x	x	x	x	x	x	x	x	x	x
SDQ52	x	x	x	x	x			x	x				x	x		x	x	x	x	x
SDQ54	x	x	x	x	x	x	x	x	x	x	x	x	x	x	x	x	x	x	x	x
SDQ56	x	x	x	x	x	x	x	x	x	x	x	x	x	x	x	x	x	x	x	
SDQ58	x	x	x	x	x	x	x	x	x	x	x	x	x		x	x	x	x	x	x
SDQ60	x	x	x	x	x	x	x	x	x	x	x	x	x	x	x	x	x	x	x	x
SDQ62	x	x	x	x	x	x	x	x	x	x	x	x	x	x	x	x	x	x	x	x
SDQ64	x	x	x	x	x	x	x	x	x	x	x	x	x	x	x	x	x	x	x	x
SDQ66	x	x	x	x	x	x	x	x	x	x	x	x	x	x	x	x		x	x	x
SDQ69	x	x	x	x		x	x	x		x	x		x	x	x	x	x		x	x

Table 8.2 M*plus* Output: Summary of Missing Data Patterns (*continued*)

	Missing Data Patterns (x = Not Missing)							
	41	42	43	44	45	46	47	48
SDQ1	x	x	x	x	x			
SDQ3	x	x	x	x		x	x	x
SDQ5	x	x			x	x	x	x
SDQ7			x			x	x	x
SDQ8	x	x	x		x	x	x	x
SDQ10	x	x	x		x	x	x	x
SDQ14	x	x	x	x	x	x	x	x
SDQ15	x	x	x	x	x	x	x	x
SDQ19	x	x	x		x	x	x	x
SDQ22	x	x	x	x	x	x		
SDQ24	x	x	x	x	x	x	x	
SDQ26	x	x	x	x	x	x	x	
SDQ28	x		x	x	x	x	x	x
SDQ32	x		x	x	x	x	x	x
SDQ34	x		x	x	x	x	x	x
SDQ36	x		x	x	x	x	x	x
SDQ38	x		x	x	x	x	x	x
SDQ40	x		x	x	x	x	x	x
SDQ42	x		x	x	x	x	x	x
SDQ44	x		x	x	x	x	x	x
SDQ46	x		x	x	x	x	x	x
SDQ48	x		x	x	x	x	x	x
SDQ50	x		x		x	x	x	x
SDQ52	x		x	x	x	x	x	
SDQ54	x	x	x	x	x	x	x	x
SDQ56	x	x	x	x	x	x	x	x
SDQ58	x	x	x	x	x	x	x	x
SDQ60	x	x	x	x	x	x	x	x
SDQ62	x	x	x	x	x	x	x	x
SDQ64	x	x	x	x	x	x	x	x
SDQ66	x	x	x	x	x	x	x	
SDQ69	x	x	x	x	x	x	x	x

Table 8.3 Mplus Output: Missing Data Pattern Frequencies

Pattern	Frequency	Pattern	Frequency	Pattern	Frequency
1	370	17	1	33	3
2	1	18	3	34	1
3	1	19	2	35	1
4	1	20	1	36	1
5	3	21	1	37	1
6	1	22	1	38	1
7	2	23	2	39	1
8	2	24	2	40	1
9	3	25	1	41	2
10	1	26	2	42	1
11	3	27	6	43	1
12	9	28	4	44	1
13	2	29	1	45	1
14	3	30	1	46	2
15	1	31	10	47	1
16	1	32	1	48	1

frequencies related to each missing data pattern. By combining information from Tables 8.2 and 8.3, for example, we are advised that for Pattern 5, three persons failed to respond to the Item SDQ62. In a second example, only one case was linked to Pattern 48, which was shown to have missing data for Items SDQ22, SDQ24, SDQ26, SDQ52, and SDQ66.

Let's return now to findings related to testing of the hypothesized model for Nigerian adolescents. In contrast to the Australian group, results revealed a substantially better fitting model, albeit still only marginally acceptable, at least in terms of the CFI (MLR$\chi^2_{[458]}$ = 726.895; CFI = 0.913; RMSEA = 0.036; SRMR = 0.052). A review of the MI values identified one parameter, in particular, that could be regarded as strongly misspecified; this parameter represented an error covariance between Items 26 and 19, which, of course, replicates the same finding for Australian adolescents. In addition, however, the MI results identified the same two cross-loadings reported for the Australian groups (F3 by SDQ38; F1 by SDQ32), as well as other moderately misspecified parameters in the model. These three parameters were each separately added to the model, and then the model was reestimated. In the interest of space, however, only results for the final model that included all three parameters are reported here. Accordingly, results led to some improvement in fit such that the model could now be regarded as moderately good (MLR$\chi^2_{[455]}$ = 665.862; CFI = 0.932; RMSEA = 0.032; SRMR = 0.047). Given no further evidence of misspecified parameters, this model was deemed the most appropriate baseline model for Nigerian adolescents.

Having established a baseline model for both groups of adolescents, we can now proceed in testing for the invariance of factor loadings, intercepts, and latent factor means across the two groups. These baseline models are schematically presented in Figure 8.2, with the broken lines representing additional parameter specifications common to both Australians and Nigerians.

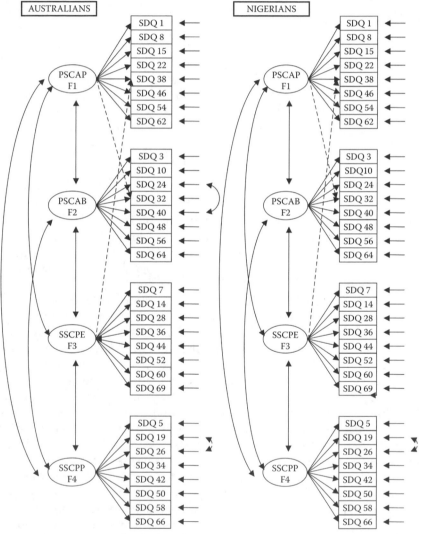

Figure 8.2. Baseline models of SDQ-I structure for Australian and Nigerian adolescents.

Mplus Input File Specification and Output File Results

Testing Invariance: The Configural Model

Input File 1

As noted in Chapter 7, the model under test in this step of the invariance-testing process is a multigroup model in which no parameter constraints are imposed. The configural model simply incorporates the baseline models pertinent to both groups and allows for their simultaneous analyses. The input file for this initial model is shown in Figure 8.3.

At first blush, you may assume that this file essentially mimics the same structure as that for the configural model in Chapter 7. Although this is basically true, one major difference between the two files is that I addressed the issue of model identification and latent variable scaling using the fixed factor, rather than the M*plus* default reference variable method. (For a review of these methods in general, together with their related references, see Chapter 2; for a perspective on use of the reference variable approach as it relates to invariance testing in particular, see Yoon & Millsap, 2007.) Specification pertinent to the fixed factor method can be evidenced under the primary MODEL command and involves two adjustments to the usual default. First, note that the first variable of each congeneric set per factor is freely estimated, as indicated by the accompanying asterisk (*). In all previous input files, with the exception of Chapter 5, specification has allowed the M*plus* default to hold, thereby fixing the value of these variables to 1.00. Second, given the free estimation of these initial variables in each congeneric set, the related factor variance must be fixed to 1.00, as indicated by the specification of F1–F4@1.

Inspection of specifications for both the factor loadings and residual covariance in the MODEL command reveals the similarity of the two baseline models. The only hypothesized difference between the two groups lies with the specification of the residual covariance of SDQ40 with SDQ24 for Australian adolescents.

Consistent with the configural model specifications noted in Chapter 7, the factor loadings are freely estimated for both adolescent groups. Thus, to offset the defaulted equality constraint for these factor-loading parameters, their specifications are repeated under the MODEL-specific command for Nigerian adolescents. Finally, note that the factor means are fixed at 0.0 ([F1–F4@0]) and the observed variable intercepts not estimated ([SDQ1–SDQ69]).

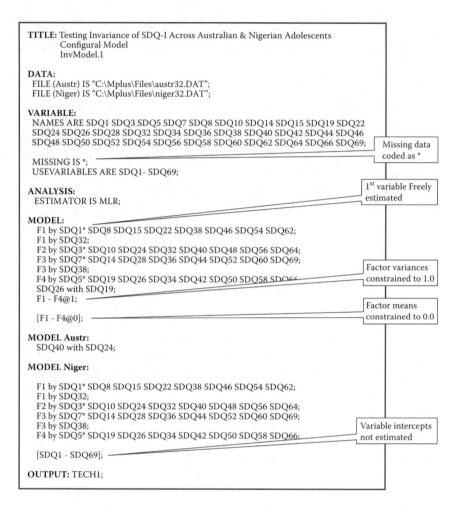

TITLE: Testing Invariance of SDQ-I Across Australian & Nigerian Adolescents
        Configural Model
        InvModel.1

DATA:
  FILE (Austr) IS "C:\Mplus\Files\austr32.DAT";
  FILE (Niger) IS "C:\Mplus\Files\niger32.DAT";

VARIABLE:
  NAMES ARE SDQ1 SDQ3 SDQ5 SDQ7 SDQ8 SDQ10 SDQ14 SDQ15 SDQ19 SDQ22
  SDQ24 SDQ26 SDQ28 SDQ32 SDQ34 SDQ36 SDQ38 SDQ40 SDQ42 SDQ44 SDQ46
  SDQ48 SDQ50 SDQ52 SDQ54 SDQ56 SDQ58 SDQ60 SDQ62 SDQ64 SDQ66 SDQ69;

  MISSING IS *;   [Missing data
  USEVARIABLES ARE SDQ1- SDQ69;   coded as *]

ANALYSIS: [1st variable Freely
  ESTIMATOR IS MLR;   estimated]

MODEL:
  F1 by SDQ1* SDQ8 SDQ15 SDQ22 SDQ38 SDQ46 SDQ54 SDQ62;
  F1 by SDQ32;
  F2 by SDQ3* SDQ10 SDQ24 SDQ32 SDQ40 SDQ48 SDQ56 SDQ64;
  F3 by SDQ7* SDQ14 SDQ28 SDQ36 SDQ44 SDQ52 SDQ60 SDQ69;
  F3 by SDQ38;   [Factor variances
  F4 by SDQ5* SDQ19 SDQ26 SDQ34 SDQ42 SDQ50 SDQ58 SDQ66   constrained to 1.0]
  SDQ26 with SDQ19;
  F1 - F4@1;   [Factor means
                                                                     constrained to 0.0]
  [F1 - F4@0];

MODEL Austr:
  SDQ40 with SDQ24;

MODEL Niger:

  F1 by SDQ1* SDQ8 SDQ15 SDQ22 SDQ38 SDQ46 SDQ54 SDQ62;
  F1 by SDQ32;
  F2 by SDQ3* SDQ10 SDQ24 SDQ32 SDQ40 SDQ48 SDQ56 SDQ64;
  F3 by SDQ7* SDQ14 SDQ28 SDQ36 SDQ44 SDQ52 SDQ60 SDQ69;   [Variable intercepts
  F3 by SDQ38;   not estimated]
  F4 by SDQ5* SDQ19 SDQ26 SDQ34 SDQ42 SDQ50 SDQ58 SDQ66;

  [SDQ1 - SDQ69];

OUTPUT: TECH1;

Figure 8.3. M*plus* input file for a test of a configural model.

Not surprisingly, results from testing of the configural model yielded goodness-of-fit statistics that were moderately acceptable (MLR$\chi^2_{[909]}$ = 1575.474). Indeed, the minimally acceptable CFI value of 0.924 was offset by the relatively good RMSEA and SRMR values of 0.039 and 0.052, respectively.

Testing Invariance: The Factor Loadings

As discussed and illustrated in Chapter 7, our next step in the invariance-testing process is to now constrain all the factor loadings equal across the two groups. Specification of this model requires that the replicated list of common factor loadings under the MODEL-specific command for the second group (in this case, for MODEL Niger;) be deleted. (For comparison, see Figure 7.3.) Removal of these parameter specifications then allows for the M*plus* default of factor-loading equality to hold.

Recall that in reviewing the MI values pertinent to these constraints, we focus on only those that are (a) related to the factor-loading matrix, and (b) actually constrained equal across groups. As such, only the BY statements are of interest here. Indeed, you may wonder why I bother to note point (b) above. The reason for this alert is because many additional factor-loading parameters will also be included in this set of MIs and can be confusing for those new to the M*plus* program. These other MI values, of course, simply suggest other parameters that if incorporated into the model would lead to a better model fit. However, our determination of best fitting models was completed with the establishment of appropriate baseline models, and thus further model fitting is not relevant here. Findings from this initial test for parameter equality identified the loading of SDQ24 on F2 as having the largest MI value, thereby indicating the severity of its noninvariance across Australian and Nigerian adolescents. Goodness-of-fit results for this model are as follows: MLR$\chi^2_{(943)}$ = 1744.821, CFI = 0.909, RMSEA = 0.042, and SRMR = 0.093. Indeed, the notable decrease in model fit compared with that of the configural model provides clear evidence of extant noninvariance in this model. This fact is further substantiated by the very large corrected MLR$\chi^2_{(34)}$ difference value of 168.681, with 34 degrees of freedom relating to the 32 initial factor loadings plus 2 cross-loadings common to each group.

Before moving on with further testing of these factor loadings, allow me to digress briefly in order to provide you with one caveat and one recommendation regarding these analyses. We turn first to the caveat. Although, admittedly, I have mentioned this caution at various stages throughout the book, I consider it important to again alert you to the fact that because the calculation of MI values is done univariately, the values can fluctuate substantially from one test of the model to another. For this reason, then, it is imperative that only one constraint be relaxed at a time and the model reestimated after each respecification. As for my recommendation, I highly suggest, particularly to those who may be new to SEM, that the TECH1 option be included on the initial execution of each set of invariance tests as it serves as a check that you have specified the model correctly. For example, in this initial test of the factor loadings, the TECH1 output reveals the numbering of estimated parameters in the factor-loading matrix to extend from 33 to 65 for the first group (in this case, the Australians). Given that these parameters are specified as being constrained equal across groups, these parameters should be likewise numbered for the Nigerians.

Continued testing for the equality of SDQ factor loadings across groups identified six additional ones to be noninvariant. In total, the seven items found to be operating nonequivalently across groups were as follows:

- SDQ24 (I enjoy sports and games) on F2
- SDQ40 (I am good at sports) on F2
- SDQ26 (My parents like me) on F4
- SDQ19 (I like my parents) on F4
- SDQ38 (Other kids think I am good looking) on F1
- SDQ52 (I have more friends than most other kids) on F3
- SDQ22 (I am a nice-looking person) on F1

The input file for this final model designed to test for factor-loading invariance is shown in Figure 8.4. Of relevance is the specification of these seven noninvariant factor loadings under the MODEL-specific command for the Nigerian group. Their specification here assures that they are not constrained equal across the two groups. Of particular note from these analyses also is the verified invariance of the two cross-loadings across Australian and Nigerian adolescents (F1 by SDQ32; F3 by SDQ38).

Goodness-of-fit statistics related to this final model are as follows: $MLR\chi^2_{(936)}$ = 1646.326, CFI = 0.919, RMSEA = 0.040, and SRMR = 0.084. Comparison of this final model having equality constraints released for seven factor loadings with the previously specified model (with six factor loadings constrained equal) yielded a corrected $MLR\Delta\chi^2_{(1)}$ value of 4.548 ($p < 0.020$). Although this value slightly exceeds the χ^2 distribution cut-point of 3.84, its z-value is nonetheless less than 1.96. Also of relevance is the difference in CFI values, which is 0.01.[3]

Testing Invariance: The Common Residual Covariance

Input File 2

As noted in Chapter 7, testing for the invariance of error covariance is considered to be extremely stringent and really unnecessary (see, e.g., Widaman & Reise, 1997). Nonetheless, given that the error covariance between Item 26 and Item 19 was found to be an important parameter in the baseline model for both Australian and Nigerian adolescents, I consider it worthwhile, from a psychometric perspective, to test for its invariance across the two groups. Given that these two parameters were already freely estimated for each group, we simply need to indicate their equality constraint by adding a parenthesized 1 to their model specification as shown in Figure 8.5. (For a more detailed explanation regarding this form of imposing equality constraints, see Chapter 7.)

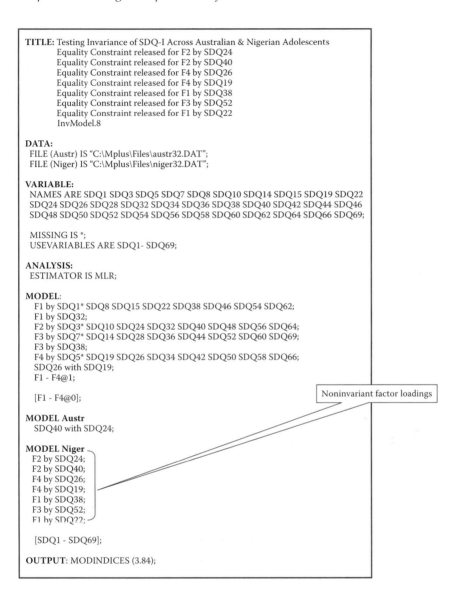

TITLE: Testing Invariance of SDQ-I Across Australian & Nigerian Adolescents
         Equality Constraint released for F2 by SDQ24
         Equality Constraint released for F2 by SDQ40
         Equality Constraint released for F4 by SDQ26
         Equality Constraint released for F4 by SDQ19
         Equality Constraint released for F1 by SDQ38
         Equality Constraint released for F3 by SDQ52
         Equality Constraint released for F1 by SDQ22
         InvModel.8

DATA:
  FILE (Austr) IS "C:\Mplus\Files\austr32.DAT";
  FILE (Niger) IS "C:\Mplus\Files\niger32.DAT";

VARIABLE:
  NAMES ARE SDQ1 SDQ3 SDQ5 SDQ7 SDQ8 SDQ10 SDQ14 SDQ15 SDQ19 SDQ22
  SDQ24 SDQ26 SDQ28 SDQ32 SDQ34 SDQ36 SDQ38 SDQ40 SDQ42 SDQ44 SDQ46
  SDQ48 SDQ50 SDQ52 SDQ54 SDQ56 SDQ58 SDQ60 SDQ62 SDQ64 SDQ66 SDQ69;

  MISSING IS *;
  USEVARIABLES ARE SDQ1- SDQ69;

ANALYSIS:
  ESTIMATOR IS MLR;

MODEL:
  F1 by SDQ1* SDQ8 SDQ15 SDQ22 SDQ38 SDQ46 SDQ54 SDQ62;
  F1 by SDQ32;
  F2 by SDQ3* SDQ10 SDQ24 SDQ32 SDQ40 SDQ48 SDQ56 SDQ64;
  F3 by SDQ7* SDQ14 SDQ28 SDQ36 SDQ44 SDQ52 SDQ60 SDQ69;
  F3 by SDQ38;
  F4 by SDQ5* SDQ19 SDQ26 SDQ34 SDQ42 SDQ50 SDQ58 SDQ66;
  SDQ26 with SDQ19;
  F1 - F4@1;

  [F1 - F4@0];   ┌──────────────────────────┐
                                                    │ Noninvariant factor loadings │
MODEL Austr   └──────────────────────────┘
  SDQ40 with SDQ24;

MODEL Niger
  F2 by SDQ24;
  F2 by SDQ40;
  F4 by SDQ26;
  F4 by SDQ19;
  F1 by SDQ38;
  F3 by SDQ52;
  F1 by SDQ22;

  [SDQ1 - SDQ69];

OUTPUT: MODINDICES (3.84);

Figure 8.4. M*plus* input file for a final test of invariant factor loadings.

   Results related to the testing of this model yielded an ever so slightly better fit to the data than was the case for the previous model, in which only seven factor loadings were constrained equal ($\text{MLR}\chi^2_{[937]}$ = 1644.489; CFI = 0.920; RMSEA = 0.040; SRMR = 0.084). The corrected difference test between these two models yielded as $\text{MLR}\Delta\chi^2_{(1)}$ = 0.279, which, of

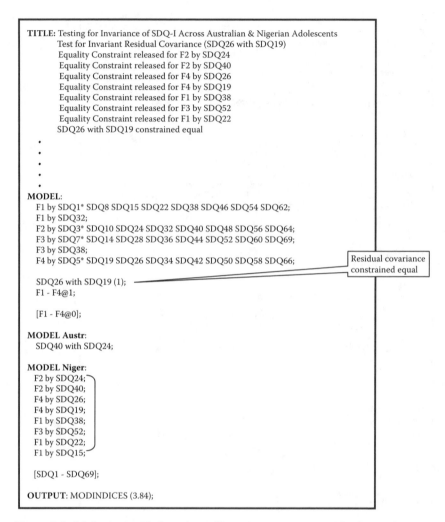

TITLE: Testing for Invariance of SDQ-I Across Australian & Nigerian Adolescents
      Test for Invariant Residual Covariance (SDQ26 with SDQ19)
      Equality Constraint released for F2 by SDQ24
      Equality Constraint released for F2 by SDQ40
      Equality Constraint released for F4 by SDQ26
      Equality Constraint released for F4 by SDQ19
      Equality Constraint released for F1 by SDQ38
      Equality Constraint released for F3 by SDQ52
      Equality Constraint released for F1 by SDQ22
      SDQ26 with SDQ19 constrained equal

    ·
    ·
    ·
    ·
    ·

MODEL:
  F1 by SDQ1* SDQ8 SDQ15 SDQ22 SDQ38 SDQ46 SDQ54 SDQ62;
  F1 by SDQ32;
  F2 by SDQ3* SDQ10 SDQ24 SDQ32 SDQ40 SDQ48 SDQ56 SDQ64;
  F3 by SDQ7* SDQ14 SDQ28 SDQ36 SDQ44 SDQ52 SDQ60 SDQ69;
  F3 by SDQ38;
  F4 by SDQ5* SDQ19 SDQ26 SDQ34 SDQ42 SDQ50 SDQ58 SDQ66;   Residual covariance
                                                         constrained equal
  SDQ26 with SDQ19 (1);
  F1 - F4@1;

  [F1 - F4@0];

MODEL Austr:
  SDQ40 with SDQ24;

MODEL Niger:
  F2 by SDQ24;
  F2 by SDQ40;
  F4 by SDQ26;
  F4 by SDQ19;
  F1 by SDQ38;
  F3 by SDQ52;
  F1 by SDQ22;
  F1 by SDQ15;

  [SDQ1 - SDQ69];

OUTPUT: MODINDICES (3.84);

Figure 8.5. M*plus* input file for a test of invariant common residual covariance.

course, is not statistically significant ($p > .05$). Thus, whereas the factor loadings for items SDQ26 (My parents like me) and SDQ19 (I like my parents), both of which load on F4, were found not to be invariant across Australian and Nigerian adolescents, the covariance between their residual terms was strong. What can we conclude from this rather intriguing finding? One suggestion is that although perception of content related to these items would appear to vary across the cultural groups (e.g., the type of parental relations that adolescents in each culture consider to be important), the degree of overlap between the content of the items is almost the same.

Testing Invariance: The Intercepts

Input File 3

To recapitulate the current invariance-testing status of the SDQ-I thus far, we have found all factor loadings except those for seven items (SDQ24, SDQ40, SDQ26, SDQ19, SDQ38, SDQ52, and SDQ22), the two cross-loadings (SDQ32 on F1; SDQ38 on F3), and the residual covariance of SDQ26 with SDQ19 to be operating equivalently across Australian and Nigerian adolescent groups. In continuing these tests for measurement invariance, we next add the observed variable intercepts to the existing model. The partial input file for this new model is shown in Figure 8.6.

Recall that, in multigroup models, M*plus* constrains intercepts of the observed variables equal across groups by default. In order to relax this constraint for the previous models, these parameters were specified within square brackets and entered under the MODEL-specific section for Nigerian adolescents. Given our focus now on testing for the invariance of these 32 SDQ-I item intercepts, however, this bracketed information has been deleted.

Results from analysis of this model were $\text{MLR}\chi^2_{(969)} = 2327.916$, CFI = 0.846, RMSEA = 0.054, and SRMR = 0.128. Even before looking at the MIs, it seems evident that this model is critically less well fitting than any of the previous models tested thus far. Thus, it seems apparent that there is likely to be substantial evidence of noninvariance of the intercepts. Indeed, comparison of this model with the previous model (seven freely estimated factor loadings, and one residual covariance constrained equal) yielded a corrected $\Delta\text{MLR}\chi^2_{(32)}$ value of 841.269 ($p < 0.001$).

Not surprisingly, examination of the MIs for this model (see Table 8.4) revealed several extremely large values, with the value for SDQ7 being the largest (MI = 56.864). Testing of a subsequent model, in which the intercept for SDQ7 was freely estimated, yielded the following goodness-of-fit indices: $\text{MLR}\chi^2_{(968)} = 2264.088$, CFI = 0.853, RMSEA = 0.053, and SRMR = 0.128. Once again, in comparing this model with the first model testing for invariant intercepts, the difference test revealed an extremely high and, of course, statistically significant corrected $\Delta\text{MLR}\chi^2_{(1)}$ value of 283.752 ($p < 0.001$).

In total, continuation of these tests for invariance revealed 27 of the 32 intercepts to be nonequivalent across the two groups. Recall that because M*plus* constrains the intercepts equal across groups by default, relaxation of these constraints requires that specification of nonequivalent intercepts be specified under the model-specific command for one of the groups (the Nigerians here). Thus, a review of these 27 nonequivalent intercepts can be seen in the input file for this final model as presented, in part, in Figure 8.7. Results bearing on this final model were as follows: $\text{MLR}\chi^2_{(942)} = 1649.972$,

---

TITLE: Testing Invariance of SDQ-I Across Australian & Nigerian Adolescents
        Intercepts Invariant

-
-
-
-
-

MODEL:
  F1 by SDQ1* SDQ8 SDQ15 SDQ22 SDQ38 SDQ46 SDQ54 SDQ62;
  F1 by SDQ32;
  F2 by SDQ3* SDQ10 SDQ24 SDQ32 SDQ40 SDQ48 SDQ56 SDQ64;
  F3 by SDQ7* SDQ14 SDQ28 SDQ36 SDQ44 SDQ52 SDQ60 SDQ69;
  F3 by SDQ38;
  F4 by SDQ5* SDQ19 SDQ26 SDQ34 SDQ42 SDQ50 SDQ58 SDQ66;
  SDQ26 with SDQ19 (1);
  F1 - F4@1;

  [F1 - F4@0];

MODEL Austr:
  SDQ40 with SDQ24;

MODEL Niger:
  F2 by SDQ24;
  F2 by SDQ40;
  F4 by SDQ26;
  F4 by SDQ19;
  F1 by SDQ38;
  F3 by SDQ52;
  F1 by SDQ22;

OUTPUT: MODINDICES (3.84);

Figure 8.6. M*plus* input file for a test of invariant observed variable intercepts.

CFI = 0.919, RMSEA = 0.040, and SRMR = 0.082. Comparison of this final model (equality constraints released for 27 intercepts) with the previously specified model (equality constraints released for 26 intercepts) yielded a corrected MLR$\Delta\chi^2_{(1)}$ value of 4.825 ($p < 0.020$). Consistent with results for the factor loadings, this value slightly exceeds the χ^2 distribution cutpoint of 3.84. However, given that its z-value is less than 1.96 and there is virtually no difference in CFI values (i.e., both are 0.919), I considered this model to represent appropriately the final test of intercepts related to the SDQ-I.

Testing Invariance: The Latent Means

Input File 4

As mentioned in this chapter, tests for the invariance of latent means are more commonly expressed as tests for latent mean differences. Recall also from earlier discussion of identification issues that because the latent factor intercepts (i.e., factor means) have an arbitrary origin when intercepts

Table 8.4 M*plus* Output:
Selected Modification Indices (MIs) for Test of Invariant Intercepts

	MI	Expected Parameter Change (EPC)	Standard EPC	StdYX EPC
Group AUSTR				
[SDQ1]	13.003	−0.090	−0.090	−0.073
[SDQ3]	11.748	−0.095	−0.095	−0.077
[SDQ7]	**56.864**	**0.156**	**0.156**	**0.162**
[SDQ10]	37.068	0.204	0.204	0.166
[SDQ15]	4.580	−0.053	−0.053	−0.042
[SDQ19]	14.904	0.058	0.058	0.086
[SDQ24]	33.327	0.106	0.106	0.120
[SDQ26]	12.094	0.058	0.058	0.078
[SDQ28]	21.511	0.086	0.086	0.092
[SDQ34]	11.599	−0.161	−0.161	−0.112
[SDQ36]	31.398	−0.178	−0.178	−0.156
[SDQ38]	19.432	−0.163	−0.163	−0.119
[SDQ44]	4.505	−0.069	−0.069	−0.059
[SDQ46]	18.476	−0.168	−0.168	−0.119
[SDQ50]	5.538	−0.072	−0.072	−0.063
[SDQ56]	11.367	−0.082	−0.082	−0.063
[SDQ58]	9.251	0.063	0.063	0.063
[SDQ60]	5.623	−0.074	−0.074	−0.061
[SDQ64]	28.469	0.144	0.144	0.129
Group NIGER				
[SDQ1]	13.003	0.122	0.122	0.095
[SDQ3]	11.748	0.155	0.155	0.109
[SDQ7]	**56.863**	**−0.476**	**−0.476**	**−0.322**
[SDQ10]	37.068	−0.333	−0.333	−0.227
[SDQ15]	4.580	0.083	0.083	0.061
[SDQ19]	14.904	−0.110	−0.110	−0.120
[SDQ24]	33.326	−0.279	−0.279	−0.213
[SDQ26]	12.094	−0.098	−0.098	−0.101
[SDQ28]	21.511	−0.231	−0.231	−0.181
[SDQ34]	11.599	0.126	0.126	0.097
[SDQ36]	31.398	0.216	0.216	0.181
[SDQ38]	19.432	0.192	0.192	0.143
[SDQ44]	4.505	0.079	0.079	0.065

Table 8.4 Mplus Output:
Selected Modification Indices (MIs) for Test of Invariant Intercepts (*continued*)

	MI	Expected Parameter Change (EPC)	Standard EPC	StdYX EPC
[SDQ46]	18.476	0.117	0.117	0.092
[SDQ50]	5.538	0.081	0.081	0.067
[SDQ56]	11.367	0.155	0.155	0.102
[SDQ58]	9.251	−0.110	−0.110	−0.094
[SDQ60]	5.623	0.097	0.097	0.075
[SDQ64]	28.469	−0.304	−0.304	−0.209

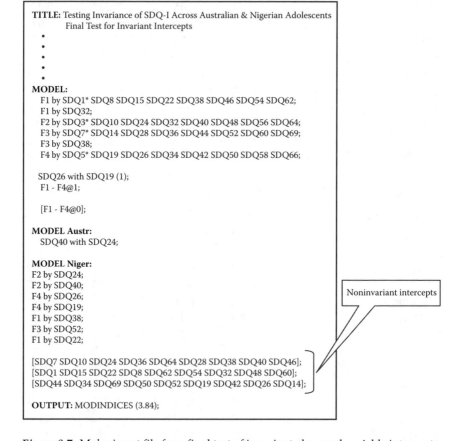

TITLE: Testing Invariance of SDQ-I Across Australian & Nigerian Adolescents
     Final Test for Invariant Intercepts
   •
   •
   •
   •
   •

MODEL:
  F1 by SDQ1* SDQ8 SDQ15 SDQ22 SDQ38 SDQ46 SDQ54 SDQ62;
  F1 by SDQ32;
  F2 by SDQ3* SDQ10 SDQ24 SDQ32 SDQ40 SDQ48 SDQ56 SDQ64;
  F3 by SDQ7* SDQ14 SDQ28 SDQ36 SDQ44 SDQ52 SDQ60 SDQ69;
  F3 by SDQ38;
  F4 by SDQ5* SDQ19 SDQ26 SDQ34 SDQ42 SDQ50 SDQ58 SDQ66;

  SDQ26 with SDQ19 (1);
  F1 - F4@1;

  [F1 - F4@0];

MODEL Austr:
  SDQ40 with SDQ24;

MODEL Niger:
F2 by SDQ24;
F2 by SDQ40;
F4 by SDQ26;
F4 by SDQ19;
F1 by SDQ38;
F3 by SDQ52;
F1 by SDQ22;

[SDQ7 SDQ10 SDQ24 SDQ36 SDQ64 SDQ28 SDQ38 SDQ40 SDQ46];
[SDQ1 SDQ15 SDQ22 SDQ8 SDQ62 SDQ54 SDQ32 SDQ48 SDQ60];
[SDQ44 SDQ34 SDQ69 SDQ50 SDQ52 SDQ19 SDQ42 SDQ26 SDQ14];

OUTPUT: MODINDICES (3.84);

Noninvariant intercepts

Figure 8.7. Mplus input file for a final test of invariant observed variable intercepts.

of the observed variables are constrained equal, the latent factor means for one group must be fixed to zero, whereas those for the other group are freely estimated. As such, one group operates as the reference group against which the other group is compared. It is important to note, however, that M*plus* automatically fixes the factor mean for the first group to zero by default (the Australian group in the present application). Given findings of noninvariance related to 7 factor loadings and 27 observed variable intercepts, our test for latent mean differences represents a partially invariant model. The input file for this test is shown, in part, in Figure 8.8.

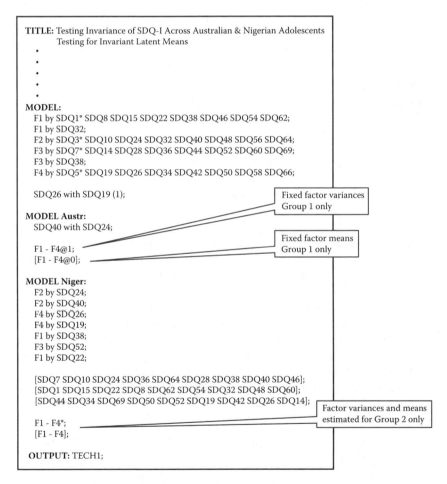

TITLE: Testing Invariance of SDQ-I Across Australian & Nigerian Adolescents
        Testing for Invariant Latent Means
  •
  •
  •
  •
  •

MODEL:
   F1 by SDQ1* SDQ8 SDQ15 SDQ22 SDQ38 SDQ46 SDQ54 SDQ62;
   F1 by SDQ32;
   F2 by SDQ3* SDQ10 SDQ24 SDQ32 SDQ40 SDQ48 SDQ56 SDQ64;
   F3 by SDQ7* SDQ14 SDQ28 SDQ36 SDQ44 SDQ52 SDQ60 SDQ69;
   F3 by SDQ38;
   F4 by SDQ5* SDQ19 SDQ26 SDQ34 SDQ42 SDQ50 SDQ58 SDQ66;

   SDQ26 with SDQ19 (1);

MODEL Austr:
   SDQ40 with SDQ24;

   F1 - F4@1;
   [F1 - F4@0];

MODEL Niger:
   F2 by SDQ24;
   F2 by SDQ40;
   F4 by SDQ26;
   F4 by SDQ19;
   F1 by SDQ38;
   F3 by SDQ52;
   F1 by SDQ22;

   [SDQ7 SDQ10 SDQ24 SDQ36 SDQ64 SDQ28 SDQ38 SDQ40 SDQ46];
   [SDQ1 SDQ15 SDQ22 SDQ8 SDQ62 SDQ54 SDQ32 SDQ48 SDQ60];
   [SDQ44 SDQ34 SDQ69 SDQ50 SDQ52 SDQ19 SDQ42 SDQ26 SDQ14];

   F1 - F4*;
   [F1 - F4];

OUTPUT: TECH1;

Fixed factor variances
Group 1 only

Fixed factor means
Group 1 only

Factor variances and means
estimated for Group 2 only

Figure 8.8. M*plus* input file for a test of invariant latent means.

THE MODEL ESTIMATION TERMINATED NORMALLY

THE STANDARD ERRORS OF THE MODEL PARAMETER ESTIMATES COULD NOT BE
COMPUTED. THE MODEL MAY NOT BE IDENTIFIED. CHECK YOUR MODEL.

PROBLEM INVOLVING PARAMETER 173.

THE CONDITION NUMBER IS -0.353D-11.

THE ROBUST CHI-SQUARE COULD NOT BE COMPUTED.

Figure 8.9. Mplus error message suggesting possible underidentification.

Review of this input file triggers several points worthy of mention. First, in contrast to all previous invariance models whereby the constraint, (F1–F4@1), was specified under the MODEL command, this specification has now been reassigned to the MODEL-specific command for the first group (Australians). Second, although the program fixes the factor mean to zero by default for this first group, as noted in this chapter, I prefer to override this default here in the interest of making this specification more explicit. Third, under the MODEL-specific command for the Nigerians, note that the specification of 7 factor loadings and 27 intercepts identifies those parameters as noninvariant, thereby allowing them to be freely estimated. Finally, also under MODEL Niger, you will see that for this group, the factor variances are freely estimated, as are the four factor means.

Execution of this file resulted in the condition code and related warning shown in Figure 8.9, which notes that the robust chi-square statistic could not be computed. As a result, of course, no goodness-of-fit statistics were reported. This warning message suggests that the model may not be identified. Indeed, given the number of freely estimated intercepts as a consequence of their noninvariance, this caveat is likely to be true as the model may be underidentified. (For an explanatory description of identification, see Chapter 2.)

Of import here is a critical criterion requiring the number of estimated intercepts to be less than the number of measured variables in the analysis of MACS models. In multigroup models, this requirement is controlled by the imposition of equality constraints across the groups. However, when these models incorporate partial measurement invariance, this balance between constrained and estimated parameters can become somewhat tenuous. Thus, it behooves us at this point to determine if, in fact, we have satisfied this criterion. The status of these parameters is as follows:

- *Intercepts*: 27 noninvariant, which translates into 27 estimated for each group (i.e., 54)
  - 5 invariant intercepts—therefore 5 estimated
  - Total number of intercepts freely estimated—59 (54+5)

- *Factor loadings*: 7 noninvariant, translating into 7 estimated for each group (i.e., 14)
  - 25 invariant factor loadings—therefore 25 estimated
  - 2 invariant cross-loadings—therefore 2 estimated
- Total number of factor loadings freely estimated = 41 (14 + 25 + 2)

Indeed, estimation of 59 intercepts versus 41 factor loadings clearly stands in violation of the dictum that the number of estimated intercepts be less than the number of estimated factor loadings. Thus, the simplest and likely most logical way to address this underidentification issue is to relax equality constraints for the 18 (59 – 41) most recently identified intercepts, thereby leaving only 9 intercepts (SDQ7–SDQ46) to be freely estimated. Consistent with analyses of the prerequisite invariance models, this respecified means model succeeded in yielding model fit that can be regarded as modestly acceptable: MLR$\chi^2_{(952)}$ = 1699.564, CFI = 0.915, RMSEA = 0.040, and SRMR = 0.057. It is interesting to compare this model in which 9 intercepts were constrained equal with the final invariance model in which 27 intercepts were constrained equal as there is virtually no difference in values of the CFI (0.915 versus 0.919) and RMSEA (0.040 versus 0.040). Results bearing on the latent factor means are presented in Table 8.5.

Given that the Australian group was designated the reference group by default and, thus, their factor means were fixed to zero, we concentrate solely on estimates as they relate to the Nigerian group. Accordingly, the results presented here tell us that whereas the means of Factor 1 (PSC: Appearance), Factor 3 (SSC: Peers), and Factor 4 (SSC: Parents) for Nigerian adolescents were significantly different from those for Australian adolescents, the mean for Factor 2 (PSC: Ability; Estimate/Standard Error [*SE*] = –1.372) was not. More specifically, these significant findings convey the notion that whereas Nigerian adolescents appear to be more positive, on average, in self-perceptions of their physical appearance and social interactions with peers than Australian adolescents, differences between the groups with respect to their self-perceptions of physical ability were negligible. On the other hand, self-perceptions of social relations with parents seem to be significantly more negative for Nigerian adolescents than for their Australian counterparts.

The interesting substantive question here is why these results should be what they are. Interpretation, of course, must be made within the context of theory and empirical research. However, when data are based on two vastly different cultural groups, as is the case here, the task can be particularly challenging. Clearly, knowledge of the societal norms, values, and identities associated with each culture would seem to be an important requisite in any speculative interpretation of these findings. (For a review of methodological issues that can bear on such analyses pertinent

Table 8.5 Mplus Output: Unstandardized and Standardized Latent Mean Estimates

	Estimate	Standard Error (SE)	Estimate/SE	Two-Tailed p-Value
Unstandardized Model Results				
Nigerians				
Means				
F1	0.970	0.062	15.527	0.000
F2	−0.097	0.072	−1.350	0.177
F3	0.383	0.070	5.509	0.000
F4	−0.167	0.066	−2.512	0.012
Standardized Model Results: STDYX Standardization				
Nigerians				
Means				
F1	1.433	0.146	9.837	0.000
F2	−0.104	0.076	−1.372	0.170
F3	0.449	0.090	4.995	0.000
F4	−0.194	0.073	−2.651	0.008

to cultural groups, readers are referred to Byrne et al., 2009; Byrne & van de Vijver, 2010; Welkenhuysen-Gybels, van de Vijver, & Cambré, 2007).

Testing Multigroup Invariance: Other Considerations

The Issue of Partial Measurement Invariance

I mentioned the issue of partial measurement invariance briefly in Chapter 7. However, I consider it instructive to provide you with a slight expansion of this topic to give you a somewhat broader perspective. As noted in Chapter 7, one of the first (if not the first) papers to discuss the issue of partial measurement invariance was that of Byrne et al. (1989). This paper addressed the difficulty commonly encountered in testing for multigroup invariance whereby certain parameters in the measurement model (typically factor loadings) are found to be noninvariant across the groups of interest. At the time of writing that paper, researchers were generally under the impression that, confronted with such results, one should not continue on to test for invariance of the structural model. Byrne and colleagues (1989) showed that, as long as certain conditions were met, tests for invariance could continue by invoking the strategy of partial measurement invariance.

More recently, however, the issue of partial measurement invariance has been subject to some controversy in the technical literature (see, e.g., Marsh & Grayson, 1994; Widaman & Reise, 1997). A review of the literature bearing on this topic reveals a modicum of experimental studies designed to test the impact of partial measurement invariance on, for example, the power of the test when group sample sizes are widely disparate (Kaplan & George, 1995); on the accuracy of selection in multiple populations (Millsap & Kwok, 2004); and on the meaningful interpretation of latent mean differences across groups (Marsh & Grayson, 1994). Substantially more work needs to be done in this area of research before we have a comprehensive view of the extent to which implementation of partial measurement invariance affects results yielded from tests for the equivalence a measuring instrument across groups.

The Issue of Statistical Versus Practical Evaluative Criteria in Determining Evidence of Invariance

In reporting on evidence of invariance, it has become customary to report the difference in χ^2 values ($\Delta\chi^2$) derived from the comparison of χ^2 values associated with various models under test. In this regard, Yuan and Bentler (2004a) have reported that for virtually every SEM application, evidence in support of multigroup invariance has been based on the $\Delta\chi^2$ test. This computed value is possible because such models are nested (for a definition, see Chapter 3, note 3). As you are now well aware, although the same comparisons can be based on the robust statistics (MLMχ^2 MLRχ^2), a correction to the value is needed as this difference is not distributed as χ^2 (Bentler, 2005; Muthén & Muthén, 2007–2010). A detailed walkthrough of this computation was provided in Chapters 6 and 7, with the latter being specific to multigroup analyses. If this difference value is statistically significant, it suggests that the constraints specified in the more restrictive model do not hold (i.e., the two models are not equivalent across groups). If, on the other hand, the $\Delta\chi^2$ value is statistically nonsignificant, this finding suggests that all specified equality constraints are tenable. Although Steiger, Shapiro, and Browne (1985) noted that, in theory, the $\Delta\chi^2$ test holds whether or not the baseline model is misspecified, Yuan and Bentler (2004a) reported findings that point to the unreliability of this test when the model is, in fact, misspecified.

This statistical evaluative strategy involving the $\Delta\chi^2$ (or its robust counterparts) represents the traditional approach to determining evidence of measurement invariance and follows from Jöreskog's (1971b) original technique in testing for multigroup equivalence. However, this strategy was based on the LISREL program, for which the only way to identify noninvariant parameters was to compare models in this manner.

Recently, however, researchers (e.g., Cheung & Rensvold, 2002; Little, 1997; Marsh, Hey, & Roche, 1997) have argued that this $\Delta\chi^2$ value is as sensitive to sample size and nonnormality as the χ^2 statistic itself, thereby rendering it an impractical and unrealistic criterion upon which to base evidence of invariance. As a consequence, there has been an increasing tendency to argue for evidence of invariance based on a more practical approach involving one, or a combination of two, alternative criteria: (a) The multigroup model exhibits an adequate fit to the data, and (b) the ΔCFI (or its robust counterpart) values between models are negligible. Although Little (1997), based on two earlier studies (McGaw & Jöreskog, 1971; Tucker & Lewis, 1973), suggested that this difference should not exceed a value of .05, other researchers have been less specific and base evidence for invariance merely on the fact that change in the CFI values between nested models is minimal. However, Cheung and Rensvold pointed out that the .05 criterion suggested by Little (1997) has neither strong theoretical nor empirical support. Thus, until their recent simulation research, use of the ΔCFI difference value has been of a purely heuristic nature. In contrast, Cheung and Rensvold examined the properties of 20 goodness-of-fit indices within the context of invariance testing, and they recommended that the ΔCFI value provides the best information for determining evidence of measurement invariance. Accordingly, they arbitrarily suggested that its difference value should not exceed .01. This recent approach to the determination of multigroup invariance, then, is considered by many to take a more practical approach to the process. (For yet another approach to the use of comparative ad hoc indices, in lieu of the $\Delta\chi^2$ test, readers are referred to MacCallum, Browne, & Cai, 2006.)

In presenting these two issues, my intent is to keep you abreast of the current literature regarding testing strategies associated with multigroup invariance. However, until such time that these issues are clearly resolved and documented with sound analytic findings, I suggest continued use of partial measurement invariance and the traditional approach in determining evidence of multigroup invariance.

Notes

1. Although M*plus* estimates these parameters by default, they are not considered in tests for invariant factor loadings.
2. Analyses were based on the EQS program (Bentler, 2005), and evidence of multivariate kurtosis based on Mardia's (1970, 1974) normalized estimate of 80.70 for the Australians and Yuan, Lambert, and Fouladi's (2004) normalized estimate of 71.20 for the Nigerians. Bentler (2005) has suggested that, in practice, Mardia's normalized values > 5.00 are indicative of data that are nonnormally distributed. The Yuan et al. (2004) coefficient is an extension of the Mardia (1970, 1974) test of multivariate kurtosis, albeit appropriate for use with missing data. Specifically, it aggregates information across the missing data patterns to yield one overall summary statistic.
3. This value is within the boundary of the suggested cutpoint from the perspective of practical significance, a topic discussed at the end of this chapter.

chapter 9

Testing the Equivalence of a Causal Structure
Full Structural Equation Model

In Chapter 4, I highlighted several problematic aspects of post hoc model fitting in structural equation modeling (SEM). One approach to addressing these issues is to apply some mode of cross-validation analysis, the focus of the present chapter. Accordingly, we examine a full structural equation model and test for its equivalence across calibration and validation samples of elementary school teachers. Before walking you through this procedure, however, allow me first to review some of the issues related to cross-validation.

Cross-Validation in Structural Equation Modeling

In applications of SEM, it is commonplace for researchers to test a hypothesized model and then, from an evaluation of various goodness-of-fit criteria, conclude that a statistically better fitting model could be attained by respecifying the model such that particular parameters previously constrained to zero are freely estimated (Breckler, 1990; MacCallum, Roznowski, Mar, & Reith, 1994; MacCallum, Roznowski, & Necowitz, 1992; MacCallum, Wegener, Uchino, & Fabrigar, 1993). During the late 1980s and much of the 1990s, this practice was the target of considerable criticism (see, e.g., Biddle & Marlin, 1987; Breckler, 1990; Cliff, 1983). As a consequence, most researchers engaged in this respecification process are now generally familiar with the issues. In particular, they are cognizant of the exploratory nature of these follow-up procedures, as well as the fact that additionally specified parameters in the model must be theoretically substantiated.

The pros and cons of post hoc model fitting have been rigorously debated in the literature. Although some have severely criticized the practice (e.g., Cliff, 1983; Cudeck & Browne, 1983), others have argued that as long as the researcher is fully cognizant of the exploratory nature of his or her analyses, the process can be substantively meaningful because practical as well as statistical significance can be taken into account (Byrne et al., 1989; Tanaka & Huba, 1984). Indeed, Jöreskog (1993) was very clear in stating, "If the model is rejected by the data, the problem is to determine what is wrong with the model and how the model should be modified to fit the data better" (p. 298). The purists would argue that once a hypothesized model is rejected, that's the end of the story. More realistically, however, other researchers in this area of study recognize the obvious impracticality in the termination of all subsequent model analyses. Clearly, in the interest of future research, it behooves the investigator to probe deeper into the question of why the model is ill fitting (see Tanaka, 1993). As a consequence of the concerted efforts of statistical and methodological SEM experts in addressing this issue, there are now several different approaches that can be used to increase the soundness of findings derived from these post hoc analyses.

Undoubtedly, post hoc model fitting in SEM is problematic. With multiple model specifications, there is the risk of capitalization on chance factors because model modification may be driven by characteristics of the particular sample on which the model was tested (e.g., sample size or sample heterogeneity) (MacCallum et al., 1992). As a consequence of this sequential testing procedure, there is increased risk of making either a Type I or Type II error, and at this point in time, there is no direct way to adjust for the probability of such error. Because hypothesized covariance structure models represent only approximations of reality and, thus, are not expected to fit real-world phenomena exactly (Cudeck & Browne, 1983; MacCallum et al., 1992), most research applications are likely to require the specification of alternative models in the quest for one that fits the data well (Anderson & Gerbing, 1988; MacCallum, 1986). Indeed, this aspect of SEM represents a serious limitation, and, thus, several alternative strategies for model testing have been proposed (see, e.g., Anderson & Gerbing, 1988; Cudeck & Henly, 1991; MacCallum et al., 1992, 1993, 1994).

One approach to addressing problems associated with post hoc model fitting is to employ a cross-validation strategy whereby the final model derived from the post hoc analyses is tested on a second (or more) independent sample(s) from the same population. Barring the availability of separate data samples, albeit a sufficiently large single sample, one may wish to randomly split the data into two (or more) parts, thereby making it possible to cross-validate the findings (see Cudeck & Browne, 1983). As such, Sample A serves as the calibration sample on which the initially hypothesized model is tested, as well as any post hoc analyses conducted in the process of attaining a well-fitting model. Once this final model is determined, the validity of its structure can then be tested based on Sample B (the validation sample). In other words, the final best fitting model for the calibration sample becomes the hypothesized model under test for the validation sample.

There are several ways by which the similarity of model structure can be tested (see, e.g., Anderson & Gerbing, 1988; Browne & Cudeck, 1989; Cudeck & Browne, 1983; MacCallum et al., 1994; Whittaker & Stapleton, 2006). For one example, Cudeck and Browne suggested the computation of a Cross-Validation Index (CVI), which measures the distance between the *restricted* (i.e., model-imposed) variance–covariance matrix for the calibration sample and the *unrestricted* variance–covariance matrix for the validation sample. Because the estimated predictive validity of the model is gauged by the smallness of the CVI value, evaluation is facilitated by their comparison based on a series of alternative models. It is important to note, however, that the CVI estimate reflects *overall* discrepancy between "the actual population covariance matrix, Σ, and the estimated population covariance matrix reconstructed from the parameter estimates obtained from fitting the model to the sample" (MacCallum et al., 1994, p. 4). More specifically, this global index of discrepancy represents combined effects arising from the discrepancy of approximation (e.g., nonlinear influences among variables) and the discrepancy of estimation (e.g., representative sample and sample size). (For a more extended discussion of these aspects of discrepancy, see Bandalos, 1993; Browne & Cudeck, 1989; Cudeck & Henly, 1991; MacCallum et al., 1994.)

More recently, Whittaker and Stapleton (2006), in a comprehensive Monte Carlo simulation study of eight cross-validation indices, determined that certain conditions played an important part in affecting their performance. Specifically, findings showed that whereas the performance of these indices generally improved with increasing factor loading and sample sizes, it tended to be less optimal in the presence of increasing non-normality. (For details related to these findings, as well as the eight cross-validation indices included in this study, see Whittaker & Stapleton, 2006.)

In the present chapter, we examine another approach to cross-validation. Specifically, we use an invariance-testing strategy to test for the replicability of a full SEM across groups. The selected application is straightforward in addressing the question of whether a model that has been specified in one sample replicates over a second independent sample from the same population (for another approach, see Byrne & Baron, 1994).

Testing Invariance Across Calibration and Validation Samples

The example presented in this chapter comes from the same original study briefly described in Chapter 6 (Byrne, 1994b), the intent of which was threefold: (a) to validate a causal structure involving the impact of organizational and personality factors on three facets of burnout for elementary, intermediate, and secondary teachers; (b) to cross-validate this model across a second independent sample within each teaching panel; and (c) to test for the invariance of common structural regression (or causal) paths across teaching panels. In contrast to Chapter 6, however, here we focus on (b) in testing for model replication across calibration and validation samples of elementary teachers. (For an in-depth examination of invariance-testing procedures within and between the three teacher groups, see Byrne, 1994b.)

It is perhaps important to note that although the present example of cross-validation is based on a full SEM, the practice is in no way limited to such applications. Indeed, cross-validation is equally as important for CFA models, and examples of such applications can be found across a variety of disciplines. For those relevant to psychology, see Byrne (1993, 1994a); Byrne and Baron (1994); Byrne, Baron, and Balev (1996, 1998); Byrne, Baron, and Campbell (1993, 1994); Byrne, Baron, Larsson, and Melin (1996); Byrne and Campbell (1999); and Byrne, Stewart, and Lee (2004). For those relevant to education, see Benson and Bandalos (1992) and Pomplun and Omar (2003). And for those relevant to medicine, see Francis, Fletcher, and Rourke (1988); as well as Wang, Wang, and Hoadley (2007). We turn now to the model under study.

The original study from which the present example is taken comprised a sample of 1,203 elementary school teachers. For purposes of cross-validation, this sample was randomly split into two; Sample A (n = 602) was used as the calibration group, and Sample B (n = 601) as the validation group.

The Hypothesized Model

The first step in the cross-validation of a model (CFA or full SEM) involves establishing a baseline model for the calibration group only. As such, we first test the hypothesized model and then modify it such that the resulting structure best fits the sample data in terms of both parsimony and goodness-of-fit. The hypothesized model under test here is schematically portrayed in Figure 9.1. As this model is taken from the same study used in Chapter 6 in which validity of causal structure was tested for a total sample of high school teachers, readers are referred to that chapter for details related to the postulated measurement and structural parameters. It is important to note that, as in Chapter 6, double-headed arrows representing correlations among the independent factors in the model are not included in Figure 9.1 in the interest of graphical clarity. Nonetheless, as you well know at this point in the book, these specifications are essential to the model and are automatically estimated by default in M*plus*.

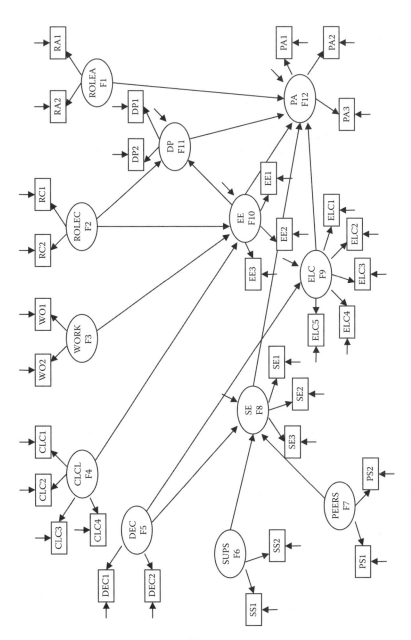

Figure 9.1. Hypothesized full SEM model of causal structure.

Mplus Input File Specification and Output File Results

Establishing the Baseline Model for the Calibration Group

Input File 1

Specification of the hypothesized model is shown in Figure 9.2. Given the known nonnormality of the data for elementary teachers, as was the case for high school teachers (see Chapter 6), the robust maximum likelihood (MLM) estimator is noted under the ANALYSIS command. Both the standardized estimates and modification indices (MIs) are requested in the OUTPUT command.

TITLE: Validating Hypothesized Causal Structure for Calibration Group

DATA:
FILE IS "C:\Mplus\Files\elemind1.dat";
FORMAT IS (19F4.2/13F4.2);

VARIABLE:
NAMES ARE ROLEA1 ROLEA2 ROLEC1 ROLEC2 WORK1 WORK2 CCLIM1 CCLIM2
CCLIM3 CCLIM4 DEC1 DEC2 SSUP1 SSUP2 PSUP1 PSUP2 SELF1 SELF2 SELF3
ELC1 ELC2 ELC3 ELC4 ELC5 EE1 EE2 EE3 DP1 DP2 PA1 PA2 PA3;
USEVARIABLES ARE ROLEA1-PA3;

ANALYSIS:
TYPE = GENERAL;
ESTIMATOR IS MLM;

MODEL:
F1 by ROLEA1-ROLEA2;
F2 by ROLEC1-ROLEC2;
F3 by WORK1-WORK2;
F4 by CCLIM1-CCLIM4;
F5 by DEC1-DEC2;
F6 by SSUP1-SSUP2;
F7 by PSUP1-PSUP2;
F8 by SELF1-SELF3;
F9 by ELC1-ELC5;
F10 by EE1-EE3;
F11 by DP1-DP2;
F12 by PA1-PA3;

F8 ON F5 F6 F7;
F9 ON F5;
F10 ON F2 F3 F4;
F11 ON F2 F10;
F12 ON F1 F8 F9 F10 F11;

OUTPUT: MODINDICES STDYX;

Figure 9.2. Mplus input file for test of hypothesized model of causal structure.

THE MODEL ESTIMATION TERMINATED NORMALLY

WARNING: THE LATENT VARIABLE COVARIANCE MATRIX (PSI) IS NOT POSITIVE DEFINITE. THIS COULD INDICATE A NEGATIVE VARIANCE/RESIDUAL VARIANCE FOR A LATENT VARIABLE, A CORRELATION GREATER OR EQUAL TO ONE BETWEEN TWO LATENT VARIABLES, OR A LINEAR DEPENDENCY AMONG MORE THAN TWO LATENT VARIABLES.

CHECK THE TECH4 OUTPUT FOR MORE INFORMATION.

PROBLEM INVOLVING VARIABLE F3.

Figure 9.3. M*plus* output file warning message related to test of hypothesized model.

Output File 1

Although the output file noted that estimation of the model terminated normally, this notification additionally included a warning that "the latent variable covariance matrix (psi) is not positive definite." This matrix represents covariances among the independent factors (F1–F7) in the model. This warning message is shown in Figure 9.3, and the related estimates in Table 9.1.

As noted in the output warning message, the likely source of the problem involves Factor 3, which, as shown in Figure 9.1, represents Work (Overload), and the likely cause is either that (a) its estimated residual is negative, or (b) its correlation with another factor exceeds a value of 1.00; both problems represent what are generally known as *Heywood cases.*[1] If essence of the difficulty involves a correlation greater than 1.00, its detection is most easily found via a review of the standardized estimates. Given that the output file indicated no negative residual or factor variances, only standardized estimates for the factor correlations are reported in Table 9.1. As you can readily see, the correlation between Factors 3 and 2 exceeds a value of 1.00. This finding indicates a definite overlapping of variance between the factors of Role Conflict and Work Overload such that divergent (i.e., discriminant) validity between these two constructs is indistinctive. As such, the validity of results based on their interpretation as separate constructs is clearly dubious. Given that measurement of these two constructs derived from subscales of the same assessment scale (the Teacher Stress Scale [TSS]; Pettegrew & Wolf, 1982), this finding is not particularly uncommon but, nonetheless, needs to be addressed.

Because, in essence, the two factors of Role Conflict and Work Overload, for all intents and purposes, are representing the same construct, one approach to resolution of the difficulty is to combine these two factors into

Table 9.1 M*plus* Output: Standardized Factor Covariance Estimates

Standardized Model Results: STDYX Standardization				
	Estimate	Standard Error (*SE*)	Estimate/*SE*	Two-Tailed *p*-Value
F2 WITH				
F1	0.802	0.028	28.610	0.000
F3 WITH				
F1	0.804	0.027	29.487	0.000
F2	1.005	0.016	62.603	0.000
F4 WITH				
F1	−0.375	0.049	−7.706	0.000
F2	−0.387	0.045	−8.617	0.000
F3	−0.460	0.050	−9.245	0.000
F5 WITH				
F1	−0.789	0.030	−26.112	0.000
F2	−0.694	0.031	−22.155	0.000
F3	−0.692	0.029	−24.094	0.000
F4	0.379	0.045	8.379	0.000
F6 WITH				
F1	−0.670	0.031	−21.453	0.000
F2	−0.572	0.032	−18.137	0.000
F3	−0.575	0.031	−18.373	0.000
F4	0.285	0.048	5.918	0.000
F5	0.950	0.012	77.888	0.000
F7 WITH				
F1	−0.520	0.043	−12.102	0.000
F2	−0.415	0.043	−9.667	0.000
F3	−0.413	0.043	−9.682	0.000
F4	0.246	0.051	4.826	0.000
F5	0.665	0.039	17.236	0.000
F6	0.503	0.041	12.332	0.000

one. As such, instead of the original causal structure involving 12 factors, we would now have one representing 11 factors. This revised model is shown in Figure 9.4. Accordingly, assignment of factor numbers has been changed such that Factor 2 now represents the combined factors of ROLEC/ WORK, as measured by their original observed variables (RC1–WO2).

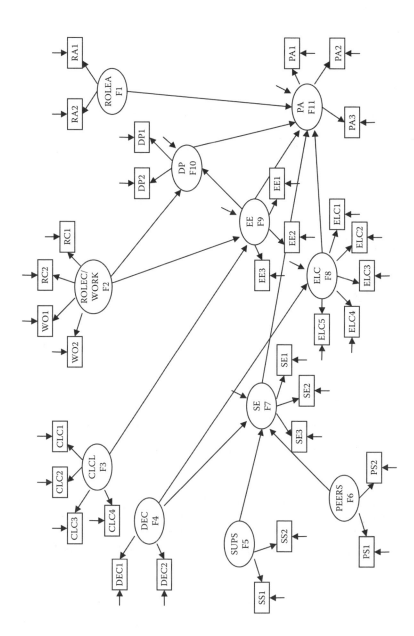

Figure 9.4. Modified hypothesized model showing constructs of role conflict and work overload combined as a single factor.

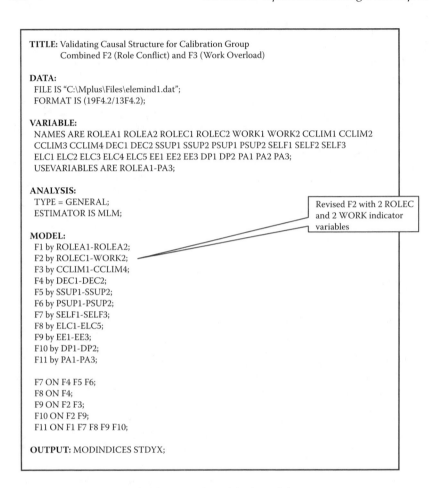

Figure 9.5. M*plus* input file for test of modified model.

Input File 2

The related input file for Figure 9.4 is shown in Figure 9.5. In particular, note that the revised Factor 2 (ROLEC/WORK) is now measured by the four observed variables ROLEC1–WORK2 (RC1–WO2), and specifications regarding all remaining factors have been renumbered accordingly.

Output Files 2–4

Goodness-of-fit statistics for this modified model were as follows: $\chi^2_{(436)}$ = 955.864, CFI= 0.943, RMSEA = 0.045, and SRMR = 0.060. As indicated by the CFI, RMSEA, and SRMR values, the model fit the calibration data relatively well. Nonetheless, a review of the MIs suggested that the inclusion of two additional parameters to the model, both of which were substantively reasonable, would lead to a better fitting model. The two MIs of interest here related to (a) the structural path of F8 on F2 (External Locus of Control on Role Conflict/Work Overload) and (b) a covariance between residuals associated with the observed variables EE1 and EE2, both of which are highlighted and flagged in the listing of all MI values in Table 9.2.

Consistent with my previous caveats concerning model modification based on MIs, each parameter was separately incorporated into the model and the model subsequently tested; results for each led to a (corrected) statistically significant difference from its preceding model (ΔMLM $\chi^2_{[1]} =$ 35.396 and ΔMLM $\chi^2_{[1]} = 29.738$, respectively). Goodness-of-fit statistics for the second of these two modified models resulted in the following: $\chi^2_{(434)} =$ 866.557, CFI= 0.953, RMSEA = 0.041, and SRMR = 0.048.

Over and above the now well-fitting model for the calibration group of elementary teachers, a review of the parameter estimates revealed five to be statistically nonsignificant. All represented structural paths in the model as follows: F7 on F6 (Self-Esteem regressed on Peer Support), F8 on F4 (External Locus of Control regressed on Decision Making), F10 on F2 (Depersonalization regressed on Role Conflict/Work Overload), F11 on F1 (Personal Accomplishment regressed on Role Ambiguity), and F11 on F8 (Personal Accomplishment regressed on External Locus of Control). Parameter estimates for all structural paths are reported in Table 9.3, with those that are nonsignificant highlighted and flagged.

In the interest of scientific parsimony, these nonsignificant paths were subsequently deleted, and the resulting model considered the established baseline model for the calibration group. As such, it serves as the model to be tested for its invariance across calibration and validation groups. However, given deletion of the paths leading from F11 to F1 and from F6 to F7, together with the fact that there are no specified relations between either F1 or F6 and any of the remaining factors, F1 and F6, most appropriately, should be deleted from the model, and the numbering of the remaining nine factors reassigned. A schematic representation of this reoriented model is shown in Figure 9.6. The dashed single-headed arrow linking the new F1 (RoleC/Work) and F6 (ELC) as well as the dashed curved arrow between EE1 and EE2 represent the newly added parameters in the model.[2]

Given a total restructuring of the baseline model to be used in testing for invariance across calibration and validation groups, it is important that we first review the related input file, which is presented in Figure 9.7. In addition to the change in factor number assignment, there are two essential modifications that must be made to the matching input file. First, with the removal of the constructs Role Ambiguity (ROLEA) and Peer Support (PSUP) from the model, their indicator variables (*ROLEA1-ROLEA2* and

Table 9.2 M*plus* Output: Selected Modification Indices

Model Modification Indices

		Estimate	Standard Error (*SE*)	Estimate/*SE*	Two-Tailed *p*-Value
BY Statements					
F1	BY ROLEC1	15.250	0.559	0.383	0.343
F1	BY WORK1	14.017	−0.540	−0.370	−0.323
F1	BY DEC2	18.240	0.611	0.419	0.337
F1	BYEE3	19.211	0.293	0.201	0.148
F2	BY DEC2	40.933	0.668	0.504	0.405
F2	BYPSUP1	10.168	−0.206	−0.155	−0.160
F2	BY EE3	15.029	0.270	0.204	0.150
F3	BY EE3	12.264	−0.433	−0.149	−0.110
F3	BY DP1	26.726	−0.663	−0.228	−0.203
F4	BY ROLEC1	16.289	−0.332	−0.257	−0.230
F4	BY EE3	10.704	−0.169	−0.131	−0.096
F5	BY ROLEC1	18.900	−0.208	−0.227	−0.204
F5	BY DEC2	37.535	1.043	1.139	0.917
F7	BY DEC2	10.171	−0.465	−0.169	−0.136
F7	BY ELC5	13.063	−0.229	−0.083	−0.122
F7	BY EE3	17.816	−0.428	−0.155	−0.114
F8	BY ROLEC1	10.655	0.343	0.144	0.129
F8	BY EE1	12.348	−0.291	−0.123	−0.090
F8	BY EE3	11.730	0.299	0.126	0.093
F8	BY PA3	10.642	−0.256	−0.108	−0.126
F9	BY ROLEC1	26.907	−0.246	−0.297	−0.266
F9	BY WORK1	24.875	0.232	0.280	0.245
F9	BY CCLIM1	11.115	−0.067	−0.081	−0.145
F9	BY PA2	11.408	0.102	0.123	0.142
F10	BY SELF3	13.268	−0.067	−0.063	−0.112
F10	BY EE3	11.751	0.200	0.188	0.138
F11	BY EE1	21.722	0.269	0.188	0.139
F11	BY EE3	35.006	−0.356	−0.249	−0.184
ON/BY Statements					
F2	ON F8 /				
F8	BY F2	24.268	0.383	0.214	0.214
F2	ON F10 /				
F10	BY F2	14.034	−0.172	−0.214	−0.214
F3	ON F9 /				
F9	BY F3	22.394	0.590	2.073	2.073

Table 9.2 M*plus* Output: Selected Modification Indices (*continued*)

			Estimate	Standard Error (*SE*)	Estimate/*SE*	Two-Tailed *p*-Value
				Model Modification Indices		
F3	ON F10	/				
F10	BY F3		23.622	−0.129	−0.353	−0.353
F4	ON F9	/				
F9	BY F4		20.048	−0.089	−0.140	−0.140
F5	ON F8	/				
F8	BY F5		25.640	0.409	0.158	0.158
F5	ON F9	/				
F9	BY F5		13.162	0.113	0.125	0.125
F7	ON F8	/				
F8	BY F7		12.349	−0.159	−0.185	−0.185
F7	ON F9	/				
F9	BY F7		18.561	−0.078	−0.259	−0.259
F7	ON F10	/				
F10	BY F7		22.155	−0.099	−0.256	−0.256
F7	ON F11	/				
F11	BY F7		14.733	0.242	0.467	0.467
F8	ON F1	/				
F1	BY F8		27.248	0.303	0.492	0.492
F8	ON F2	/				
→F2	**BY F8**		**46.778**	**0.281**	**0.503**	**0.503**
F8	ON F5	/				
F5	BY F8		36.124	0.384	0.994	0.994
F8	ON F7	/				
F7	BY F8		25.588	−0.306	−0.263	−0.263
F8	ON F9	/				
F9	BY F8		12.077	0.063	0.180	0.180
F8	ON F11	/				
F11	BY F8		19.307	−0.256	−0.426	−0.426
F9	ON F7	/				
F7	BY F9		21.825	−0.679	−0.204	−0.204
F9	ON F10	/				
F10	BY F9		31.395	−2.136	−1.657	−1.657
F10	ON F3	/				
F3	BY F10		31.394	−0.796	−0.292	−0.292
F10	ON F7	/				
F7	BY F10		13.471	−0.454	−0.176	−0.176
F10	ON F11	/				
F11	BY F10		18.020	−1.293	−0.967	−0.967

Table 9.2 M*plus* Output: Selected Modification Indices (*continued*)

		Estimate	Standard Error (*SE*)	Estimate/*SE*	Two-Tailed *p*-Value
WITH Statements					
SSUP2	WITH DEC1	17.974	−0.099	−0.099	−0.335
SSUP2	WITH DEC2	26.130	0.137	0.137	0.466
PSUP2	WITH SSUP1	13.980	−0.062	−0.062	−0.273
PSUP2	WITH SSUP2	10.569	0.052	0.052	0.325
ELC2	WITH ELC1	18.927	0.048	0.048	0.225
EE1	WITH WORK1	19.457	0.114	0.114	0.245
EE1	WITH WORK2	10.448	0.098	0.098	0.170
→**EE2**	**WITH EE1**	**42.403**	**0.297**	**0.297**	**0.876**
F8	WITH F2	24.268	0.054	0.191	0.191
F8	WITH F5	25.640	0.058	0.141	0.141
F8	WITH F7	12.349	−0.022	−0.194	−0.194
F9	WITH F3	22.396	0.483	1.553	1.553
F9	WITH F4	20.048	−0.073	−0.105	−0.105
F9	WITH F5	13.162	0.092	0.094	0.094
F9	WITH F7	16.525	−0.062	−0.221	−0.221
F10	WITH F2	11.358	−0.092	−0.171	−0.171
F10	WITH F3	28.467	−0.073	−0.297	−0.297
F10	WITH F9	31.394	−1.091	−1.687	−1.687

Model Modification Indices

PSUP1-PSUP2, respectively) will no longer be used in subsequent analyses; thus, they need to be deleted from the USEVARIABLES subcommand. Second, these four variables, likewise, will not be included in the MODEL command.

Goodness-of fit statistics for this revised baseline model were $\chi^2_{(333)}$ = 726.511, CFI = 0.950, RMSEA = 0.044, and SRMR = 0.051. However, a review of the estimated parameters revealed an estimated residual covariance between F6 and F9,[3] which, of course, was not specified. In seeking the reason for this rather strange occurrence, I was advised that M*plus* estimates the residual covariance between final dependent variables by default (M*plus* Product Support, December 10, 2010). Of course, this unwanted parameter can be fixed to zero, and, thus, a second estimation of the baseline model was conducted with F6 with F9 constrained to 0.0. Results pertinent to this latter model were as follows: $\chi^2_{(334)}$ = 728.213, CFI = 0.950, RMSEA = 0.044, and SRMR = 0.051. Although all parameters were statistically significant, only results for the standardized structural regression paths and factor correlations are presented in Table 9.4.

Table 9.3 M*plus* Output: Statistically Nonsignificant Parameters

		Model Results		
	Estimate	Standard Error (*SE*)	Estimate/*SE*	Two-Tailed *p*-Value
F7 ON				
F4	1.072	0.337	3.181	0.001
F5	−0.588	0.203	−2.900	0.004
→F6	**−0.104**	**0.083**	**−1.258**	**0.208**
F8 ON				
→F4	**−0.047**	**0.032**	**−1.473**	**0.141**
F2	0.276	0.036	7.708	0.000
F9 ON				
F2	0.838	0.077	10.895	0.000
F3	−0.685	0.136	−5.034	0.000
F10 ON				
→F2	**0.081**	**0.080**	**1.012**	**0.311**
F9	0.525	0.052	10.046	0.000
F11 ON				
→F1	**−0.107**	**0.070**	**−1.532**	**0.126**
F7	0.299	0.101	2.962	0.003
→F8	**−0.058**	**0.082**	**−0.703**	**0.482**
F9	−0.115	0.043	−2.661	0.008
F10	−0.221	0.059	−3.773	0.000

Testing Multigroup Invariance

Having established a well-fitting and parsimonious baseline model for the calibration group, we are now ready to move on in testing for the equivalence of this causal structure across the validation group of elementary teachers. Consistent with the tests for invariance addressed in Chapters 7 and 8, our first step is to test the multigroup configural model in which no parameter constraints are specified.

Input File 1

In reviewing the input file for this configural model in Figure 9.8, you will note that, with one particular exception, the overall MODEL command reflects specification pertinent to the final baseline model for the calibration group as noted in Figure 9.7. The one exception refers to the

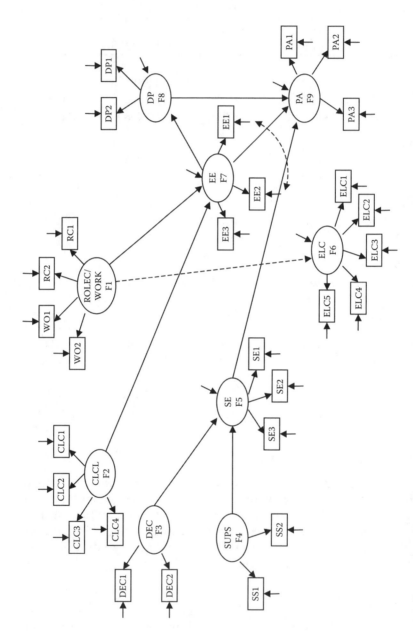

Figure 9.6. Restructured baseline model to be used in testing for invariance across calibration and validation groups.

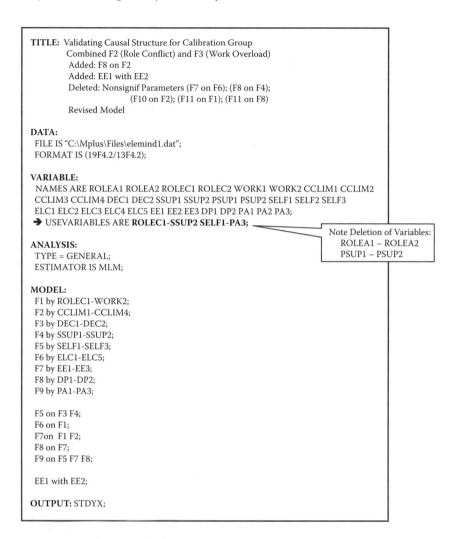

TITLE: Validating Causal Structure for Calibration Group
Combined F2 (Role Conflict) and F3 (Work Overload)
Added: F8 on F2
Added: EE1 with EE2
Deleted: Nonsignif Parameters (F7 on F6); (F8 on F4);
(F10 on F2); (F11 on F1); (F11 on F8)
Revised Model

DATA:
FILE IS "C:\Mplus\Files\elemind1.dat";
FORMAT IS (19F4.2/13F4.2);

VARIABLE:
NAMES ARE ROLEA1 ROLEA2 ROLEC1 ROLEC2 WORK1 WORK2 CCLIM1 CCLIM2
CCLIM3 CCLIM4 DEC1 DEC2 SSUP1 SSUP2 PSUP1 PSUP2 SELF1 SELF2 SELF3
ELC1 ELC2 ELC3 ELC4 ELC5 EE1 EE2 EE3 DP1 DP2 PA1 PA2 PA3;
➔ USEVARIABLES ARE **ROLEC1-SSUP2 SELF1-PA3;**

Note Deletion of Variables:
ROLEA1 – ROLEA2
PSUP1 – PSUP2

ANALYSIS:
TYPE = GENERAL;
ESTIMATOR IS MLM;

MODEL:
F1 by ROLEC1-WORK2;
F2 by CCLIM1-CCLIM4;
F3 by DEC1-DEC2;
F4 by SSUP1-SSUP2;
F5 by SELF1-SELF3;
F6 by ELC1-ELC5;
F7 by EE1-EE3;
F8 by DP1-DP2;
F9 by PA1-PA3;

F5 on F3 F4;
F6 on F1;
F7on F1 F2;
F8 on F7;
F9 on F5 F7 F8;

EE1 with EE2;

OUTPUT: STDYX;

Figure 9.7. M*plus* input file for restructured baseline model.

specification of [F1-F11@0], which indicates that the factor means are constrained to a value of zero.

Again, consistent with multigroup model specifications in Chapters
7 and 8, the input file for the configural model also includes two model-
specific commands; in the present case, one for the calibration group and
one for the validation group. Recall that these model-specific command
sections serve two purposes: (a) to neutralize M*plus*-invoked default
parameter estimation and/or equivalence across groups, and (b) to
specify parameter estimation pertinent to only certain groups (i.e., not

Table 9.4 M*plus* Output: Standardized Parameter Estimates for Structural
Regression Paths, Factor Correlations, and Residual Covariance

| | | STDYX Standardization | | |
	Estimate	Standard Error (*SE*)	Estimate/*SE*	Two-Tailed *p*-Value
F5 ON				
F3	2.076	0.501	4.147	0.000
F4	−1.725	0.509	−3.391	0.001
F6 ON				
F1	0.563	0.036	15.718	0.000
F7 ON				
F1	0.591	0.034	17.202	0.000
F2	−0.210	0.038	−5.473	0.000
F8 ON				
F7	0.668	0.030	22.533	0.000
F9 ON				
F5	0.184	0.043	4.278	0.000
F7	−0.239	0.064	−3.722	0.000
F8	−0.298	0.073	−4.070	0.000
F9 WITH				
F6	0.000	0.000	999.000	999.000
F2 WITH				
F1	−0.412	0.046	−8.969	0.000
F3 WITH				
F1	−0.693	0.033	−20.797	0.000
F2	0.368	0.047	7.896	0.000
F4 WITH				
F1	−0.577	0.032	−18.171	0.000
F2	0.287	0.048	5.963	0.000
F3	0.974	0.010	95.916	0.000
EE1 WITH				
EE2	0.459	0.047	9.803	0.000

common to all groups). Because model specification for the calibration
group is consistent with that shown under the overall MODEL command
(i.e., there are no parameter specifications that are relevant only to the
calibration group), this section remains void of specification information.

In contrast, the model-specific section of the input file pertinent to the validation group specifies all factor loadings and observed variable intercepts that would automatically be constrained equal by default. As mentioned above, their specification here negates their defaulted equivalence across groups. Finally, although noted in Chapters 7 and 8, I once again draw your attention to the importance of *not* including the reference variable loading (i.e., the factor loading constrained to 1.0 for purposes of model identification and scaling) in the model-specific section, because otherwise this parameter will be excluded from the model, thereby resulting in an error message alerting you that the model is underidentified.

Output File 1

Of import for the configural model is the extent to which it fits the data for both the calibration and validation groups simultaneously; these goodness-of-fit results are reported in Table 9.5. As you will observe from the separately reported χ^2 values in this multigroup analysis, although model fit for the calibration group ($\chi^2 = 729.143$) was slightly better than it was for the validation group ($\chi^2 = 768.829$), overall model fit to their combined data yielded goodness-of-fit statistics that were negligibly different from those reported earlier for this same (baseline) model derived from the single-group analysis for the calibration group. More specifically, whereas the CFI, RMSEA, and SRMR values were 0.950, 0.044, and 0.051 respectively, when this model was tested separately for the calibration group, they remained minimally different (by only the third decimal place) when tested for both groups simultaneously.

Provided with evidence of a well-fitting model for the combined calibration and validation groups, we can now proceed with testing for the equivalence of the factor loadings, observed variable intercepts, and structural regression paths across the two groups. The input file addressing these equality constraints is presented in Figure 9.9.

Input File 2

There are several important aspects of this input file to be noted. First, given that precisely the same model is specified across groups, there are no model-specific components included in this file. Second, given that the observed variable intercepts are constrained equal by default, these parameters are not specified. Third, there are nine structural paths in the model under test, each of which will be tested for its equivalence across groups and, as such, has been assigned a specific number within parentheses. Fourth, the error covariance between EE1 and EE2 is not included in the tests for group invariance. Fifth, note that the factor means remain fixed to a value of zero and, thus, are not estimated; likewise for the default covariance between F6 and F9. Finally, I have included the specification of

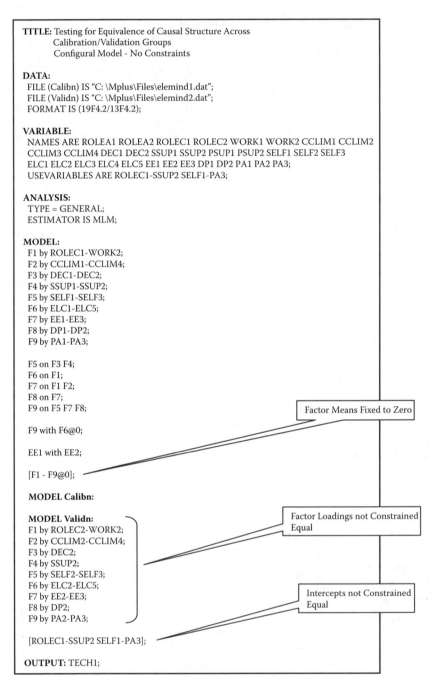

TITLE: Testing for Equivalence of Causal Structure Across
            Calibration/Validation Groups
            Configural Model - No Constraints

DATA:
  FILE (Calibn) IS "C: \Mplus\Files\elemind1.dat";
  FILE (Validn) IS "C: \Mplus\Files\elemind2.dat";
  FORMAT IS (19F4.2/13F4.2);

VARIABLE:
  NAMES ARE ROLEA1 ROLEA2 ROLEC1 ROLEC2 WORK1 WORK2 CCLIM1 CCLIM2
  CCLIM3 CCLIM4 DEC1 DEC2 SSUP1 SSUP2 PSUP1 PSUP2 SELF1 SELF2 SELF3
  ELC1 ELC2 ELC3 ELC4 ELC5 EE1 EE2 EE3 DP1 DP2 PA1 PA2 PA3;
  USEVARIABLES ARE ROLEC1-SSUP2 SELF1-PA3;

ANALYSIS:
  TYPE = GENERAL;
  ESTIMATOR IS MLM;

MODEL:
  F1 by ROLEC1-WORK2;
  F2 by CCLIM1-CCLIM4;
  F3 by DEC1-DEC2;
  F4 by SSUP1-SSUP2;
  F5 by SELF1-SELF3;
  F6 by ELC1-ELC5;
  F7 by EE1-EE3;
  F8 by DP1-DP2;
  F9 by PA1-PA3;

  F5 on F3 F4;
  F6 on F1;
  F7 on F1 F2;
  F8 on F7;
  F9 on F5 F7 F8;

  F9 with F6@0;

  EE1 with EE2;

  [F1 - F9@0];   Factor Means Fixed to Zero

  MODEL Calibn:

  MODEL Validn: Factor Loadings not Constrained
  F1 by ROLEC2-WORK2;   Equal
  F2 by CCLIM2-CCLIM4;
  F3 by DEC2;
  F4 by SSUP2;
  F5 by SELF2-SELF3;
  F6 by ELC2-ELC5;
  F7 by EE2-EE3;
  F8 by DP2;   Intercepts not Constrained
  F9 by PA2-PA3;   Equal

  [ROLEC1-SSUP2 SELF1-PA3];

  OUTPUT: TECH1;

Figure 9.8. M*plus* input file for test of configural model.

Table 9.5 M*plus* Output:
Selected Goodness-of-Fit Statistics for Configural Model

Tests of Model Fit	
Chi-Square Test of Model Fit	
Value	1497.972*
Degrees of freedom	668
p-value	0.0000
Scaling Correction Factor for MLM	1.083
Chi-Square Contributions From Each Group	
CALIBN	729.143
VALIDN	768.829
CFI/TLI	
CFI	0.948
TLI	0.941
Root Mean Square Error of Approximation (RMSEA)	
Estimate	0.045
Standardized Root Mean Square Residual (SRMR)	
Value	0.056

TECH1 in the OUTPUT command as this option is invaluable in helping you to determine if, in fact, the model has been specified as per your intent. It is particularly helpful in situations such as we have here in testing for the invariance of a full SEM model.

Output File 2

Prior to reviewing the output results, it is perhaps instructive to first examine the difference in degrees of freedom (*df*) between this model in which the factor loadings, intercepts, and structural regression paths were constrained equal (*df* = 724) and the configural model in which these parameters were freely estimated (*df* = 668). Indeed, this difference of 56 is accounted for by the equating of 19 factor loadings, 28 intercepts, and 9 structural regression paths.

That these parameters were constrained equal can also be confirmed by a review of the TECH1 output. For example, the numbering of parameters in the Nu matrix (representing the observed variable intercepts) ranged from 1 through 28 inclusively, in the Lambda matrix (representing the factor loadings) from 29 through 47 inclusively, and in the Beta matrix (representing the structural regression paths) from 77 through 85 inclusively. Given that these parameters are estimated for the first group (the

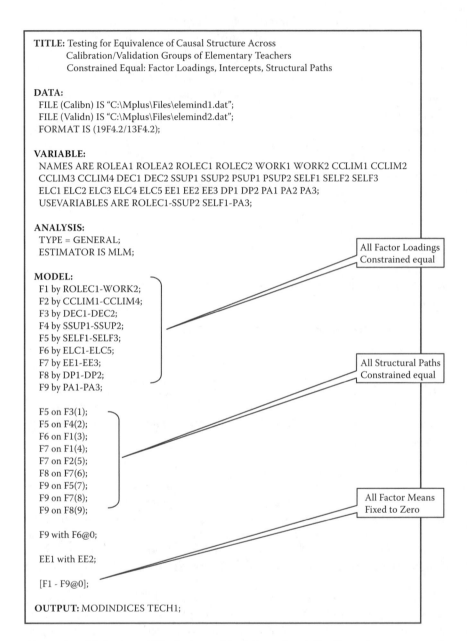

TITLE: Testing for Equivalence of Causal Structure Across
        Calibration/Validation Groups of Elementary Teachers
        Constrained Equal: Factor Loadings, Intercepts, Structural Paths

DATA:
  FILE (Calibn) IS "C:\Mplus\Files\elemind1.dat";
  FILE (Validn) IS "C:\Mplus\Files\elemind2.dat";
  FORMAT IS (19F4.2/13F4.2);

VARIABLE:
  NAMES ARE ROLEA1 ROLEA2 ROLEC1 ROLEC2 WORK1 WORK2 CCLIM1 CCLIM2
  CCLIM3 CCLIM4 DEC1 DEC2 SSUP1 SSUP2 PSUP1 PSUP2 SELF1 SELF2 SELF3
  ELC1 ELC2 ELC3 ELC4 ELC5 EE1 EE2 EE3 DP1 DP2 PA1 PA2 PA3;
  USEVARIABLES ARE ROLEC1-SSUP2 SELF1-PA3;

ANALYSIS:
  TYPE = GENERAL;
  ESTIMATOR IS MLM;

> All Factor Loadings
> Constrained equal

MODEL:
  F1 by ROLEC1-WORK2;
  F2 by CCLIM1-CCLIM4;
  F3 by DEC1-DEC2;
  F4 by SSUP1-SSUP2;
  F5 by SELF1-SELF3;
  F6 by ELC1-ELC5;
  F7 by EE1-EE3;
  F8 by DP1-DP2;
  F9 by PA1-PA3;

> All Structural Paths
> Constrained equal

  F5 on F3(1);
  F5 on F4(2);
  F6 on F1(3);
  F7 on F1(4);
  F7 on F2(5);
  F8 on F7(6);
  F9 on F5(7);
  F9 on F7(8);
  F9 on F8(9);

> All Factor Means
> Fixed to Zero

  F9 with F6@0;

  EE1 with EE2;

  [F1 - F9@0];

OUTPUT: MODINDICES TECH1;

Figure 9.9. M*plus* input file for test of invariant factor loadings, intercepts, and structural regression paths.

Table 9.6 M*plus* Output:
Selected Goodness-of-Fit Statistics for Equality Constraints Model

Tests of Model Fit	
Chi-Square Test of Model Fit	
Value	1554.974*
Degrees of freedom	724
p-value	0.0000
Scaling Correction Factor for MLM	1.082
Chi-Square Contributions From Each Group	
CALIBN	758.470
VALIDN	796.504
CFI/TLI	
CFI	0.948
TLI	0.946
Root Mean Square Error of Approximation (RMSEA)	
Estimate	0.044
Standardized Root Mean Square Residual (SRMR)	
Value	0.058

calibration group in the present case), albeit constrained equal for the second group, these numbers will remain the same under the TECH1 results for the validation group. That the numbers differ across the same matrices represents a clear indication that the model specification is incorrect.

A review of the results related to this equality constraints model revealed both an exceptionally good fit to the data and no suggestion of potential parameter misspecification as might be indicated by the MIs. Model goodness-of-fit statistics are reported in Table 9.6.

That the CFI value remained unchanged from the one reported for the configural model speaks well for cross-group equality of the factor loadings, intercepts, and structural regression paths specified in Model 9.6. Furthermore, given that both the RMSEA and SRMR values also remain virtually unchanged (i.e., only values at the third decimal place changed), we can conclude that these parameters are operating equivalently across calibration and validation groups. Verification of these conclusions, of course, can be evidenced from computation of the corrected MLM chi-square difference test, which is found to be statistically nonsignificant ($\Delta\chi^2_{[56]} = 56.172$). Indeed, based on Meredith's (1993) categorization of weak, strong, and strict invariance, these results would indicate clear evidence of strong measurement and structural invariance.

Notes

1. Heywood cases represent out-of-range estimated values such as negative error (i.e., residual) variances and correlations greater than 1.00.

2. Deletion of these parameters could also be accomplished in two alternative ways: (a) by fixing each of the nonsignificant paths to zero, or (b) by simply not estimating the nonsignificant paths. Both approaches, however, result in a less parsimonious model than the one shown in Figure 9.6 and tested here. In addition, be aware that estimation of the model via the (b) approach leads to a difference of four degrees of freedom, rather than five, due to the M*plus* default noted here with the reoriented model.

3. We know this parameter represents a residual covariance and not a factor variance as only the covariances of independent continuous factors in the model are estimated by default.

section IV

Other Important Topics

chapter 10

Testing Evidence of Construct Validity
The Multitrait–Multimethod Model

The application illustrated in this chapter uses confirmatory factor analysis (CFA) procedures to test hypotheses bearing on construct validity. Specifically, hypotheses are tested within the framework of a multitrait–multimethod (MTMM) design by which multiple traits are measured by multiple methods. Following from the seminal work of Campbell and Fiske (1959), construct validity research typically focuses on the extent to which data exhibit evidence of (a) convergent validity, the extent to which different assessment methods concur in their measurement of the same trait (i.e., construct; ideally, these values should be moderately high); (b) discriminant validity, the extent to which independent assessment methods diverge in their measurement of different traits (ideally, these values should demonstrate minimal convergence); and (c) method effects, an extension of the discriminant validity issue. Method effects represent bias that can derive from use of the same method in the assessment of different traits; correlations among these traits are typically higher than those measured by different methods.

In the time since its inception, the original MTMM design (Campbell & Fiske, 1959) has been the target of much criticism as methodologists uncovered a growing number of limitations in its basic analytic strategy (see, e.g., Marsh, 1988, 1989; Schmitt & Stults, 1986). Although several alternative MTMM approaches have been proposed in the interim, the analysis of MTMM data within the framework of covariance structure modeling has gained the most prominence and has been the most widely applied methodological strategy (Eid et al., 2008). Within this analytic context, some argue for the superiority of the correlated uniquenesses (CU) model (Kenny, 1976, 1979; Kenny & Kashy, 1992; Marsh, 1989), whereas others support the general CFA (Conway, Scullen, Lievens, & Lance, 2004; Lance, Noble, & Scullen, 2002) or composite direct product models (Browne, 1984b). Nonetheless, a review of the applied MTMM literature reveals that the general CFA model[1] has been, and continues to be, the method of choice (Kenny & Kashy, 1992; Marsh & Grayson, 1995). The popularity of this approach likely derives from Widaman's (1985) seminal paper in which he proposed a taxonomy of nested model comparisons. (For diverse comparisons of the correlated uniquenesses, composite direct product, and general CFA models, readers are referred to Bagozzi, 1993; Bagozzi & Yi, 1990; Byrne & Goffin, 1993; Coenders & Saris, 2000; Hernández & González-Romá, 2002; Lance et al., 2002; Marsh & Bailey, 1991; Marsh, Byrne, & Craven, 1992; Marsh & Grayson, 1995; Tomás, Hontangas, & Oliver, 2000; Wothke, 1996). More recent MTMM research, however, has tested various aspects of the correlated traits–correlated methods minus one (CT–C[M–1]) model introduced by Eid (2000; see also Geiser, Eid, & Nussbeck, 2008; Maydeu-Olivares & Coffman, 2006; Pohl & Steyer, 2010): these include examination of specified correlated residuals (Cole, Ciesla, & Steiger, 2007; Saris & Aalberts, 2003), and applications to longitudinal (Courvoisier, Nussbeck, Eid, Geiser, & Cole, 2008; Grimm, Pianta, & Konold, 2009; LaGrange & Cole, 2008) and multilevel (Hox & Kleiboer, 2007) data. (For comparisons of diverse variants of these models, readers are referred to Eid et al., 2008; Pohl & Steyer, 2010; Saris & Aalberts, 2003.)

The present application is taken from a study by Byrne and Bazana (1996), which was based on the general CFA approach to MTMM analysis and based on the early work of Widaman (1985). The primary intent of the original study was to test for evidence of convergent validity, discriminant validity, and method effects related to four facets of perceived competence (social, academic, English, and mathematics) as measured by self-, teacher, parent, and peer ratings for early and late preadolescents and for adolescents in grades 3, 7, and 11, respectively. For our purposes here, however, we focus only on data for late preadolescents (grade 7; $n = 193$). (For further elaboration of the sample, instrumentation, and analytic strategy, see Byrne & Bazana, 1996.) In addition, however, given that the CU model has become a topic of considerable interest and debate over the past few years, I consider it worthwhile to include this model also in the present chapter. However, given that the CU model represents a special case of, rather than a nested model within, the general CFA framework, I delay discussion and application of this model until later in the chapter.

Rephrased within the context of an MTMM design, the model of interest in this chapter is composed of four traits (social competence, academic competence, English competence, and math competence) and four methods (self-ratings, teacher ratings, parent ratings, and peer ratings). A schematic portrayal of this model is presented in Figure 10.1.

The General CFA Approach to MTMM Analyses

In testing for evidence of construct validity within the framework of the general CFA model, it has become customary to follow guidelines set forth by Widaman (1985). As such, the hypothesized MTMM model is

Figure 10.1. Hypothesized correlated traits/correlated methods (CTCM) MTMM model.

compared with a nested series of more restrictive models in which specific parameters are either eliminated or constrained equal to zero or 1.0. The difference in χ^2 ($\Delta\chi^2$) between these competing models provides the yardstick by which to judge evidence of convergent and discriminant validity. Although these evaluative comparisons are made solely at the matrix level, the CFA format allows for an assessment of construct validity at the individual parameter level. A review of the literature bearing on the CFA approach to MTMM analyses indicates that assessment is typically formulated at both the matrix and the individual parameter levels; we examine both in the present application.

The Hypothesized Model

The MTMM model portrayed in Figure 10.1 represents the hypothesized model and serves as the baseline against which all other alternatively nested models are compared in the process of assessing evidence of construct and discriminant validity. Clearly, this CFA model represents a much more complex structure than any of the CFA models examined thus far in this book. This complexity arises primarily from the loading of each observed variable onto *both* a trait and a method factor. In addition, the model postulates that, although the traits are correlated among themselves, as are the methods, any correlations between traits and methods are assumed to be zero.[2]

Testing for evidence of convergent and discriminant validity involves comparisons between the hypothesized model (Model 1) and three alternative MTMM models. We turn now to a description of these four nested models; they represent those most commonly included in CFA MTMM analyses.

Model 1: Correlated Traits and Correlated Methods (CTCM)

The first model to be tested (Model 1) represents the hypothesized model shown in Figure 10.1 and serves as the baseline against which the three alternative general CFA models are compared. As noted earlier, because its specification includes both trait and method factors, and allows for correlations among traits and among methods, this model is typically the least restrictive.

Before working through these analyses, however, I need first to clarify both the names of the variables and one aspect of the model structure. First, the observed variables occupying the first small rectangle in each set of four rectangles shown in the center of the figure (*SCSelf, SCTch, SCPar, SCPeer*) represent general Social Competence (SC) scores as derived from self-, teacher, parent, and peer ratings. Likewise, for each of the remaining traits (Academic SC, English SC, and Math SC) there are ratings by self, teacher, parents, and peers. Second, note that although the traits and methods are correlated among themselves, there are no double-headed curved arrows indicating correlations among traits and methods.

Mplus Input File Specifications
and Output File Results

Let's move on now to a review of the input file for Model 1, which is shown in Figure 10.2.

Input File 1

At least four aspects of this first input file are of particular import. First, although I have referred to this model as Model 1 in the group of four general CFA models to be tested, I caution you not to include the term *Model 1* in the TITLE command as it triggers the program to think you are working with a multigroup model. As a result, you will receive the following error message:

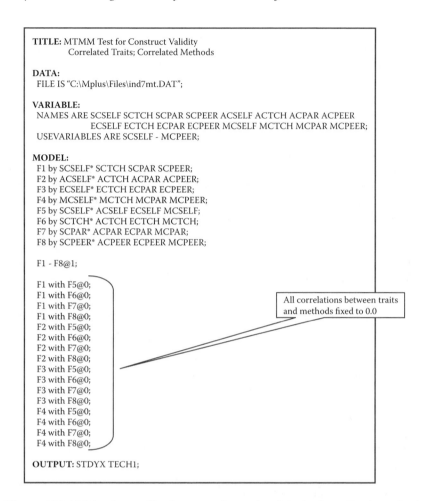

TITLE: MTMM Test for Construct Validity
          Correlated Traits; Correlated Methods

DATA:
  FILE IS "C:\Mplus\Files\ind7mt.DAT";

VARIABLE:
  NAMES ARE SCSELF SCTCH SCPAR SCPEER ACSELF ACTCH ACPAR ACPEER
            ECSELF ECTCH ECPAR ECPEER MCSELF MCTCH MCPAR MCPEER;
  USEVARIABLES ARE SCSELF - MCPEER;

MODEL:
  F1 by SCSELF* SCTCH SCPAR SCPEER;
  F2 by ACSELF* ACTCH ACPAR ACPEER;
  F3 by ECSELF* ECTCH ECPAR ECPEER;
  F4 by MCSELF* MCTCH MCPAR MCPEER;
  F5 by SCSELF* ACSELF ECSELF MCSELF;
  F6 by SCTCH* ACTCH ECTCH MCTCH;
  F7 by SCPAR* ACPAR ECPAR MCPAR;
  F8 by SCPEER* ACPEER ECPEER MCPEER;

  F1 - F8@1;

  F1 with F5@0;
  F1 with F6@0;
  F1 with F7@0;
  F1 with F8@0;
  F2 with F5@0;
  F2 with F6@0;
  F2 with F7@0;
  F2 with F8@0;
  F3 with F5@0;
  F3 with F6@0;
  F3 with F7@0;
  F3 with F8@0;
  F4 with F5@0;
  F4 with F6@0;
  F4 with F7@0;
  F4 with F8@0;

  All correlations between traits
  and methods fixed to 0.0

OUTPUT: STDYX TECH1;

Figure 10.2. M*plus* input file for test of correlated traits/correlated methods (CTCM) MTMM model.

*** ERROR in MODEL command
Unknown group name 1 specified in group-specific MODEL command.

Second, note that the first variable in each congeneric set of indicator variables (e.g., SCSELF) is accompanied by an asterisk, thereby indicating that it is to be freely estimated rather than fixed to a value of 1.0 by default. Alternatively, as in Chapter 8, model identification is accomplished by fixing each of the factor variances to 1.0 (F1 – F8@1).

Third, as noted earlier and consistent with Figure 10.1, all correlations among trait and method factors are fixed to zero. Finally, given the complexity of this hypothesized model, I strongly recommend that you include the TECH1 option in the OUTPUT command as it is a boon in helping you to determine if you have specified the model correctly.

Output File 1

In reviewing results related to this initial test of the CTCM model, we find that although model estimation terminated normally, the output included the two warning messages shown in Figure 10.3. Both warnings address the issue of nonpositive matrices and represent a common occurrence in analysis of MTMM models based on the general CFA model. Indeed, so pervasive is this problem that the estimation of proper solutions may be regarded as a rare find (see, e.g., Kenny & Kashy, 1992; Marsh, 1989). Although these results can be triggered by a number of factors, one likely cause in the case of MTMM models is overparameterization of the model (Wothke, 1993), with this condition likely occurring as a function of the complexity of model specification. It is the very commonality of these improper solutions that has motivated researchers, such as those noted earlier, to seek alternative approaches to the analysis of MTMM data.

Typically, when these improper solutions occur, the offending parameter represents a negative variance associated either with a residual or with a factor, which is consistent with the messages reported in Figure 10.3. Indeed, a review of the parameter estimates revealed a negative variance associated with the residual *ACSELF* as reported in Table 10.1.

THE MODEL ESTIMATION TERMINATED NORMALLY

WARNING: THE RESIDUAL COVARIANCE MATRIX (THETA) IS NOT POSITIVE DEFINITE. THIS COULD INDICATE A NEGATIVE VARIANCE/RESIDUAL VARIANCE FOR AN OBSERVED VARIABLE, A CORRELATION GREATER OR EQUAL TO ONE BETWEEN TWO OBSERVED VARIABLES, OR A LINEAR DEPENDENCY AMONG MORE THAN TWO OBSERVED VARIABLES.
CHECK THE RESULTS SECTION FOR MORE INFORMATION.
PROBLEM INVOLVING VARIABLE ACSELF.

WARNING: THE LATENT VARIABLE COVARIANCE MATRIX (PSI) IS NOT POSITIVE DEFINITE. THIS COULD INDICATE A NEGATIVE VARIANCE/RESIDUAL VARIANCE FOR A LATENT VARIABLE, A CORRELATION GREATER OR EQUAL TO ONE BETWEEN TWO LATENT VARIABLES, OR A LINEAR DEPENDENCY AMONG MORE THAN TWO LATENT VARIABLES.
CHECK THE TECH4 OUTPUT FOR MORE INFORMATION.
PROBLEM INVOLVING VARIABLE F8.

Figure 10.3. M*plus* output file warning message related to test of correlated traits/correlated methods (CTCM) MTMM model.

Table 10.1 M*plus* Output:
Residual Error Variance and *R*-Square Estimates for Model 1
(Correlated Traits/Correlated Methods)

		Model Results		
	Estimate	Standard Error (*SE*)	Estimate/*SE*	Two-Tailed *p*-Value
Residual Variances				
SCSELF	0.275	0.131	2.093	0.036
SCTCH	0.754	0.064	11.751	0.000
SCPAR	0.514	0.080	6.430	0.000
SCPEER	0.733	0.063	11.616	0.000
→**ACSELF**	**−0.380**	**999.000**	**999.000**	**999.000**
ACTCH	0.106	0.059	1.802	0.072
ACPAR	0.339	0.081	4.207	0.000
ACPEER	0.100	0.058	1.733	0.083
ECSELF	0.311	0.237	1.309	0.190
ECTCH	0.331	0.061	5.419	0.000
ECPAR	0.388	0.112	3.469	0.001
ECPEER	0.515	0.061	8.380	0.000
MCSELF	0.336	0.079	4.240	0.000
MCTCH	0.417	0.055	7.641	0.000
MCPAR	0.212	0.058	3.673	0.000
MCPEER	0.429	0.056	7.656	0.000
R-**square**				
SCSELF	0.725	0.131	5.528	0.000
SCTCH	0.246	0.064	3.828	0.000
SCPAR	0.486	0.080	6.082	0.000
SCPEER	0.267	0.063	4.225	0.000
→**ACSELF**	**Undefined 0.13796E+01**			
ACTCH	0.894	0.059	15.163	0.000
ACPAR	0.661	0.081	8.198	0.000
ACPEER	0.900	0.058	15.652	0.000
ECSELF	0.689	0.237	2.902	0.004
ECTCH	0.669	0.061	10.930	0.000
ECPAR	0.612	0.112	5.483	0.000
ECPEER	0.485	0.061	7.883	0.000
MCSELF	0.664	0.079	8.361	0.000
MCTCH	0.583	0.055	10.694	0.000
MCPAR	0.788	0.058	13.684	0.000
MCPEER	0.571	0.056	10.182	0.000

Table 10.2 M*plus* Output:
Selected Goodness-of-Fit Statistics for Model 1
(Correlated Traits/Correlated Methods)

The Model Estimation Terminated Normally: Tests of Model Fit	
Chi-Square Test of Model Fit	
Value	77.164
Degrees of freedom	77
p-value	0.4733
CFI/TLI	
CFI	1.000
TLI	1.000
Root Mean Square Error of Approximation (RMSEA)	
Estimate	0.003
90 percent confidence interval (CI)	0.000 0.041
Probability RMSEA <= .05	0.990
Standardized Root Mean Square Residual (SRMR)	
Value	0.042

One approach to the resolution of this improper outcome is to impose an equality constraint between parameters having similar estimates (Marsh et al., 1992). However, specification of an equality constraint between the residuals of *ACSELF* and *ECSELF* (see the similarity of estimates in Table 10.1) only yielded a different error message that there was no convergence. A second approach to addressing the presence of a negative variance, however, is to simply fix the parameter to a value of zero. Addition of this constraint for the *ACSELF* residual led to a proper solution. Goodness-of-fit statistics for this model are reported in Table 10.2.

As evidenced from these results, the fit between this respecified CTCM model and the data must be considered perfect. Indeed, had additional parameters been added to the model as a result of post hoc analyses, I would have concluded that the results were indicative of an overfitted model. However, because this was not the case, I can only presume that the model fits the data exceptionally well. We turn now to an examination of Model 2, the first of three MTMM models against which the modified Model 1 will be compared.

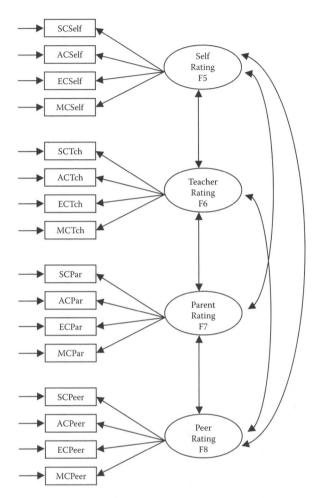

Figure 10.4. Hypothesized no traits/correlated methods (NTCM) MTMM model.

Model 2: No Traits/Correlated Methods (NTCM)

Specification of parameters for this model is portrayed schematically in Figure 10.4 and, within the context of the related M*plus* input file, in Figure 10.5. Of major importance with this model is the total absence of trait factors. It is important to note also that for purposes of comparison across all four general CFA MTMM models, the constraint of *ACSELF* at zero was maintained throughout. Goodness-of-fit for this NTCM model proved to be poor ($\chi^2_{[99]}$ = 335.635; CFI = 0.829; RMSEA = 0.111; SRMR = 0.084).

```
TITLE: MTMM Test for Construct Validity
       No Traits; Correlated Methods

DATA:
    FILE IS "C:\Mplus\Files\ind7mt.DAT";

VARIABLE:
    NAMES ARE SCSELF SCTCH SCPAR SCPEER ACSELF ACTCH ACPAR ACPEER
            ECSELF ECTCH ECPAR ECPEER MCSELF MCTCH MCPAR MCPEER;
    USEVARIABLES ARE SCSELF - MCPEER;

MODEL:
    F5 by SCSELF* ACSELF ECSELF MCSELF;
    F6 by SCTCH* ACTCH ECTCH MCTCH;
    F7 by SCPAR* ACPAR ECPAR MCPAR;
    F8 by SCPEER* ACPEER ECPEER MCPEER;

    F5 - F8@1;

    ACSELF@0;

OUTPUT: STDYX TECH1;
```

Figure 10.5. M*plus* input file for test of no traits/correlated methods (NTCM) MTMM model.

Model 3: Perfectly Correlated Traits/Freely Correlated Methods (PCTCM)

In reviewing the schematic presentation of Model 3 in Figure 10.6, together with its input file specification in Figure 10.7, we can see that, as with the hypothesized CTCM model (Model 1), each observed variable loads on both a trait and a method factor. However, in stark contrast to the CTCM Model 1, this MTMM model argues for trait correlations that are perfect (i.e., they are equal to 1.0); consistent with both Models 1 and 2, the method factors are freely estimated.

In reviewing the input file in Figure 10.7, you will quickly note that, as with specification for Model 1 (see Figure 10.2), all correlations between traits and methods are fixed to 0.0. In addition, however, all correlations among the traits are fixed to a value of 1.00, and, as noted above, *ACSELF* was fixed at zero. Although goodness-of-fit results for this model (Model 3) were *substantially* better than for Model 2, they nonetheless were indicative of only a marginally well-fitting model and one that was somewhat less well fitting than Model 1($\chi^2_{[83]}$ = 216.164; CFI = 0.904; RMSEA = 0.091; SRMR = 0.071).

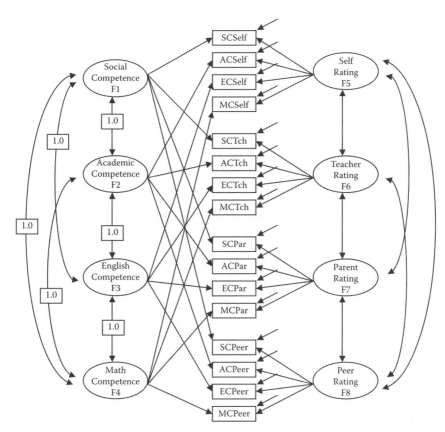

Figure 10.6. Hypothesized perfectly correlated traits/correlated methods (CTCM) MTMM model.

Model 4: Freely Correlated Traits/Uncorrelated Methods (CTUM)

This final MTMM model is portrayed in Figure 10.8 and specified in its related input file (see Figure 10.9). It differs from Model 1 only in the absence of specified correlations among the method factors. Goodness-of-fit results for this model revealed an exceptionally good fit to the data ($\chi^2_{[83]}$ = 111.117; CFI = 0.980; RMSEA = 0.042; SRMR = 0.067).

Examining Evidence of Construct Validity at the Matrix Level

Now that we have examined goodness-of-fit results for each of the four general CFA MTMM models, we can turn to the task of determining evidence of construct and discriminant validity. Accordingly, we ascertain

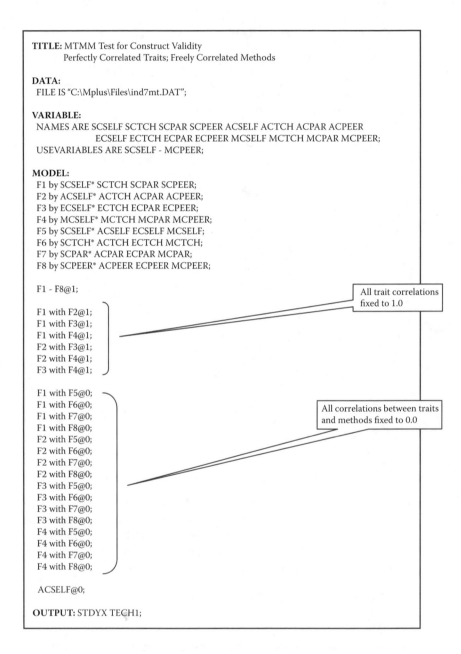

```
TITLE: MTMM Test for Construct Validity
       Perfectly Correlated Traits; Freely Correlated Methods

DATA:
 FILE IS "C:\Mplus\Files\ind7mt.DAT";

VARIABLE:
 NAMES ARE SCSELF SCTCH SCPAR SCPEER ACSELF ACTCH ACPAR ACPEER
          ECSELF ECTCH ECPAR ECPEER MCSELF MCTCH MCPAR MCPEER;
 USEVARIABLES ARE SCSELF - MCPEER;

MODEL:
 F1 by SCSELF* SCTCH SCPAR SCPEER;
 F2 by ACSELF* ACTCH ACPAR ACPEER;
 F3 by ECSELF* ECTCH ECPAR ECPEER;
 F4 by MCSELF* MCTCH MCPAR MCPEER;
 F5 by SCSELF* ACSELF ECSELF MCSELF;
 F6 by SCTCH* ACTCH ECTCH MCTCH;
 F7 by SCPAR* ACPAR ECPAR MCPAR;
 F8 by SCPEER* ACPEER ECPEER MCPEER;

 F1 - F8@1;

 F1 with F2@1;                      [All trait correlations
 F1 with F3@1;                       fixed to 1.0]
 F1 with F4@1;
 F2 with F3@1;
 F2 with F4@1;
 F3 with F4@1;

 F1 with F5@0;
 F1 with F6@0;
 F1 with F7@0;                      [All correlations between traits
 F1 with F8@0;                       and methods fixed to 0.0]
 F2 with F5@0;
 F2 with F6@0;
 F2 with F7@0;
 F2 with F8@0;
 F3 with F5@0;
 F3 with F6@0;
 F3 with F7@0;
 F3 with F8@0;
 F4 with F5@0;
 F4 with F6@0;
 F4 with F7@0;
 F4 with F8@0;

 ACSELF@0;

OUTPUT: STDYX TECH1;
```

Figure 10.7. M*plus* input file for perfectly correlated traits/correlated methods (CTCM) MTMM model.

Figure 10.8. Hypothesized correlated traits/uncorrelated methods (CTUM) MTMM model.

information at the matrix level only through the comparison of particular pairs of models. A summary of goodness-of-fit statistics related to all four MTMM models is presented in Table 10.3, and a summary of model comparisons in Table 10.4.

Determining Evidence of Convergent Validity

As noted earlier, one criterion of construct validity bears on the convergent validity, the extent to which *independent measures* of the *same trait* are correlated (e.g., teacher and self-ratings of social competence); these values should be substantial and statistically significant (Campbell & Fiske, 1959). Using Widaman's (1985) paradigm, evidence of convergent validity can be tested by comparing a model in which traits are specified (Model 1) with one in which they are not (Model 2), the difference in χ^2 ($\Delta\chi^2$) between these

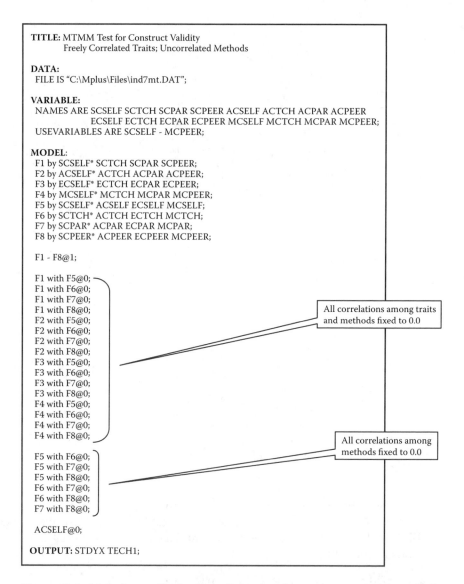

TITLE: MTMM Test for Construct Validity
        Freely Correlated Traits; Uncorrelated Methods

DATA:
FILE IS "C:\Mplus\Files\ind7mt.DAT";

VARIABLE:
NAMES ARE SCSELF SCTCH SCPAR SCPEER ACSELF ACTCH ACPAR ACPEER
              ECSELF ECTCH ECPAR ECPEER MCSELF MCTCH MCPAR MCPEER;
USEVARIABLES ARE SCSELF - MCPEER;

MODEL:
F1 by SCSELF* SCTCH SCPAR SCPEER;
F2 by ACSELF* ACTCH ACPAR ACPEER;
F3 by ECSELF* ECTCH ECPAR ECPEER;
F4 by MCSELF* MCTCH MCPAR MCPEER;
F5 by SCSELF* ACSELF ECSELF MCSELF;
F6 by SCTCH* ACTCH ECTCH MCTCH;
F7 by SCPAR* ACPAR ECPAR MCPAR;
F8 by SCPEER* ACPEER ECPEER MCPEER;

F1 - F8@1;

F1 with F5@0;
F1 with F6@0;
F1 with F7@0;
F1 with F8@0;
F2 with F5@0;
F2 with F6@0;
F2 with F7@0;
F2 with F8@0;
F3 with F5@0;
F3 with F6@0;
F3 with F7@0;
F3 with F8@0;
F4 with F5@0;
F4 with F6@0;
F4 with F7@0;
F4 with F8@0;

F5 with F6@0;
F5 with F7@0;
F5 with F8@0;
F6 with F7@0;
F6 with F8@0;
F7 with F8@0;

ACSELF@0;

OUTPUT: STDYX TECH1;

> All correlations among traits and methods fixed to 0.0

> All correlations among methods fixed to 0.0

Figure 10.9. M*plus* input file for test of correlated traits/uncorrelated methods (CTUM) MTMM model.

two nested models providing the basis for judgment; a significant difference in χ^2 values supports evidence of convergent validity. In an effort to provide indicators of nested model comparisons that were more realistic than those based on the χ^2 statistic, Bagozzi and Yi (1990), Widaman (1985), and others have examined differences in CFI values. However, until the

Table 10.3 Summary of Goodness-of-Fit Statistics for General Confirmatory Factor Analysis (CFA) Multitrait–Multimethod (MTMM) Models

Model	χ^2	Degrees of Freedom	Comparative Fit Index (CFI)	Root Mean Square Error of Approximation (RMSEA)	RMSEA 90% Confidence Interval (CI)	Standardized Root Mean Square Residual (SRMR)
1. Freely correlated traits;[a] freely correlated methods	77.164	77	1.000	0.003	0.000, 0.041	0.042
2. No traits;[a] freely correlated methods	335.635	99	0.829	0.111	0.098, 0.124	0.084
3. Perfectly correlated traits;[a] freely correlated methods	216.164	83	0.904	0.091	0.076, 0.106	0.071
4. Freely correlated traits;[a] uncorrelated methods	111.117	83	0.980	0.042	0.017, 0.061	0.067

[a] Represents respecified model with one residual (ACSELF) fixed at 0.0.

Table 10.4 Differential Goodness-of-Fit Indices
for General CFA MTMM Nested Model Comparisons

	Difference in			
Model Comparisons	χ^2	df	CFI	p
Test of Convergent Validity				
Model 1 versus Model 2 (traits)	258.471	22	0.171	< 0.001
Test of Discriminant Validity				
Model 1 versus Model 3 (traits)	139.000	6	0.096	< 0.001
Model 1 versus Model 4 (methods)	33.953	6	0.020	< 0.001

df = degrees of freedom

work of Cheung and Rensvold (2002), these ΔCFI values have served in
only a heuristic sense as an evaluative base upon which to determine
evidence of convergent and discriminant validity. As noted in Chapter
9, these authors examined the properties of 20 goodness-of-fit indices
within the context of invariance testing and arbitrarily recommended that
ΔCFI values should not exceed 0.01. Although the present application does
not include tests for invariance, the same principle holds regarding model
comparisons. As shown in Table 10.4, the $\Delta\chi^2$ is highly significant ($\chi^2_{[22]}$ =
258.471, $p < 0.001$),[3] and the difference in practical fit (ΔCFI = 0.171) substantial, thereby arguing for the tenability of this criterion (i.e., evidence
of convergent validity).

Determining Evidence of Discriminant Validity

Discriminant validity is typically assessed in terms of both traits and
methods. In testing for evidence of trait discriminant validity, interest
focuses on the extent to which *independent measures* of *different traits* are
correlated; these values should be negligible. When the independent measures represent different methods, correlations bear on the discriminant
validity of traits; when they represent the same method, correlations bear
on the presence of method effects, another aspect of discriminant validity.

In testing for evidence of discriminant validity among traits, we
compare a model in which traits correlate freely (Model 1) with one in
which they are perfectly correlated (Model 3); the larger the discrepancy
between the χ^2 and CFI values, the stronger the support for evidence of
discriminant validity. Accordingly, this comparison yielded a $\Delta\chi^2$ value
that was statistically significant ($\chi^2_{[6]}$ = 139.000, $p < 0.001$) and a difference
in practical fit that was fairly large (ΔCFI = 0.096), thereby suggesting only
modest evidence of discriminant validity.

Based on the same logic, albeit in reverse, evidence of discriminant validity related to method effects can be tested by comparing a model in which method factors are freely correlated (Model 1) with one in which they are uncorrelated (Model 4). As such, a large $\Delta\chi^2$ (or substantial ΔCFI) argues for the lack of discriminant validity and, thus, for common method bias across methods of measurement. On the strength of both statistical ($\Delta\chi^2_{[6]}$ = 33.953) and nonstatistical (ΔCFI = 0.020) criteria, as shown in Table 10.4, it seems reasonable to conclude that evidence of discriminant validity for the methods was substantially stronger than it was for the traits.

Examining Evidence of Construct Validity at the Parameter Level

A more precise assessment of trait- and method-related variance can be ascertained by examining individual parameter estimates. Specifically, the factor loadings and factor correlations of the CTCM model (Model 1) provide the focus here. Because it is difficult to envision the MTMM pattern of factor loadings and correlations from the output when more than six factors are involved, these values have been tabled to facilitate the assessment of convergent and discriminant validity; standardized estimates for the factor loadings are summarized in Table 10.5, and for the factor correlations in Table 10.6. (For a more extensive discussion of these MTMM findings, see Byrne & Bazana, 1996.) We turn first to a review of the trait and method factor loadings reported in Table 10.5.

Determining Evidence of Convergent Validity

In examining individual parameters, convergent validity is reflected in the magnitude of the trait loadings. As indicated in Table 10.5, all trait loadings related to Academic Competence, in addition to English Competence as measured by peers, were found not to be statistically significant. In a comparison of factor loadings across traits and methods, we see that method variance exceeds trait variance in a little over half of the ratings; these include self-ratings of Academic Competence; teacher ratings of Academic, English, and Math Competence; parent ratings of Academic Competence; and peer ratings of all four competence traits.[4] Thus, although at first blush evidence of convergent validity appeared to be fairly good at the matrix level, more in-depth examination at the individual parameter level reveals the attenuation of traits by method effects related mainly to teacher and peer ratings, thereby tempering evidence of convergent validity (see also Byrne & Goffin, 1993, with respect to adolescents).

Table 10.5 Trait and Method Loadings for General CFA MTMM Model 1
(Correlated Traits/Correlated Methods)[a]

	SC	AC	EC	MC	SR	TR	PAR	PER
Self-Ratings (SR)								
Social Competence	0.806				0.265			
Academic Competence		0.472[b]			0.882			
English Competence			0.726		0.382[b]			
Math Competence				0.674	0.479			
Teacher Ratings (TR)								
Social Competence	0.408					0.283		
Academic Competence		0.176[b]				0.939		
English Competence			0.250			0.776		
Math Competence				0.450		0.609		
Parent Ratings (PAR)								
Social Competence	0.584						0.387	
Academic Competence		0.483[b]					0.663	
English Competence			0.646				0.468	
Math Competence				0.730			0.529	
Peer Ratings (PER)								
Social Competence	0.311							0.416
Academic Competence		0.151[b]						0.931
English Competence			0.210[b]					0.674
Math Competence				0.298				0.700

[a] Standardized estimates.
[b] Not statistically significant ($p < .05$).

Determining Evidence of Discriminant Validity

Discriminant validity bearing on particular traits and methods can be
evaluated by examining the factor correlation matrices. Although, conceptually, correlations among traits should be negligible in order to satisfy
evidence of discriminant validity, such findings are highly unlikely in
general, and with respect to psychological data in particular. Although
these findings, as reported in Table 10.6, suggest that relations between
perceived Academic Competence (AC) and the subject-specific competencies of English (EC) and Math (MC) are most detrimental to the attainment of trait discriminant validity, they are nonetheless consistent with
construct validity research in this area as it relates to late preadolescent
children (see Byrne & Worth Gavin, 1996).

Table 10.6 Trait and Method Correlations for General CFA MTMM Model 1
(Correlated Traits/Correlated Methods)[a]

	Traits				Methods			
	SC	AC	EC	MC	SR	TR	PAR	PER
Social Competence (SC)	1.000							
Academic Competence (AC)	0.213[b]	1.000						
English Competence (EC)	0.087[b]	0.770	1.000					
Math Competence (MC)	0.157[b]	0.786	0.337[b]	1.000				
Self-Ratings (SR)					1.000			
Teacher Ratings (TR)					0.423	1.000		
Parent Ratings (PAR)					0.432[b]	0.626	1.000	
Peer Ratings (PER)					0.396	0.439	0.282[b]	1.000

[a] Standardized estimates.
[b] Not statistically significant ($p < .05$).

We turn next to a review of the method factor correlations. Estimated values of these parameters reflect on their discriminability and thus on the extent to which the methods are maximally dissimilar, an important underlying assumption of the MTMM strategy (see Campbell & Fiske, 1959). Given the obvious dissimilarity of self-, teacher, parent, and peer ratings, it is somewhat surprising to find a correlation of .626 between teacher and parent ratings of competence. One possible explanation of this finding is that, except for minor editorial changes necessary in tailoring the instrument to either the teacher or parent as respondents, the substantive content of all comparable items in the teacher and parent rating scales were identically worded, the rationale here being to maximize responses by different raters of the same student.

The Correlated Uniquenesses Approach to MTMM Analyses

As noted earlier, the CU model represents a special case of the general CFA model. Building upon the early work of Kenny (1976, 1979), Marsh (1988, 1989) proposed this alternative MTMM model in answer to the numerous estimation and convergence problems encountered with analyses of general CFA models and, in particular, of the CTCM model (Model 1 in this application). More recently, however, research has shown that the CU model also is not without its own problems, and researchers have proposed a number of specification alternatives to the general CU model (see, e.g., Cole et al., 2007; Conway et al., 2004; Corten, Saris, Coenders, van der Veld, Aalberts, & Kornelis, 2002; Lance et al., 2002). The hypothesized CU model tested here, however, is based on the originally postulated CU model (see, e.g., Kenny, 1976, 1979; Kenny & Kashy, 1992; Marsh, 1989). A schematic representation of this model is shown in Figure 10.10.

In reviewing the model depicted in Figure 10.10, you will note that it embodies just the four correlated trait factors; in this aspect only, it is consistent with the model shown in Figure 10.1. The notably different feature about the CU model, however, is that although no method factors are specified per se, their effects are implied from the specification of correlated residual terms (the uniquenesses)[5] associated with each set of observed variables embracing the same method. For example, as indicated in Figure 10.10, all residuals associated with self-rating measures of Social Competence are correlated with one another; likewise, those associated with teacher, parent, and peer ratings are intercorrelated.

Consistent with the CTUM model (Model 4 in this application), the CU model assumes that effects associated with one type of method are uncorrelated with those of the other methods (Marsh & Grayson, 1995). However, one critically important difference between the CU model and both the CTCM (Model 1) and CTUM (Model 4) models involves the assumed unidimensionality of the method factors. Whereas Models 1 and 4 implicitly assume that the method effects associated with a particular method are unidimensional (i.e., they can be explained by a single latent method factor), the CU model makes no such assumption (Marsh & Grayson, 1995). These authors further noted that when an MTMM model includes *more than* three trait factors, this important distinction can be tested. However, when the number of traits equals three, the CU model is formally equivalent to the other two in the sense that the "number of estimated parameters and model goodness-of-fit are the same, and parameter estimates from one can be transformed into the other" (Marsh & Grayson, 1995, p. 185).

Of course, from a practical perspective, the most important distinction between the CU model and Models 1 and 4 is that it typically results in a proper solution (Kenny & Kashy, 1992; Marsh, 1989; Marsh & Bailey, 1991). The CTCM model (Model 1), on the other hand, is now notorious for its tendency to yield inadmissible solutions, as we observed in the present application. As a case in point, Marsh and Bailey, in their analyses of 435 MTMM matrices based on both real and simulated data, reported that whereas the CTCM model resulted in improper solutions 77% of the time, the CU model yielded proper solutions nearly every time (98%). (For additional examples of the incidence of improper solutions with respect to Model 1, see Kenny & Kashy, 1992.) We turn now to the analyses based on the CU model.

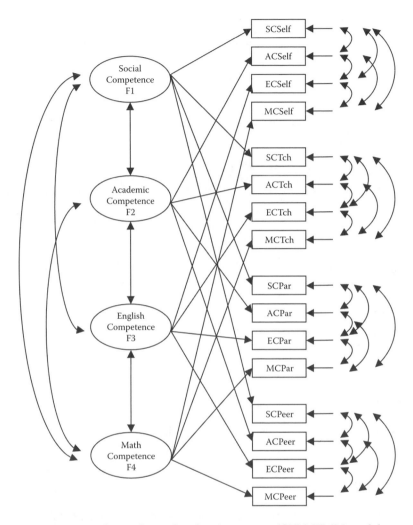

Figure 10.10. Hypothesized correlated uniquenesses (CU) MTMM model.

Input File

Reviewing, once again, the model depicted in Figure 10.10, we see that there are four trait factors and that these factors are hypothesized to correlate among themselves. In lieu of the method factors specified for the general CFA models, however, the correlated residuals for each set of observed variables measuring the same method of measurement are considered to reflect these method effects. The related input file is shown in Figure 10.11. Of particular note here, of course, is the specific correlations among each set of residuals.

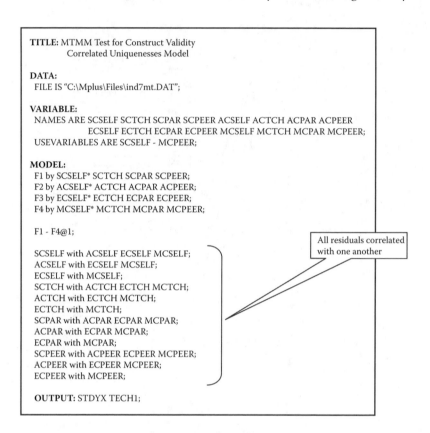

Figure 10.11. M*plus* input file for test of correlated uniquenesses (CU) MTMM model.

Output File

In reviewing results for the CU model, we turn first to the goodness-of-fit statistics, which are presented in Table 10.7. As shown here, it is easy to see that this model represents an excellent fit to the data. Furthermore, consistent with past reported results (e.g., Kenny & Kashy, 1992; Marsh & Bailey, 1991), this solution resulted in no lack of convergence or problematic parameter estimates.

Assessment of convergent and discriminant validity for the CU model can be accomplished in the same way that it was for the General CFA model when focused at the individual parameter level. As shown in Table 10.8, evidence related to the convergent validity of the traits, not surprisingly, was substantial and somewhat higher than for the CTCM model (Model 1; see Table 10.5). Indeed, there are two notable and interesting differences

Table 10.7 M*plus* Output:
Selected Goodness-of-Fit Statistics for the Correlated Uniquenesses Model

Tests of Model Fit	
Chi-Square Test of Model Fit	
Value	96.975
Degrees of freedom	74
p-value	0.0379
CFI/TLI	
CFI	0.983
TLI	0.973
Root Mean Square Error of Approximation (RMSEA)	
Estimate	0.040
90 percent confidence interval (CI)	0.010 0.061
Probability RMSEA <= .05	0.766
Standardized Root Mean Square Residual (SRMR)	
Value	0.067

between these two models. First, whereas the CTCM model resulted in five trait-loading estimates that were not statistically significant, the CU model resulted in all estimates being statistically significant. Second, with the exception of all ratings pertinent to Social Competence, as well as self-ratings of English Competence, all remaining trait loadings for the CU model were higher than those for the CTCM model.

Let's look now at the factor correlations relevant only to the traits; these estimates are presented in Table 10.9. In reviewing these values, we see that all but one estimated correlation are statistically significant, and virtually all trait estimates higher than they were for the CTCM model. One commonality between the two models, however, was the nonsignificant estimate of the correlation between Social Competence and English Competence.

Method effects in the CU model are determined by the degree to which the residuals terms are correlated with one another (Kenny & Kashy, 1992), and these estimates for the CU model are presented in Table 10.10. It is interesting to note that the strongest method effects are clearly associated with teacher and peer ratings of the two specific academic competencies of English (0.684 and 0.579, respectively) and math (0.511 and 0.652, respectively). Indeed, from a substantive standpoint, these findings certainly seem perfectly reasonable. On the other hand, the strong method effects shown by self- and parent ratings of only the academic

Table 10.8 Trait-Loading Estimates for Correlated Uniquenesses Model[a]

	SC	AC	EC	MC
Self-Ratings (SR)				
Social Competence	0.757			
Academic Competence		0.766		
English Competence			0.683	
Math Competence				0.743
Teacher Ratings (TR)				
Social Competence	0.464			
Academic Competence		0.593		
English Competence			0.582	
Math Competence				0.634
Parent Ratings (PAR)				
Social Competence	0.679			
Academic Competence		0.647		
English Competence			0.720	
Math Competence				0.796
Peer Ratings (PER)				
Social Competence	0.362			
Academic Competence		0.423		
English Competence			0.412	
Math Competence				0.442

[a] Standardized estimates.

Table 10.9 Trait Correlation Estimates for Correlated Uniquenesses Model[a]

	Traits			
Measures	SC	AC	EC	MC
Social Competence (SC)	1.000			
Academic Competence (AC)	0.356	1.000		
English Competence (EC)	0.167[b]	0.868	1.000	
Math Competence (MC)	0.325	0.800	0.591	1.000

[a] Standardized estimates.
[b] Not statistically significant ($p < .05$).

Table 10.10 Residual Correlation Estimates for Correlated Uniquenesses Model[a]

	SCSelf	ACSelf	ECSelf	MCSelf	SCTchr	ACTchr	ECTchr	MCTchr	SCPar	ACPar	ECPar	MCPar	SCPeer	ACPeer	ECPeer	MCPeer
SCSelf	1.000															
ACSelf	0.338	1.000														
ECSelf	0.375	0.389	1.000													
MCSelf	0.072[b]	0.556	0.173[b]	1.000												
SCTchr					1.000											
ACTchr					0.238	1.000										
ECTchr					0.132[b]	0.684	1.000									
MCTchr					0.046[b]	0.511	0.386	1.000								
SCPar									1.000							
ACPar									0.220	1.000						
ECPar									0.172[b]	0.250	1.000					
MCPar									0.176[b]	0.467	0.160[b]	1.000				
SCPeer													1.000			
ACPeer													0.361	1.000		
ECPeer													0.280	0.579	1.000	
MCPeer													0.206	0.652	0.434	1.000

[a] Standardized estimates.
[b] Not statistically significant ($p < .05$).

area of Math Competence (0.556 and 0.467, respectively) are intriguing. One possible explanation may lie in the fact that perceptions of Academic Competence are unintentionally equated with Math Competence. In other words, self-perceptions as well as parental perceptions of academic competence appear to be defined in terms of one's competence in math.

In contrast to the CTCM model, the CU model makes no assumption that each method factor remains the same for all measures embracing the same method. Rather, as Kenny and Kashy (1992) explained, "In the Correlated Uniqueness model, each measure is assumed to have its own method effect, and the covariances between measures using the same method assess the extent to which there is a common method factor" (p. 169). In other words, as Kenny and Kashy further noted, whereas the General CFA MTMM model assumes that method effects are invariant across traits, the CU model allows for the multidimensionality of method effects. (For critiques of these effects, see Conway et al., 2004; Lance et al., 2002. For an attempt to understand the substance of these correlated residual terms, see Saris & Aalberts, 2003.)

In closing out this chapter, it is worthwhile to underscore Marsh and Grayson's (1995) recommendation regarding the analysis of MTMM data. As they emphasized, "MTMM data have an inherently complicated structure that will not be fully described in all cases by any of the models or approaches typically considered. There is, apparently, no 'right' way to analyze MTMM data that works in all situations" (Marsh & Grayson, 1995, p. 198). Consequently, Marsh and Grayson (1995), supported by Cudeck (1989), strongly advised that in the study of MTMM data, researchers should always consider alternative modeling strategies (see, e.g., Cole et al., 2007; Eid et al., 2008; Pohl & Steyer, 2010). In particular, Marsh and Grayson (1995) suggested an initial examination of data within the framework of the original Campbell-Fiske guidelines. This analysis should then be followed by the testing of a subset of at least four CFA models (including the CU model); for example, the five models considered in the present application would constitute an appropriate subset. Finally, given that the composite direct product model[6] is designed to test for the presence of multiplicative rather than additive effects, it should also be included in the MTMM analysis alternative approach strategy. (But, for a critique of this approach, readers are referred to Corten et al., 2002.). In evaluating results from each of the covariance structure models noted here, Marsh and Grayson (1995) cautioned that, in addition to technical considerations such as convergence to proper solutions and goodness-of-fit, researchers should place a heavy emphasis on substantive interpretations and theoretical framework.

Notes

1. The term *general* is used to distinguish the generic CFA model from other special cases, such as the CU model (see Marsh, 1989).
2. As a consequence of problems related to both the identification and estimation of CFA models, trait–method correlations cannot be freely estimated (see Schmitt & Stults, 1986; Widaman, 1985).
3. Given that the data were normally distributed, analyses were based on maximum likelihood (ML) estimation. Thus, the chi-square difference value required no scaling correction.
4. Trait and method variance, within the context of the general CFA MTMM model, equals the factor loading squared.
5. As noted in Chapter 3, the term *uniqueness* is used in the factor analytic sense to mean a composite of random measurement error and specific measurement error associated with a particular measuring instrument.
6. Whereas CFA models assume that test scores represent the sum of trait and method components (i.e., additive effects), the composite direct product model assumes that they derive from the product of the trait and method components (i.e., multiplicative effects).

chapter 11

Testing Change Over Time
The Latent Growth Curve Model

Latent growth curve (LGC) modeling within the framework of structural equation modeling (SEM) is now considered one of the most powerful and informative approaches to the analysis of longitudinal data (see, e.g., Curran & Hussong, 2003). Whereas this methodological approach enables researchers to test for differences in developmental trajectories across time, conventional repeated measures analyses (e.g., analysis of variance [ANOVA], analysis of covariance [ANCOVA], and multivariate analysis of covariance [MANOVA]) fail to provide this opportunity. More specifically, although these traditional statistical strategies are capable of describing an individual's developmental trajectory, they are incapable of capturing individual differences in these trajectories over time (Curran & Hussong, 2003; Duncan & Duncan, 1995; Fan, 2003; Willett & Sayer, 1994). Thus, they are increasingly becoming perceived as somewhat inadequate in that they prevent researchers from seeking answers to interesting and important questions bearing on such differences. For example, it might be interesting to ask, "Is there a difference in the rate of change in one's perceived body image for breast cancer patients who have undergone lumpectomy as opposed to mastectomy surgery?"

Fortunately, as a result of breakthroughs in both mathematical statistics and computer technology, a plethora of analytic designs capable of addressing this apparent weakness in longitudinal research have been advanced (Curran & Hussong, 2003). (For examples of a few of these methods, see Collins & Sayer, 2001; Little, Schnabel, & Baumert, 2000.) Of these newer statistical methods, perhaps most have fallen within the frameworks of hierarchical linear modeling (HLM; Raudenbush & Bryk, 2002) and SEM (McArdle & Epstein, 1987; Meredith & Tisak, 1990). HLM was originally designed as a means to accounting more precisely for nested (or hierarchical) data structures (i.e., multiple levels of one entity nested within a single level of another); examples include students nested within classrooms or patients nested within hospitals. Subsequently, it was shown that these structures also could take the form of repeated measures within individuals (Bryk & Raudenbush, 1987) and as such could be used to study individual trajectories over time. In contrast, the SEM approach to longitudinal analyses was developed as a generalized method for model-ing growth (Chou, Bentler, & Pentz, 1998), and, thus, these models became known as *latent growth curve* (LGC) models. Whereas the HLM model con-siders time as a predictor variable, the LGC model parameterizes it via the factor loadings that relate the repeated measures to the latent factors representing the intercept and slope (Curran & Hussong, 2003; Meredith & Tisak, 1990).

Although both the HLM and SEM frameworks serve as flexible mech-anisms for examining complex longitudinal data structures in a feasible way, they are not completely interchangeable from the perspective of prac-tical data analyses. Indeed, several researchers have compared the two statistical strategies and reported that under certain conditions, the HLM and SEM frameworks yield approximately the same results, albeit under other conditions they do not (see, e.g., Chou et al., 1998; MacCallum, Kim, Malarkey, & Kiecolt-Glaser, 1997; Willett & Sayer, 1994). Thus, despite their similarities, the two techniques can often operate very differently depend-ing on the data analyzed, thereby leading Schnabel, Little, and Baumert (2000) to have termed them aptly as the "unequal twins" (p. 12). Indeed, a full comparison of the HLM and SEM approaches to longitudinal analy-ses is beyond the scope of this chapter. However, interested readers are referred to MacCallum et al. (1997) for an excellent description and thor-ough discussion of the comparative issues, and to Wu, West, and Taylor (2009) for a comprehensive and intriguing comparison of the extent to which the two methodologies address the challenges of different types of longitudinal data, sources of misspecification, and assessment of model fit.

Only SEM-based LGC modeling is addressed in this chapter; the application demonstrated is based on a study of 405 Hong Kong Chinese women who underwent breast cancer surgery (see Byrne, Lam, & Fielding, 2008). Of primary interest in this study was the extent to which the women exhibited evidence of the extent and rate of change in their mood[1] and social adjustment at 1, 4, and 8 months post surgery. Of the numerous different types of LGC models capable of being tested with M*plus* (see Muthén & Muthén, 2007–2010), the current application represents a linear growth model with continuous outcomes.

Consistent with most longitudinal research, some subject attrition occurred over the 8-month period. Missingness, based on continuous data, is easily addressed in M*plus* through use of the robust maximum likelihood (MLR) estimator, and this is the case here. In a repetition of my caveat noted in Chapter 8, I again urge you to familiarize yourself with pitfalls that might be encountered if you work with incomplete data in the analysis of SEM models (see, e.g., Muthén, Kaplan, & Hollis, 1987), as well as with strategies that can be used in analyses of LGC models with miss-ing data in general (see Byrne & Crombie, 2003; Duncan & Duncan, 1994;

Duncan, Duncan, & Stryker, 2006) and with use of the M*plus* program in particular (see Muthén & Muthén, 2007–2010).

Historically, researchers have typically based analyses of change on two-wave panel data, a strategy that Willett and Sayer (1994) deemed inadequate because of limited information. Addressing this weakness in longitudinal research, Willett (1988) and others (Bryk & Raudenbush, 1987; Rogosa, Brandt, & Zimowski, 1982; Rogosa & Willett, 1985) outlined methods of individual growth modeling that, in contrast, capitalized on the richness of multiwave data, thereby allowing for more effective testing of systematic interindividual differences in change. (For a comparative review of the many advantages of LGC modeling over the former approach to the study of longitudinal data, see Tomarken & Waller, 2005.)

In a unique extension of this earlier work, researchers (e.g., McArdle & Epstein, 1987; Meredith & Tisak, 1990; Muthén, 1997) have shown how individual growth models can be tested using the analysis of means and covariance structures (MACS) within the framework of SEM. Considered within this context, it has become customary to refer to such models as *LGC models*. Of the many advantages in testing for change within the framework of SEM over other longitudinal strategies, two are of primary importance. First, this approach is based on the analysis of MACS and, as such, can distinguish group effects observed in means from individual effects observed in covariances. Second, a distinction can be made between observed and unobserved (or latent) variables in the specification of models. This capability allows for both the modeling and estimation of measurement error. Given its many appealing features (for an elaboration, see Willett & Sayer, 1994), together with the ease with which researchers can tailor its basic structure for use in innovative applications, it seems evident that LGC modeling has the potential to revolutionize analyses of longitudinal research (see, e.g., Benner & Graham, 2009; Cheong, MacKinnon, & Khoo, 2003; Curran, Bauer, & Willoughby, 2004; Duncan, Duncan, Okut, Strycker, & Li, 2002; Hancock, Kuo, & Lawrence, 2001; Li et al., 2001; Muthén, 2004; Muthén & Curran, 1997; Muthén & Muthén, 2000; Pettit, Keiley, Laird, Bates, & Dodge, 2007).

In introducing you to the topic of LGC modeling, I like to use the two-step approach taken by Willett and Sayer (1994) in describing the processes involved; these include evaluating first the extent of *intraindividual* change, followed by evaluation of *interindividual* change. Thus, in this chapter, I present the model to be demonstrated based on three gradations of conceptual understanding. First, I present a general overview of measuring change over an 8-month period in individual perceptions of mood and social adjustment by women who recently (1 month previous) underwent breast cancer surgery (intraindividual change). Next, I focus on the portion of the LGC model that measures differences in such change across all subjects (interindividual change). Finally, I demonstrate the addition of age and type of surgical treatment to the model as possible time-invariant predictors that may account for any change in the individual growth trajectories (i.e., intercept and slope) of mood and social adjustment.

Measuring Change in Individual Growth Over Time: The General Notion

In answering questions of individual change related to one or more domains of interest, a representative sample of individuals must be observed systematically over time and their status in each domain measured on several temporally spaced occasions, albeit these intervals need not necessarily be equal (Willett & Sayer, 1994). Although earlier applications of LGC modeling required that several additional conditions be met, recent statistical and methodological advancements in the field have addressed many of these issues, and, as a result, they are less in number. Nonetheless, at least two important provisos remain: (a) Data must be obtained for each individual on three or more occasions, and (b) sample size must be large enough to allow for the detection of person-level effects (Willett & Sayer, 1994). Furthermore, when analyses are based on SEM, sample size requirements become even more critical due to the underlying assumption of multivariate normality. Thus, one would expect minimum sample sizes of not less than 200 at each time point (see Boomsma, 1985; Boomsma & Hoogland, 2001).

The Hypothesized Dual-Domain LGC Model

Given that the hypothesized model under study in this chapter encompasses the two constructs of mood and social adjustment, I refer to this model as a *dual domain model*. Another way of conceptualizing this model is to think of it as a single model of growth in two variables; as such, we are fitting two simultaneous growth curves and estimating covariances among their growth factors. Borrowing from the work of Willett and Sayer (1994), we can consider the basic building blocks of this hypothesized LGC model to comprise two underpinning submodels that we'll call *Level 1* and *Level 2* models. The Level 1 model can be thought of as a "within-person" regression model that represents individual change over time with respect to (in the present instance) self-ratings pertinent to two outcome variables, *mood* and *social adjustment*. As noted earlier, the focus of Level 1 analyses is on intraindividual change. In contrast, the Level 2 model can be viewed as a "between-person" model that focuses on interindividual differences in change with respect to these outcome variables.

Modeling Intraindividual Change

The first step in building an LGC model is to examine the within-person growth trajectory. In the present case, this task translates into determining, for each woman, the direction and extent to which scores for *mood* and *social adjustment* change across 1 month, 4 months, and 8 months post surgery. If the trajectory of hypothesized change is considered to be linear, then the specified model will include two growth parameters: (a) an intercept parameter representing a woman's score on the outcome variable at Time 1, and (b) a slope parameter representing her rate of change over the time period of interest. Within the context of the present data, the intercept represents the woman's *mood* and *social adjustment* 1 month following surgery; the slope represents the rate of change in these values over the course of an 8-month period.

If, on the other hand, change over time were to be better described by a nonlinear (i.e., curvilinear) rather than a linear trajectory, the LGC model would include a third latent factor, termed a *quadratic factor*, capable of capturing any curvature that might be present in the individual trajectories. (For an elaboration and illustrated application of nonlinear LGC models, readers are referred to Byrne & Crombie, 2003; Duncan & Duncan, 1995; Duncan et al., 2006; Grimm & Ramm, 2009; Muthén & Muthén, 2010; Willett & Sayer, 1994.) The data used in this chapter are linear.

With these basic concepts in hand, let's turn now to Figure 11.1, where the hypothesized dual domain model to be tested is schematically presented. In reviewing this model, focus first on the six outcome (i.e., observed) variables enclosed in rectangles at the bottom of the path diagram. Each variable constitutes a subscale score at one of three time points, with the first three representing *mood* and the latter three *social adjustment*. As usual, the single-headed arrows leading to each of the outcome variables represent the influence of random measurement error (i.e., residuals in M*plus*). Moving up to the top of the model, we find two latent variables (or factors) associated with each of these *mood* and *social adjustment* domains; they represent the Intercept and Slope factors for each of these two domains. The arrows leading from each of the four latent factors to their related outcome variables represent the regression of observed scores at each of three time points onto their appropriate Intercept and Slope factors. Finally, linking the Intercept and Slope factors for each domain is a double-headed arrow indicating their covariance. These factor covariances are assumed in the specification of LGC models. In addition, however, consistent with Willett and Sayer's (1994) caveat that in multiple-domain LGC models, covariation across domains should be considered, M*plus* estimates these factor covariances by default; these parameters are represented in Figure 11.1 by broken two-headed arrows.

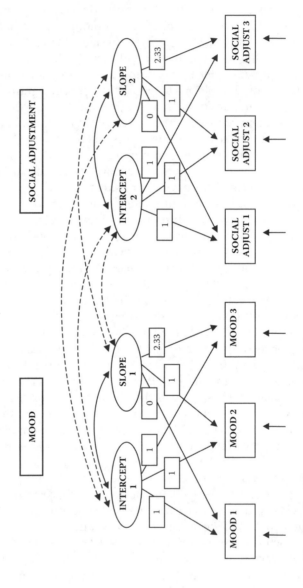

Figure 11.1. Hypothesized latent growth curve model.

The numerical values assigned to the paths flowing from the Intercept and Slope factors to the observed variables represent fixed parameters in the model. The 1's specified for the paths flowing from each Intercept factor to each of its related outcome variables indicate that each is constrained to a value of 1.0. This constraint reflects the fact that the intercept value remains constant across time for each individual (Duncan et al., 2006). The values of 0, 1, and 2.33 assigned to the Slope regression paths represent Times 1, 2, and 3, respectively. These constraints address the issue of model identification; they also ensure that these factors can be interpreted as slopes. Three important points are of interest with respect to these fixed slope values. First, technically speaking, the first path (assigned a zero value) is really nonexistent and, therefore, has no effect. Although it would be less confusing to simply eliminate this parameter, it has become customary to include this path in the model, albeit with an assigned value of zero (Bentler, 2005). Second, these values represent the time intervals of 1, 4, and 8 months following surgery, albeit adjusted to take into account that, for our purposes here, Time 1 actually begins 1 month following the true initial testing point of 1 week following surgery. Unfortunately, due to the absence of scores for *social adjustment* at baseline (i.e., 1 week post surgery), only three of the four actual time points can be considered. As such, the values of 0, 1, and 2.33 represent a linear transformation of scores at Times 2, 3, and 4 (i.e., 1, 4, and 8 months post surgery) in order to establish initial status.[2] Finally, although the choice of fixed values assigned to the Slope factor loadings is arbitrary, it is important to realize that the Intercept factor is tied to a time scale (Duncan et al., 2006). Thus, any shift in fixed loading values on the Slope factor will necessarily modify the scale of time bearing on the Intercept factor, which, in turn, will influence interpretations related to the Intercept mean and variance. Relatedly, the variances and correlations among the factors in the model will change depending on the chosen coding (see, e.g., Biesanz, Deeb-Sossa, Papadakis, Bollen, & Curran, 2004; Blozis & Cho, 2008).

In this section, our focus is on the modeling of intraindividual change. Within the framework of SEM, this focus is captured by the *measurement model*, the portion of a model that, as you well know at this point in the book, incorporates only linkages between the observed (i.e., outcome) variables and their underlying unobserved factors. As such, the only parts of the model in Figure 11.1 that are relevant to intraindividual change are (a) the regression paths linking the six outcome variables to the two Intercept and two Slope factors, (b) the factor variances and covariances, and (c) the related residuals associated with the outcome variables.

Essentially, we can think of this part of the model as an ordinary factor analysis model with two special features. First, all the loadings are fixed; that is, there are no unknown factor loadings. Second, the particular pattern of fixed loadings plus the mean structure allows us to interpret the factors as Intercept and Slope factors. As in all factor models, the present case argues that each woman's *mood* and *social adjustment* scores, at each of three time points (Time 1 = 0; Time 2 = 1; Time 3 = 2.33), are a function of three distinct components: (a) a factor loading matrix of constants (1; 1; 1) and known time values (0; 1; 2.33) that remain invariant across all individuals, multiplied by (b) an LGC vector containing individual-specific and unknown factors that in LGC models are called *individual growth parameters* (Intercept, Slope), plus (c) a vector of individual-specific and unknown errors of measurement (residuals of the outcome variables). Whereas the LGC vector represents the within-person *true* change in (self-perceived) *mood* and *social adjustment* over time, the residual or error vector represents the within-person *noise* that serves to erode these true change values (Willett & Sayer, 1994).

In preparing for transition from the modeling of intraindividual change to the modeling of interindividual change, it is important that we review briefly the basic concepts underlying the analyses of MACS in SEM (see also Chapter 8). When population means are of no interest in a model, analysis is based on only covariance structure (COVS) parameters. As such, all scores are considered to be deviations from their means, and, thus, the constant term (represented as α in a regression equation) equals zero. Given that mean values played no part in the specification of the Level 1 (or within-person) portion of our LGC model, the analysis of COVS was sufficient. However, in moving to Level 2, the between-person portion of the model, interest focuses on mean values associated with the Intercept and Slope growth factors; these values in turn influence the means of the outcome variables. Because both levels are involved in the modeling of interindividual differences in change, analyses are now based on MACS.

Modeling Interindividual Differences in Change

Level 2 argues that, over and above hypothesized linear change in *mood* and *social adjustment* over time, trajectories will necessarily vary across all Hong Kong women as a consequence of different intercepts and slopes. Within the framework of SEM, this portion of the model reflects that which we recognize as the *structural model* in that it typically represents relations among unobserved factors. However, in LGC models, structure is limited to only the means and variances of the Intercept and Slope growth factors. Whereas the means convey information regarding average intercept and slope values, the variances yield information related to individual differences in intercept and slope values. Specification of these parameters, then, makes possible the estimation of interindividual differences in change.

Let's now reexamine Figure 11.1 in more specific terms in order to clarify information bearing on possible differences in change across time. Within the context of only the first domain of *mood*, interest focuses on five parameters that are key to determining between-person differences in change: two means (Intercept1; Slope1), two variances (Intercept1; Slope1), and one covariance (between Intercept1 and Slope1). The means represent the average population values for the Intercept and Slope and answer the questions "What is the population initial level of *mood* at one month post surgery?" and "What is the population trajectory of true change in *mood* across 8 months post surgery?" The variances represent deviations of the individual Intercepts and Slopes from their population means, thereby reflecting population interindividual differences in the initial (1 month post surgery) *mood* self-rating scores and the rate of change in these scores, respectively. Addressing the issue of variability, these key parameters answer the question "Are there interindividual differences in the starting point and growth trajectories of *mood* in the population?" Finally, the Intercept–Slope covariance represents the population covariance between any deviations in initial status and rate of change and answers the question "Is there any evidence of interindividual differences in the association between initial status and rate of change in *mood* across an 8-month time span?"

Now that you have a basic understanding of LGC modeling in general and as it bears specifically on the hypothesized dual domain model shown in Figure 11.1, let's turn next to the M*plus* input file and testing of this model.

Mplus Input File Specification and Output File Results

Testing for Validity of the Hypothesized Model

Input File 1

Displayed in Figure 11.2, you will see two input files related to this initial testing of the model. Whereas the one on the top left represents the short and preferred LGC specification, the one on the bottom right (labeled in the TITLE as Alternative Specification) specifies the model in a logical step-by-step manner that is relatively straightforward and perhaps easier to follow. Regardless of which form of specification is used, both input files generate the same output file. Turning first to the VARIABLE command, you will see that the data comprise 11 variables, only 6 of which will be used in this initial analysis (*MOOD2, MOOD3, MOOD4, SOCADJ2, SOCADJ3,* and *SOCADJ4*).[3] Second, as noted in this chapter, due to a relatively minor degree of attrition, there are missing scores in the data. We

TITLE: HK Cancer Study "HKcancer1"
 Initial Model

DATA:
 FILE IS "C:\Mplus\Files\hkcancer_red2.dat";

VARIABLE:
 NAMES ARE AGE_GP SURG_TX MOOD2 MOOD3 MOOD4
  SOCADJ2 SOCADJ3 SOCADJ4 AGE AGE2
  SURG_TX2;

 USEVARIABLES ARE MOOD2 MOOD3 MOOD4
  SOCADJ2 SOCADJ3 SOCADJ4;
 MISSING IS *;

ANALYSIS:
 ESTIMATOR IS MLR;

MODEL:
 I1 S1 | MOOD2@0 MOOD3@1 MOOD4@2.33;
 I2 S2 | SOCADJ2@0 SOCADJ3@1 SOCADJ4@2.33;

OUTPUT: PATTERNS SAMPSTAT MODINDICES;

TITLE: HK Cancer Study "HKcancer1A"
 Initial Model (Alternative Specification)

DATA:
 FILE IS "C:\Mplus\Files\hkcancer_red2.dat";

VARIABLE:
 NAMES ARE AGE_GP SURG_TX MOOD2 MOOD3 MOOD4
 SOCADJ2 SOCADJ3 SOCADJ4 AGE AGE2
 SURG_TX2;

 USEVARIABLES ARE MOOD2 MOOD3 MOOD4
  SOCADJ2 SOCADJ3 SOCADJ4;
 MISSING IS *;

ANALYSIS:
 ESTIMATOR IS MLR;

MODEL:
 I1 by MOOD2@1 MOOD3@1 MOOD4@1;
 S1 by MOOD2@0 MOOD3@1 MOOD4@2.33;
 I2 by SOCADJ2@1 SOCADJ3@1 SOCADJ4@1;
 S2 by SOCADJ2@0 SOCADJ3@1 SOCADJ4@2.33;

 I1 with S1;
 I2 with S2;

 [MOOD2-MOOD4@0];
 [SOCADJ2-SOCADJ4@0];

 [I1 S1];
 [I2 S2];

OUTPUT: PATTERNS SAMPSTAT MODINDICES;

Figure 11.2. M*plus* input files for model 1 shown in short (on the left) and long forms.

alert the program to these missing values through use of the MISSING option, which in these data can be identified by the presence of an asterisk (*). This identification process is applied to all variables in the data.

As discussed in Chapter 8, when continuous variable data are missing, whether they are missing completely at random (MCAR) or missing at random (MAR), M*plus* is capable of taking such missingness into account through specification of the MLR estimator for which the standard errors are robust. Thus, under the ANALYSIS command, you will see that the ESTIMATOR option has been invoked and use of MLR estimation specified.

Thus far, our review of specifications in the two input files comprising Figure 11.2 has revealed them to be identical. However, in moving on to the MODEL command, they become substantially different. Because I believe you may find the alternative specification on the bottom right to be the easier of the two to follow, let's turn our attention to this input file first, accompanied by the portrayal of the model itself in Figure 11.1. The first four lines of specifications are pertinent to the regression paths flowing from the Intercept and Slope associated with each of the two domains of interest, *mood* and *social adjustment*. The first line specifies that the intercept for *mood* (I1) is measured by *MOOD2*, *MOOD3*, and *MOOD4* (albeit labelled as MOOD1, MOOD2, and MOOD3 in Figure 11.1 for purpose of the introductory model; see Note 3). Likewise, the second line specifies that *MOOD2* through *MOOD4* also measure the slope for MOOD (S1). In both cases, each of the regression paths is specified as a fixed parameter in the model. Whereas the regression paths associated with I1 are constrained to a value of 1.00 (MOOD2@1 − MOOD3@1), those associated with S1 are constrained to values of 0.00, 1.00, and 2.33 for *MOOD2* through *MOOD4*, respectively. The next two lines, of course, follow the same pattern for the second domain of *social adjustment*.

The two WITH statements in Lines 5 and 6 under the MODEL command specify that the Intercept and Slope factors covary for both the *mood* and *social adjustment* domains. Because this covariance is assumed in LGC modeling, as noted, it is default in M*plus*.

The parenthesized information appearing in Lines 7 and 8 merely serves to group the variables according to their function as outcome variables in the model. As indicated, each of these six outcome variables is fixed at a value of zero. This specification relates to the intercepts of these variables, which are fixed at zero by default.

The final two parenthesized statements indicate that the Intercept and Slope for *mood* ([I1, S1]) serve as a set of parameters in the model; likewise the Intercept and Slope factors for *social adjustment* ([I2 S2]).

Now that we have dissected the longer specification of our dual domain LGC model, let's turn back to the input file on the upper left-hand side of Figure 11.2 and focus on the much abbreviated MODEL command. Here we find only two statements—one pertinent to *mood*, and the other to *social adjustment*. These two statements represent exactly the same model specifications as the longer form in the alternative input file. This more concise specification is made possible through implementation of several related Mplus defaults. With respect to the dual domain LGC model hypothesized and tested in this chapter, these defaults are as follows: (a) The coefficients of each intercept factor are fixed at 1.00, (b) the intercepts of the outcome variables are fixed to zero, (c) the means and variances of both the Intercept and Slope factors are estimated, (d) the factor covariance between each Intercept–Slope pair is estimated, (e) cross-domain factor covariances are estimated, (f) residual variances of the outcome variables are estimated and allowed to vary across time points, and (g) residual covariances are assumed to be zero.

The | symbol is used to name and define the Intercept and Slope factors comprising the LGC model. Appearing on the left side of the | symbol are the names of the Intercept and Slope factors pertinent to each domain of interest. Thus, in the present case, we see I1 S1 specific to *mood*, and I2 S2 specific to *social adjustment*. Appearing on the right side of the | symbol are the outcome variable names together with time scores for the LGC model. As with the longer version of this input file, time scores for the Slopes are fixed at 0, 1, and 2.33 and, as such, make it possible to define a linear growth model with nonequidistant time points.

Finally, because the data used for this application have missing values, the option of PATTERNS has been requested, along with SAMPSTATS and MODINDICES. As we observed in Chapter 8, this option provides us with an informed picture of the configuration and extent to which the data are incomplete.

Output File 1

Having reviewed the two alternative input files for our LGC model, let's turn next to Table 11.1, where a summary of the missing data results in the output file is presented. Identified first in the output is the number of missing data patterns, which is shown to be 15. This summary information is followed by a detailed breakdown of these 15 patterns, together with the score frequency for each pattern. Given that an *x* represents no missing data, we can see that Pattern 1, for example, represents the case for complete data and has a frequency of 307 scores. Given a total sample of 405 cases, we now know that there are 98 women for whom there are missing scores and that these missing scores are represented by 14 different patterns. A review of the pattern frequencies helps to fill in the blanks on this information. For example, whereas Pattern 9 reveals that 23 women had complete scores for only *MOOD2* and *SOCADJ2*, Pattern

Table 11.1 Mplus Output for Model 1: Missing Data Statistics

Summary of Data	
Number of missing data patterns	15

Summary of Missing Data Patterns

Missing Data Patterns (x = Not Missing)

	1	2	3	4	5	6	7	8	9	10	11	12	13	14	15
MOOD2	x	x	x	x	x	x	x	x	x						
MOOD3	x	x	x	x						x	x	x			
MOOD4	x			x	x					x	x		x		
SOCADJ2	x	x	x	x	x	x	x	x	x	x			x		
SOCADJ3	x	x	x		x		x			x	x	x			x
SOCADJ4	x	x		x	x	x	x			x	x		x		

Missing Data Pattern Frequencies

Pattern	Frequency	Pattern	Frequency	Pattern	Frequency
1	307	6	20	11	6
2	2	7	1	12	3
3	12	8	1	13	4
4	1	9	23	14	1
5	3	10	1	15	1

Covariance Coverage of Data

Minimum covariance coverage value	0.100

Proportion of Data Present

	Covariance Coverage					
	MOOD2	MOOD3	MOOD4	SOCADJ2	SOCADJ3	SOCADJ4
MOOD2	0.959					
MOOD3	0.834	0.860				
MOOD4	0.855	0.813	0.883			
SOCADJ2	0.959	0.837	0.858	0.964		
SOCADJ3	0.842	0.858	0.821	0.845	0.870	
SOCADJ4	0.865	0.819	0.883	0.868	0.829	0.894

Table 11.2 Mplus Output for Model 1: Sample Statistics

Estimated Sample Statistics

Means

	MOOD2	MOOD3	MOOD4	SOCADJ2	SOCADJ3	SOCADJ4
	21.336	21.140	20.070	101.024	99.928	100.320

Covariances

	MOOD2	MOOD3	MOOD4	SOCADJ2	SOCADJ3	SOCADJ4
MOOD2	40.260					
MOOD3	24.144	43.161				
MOOD4	21.051	24.510	35.351			
SOCADJ2	−22.352	−19.480	−17.693	94.987		
SOCADJ3	−23.924	−31.640	−21.667	69.774	108.343	
SOCADJ4	−18.018	−18.610	−21.081	47.228	61.547	79.812

Correlations

	MOOD2	MOOD3	MOOD4	SOCADJ2	SOCADJ3	SOCADJ4
MOOD2	1.000					
MOOD3	0.579	1.000				
MOOD4	0.558	0.627	1.000			
SOCADJ2	−0.361	−0.304	−0.305	1.000		
SOCADJ3	−0.362	−0.463	−0.350	0.688	1.000	
SOCADJ4	−0.318	−0.317	−0.397	0.542	0.662	1.000

15 reveals that it has complete data for only one of the six variables (*SOCADJ3*); each of the remaining variables has missing data. The final piece of information for this section of the output file reports on the proportion of data present. As can be seen in the table, the largest proportion of data is provided at Time 1 with 95.9% scores present for *MOOD2* and 96.4% for *SOCADJ2*.

Presented next, in Table 11.2, are the estimated sample statistics for these data. Turning first to the means of the outcome variables, we can see that there is minimal fluctuation across the 8 months for both *mood* and *social adjustment*. In fact, there appears to be virtually no difference in the *mood* scores between those collected at 1 month post surgery and those collected after 4 months; scores at Time 3 (i.e., after 8 months post surgery) were slightly lower. *Social adjustment* also showed little change over the 8-month period, albeit the lowest score here occurred at the second time point (4 months post surgery). These mean scores suggest that evidence of change in the slopes related to both constructs across an 8-month postsurgery period will likely be minimal.

Appearing next in Table 11.2 is the covariance matrix. In reviewing the variances on the main diagonal of this matrix, we can see that for both *mood* and *social adjustment*, scores collected 4 months post surgery exhibited the most variability across the women, dropping off substantially at 8 months post surgery. That a wide fluctuation of individual trajectories occurred at time point 2 (4 months post surgery) seems to suggest that it is at the midpoint of the healing process when the perceptions of the women varied widely in terms of both their emotional well-being and their ability to cope with the situation socially. Appearing last in Table 11.2 is the correlation matrix, where we can observe the strongest association to be between *SOCADJ2* and *SOCADJ3*, the intersection between perceptions of social adjustment at Time 1 and Time 2.

Before turning to SEM results related to the testing of the hypothesized model, I wish to show you an example of the PLOT command provided by M*plus* as it works easily and well in enabling you to have a more detailed look at your data. Details related to this facility were outlined in Chapter 2. Graphical presentations resulting from the PLOT command can be inspected following completion of the analyses using a dialog-based postprocessing graphics module. These graphical presentations are tagged as .gph files and are accessed in the same way as both the model input and output files. The input file related to specification of the PLOT command is presented in Figure 11.3, and the process of accessing the graph file shown in Figure 11.4.

Once you access a graph file, you are offered the choice of viewing variables within the context of a histogram or scatterplot (sample values), or as observed individual values; you can also select the number of cases to be included in the graph, as well as whether they should be selected consecutively or randomly. Presented in Figures 11.5, 11.6, and 11.7 are three different views of individual values pertinent to the first 15 women in our breast cancer database. Turning first to Figure 11.5, note first (on the bar under the toolbar) the term *Process 1*. Accordingly, this first graph limits the trajectories to only the first domain of *mood*. However, right-clicking on any of the points will provide you with extended information related to scores for any particular case. As illustrated in Figure 11.5, right-clicking on the highest score for Time 1 revealed this trajectory to belong to Individual 3, along with the other scores on both domains for this person. Figure 11.6 shows the trajectories for the same Individual 3, albeit specific to Domain 2, *social adjustment*. Note that the bar at the top of this set is labeled *Process 2*. Again, right-clicking on the initial score of 80.667 listed all scores for this individual. Finally, Figure 11.7 shows you how to access further information, which in this case is how to move to another

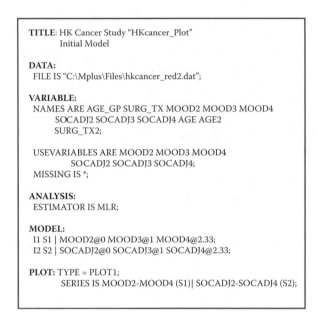

```
TITLE: HK Cancer Study "HKcancer_Plot"
       Initial Model

DATA:
  FILE IS "C:\Mplus\Files\hkcancer_red2.dat";

VARIABLE:
  NAMES ARE AGE_GP SURG_TX MOOD2 MOOD3 MOOD4
         SOCADJ2 SOCADJ3 SOCADJ4 AGE AGE2
         SURG_TX2;

  USEVARIABLES ARE MOOD2 MOOD3 MOOD4
         SOCADJ2 SOCADJ3 SOCADJ4;
  MISSING IS *;

ANALYSIS:
  ESTIMATOR IS MLR;

MODEL:
  I1 S1 | MOOD2@0 MOOD3@1 MOOD4@2.33;
  I2 S2 | SOCADJ2@0 SOCADJ3@1 SOCADJ4@2.33;

PLOT: TYPE = PLOT1;
       SERIES IS MOOD2-MOOD4 (S1)| SOCADJ2-SOCADJ4 (S2);
```

Figure 11.3. M*plus* input file showing the PLOT command.

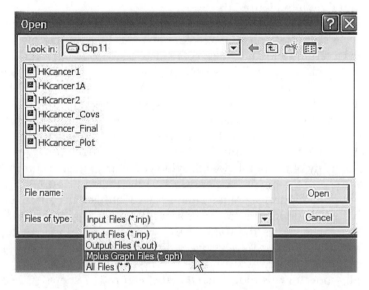

Figure 11.4. M*plus* dropdown menu for retrieval of graphical output.

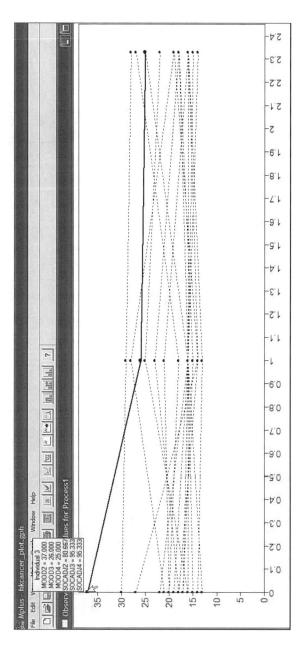

Figure 11.5. M*plus* graphical output: Individual plot showing scores for first 15 subjects over three time points for mood.

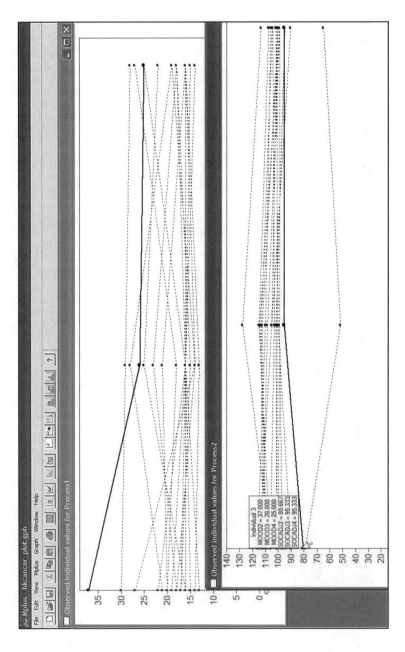

Figure 11.6. Mplus graphical output: Individual plot showing in the foreground scores for first 15 subjects over three time points for social adjustment.

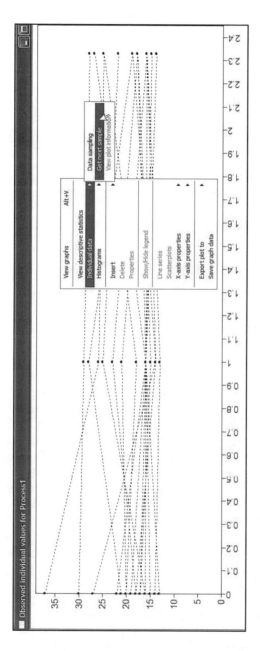

Figure 11.7. Mplus graphical output showing method for obtaining plot for an alternative set of scores.

Table 11.3 M*plus* Output for Model 1: Selected Goodness-of-Fit Statistics

Tests of Model Fit

Chi-Square Test of Model Fit

Value	36.036*
Degrees of freedom	7
p-value	0.0000
Scaling Correction Factor for MLR	1.118

CFI/TLI

CFI	0.944
TLI	0.879

Root Mean Square Error of Approximation (RMSEA)

Estimate	0.104
90 percent confidence interval (CI)	0.072 0.138
Probability RMSEA <= .05	0.004

Standardized Root Mean Square Residual (SRMR)

Value	0.086

* The chi-square value for MLM, MLMV, MLR, ULSMV, WLSM, and WLSMV cannot be used for chi-square difference tests. MLM, MLR, and WLSM chi-square difference testing is described in the M*plus* "Technical Appendices" at www.statmodel.com. See chi-square difference testing in the index of the M*plus User's Guide* (Muthén & Muthén, 2007–2010).

set of 15 individuals. Because I opted for consecutive selection, this next sample would comprise scores for Individuals 16 through 30.

At this point, I think we're ready to move on to examining results from our test of the hypothesized model. Presented in Table 11.3 are the key goodness-of-fit statistics. Recall that due to the presence of incomplete data, we selected the MLR estimator as it can correct the maximum likelihood (ML) chi-square (χ^2) statistic to take this missingness into account. Here we find a corrected χ^2 value of 36.036 with seven degrees of freedom; the scaling correction factor is reported to be 1.118. Consistent with notation of this caveat elsewhere in the book, the * accompanying the χ^2 statistic serves as a reminder that calculation of χ^2 difference tests based on (in this case) the MLR estimator between any two competing models is inappropriate.

Before reviewing the remaining fit statistics, however, I think it's important that you clearly understand the source of the seven degrees of freedom. First, let's think about the number of pieces of information with which we have to work here. With LGC models, we are dealing with both the means as well as the covariances of the outcome variables. Thus, given six outcome variables, the number of covariances will be 6 (6 + 1)/2, which equals 21; taking into consideration the six observed means, we have a total of 27 pieces of information upon which the analyses will be based. Consider now the number of freely estimated parameters in the model (see Figure 11.1); these are as follows:

- Four factor means (I1, S1, I2, and S2)
- Four factor variances (I1, S1, I2, and S2)
- Six residual variances (MOOD2, MOOD3, MOOD4, SOCADJ2, SOCADJ3, and SOCADJ4)
- Two factor covariances (I1 with S1; and I2 with S2)
- Four cross-domain factor covariances (I1 with I2; I1 with S2; S1 with S2; and S1 with I2)

Accordingly, given 27 pieces of information and 20 estimated parameters, the number of degrees of freedom should be seven, which indeed it is.

Moving on to the remainder of Table 11.3, we find values of 0.944 and 0.879 for the CFI and TLI, respectively. Although the CFI value is moderately good, the TLI value is clearly unacceptable. Likewise, the Root Mean Square Error of Approximation (RMSEA) value of 0.104 and Standardized Root Mean Square Residual (SRMR) value of 0.086 are also less than acceptable. Thus, it is clear that some modification to the model is needed.

Shown in Table 11.4 is the listing of only one modification index suggesting that specification of a covariance between the residual variances associated with *SOCADJ3* and *MOOD3* would lead to a substantially better fit to the hypothesized model. Indeed, the expected parameter change (EPC) value of −9.657 suggests a fairly strong relation between these two outcome variables. Given that *mood* was measured by the 12-item Chinese Health Questionnaire (Cheng & Williams, 1986), which taps into symptoms of anxiety and depression, low scores are indicative of a more positive mood; the resulting negative EPC value therefore is reasonable. Given both the estimated size of this covariance parameter, together with its substantive plausibility, the hypothesized model was respecified and reestimated accordingly.

Table 11.4 Mplus Output for Model 1: Modification Indices (MIs)

		Model Modification Indices		
	MI	Expected Parameter Change (EPC)	Standard EPC	StdYX EPC
WITH Statements				
SOCADJ3 WITH MOOD3	26.452	−9.637	−9.637	−0.361

Table 11.5 Mplus Output for Model 2: Selected Goodness-of-Fit Statistics

Tests of Model Fit	
Chi-Square Test of Model Fit	
Value	6.590
Degrees of freedom	6
p-value	0.3605
Scaling Correction Factor for MLR	1.085
CFI/TLI	
CFI	0.999
TLI	0.997
Root Mean Square Error of Approximation (RMSEA)	
Estimate	0.016
90 percent confidence interval (CI)	0.000 0.069
Probability RMSEA <= .05	0.806
Standardized Root Mean Square Residual (SRMR)	
Value	0.042

Testing for Validity of Model 2

Let's now review goodness-of-fit statistics related to this modified model, which are reported in Table 11.5. Clearly, the addition to Model 1 of the residual covariance between *MOOD3* and *SOCADJ3* resulted in a highly improved fit to the data, as evidenced from the CFI = 0.999, TLI = 0.997, RMSEA = .016, and SRMR = 0.042. Now that we have an extremely well-fitting model, let's review parameter estimates as a check for any that may be nonsignificant, thereby allowing us to obtain a more parsimonious model through their deletion; this search is limited to only modeled covariances, as all other parameters must remain intact. These estimated values are presented in Table 11.6.

In reviewing these estimates in Table 11.6, you will readily note that all statistically significant covariance estimates have been highlighted in bold. Accordingly, in addition to the residual covariance added in Model 2, there are only two other covariance estimates that are statistically significant: (a) the originally hypothesized association between the intercept and slope for *social adjustment* (S2, I2), and (b) an association between the intercepts for *social adjustment* and *mood* (I2, I1). Given the substantive rationality of this latter covariance, it is reasonable to retain this parameter in the model. Thus, in the interest of parsimony, a final LGC model was specified in which the following covariances were deleted: (a) the slope

Table 11.6 M*plus* Output for Model 2: Selected Parameter Estimates

		Estimate	Standard Error (*SE*)	Estimate/*SE*	*p*-Value
S1	WITH				
	I1	−1.958	1.642	−1.193	0.233
I2	WITH				
	I1	−22.352	4.002	−5.585	0.000
	S1	1.917	1.737	1.104	0.270
S2	WITH				
	I1	1.998	1.584	1.262	0.207
	S1	−1.426	0.750	−1.902	0.057
	I2	−15.482	4.530	−3.418	0.001
MOOD3	WITH				
	SOCADJ3	−10.371	2.495	−4.156	0.000

and intercept for *mood* (S1, I1), (b) the slope for *mood* and the intercept for *social adjustment* (S1, I2), (c) the slope for *social adjustment* and the intercept for *mood* (S2, I1), and (d) the slopes for *social adjustment* and *mood* (S2, S1).

Testing for Validity of the Final Model

Output File 2

Turning first to the goodness-of-fit statistics for this final model (see Table 11.7), we note that, except for the MLR chi-square value, which now has 10, rather than 6 degrees of freedom (due to deletion of the four covariance parameters), the remaining CFI, TLI, RMSEA, and SRMR results remained close to the former values for Model 2. As such, we can feel confident that interpretations of the final growth results are based on an extremely well-fitting model.

Let's now examine the resulting parameter estimates, which are reported in Table 11.8. Presented first are the factor covariance estimates, which of course are all significant. Turning first to the between-domain covariance of I2 with I1, we find the negative value of −19.870. This result suggests that for women whose scores for *mood* were high at Time 1 (1 month following surgery), their scores for *social adjustment* were low. Given my earlier explanation regarding the assessment scale used in measuring *mood*, this inverse relation between the two domains is both logical and reasonable.

Table 11.7 Mplus Output for Final Model: Selected Goodness-of-Fit Statistics

Tests of Model Fit	
Chi-Square Test of Model Fit	
Value	13.530
Degrees of freedom	10
p-value	0.1955
Scaling Correction Factor for MLR	1.247
CFI/TLI	
CFI	0.993
TLI	0.990
Root Mean Square Error of Approximation (RMSEA)	
Estimate	0.030
90 percent confidence interval (CI)	0.000 0.067
Probability RMSEA <= .05	0.778
Standardized Root Mean Square Residual (SRMR)	
Value	0.040

The second reported covariance represents the within-domain link between scores on *social adjustment* at Time 1 and at Time 3 (i.e., 8 months later). That these scores are also negative is rather interesting as they suggest that for women who perceived their future social interaction among friends and family in a rather pessimistic light at 1 month following breast cancer surgery, the reverse situation occurred; that is, these perceptions became more optimistic over the 8-month postsurgery period. Likewise, the reverse perceptions were realized.

The third covariance reported relates to the subsequently specified residual covariance between *mood* and *social adjustment* at Time 2, which is shown to be statistically significant.

The next two categories of results reported in Table 11.8 (Means and Variances) are typically of most importance in LGC modeling. All statistically significant estimates have been highlighted in bold. We turn first to results for the Intercept and Slope means. These estimates convey information related to both the average scores on *mood* and *social adjustment* at Time 1 and the average rate of change in these scores across the 8-month period. As shown in Table 11.8, only the estimated slope for *social adjustment* was found to be nonsignificant. Let's look first at the results for *mood*. These estimates indicate that, although the average self-reported score at 1 month post surgery was 21.397 (the Intercept), this score decreased, on average, by 0.550 (the Slope) over the subsequent 8 months. This finding

Table 11.8 M*plus* Output for Final Model: Selected Parameter Estimates

		Model Results		
	Estimate	Standard Error (*SE*)	Estimate/*SE*	*p*-Value
I2 WITH				
I1	−19.870	2.866	−6.933	0.000
S2 WITH				
I2	−15.469	4.492	−3.444	0.001
MOOD3 WITH				
SOCADJ3	−10.647	2.540	−4.192	0.000
Means				
I1	**21.397**	**0.313**	**68.313**	**0.000**
S1	**−0.550**	**0.131**	**−4.188**	**0.000**
I2	**100.926**	**0.503**	**200.673**	**0.000**
S2	−0.268	0.207	−1.293	0.196
Variances				
I1	**21.962**	**2.722**	**8.068**	**0.000**
S1	0.887	0.763	1.163	0.245
I2	**83.396**	**13.060**	**6.385**	**0.000**
S2	**12.490**	**3.429**	**3.643**	**0.000**
Residual Variances				
MOOD2	**18.101**	**2.245**	**8.064**	**0.000**
MOOD3	**18.627**	**2.526**	**7.375**	**0.000**
MOOD4	**9.479**	**3.636**	**2.607**	**0.009**
SOCADJ2	11.365	7.454	1.525	0.127
SOCADJ3	**41.358**	**7.331**	**5.642**	**0.000**
SOCADJ4	1.193	10.978	0.109	0.913

implies that as time following surgery increases, women tend gradually to report a more positive mood. With respect to *social adjustment*, we note that, on average, the score at 1 month following surgery was 100.926, albeit with negligible change over the next 8 months.

Turning next to the variances, we see that again we have one statistically nonsignificant estimate (S1), the Slope for *mood*. As noted earlier, these parameters represent deviation from the average intercept and slope in the population and, as such, yield information on interindividual differences both in the initial status of *mood* and *social adjustment* and in their change over time from 1 month to 8 months post surgery. Such evidence provides strong justification for the incorporation of predictor variables in subsequent analyses in an effort to explain this variation. We address this issue following this review of the parameter estimates.

Finally, the last six entries in Table 11.8 provide estimates of the residual variance associated with each occasion of measurement for *mood* and *social adjustment*. Although these error terms were statistically significant with respect to *mood* at each of the three time points, they were only so for Time 2 (4 months post surgery) for *social adjustment*.

Hypothesized Covariate Model: Age and Surgery as Predictors of Change

As noted earlier in the chapter, provided with evidence of interindividual differences, we can then ask whether, and to what extent, one or more predictors might explain this heterogeneity. For our purposes here, we ask whether statistically significant heterogeneity in the individual growth trajectories (i.e., intercept and slope) of *mood* and *social adjustment* can be explained by age and/or type of surgery performed. As such, two questions that we might ask are "Do self-perceptions of *mood* and *social adjustment* following breast cancer surgery differ for Hong Kong women according to their age (0 = < 51 years; 1 = > 50 years) and/or type of surgical treatment (0 = lumpectomy; 1 = mastectomy)[4] at Time 1 (1 month following surgery)?" and "Does the rate at which self-perceived mood and social adjustment change over time differ according to age and/or type of surgery?" To answer these questions, the predictor variables of *age* and *surgery* were incorporated into the model. This covariate model represents an extension of our final best fitting model and is shown schematically in Figure 11.8.

In reviewing this path diagram, I draw your attention to the addition of three new components: (a) the four regression paths leading from each of the predictor variables (*age* and *surgery*) to the Intercept and Slope factors associated with *mood* and *social adjustment*, (b) the double-headed arrow representing the covariance between I1 and I2, and (c) the double-headed arrow representing the covariance between the residual variances for *MOOD3* and *SOCADJ3*. Note also that, given findings of a nonsignificant estimate for the postulated covariance between the intercept and slope for *mood* in the initially hypothesized model, this parameter does not appear in this covariate model. Of primary interest here are the regression paths that flow from the predictor variables to I1, S1, I2, and S2 for the two domains of *mood* and *social adjustment* as they hold the key in answering the question of whether the trajectories of *mood* and

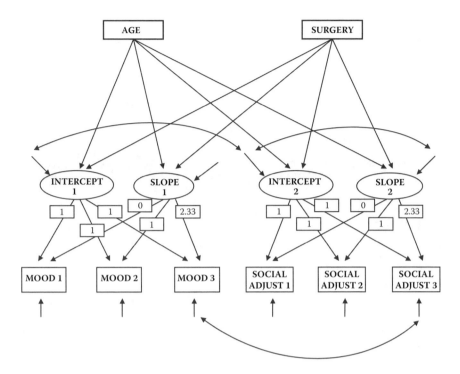

Figure 11.8. Hypothesized covariate model showing *age* and *surgery* as predictor variables.

social adjustment differ across *age* and *surgery*. Also worthy of note is the fact that, with the addition of the two predictor variables to the model, interpretation of the Intercept and Slope residual variances necessarily changes. Whereas these parameters in the previous model (in which no predictors were specified) represented deviations between the Intercept and Slope factors, and their population means, within the framework of the current model they now represent variation remaining in the intercepts and slopes *after* all variability in their prediction by *age* and *surgery* has been explained. That is, they represent the adjusted values of the factor intercepts and slopes after partialing out the linear effect of the predictors of change (Willett & Keiley, 2000).

Input File

Before examining the results of analyses stemming from the test of this covariate model, let's first review the related input M*plus* file presented in Figure 11.9. Three specifications are of prime interest here. First, note under the VARIABLE command that the USEVARIABLES option now includes the variables *AGE2* and *SURG_TX2*, the two predictor variables.

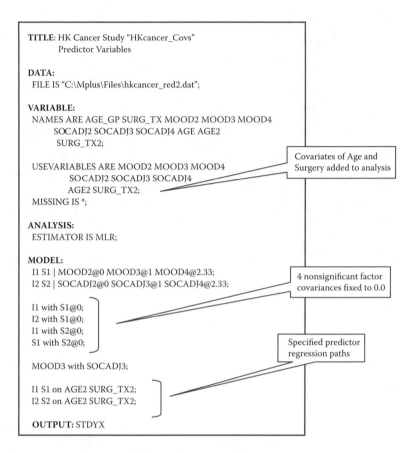

Figure 11.9. M*plus* input file for covariate model.

Of import here is that although these two variables are categorical, there is no need to specify this information as they operate as only *independent* variables in the model. Second, recall that in our testing of the initially hypothesized model, we found four factor covariance parameters to be nonsignificant, and in the interest of parsimony they were subsequently deleted; in M*plus*, this deletion is accomplished by fixing the related parameters to zero. Accordingly, the four WITH statements representing these nonsignificant covariance parameters appear in lines 4 through 7 under the MODEL command. Finally, the last two lines of model input represent specifications related to the two predictor regression paths. As such, the Intercept and Slope factors for both *mood* and *social adjustment* are shown to load on predictor variables labeled in the data set as *AGE2* and *SURG_TX2*.

Table 11.9 Mplus Output for Covariate Model: Selected Goodness-of-Fit Statistics

Tests of Model Fit	
Chi-Square Test of Model Fit	
Value	16.622
Degrees of freedom	14
p-value	0.2769
Scaling Correction Factor for MLR	1.147
CFI/TLI	
CFI	0.996
TLI	0.992
Root Mean Square Error of Approximation (RMSEA)	
Estimate	0.022
90 percent confidence interval (CI)	0.000 0.055
Probability RMSEA <= .05	0.911
Standardized Root Mean Square Residual (SRMR)	
Value	0.033

Output File

We turn now to the results for this covariance model and look first at the goodness-of fit statistics, which are presented in Table 11.9. Here again, we find an exceptionally good fit to the data (MLR $\chi^2_{[14]}$ = 16.622; CFI = 0.996; TLI = 0.992; RMSEA = 0.022; SRMR = 0.033). In the interest of space restrictions and because the parameters of primary interest with this model are the factor regression paths of individual change on the predictor variables of *age* and *surgery*, only findings related to these parameters are presented in Table 11.10.

Turning first to results for *mood*, we find that whereas *age* was a statistically significant predictor of initial status (I1 on *AGE2*; –1.637, estimate/standard error [SE] = –2.647), it was not so for rate of change (S1 on *AGE2*; –0.207, estimate/*SE* = –0.795). Given a coding of 0 for women < 51 years and 1 for women > 50 years, these findings suggest that reported *mood* scores, on average, were lower at Time 1 (by 1.637 units) for women over the age of 50 than they were for younger women. The nonsignificant findings related to the slope suggest that any differences in the rate of change in these scores across the 8-month period between the two age groups were negligible. Likewise, type of SURGERY appeared to have no effect on either the initial status of *mood* (I1 ON *SURG_TX2*; –0.027, estimate/*SE* = –0.036) or its rate of change across time (S1 on *SURG_TX2*; –0.339, estimate/*SE* = –1.006).

Table 11.10 M*plus* Output for Covariate Model: Selected Parameter Estimates

Model Results

	Estimate	Standard Error (*SE*)	Estimate/*SE*	Two-Tailed *p*-Value
Unstandardized Parameters				
I1 ON				
AGE2	**−1.637**	**0.618**	**−2.647**	**0.008**
SURG_TX2	−0.027	0.750	−0.036	0.972
S1 ON				
AGE2	−0.207	0.260	−0.795	0.427
SURG_TX2	−0.339	0.337	−1.006	0.315
I2 ON				
AGE2	−0.968	0.989	−0.979	0.328
SURG_TX2	**−3.327**	**1.056**	**−3.151**	**0.002**
S2 ON				
AGE2	0.405	0.405	1.000	0.318
SURG_TX2	**1.253**	**0.486**	**2.577**	**0.010**
Standardized Parameters (STDYX Standardization)				
I1 ON				
AGE2	**−0.175**	**0.064**	**−2.733**	**0.006**
SURG_TX2	−0.002	0.063	−0.036	0.972
S1 ON				
AGE2	−0.119	0.162	−0.737	0.461
SURG_TX2	−0.155	0.167	−0.930	0.352
I2 ON				
AGE2	−0.053	0.053	−0.997	0.319
SURG_TX2	**−0.144**	**0.044**	**−3.257**	**0.001**
S2 ON				
AGE2	0.057	0.059	0.974	0.330
SURG_TX2	**0.140**	**0.055**	**2.563**	**0.010**

In contrast, results related to *social adjustment* revealed type of SURGERY to be a significant predictor of both initial status (I2 on *SURG_TX2*; –3.327, estimate/*SE* = –3.151) and its rate of change across the 8-month period (S2 on *SURG_TX2*; 1.253, estimate/*SE* = 2.577). Based on the coding system of 0 for women who underwent lumpectomy and 1 for those who underwent mastectomy, these findings suggest that whereas women who underwent a mastectomy had lower scores on *social adjustment* at initial status than women who underwent a lumpectomy (by –3.327), their rate of change in this perception over the 8-month period was somewhat faster (by 1.253). Thus, although initially social adjustment among women having a lumpectomy was better than it was among women having a mastectomy, over time this advantage diminished. Finally, age was found not to be a significant predictor of either initial status (I2 on AGE2; –0.968, estimate/*SE* = –0.979) or rate of change (S2 on AGE2; 0.405, estimate/*SE* = 1.000) for *social adjustment*.

In closing out this chapter, I draw from the work of Willett and Sayer (1994, 1996) in highlighting several important features captured by the LGC modeling approach in the investigation of change. First, the methodology can accommodate anywhere from 3 to 30 waves of longitudinal data equally well. Willett (1988, 1989) has shown, however, that the more waves of data collected, the more precise will be the estimated growth trajectory and the higher will be the reliability for the measurement of change. Second, there is no requirement that the time lag between each wave of assessments be equivalent. Indeed, LGC modeling can easily accommodate irregularly spaced measurements, but with the caveat that all subjects are measured on the same set of occasions. Third, individual change can be represented by either a linear or a nonlinear growth trajectory. Although linear growth is typically assumed by default, this assumption is easily tested and the model respecified to address curvilinearity if need be. Fourth, in contrast to traditional methods used in measuring change, LGC models allow not only for the estimation of measurement residual (i.e., error) variances, but also for their autocorrelation and fluctuation across time in the event that tests for the assumptions of independence and homoscedasticity are found to be untenable. Fifth, multiple predictors of change can be included in the LGC model. They may be time invariant, as in the case of gender, and as applied in the present chapter, or they may be time varying (see, e.g., Curran, Muthén, & Harford, 1998; Willett & Keiley, 2000). Finally, the three key statistical assumptions associated with LGC modeling (linearity, independence of measurement error variances, and homoscedasticity of measurement error variances), although not demonstrated in this chapter, can be easily tested via a comparison of nested models (see Duncan et al., 2006).

Notes

1. In the original study, this construct was termed *psychological morbidity*.
2. Had all time points been used, these values would have been 0, 1, 2, and 3.
3. Recall that, for our purposes here, analyses are based on scores from the second through fourth time points, as noted in this chapter (albeit we have considered them to represent Times 1 through 3 for convenience here), hence the numbered labels 2 through 4.
4. The two categories of *age* were formulated on the basis of average physiological age of menopause, thereby yielding a premenopausal group (< 51 years, coded as 0) and a postmenopausal group (> 50 years, coded as 1). The two categories of *surgery* type comprised women whose breast cancer involved a lumpectomy (coded as 0) and those for whom surgery involved a mastectomy (coded as 1).

chapter 12

Testing Within- and Between-Level Variability
The Multilevel Model

In contrast to the multigroup models illustrated in Chapters 7, 8, and 9 in which analyses were based on data representing different populations, the multigroup model examined in this chapter focuses on a single population that is hierarchically structured. Such models are termed *multilevel* (MLV) models because the data lend themselves to more than one level of analyses. Most commonly, examples of hierarchically structured data are (a) students nested within schools, (b) patients nested within clinics, (c) employees nested within firms or corporations, and (d) children and adults nested within families, among others. Such hierarchical structures are often termed *nested data* or *clustered data*. In essence, however, hierarchical structures may involve more than two levels of analysis. For example, building upon these earlier examples, data could be extended to include schools nested within districts, and districts nested within states; or employees nested within departments, departments nested within business organizations, organizations nested within regions, and so on.

Beyond these examples, however, substantial methodological research over this past decade has shown that hierarchical structures can be studied from a wide variety of perspectives. Although this work clearly exceeds the scope of the present volume, I highly recommend that you review at least a few of these intriguing, albeit ever-growing applications of MLV modeling within the framework of structural equation modeling (SEM).[1] For readers interested in *longitudinal analyses* in general, and/or *latent growth curve modeling* in particular, see Baumler, Harrist, and Carvajal (2003); Chen, Kwok, Luo, and Willson (2010); Chou, Bentler, and Pentz (2000); Ecob and Der (2003); Heck and Thomas (2009); Hoffman (2007); Hox (2000, 2002, 2010); Hung (2010); Jo and Muthén (2003); Kaplan, Kim, and Kim (2009); Kwok, West, and Green (2007); Little, Schnabel, and Baumert (2000); MacCallum and Kim (2000); and Muthén, Khoo, Francis, and Boscardin (2003). More recently, enormous progress has been made in advancing MLV modeling applications to numerous other areas of research. Suggested publications on these specific topics are as follows:

multitrait–multimethod analyses (Hox & Kleiboer, 2007), *mediation analyses* (Preacher, Zyphur, & Zhang, 2010), *item response theory analyses* (Hsieh, von Eye, & Maier, 2010), and *meta-analyses* (Hox, 2010; Hox & de Leeuw, 2003). Finally, other MLV modeling issues capturing the interests of methodological researchers have focused on use of *categorical data* (see Fielding, 2003; Heck & Thomas, 2009; Hox, 2010; Hung, 2010; Kaplan et al., 2009), determination of *reliability* (Raykov & Penev, 2010), and *specification searches* (Peugh & Enders, 2010).

The application illustrated in the present chapter represents a two-level analysis (CFA) model based on item responses to the Family Values (FV) Scale (Georgas, 1999) for 5,482 university students (2,070 males and 3,160 females) from 27 countries; gender scores were missing for Germany (n = 7), India (n = 1), Mexico (n = 1), Nigeria (n = 3), Ukraine (n = 1), and Indonesia (n = 239).[2] The example presented here extends the work of Byrne and van de Vijver (2010) that probed the many complexities associated with testing for measurement invariance across diverse cultural groups. (For details related to sample size, gender composition, and mean age by country, see Byrne & van de Vijver, 2010.)

Overview of Multilevel Modeling

As noted by Selig, Card, and Little (2008), in general terms, "[A]ny model that can be depicted as a multigroup SEM, can also be defined as a multilevel SEM, given that the data are hierarchically clustered as individuals within groups" (p. 102). In its simplest form, the data are represented by a two-level structure, with the lower level representing individuals (e.g., students and employees) and the upper level representing groups (e.g., schools and companies). Taken together, the primary objective of MLV modeling is to summarize within-group variability at the individual (or lower) level and between-group variability at the group (or higher) level. These levels are often referred to as *Level 1* and *Level 2*, respectively.

Over this past decade, MLV modeling has been increasingly recognized as one of the most effective means to investigating hierarchical data. Until relatively recently, however, practical application of MLV modeling has tended to lag behind the substantive theory to which it is grounded. This delay in the use of MLV modeling can be linked to the inability of earlier SEM software packages to adequately address complexities such as the computation of separate covariance matrices for sampling units of varying sample sizes and the provision of appropriate estimators (Heck & Thomas, 2009; Hox, 2002; McArdle & Hamagami, 1996). As a consequence, researchers working with hierarchical data had no choice but to disregard the rich source of potential information provided by such data, thereby limiting their investigation to single-level analyses either on the lowest level of measurement (e.g., students) or on the highest level of measurement (e.g., schools). Rephrased differently, researchers needed either to disaggregate or to aggregate variables from their nested data in order to enable single-level analyses (Heck, 2001). Importantly, however, when such hierarchical structure is ignored, problematic repercussions necessarily occur at both the individual (i.e., disaggregated) and group (i.e., aggregated) levels, thereby leading to several analytic and interpretation difficulties, a topic to which we now turn.

Single-Level Analyses of Hierarchical Data: Related Problems

The Disaggregation Approach

In using this approach, analyses focus on the individual (or lower) level of the hierarchy and necessarily lead to violation of two major statistical assumptions: (a) that all observations are independent, and (b) that all random errors are independent, normally distributed, and homoscedastic. Violation of the first assumption implies that all individuals within similar organizational or societal units share no common characteristics, which of course is totally unreasonable (Heck, 2001; Julian, 2001). Indeed, Muthén and Satorra (1995) reported that the more pronounced the similarities among individuals within groups, the more biased will be the parameter estimates, standard errors, and related tests for significance. Violation of the second assumption, on the other hand, suggests no systematic influence of variables at the higher level, which again is erroneous and unrealistic (Kreft & de Leeuw, 1998). Taken as a whole, disregard for hierarchical structure of the data has the potential to yield underestimated standard errors and, as a result, an inflated Type I error rate (Bovaird, 2007).

The Aggregated Approach

In like manner, single-level analyses of data that focus on the group (or higher) level are equally problematic. As such, the groups (e.g., schools) form the unit of analysis with the individual data used to develop mean scores on the variables as they relate to each organization (Heck, 2001). Again, there are at least three limitations associated with these higher level analyses: (a) Given that all variability within each organizational unit is reduced to a single mean, any differences found at the group level will appear stronger than would be the case if within-organizational (i.e., individual) variability were also incorporated into the analysis (Kaplan & Elliott, 1997);[3] (b) in situations where the individual-level data for particular variables (e.g., socioeconomic status) may be scant in some groups, the attainment of efficient estimates is made more difficult, thereby resulting in less efficient prediction equations for these groups (Bryk & Raudenbush,

1992); and (c) aggregated analyses can lead to reduced statistical power, inaccurate representations of group-level relations, and increased risk of incorrectly drawing causal inferences from individual-level behavior based on group-level data (Bovaird, 2007). Given substantial focus on cross-cultural mean comparisons, this latter point, termed the *ecological fallacy* (Robinson, 1950), remains one of the most notable problems associated with cross-cultural research.

Multilevel Analyses of Hierarchical Data

In contrast to single-level analyses, MLV modeling allows the researcher to consider *both* levels of the hierarchically structured data simultaneously. In particular, it enables the partitioning of total variance into within- and between-group components and allows a separate structural model to be specified at each level. For example, in the case of students nested within schools, this would mean that the total covariance matrix, Σ, is partitioned into a within-covariance matrix (Σ_W) and a between-covariance matrix (Σ_B). The Σ_W matrix represents covariation at the individual level (i.e., individual differences in, say, math self-concept) and their correlates, albeit controlling for variation across schools. In contrast, the Σ_B matrix represents covariation at the school level (i.e., differences across schools in, say, school climate) and their correlates. The Σ_W and Σ_B covariance matrices may have similar or totally different model structures. For each student, then, the total score is decomposed into an individual component (i.e., individual deviation from the group mean) and a group component (i.e., the disaggregated school group mean). It is via this individual decomposition that the separate within- and between-group covariance matrices are computed (Heck, 2001; Hox, 2002). Not surprisingly, the related effects are termed *within-cluster* and *between-cluster* effects (see Bentler, 2005). If a mean structure is needed, it is used to model the between-group means.

As an aid to conceptualizing the MLV model, McArdle and Hamagami (1996) suggested that one think of it as a typical multisample analysis. The rationale underlying this proposal stems from the fact that analyses focus on the estimation of two unstructured matrices, Σ_W and Σ_B, each of which represents a separate model. Although the standard statistical assumption of independent groups, of course, cannot be made, such a model can nonetheless be thought of as a two-group multigroup model (Bentler, 2005).

MLV Model Estimation

In the early years of MLV modeling within the framework of SEM, analytic approaches to the estimation of parameters involved mainly full information maximum likelihood (FIML; hereafter shortened to maximum likelihood [ML]) estimation and Muthén's (1994) approximate maximum likelihood (MUML) estimation. Whereas ML estimation demanded that group sizes be balanced (i.e., into clusters of equal size), MUML estimation represented a limited ML method of analyses that allowed for unbalanced groups (i.e., with clusters of unequal sizes). More specifically, whereas ML estimation based on data representing unbalanced groups yielded incorrect χ^2 values, fit indices, and standard errors (Kaplan, 1998; Muthén, 1994), the MUML estimator did not exhibit this limitation. On the other hand, when used with balanced groups, the MUML estimator virtually operates as ML.

More recently, advancements in statistical and methodological research pertinent to MLV modeling have led to important refinements in ML estimation (Heck & Thomas, 2009; Kaplan et al., 2009). In particular, Kaplan et al. noted that three recently developed expectation maximization (EM) algorithms[4] based on ML estimation are now available to users of the M*plus* program. These newer estimation methods can be distinguished on the basis of their approach to the computation of standard errors. The first of these methods is based on the MLF estimator; the second is based on the usual ML estimator but on the second-order derivatives; and the third is based on the MLR estimator, which is known not only to be robust to non-normality but also to allow for MLV analyses based on unbalanced groups. Given these capabilities, Yuan and Hayashi (2005) suggested that use of the MUML estimator may no longer be needed. A final benefit of current ML estimation is its allowance for random path coefficients. (For a more comprehensive and very readable review of MLV modeling estimation in general, as well as for these latter three estimators in particular, readers are referred to Bovaird, 2007; Heck & Thomas, 2009; Kaplan et al., 2009. For a more mathematical treatment of the topic, see Yuan & Hayashi, 2005.)

Clearly, these updated estimation options have increased the flexibility of SEM MLV modeling in the sense that they offer greater computational efficiency and provide increased options for model estimation (Heck & Thomas, 2009). Nonetheless, one major obstacle in using ML estimation is the need for large sample sizes, particularly at the highest level of a hierarchical structure, in order to ensure that estimates have desirable asymptotic properties (Heck, 2001; Hox, 2002; Hox & Maas, 2001; Muthén, 1994; Yuan & Bentler, 2002, 2004b). Indeed, Hox and Maas suggested that, ideally, the group-level sample size should be approximately 100.

MLV Model-Testing Approaches

Traditionally, there have been three approaches to the analysis of MLV models (Selig et al., 2008). The first of these has been, until relatively recently, the four-stage method proposed by Muthén (1994). However, as noted above, advancements in the development and refinement of MLV modeling estimation, as well as that of related statistical software

(Kaplan et al., 2009), have necessarily reduced the need for this method as originally implemented. As such, the original Steps 2 through 4 of these analyses have gradually become integrated into the M*plus* program such that they are now fully embedded in the current Version 6. The second approach, proposed by Hox (2002), is based on the establishment of a set of benchmark models, each of which tests key assumptions associated with ML modeling. Finally, the third approach was introduced by Mehta and Neale (2005) and is based on a three-step process that involves the fitting of univariate random intercepts to the data. Although Selig et al. (2008) contended that the Hox approach is the most straightforward and easiest to implement, Cheung and Au (2005) noted that the original Muthén (1994) approach nonetheless remains the most commonly used. (For a brief summary of all three approaches, see Selig et al., 2008.)

Following this introductory synopsis of MLV modeling, let's move on to an examination of the application under study in this chapter. Further details related to MLV analyses will emerge as we work through the various analytic stages. However, for more comprehensive coverage of the theory, related issues, and practice of MLV modeling, readers are referred to these excellent resources: Bovaird (2007), Heck (2001), Heck and Thomas (2009), Hox (2002, 2010), Kaplan et al. (2009), Little et al. (2000), Reise and Duan (2003), and Selig et al. (2008).

The Hypothesized Model

Despite an ever-growing number of possible MLV modeling applications involving variants of two-level CFA and path models, few appear to have had a psychometric focus (Dedrick & Greenbaum, 2010). The model under study in this chapter falls into this latter psychometric category. Specifically, the model of interest here is a two-level, two-factor CFA model representing the hypothesized factorial structure of the FV Scale. The purpose of this application is to illustrate initial tests of its factorial structure within the framework of MLV modeling. Although a comprehensive construct validity study of the FV Scale would necessarily entail many additional analyses conducted separately at the individual and group levels, these extensions clearly exceed the scope of this chapter. (Two potential follow-up analyses are suggested following these initial analyses.) The present analyses, then, serve only to provide an introduction to the initial stages in seeking evidence of construct validity for the FV Scale when used with data that are logically hierarchically structured.

The FV Scale is an 18-item measure having a 7-point Likert scale that ranges from 1 (*strongly disagree*) to 7 (*strongly agree*). Items were derived from an original 64-item pool and selected in such a way that the expected factors (Family Roles Hierarchy and Family/Kin Relationships) would be well represented. Based on exploratory factor analysis (EFA) findings that revealed near-zero loadings for four items (see van de Vijver, Mylonas, Pavlopoulos, & Georgas, 2006), Byrne and van de Vijver (2010) based their analyses on the resulting 14-item scale. (For a review of content related to all 18 items, readers are referred to the Byrne and van de Vijver [2010] article.)

Typically, the prime focus in cross-cultural research is on mean group comparisons across countries. As such, this type of research clearly represents single-level analyses conducted at the higher level of hierarchically structured data. A strong assumption of such analyses, however, is that both the measuring instrument and its underlying constructs are operating equivalently across cultural contexts. That is to say, items comprising the instrument are being perceived in exactly the same way across groups, and the structure and meaningfulness of the constructs being measured are the same across groups. The intent of this application is to test the extent to which the postulated two-factor structure of the FV Scale holds at both the individual and country levels. A schematic representation of this hypothesized MLV model is shown in Figure 12.1.

As you can see in Figure 12.1, the within-level and between-level models are identical in representing a two-factor CFA model, with Items 1, 3, 4, 6, 15, and 18 loading on Family Roles Hierarchy (Factor 1) and Items 2, 5, 8, 9, 10, 11, 12, and 14 loading on Family/Kin Relations (Factor 2). Of important note, however, are two distinctive differences implemented here for purposes of conceptual understanding and ease of analyses. First, although factorial structure is identical across levels, its graphical representation differs with respect to the depiction of the FV Scale items. Essentially, the model shown at the individual level, consistent with the measurement models of all preceding chapters in this book, characterizes a conventional two-factor structure, with the rectangles representing directly observed variables (i.e., the items). Although the model, at the group level, represents the same two-factor structure, the items are enclosed in ellipses that, in turn, are shown to impact their observed variable counterparts, thereby indicating that the latter are functions of both the within and between components (Muthén, 1994). Second, for specification clarity, notation related to the factor names at the higher level is labeled as BF1 and BF2 (with *B* representing the between component).

As noted earlier, the data to be used in this application comprise item responses to the FV Scale for 5,482 university students (2,070 males and 3,160 females) drawn from 27 geographically and culturally diverse countries from around the globe.[5] Of import here, however, is the notably small sample size (27 cultures) at the group (i.e., country) level. (Recall Hox & Maas's [2001] recommended number of 100, noted earlier.) Relatedly, however, Cheung and Au (2005) astutely noted that with only 200 countries in the entire world, many of which are small and developing, the chances

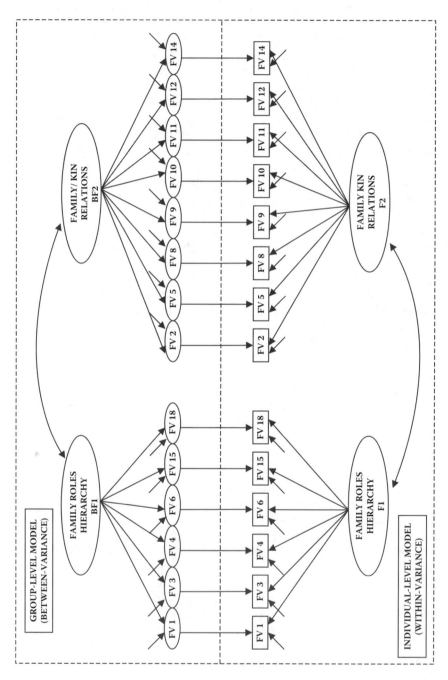

Figure 12.1. Hypothesized multilevel model of factorial structure for the Family Values Scale (Georgas, 1999).

of garnering group-level samples of this size when groups involve cross-cultural entities are highly unlikely. Indeed, based on a sample of 15,244 individuals drawn from 27 nations, Cheung and Au reported findings that revealed (a) individual-level results to be quite stable, and (b) results held even with small individual-level sample sizes.

Current Approach to Analyses of the Hypothesized MLV Model

Prior to walking you through stages of analyses related to this application, I wish first to summarize characteristics of the data as this may be instructive in helping you understand why I chose the analytic approach taken here; these are as follows.

Sample Size

Because 5,482 university students from 27 countries responded to 14 items on the FV Scale, sample size for the individual (or lower) level of the hierarchical structure is 5,482 and that of the group (or higher) level is 27. As data preparation in the original study of the FV Scale across cultures (Georgas, Berry, van de Vijver, Kagitcibasi, & Poortinga, 2006) involved replacement of the relatively few missing values with regression-based estimates to which an error component was added, all FV Scale item scores are complete.

Item Scaling

Although items on the FV Scale are admittedly categorical, the number of scale points is seven. Given evidence that, as the number of scale points increases, ordinal data behave more closely to interval data (Boomsma, 1987; Rigdon, 1998), outcome variables in the present analyses are treated as if they are continuous.

Estimation

Given that the MLR estimator is now default in M*plus* for MLV modeling and is becoming the preferred approach to these analyses, this estimator is used first in MLV analyses of the FV Scale. However, if presented with analytic difficulties, possibly due to the small sample size at the higher level, analyses are subsequently based on the MUML estimator.

The Analytic Process

Analyses of the data are conducted in three different stages. First, based on the full sample covariance matrix that ignores the grouping aspect of the data, we conduct a CFA as a means of testing the validity of the hypothesized two-factor structure shown in Figure 12.1. In the event that this analysis suggests model modifications that are rational and substantively defensible, the model is modified accordingly.

Second, provided with evidence of adequate fit of the single-level CFA model, the factor structure pertinent to both the individual and group levels of the data is tested in a simultaneous analysis of the MLV model based on MLR estimation.

Third, given that intraclass correlation coefficients (ICCs) of the observed variables (the items) are automatically reported in the simultaneous analysis conducted at Step 2, these values are examined as a means of justification (or nonjustification) of continued analyses of the MLV model. ICC values range from 0.0 to 1.0 and represent the proportion of between-group variance compared with total variance. Given findings of ICCs close to zero, it is meaningless to model within and between levels of the structure, and, thus, a conventional SEM approach to the analyses will yield reasonable and unbiased estimates (Julian, 2001). Muthén (1997) noted that, typically, ICC values tend to range from 0.00 to 0.50 and suggested that when group sizes exceed 15 and findings yield ICC values of 0.10 or larger, the multilevel structure of the data should definitely be modeled. More recently, however, Julian (2001) and Selig et al. (2008) have recommended that even with findings of ICC values less than 0.10, the hierarchical structure should not be ignored.

Finally, as noted earlier, in the event that MLV modeling of the data rendered reasonable results, two suggestions are provided regarding subsequent analyses that might be considered in an attempt to gather further evidence of construct validity related to the FV Scale.

Mplus Input File Specification and Output File Results

CFA of FV Scale Structure

Input File

As noted earlier, initial analysis of the data involved testing for the validity of the hypothesized structure of the FV Scale based on the total covariance matrix with no concern regarding hierarchical structure. The input file for this initial analysis is shown in Figure 12.2. Given that you are now very familiar with CFA Mplus model specification, I draw your attention to only two aspects of this file. First, note that the variable COUNTRY is not included in the USEVARIABLES command as it is not, of course, part of the factor analytic structure of the FV Scale. Second, given that the data are nonnormally distributed, the MLM estimator is used.

A review of the output file for this analysis reveals a fairly well-fitting model as follows: $\chi^2_{(76)} = 1470.341$, Comparative Fit Index (CFI) = 0.938, Root Mean Square Error of Approximation (RMSEA) = 0.058, and Standardized Root Mean Square Residual (SRMR) = 0.051. Not surprisingly, given the

---

TITLE: Testing the Full Sample CFA Model

DATA:
    FILE IS "C:\Mplus\Files\FVScale.DAT";

VARIABLE:
    NAMES ARE COUNTRY FV1 - FV18;
    USEVARIABLES ARE FV1 FV2 FV3 FV4 FV5 FV6 FV8
                    FV9 FV10 FV11 FV12 FV14 FV15 FV18;
ANALYSIS:
    ESTIMATOR IS MLM;

MODEL:
    F1 by FV1 FV3 FV4 FV6 FV15 FV18;
    F2 by FV2 FV5 FV8 - FV12 FV14;

OUTPUT: MODINDICES;

Figure 12.2. M*plus* input file for test of confirmatory factor analysis (CFA) model for full sample.

total sample size, all parameters were found to be statistically significant. Although these results are supportive of the hypothesized factor structure, a review of the modification indices (MIs) indicated the need for possible respecification of the model. These MI values are presented in Table 12.1.

In examining these MIs, you will note five very large values that appear in bolded text—three representing possible cross-loadings (F1 by FV9; F1 by FV14; F2 by FV1) and two possible residual covariances (FV12 with FV9; FV15 with FV11). Because particular items will be of interest at various stages of these MLV analyses, abbreviated content of all 14 FV items used in this application (see earlier explanation of this number) is presented in Table 12.2. Thus, essence of the items pertinent to these large MI values can be observed in this table.

As I have stressed throughout this book, however, any modifications to a postulated model should be made only on the basis of substantive meaningfulness. Adhering to this edict, I consider modifications based on only the first two MIs in Table 12.1 to fall into this category as each would appear to represent an aspect of familial hierarchical structure. Accordingly, these two cross-loadings represent the regression of FV9 and FV14 on Factor 1 (Family Roles Hierarchy).

Provided with substantive justification for modification of the hypothesized CFA structure, the model was subsequently respecified to include these two additional parameters, albeit pertinent to the individual level only. Goodness-of-fit indices related to this respecified model were $\chi^2_{(74)}$ = 1101.256, CFI = 0.954, RMSEA = 0.050, and SRMR = 0.038. Both cross-loadings were found to be statistically significant. A schematic representation of this modified model is shown in Figure 2.3.

Table 12.1 M*plus* Output:
Selected Modification Indices (MIs)

			Expected Parameter Change (EPC)	Standard EPC	StdYX EPC
		MI			
BY Statements					
F1	BY FV5	23.628	−0.062	−0.097	−0.102
F1	BY FV8	62.855	0.131	0.206	0.161
F1	**BY FV9**	**169.918**	**−0.194**	**−0.306**	**−0.283**
F1	BY FV11	52.486	0.122	0.192	0.137
F1	BY FV12	93.398	0.153	0.242	0.179
F1	**BY FV14**	**142.020**	**−0.152**	**−0.239**	**−0.236**
F2	**BY FV1**	**114.214**	**0.531**	**0.337**	**0.174**
F2	BY FV3	96.156	−0.603	−0.383	−0.184
F2	BY FV6	38.556	−0.308	−0.195	−0.103
F2	BY FV15	39.169	0.315	0.200	0.107
F2	BY FV18	11.040	−0.172	−0.109	−0.054
WITH Statements					
FV2	WITH FV1	41.917	0.132	0.132	0.119
FV4	WITH FV1	56.937	−0.260	−0.260	−0.150
FV4	WITH FV3	47.323	0.289	0.289	0.124
FV6	WITH FV2	22.246	−0.097	−0.097	−0.086
FV8	WITH FV4	36.322	0.167	0.167	0.105
FV9	WITH FV5	15.819	0.054	0.054	0.068
FV9	WITH FV6	18.119	−0.085	−0.085	−0.076
FV9	WITH FV8	31.469	0.098	0.098	0.097
FV10	WITH FV2	11.652	−0.055	−0.055	−0.060
FV10	WITH FV3	21.416	−0.115	−0.115	−0.081
FV10	WITH FV6	11.722	−0.067	−0.067	−0.063
FV10	WITH FV9	21.664	0.073	0.073	0.080
FV11	WITH FV1	29.555	0.117	0.117	0.106
FV11	WITH FV3	10.691	−0.089	−0.089	−0.060
FV11	WITH FV4	27.110	−0.142	−0.142	−0.095
FV11	WITH FV8	59.220	−0.151	−0.151	−0.150
FV11	WITH FV9	23.459	0.085	0.085	0.090
FV12	WITH FV1	20.725	0.091	0.091	0.091
FV12	WITH FV2	15.041	−0.067	−0.067	−0.077

Table 12.1 Mplus Output:
Selected Modification Indices (MIs) (*continued*)

		MI	Expected Parameter Change (EPC)	Standard EPC	StdYX EPC
FV12	**WITH FV9**	**120.200**	**−0.180**	**−0.180**	**−0.210**
FV12	WITH FV10	35.231	0.099	0.099	0.120
FV14	WITH FV2	81.742	0.126	0.126	0.163
FV14	WITH FV3	25.502	−0.107	−0.107	−0.089
FV14	WITH FV4	10.310	−0.068	−0.068	−0.057
FV14	WITH FV5	14.467	0.044	0.044	0.068
FV14	WITH FV9	37.706	0.083	0.083	0.108
FV15	WITH FV5	34.699	−0.102	−0.102	−0.105
FV15	WITH FV8	27.183	−0.116	−0.116	−0.094
FV15	**WITH FV11**	**127.152**	**0.247**	**0.247**	**0.214**
FV18	WITH FV4	16.803	0.147	0.147	0.081
FV18	WITH FV8	16.552	0.092	0.092	0.075
FV18	WITH FV9	23.349	−0.101	−0.101	−0.087

Table 12.2 Abbreviated FV Scale Item Content

Item	Abbreviated Content
1	Father should be head of family.
2	Should maintain good relationships with relatives.
3	Mother's place is at home.
4	In family disputes, mother should be go-between.
5	Parents should teach proper behavior.
6	Father should handle the money.
8	Children should take care of old parents.
9	Children should help with chores.
10	Problems should be resolved within the family.
11	Children should obey parents.
12	Children should honor family's reputation.
14	Children should respect grandparents.
15	Mother should accept father's decisions.
18	Father should be breadwinner

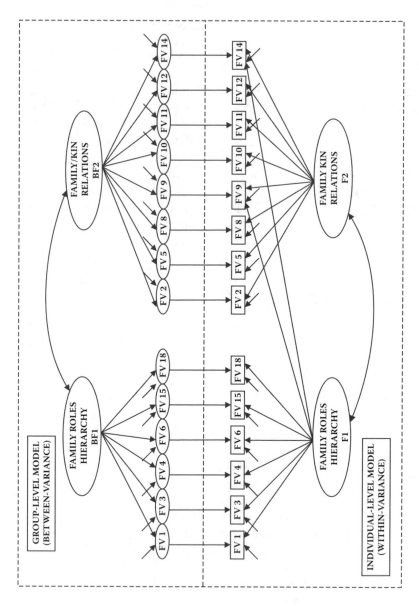

Figure 12.3. Multilevel model respecified at the individual level.

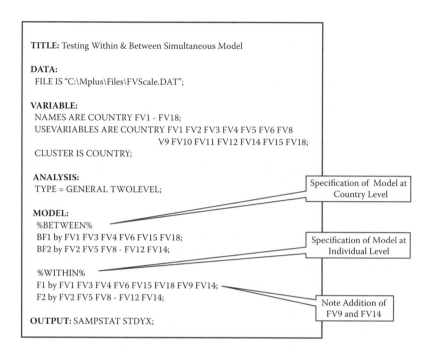

Figure 12.4. M*plus* input file for test of modified multilevel model based on MLR estimation.

MLV Model of FV Scale Structure

Input File

Having established a better fitting model in representing the FV Scale factor structure, we are now ready to conduct a simultaneous analysis of this structure relative to both the individual and country levels of the data. The input file pertinent to this analysis is presented in Figure 12.4.

In reviewing this file, there are several points to note. First, in contrast to the input file for full-sample tests of the CFA model (see Figure 12.2), the variable of *Country* has been added to the USEVARIABLES subcommand. Second, there is now a CLUSTER subcommand appearing under the VARIABLE command that is used to identify the grouping variable. Third, the ANALYSIS command identifies the TYPE of analysis to be GENERAL as applied to a two-level model. It should be noted, however, that if a breakdown of sample size per group is of interest, this information can be obtained simply by replacing the term *GENERAL* with *BASIC*. No estimator is noted here as analyses are based on robust maxium likelihood (MLR) estimation, which is default. Fourth, under the MODEL command, as indicated in Figure 12.4, the %BETWEEN% and %WITHIN%.

THE STANDARD ERRORS OF THE MODEL PARAMETER ESTIMATES MAY NOT BE
TRUSTWORTHY FOR SOME PARAMETERS DUE TO A NON-POSITIVE DEFINITE
FIRST-ORDER DERIVATIVE PRODUCT MATRIX. THIS MAY BE DUE TO THE STARTING
VALUES BUT MAY ALSO BE AN INDICATION OF MODEL NONIDENTIFICATION. THE
CONDITION NUMBER IS -0.999D-16. PROBLEM INVOLVING PARAMETER 29.

THE NONIDENTIFICATION IS MOST LIKELY DUE TO HAVING MORE PARAMETERS THAN
THE NUMBER OF CLUSTERS. REDUCE THE NUMBER OF PARAMETERS.

THE MODEL ESTIMATION TERMINATED NORMALLY

Figure 12.5. M*plus* output file: Error message associated with (MLR) estimated model.

subcommands provide for specification of the country (higher) and individual (lower) levels of the MLV model, respectively. Finally, note the
additional specification of FV9 and FV14 as factor loadings on Factor 1 at
the individual level, but not at the country level.

Unfortunately, although the model terminated normally, an error
message related to the higher level of the model appeared in the output.
This message is presented in Figure 12.5.

As you can see from the error message text, the problem involves a
condition of nonidentification at the higher level likely due to the small
number of countries included in the higher level sample. Indeed, a review
of model specifications reveals the number of estimated parameters (43)
to exceed the number of groups (27); the estimated parameters comprise
14 item intercepts, 12 factor loadings, 14 residuals, 2 factor variances, and
1 factor covariance. To obtain an overidentified model, I would therefore need to delete at least 17 parameters from the estimation process.
Considering only the item intercepts and three residual variances to be
the most logical and reasonable parameters eligible for deletion, I subsequently modified the input file to exclude estimation of the 14 item intercepts as well as the three residual variances having the lowest estimated
values from this first analysis (FV5, FV14, and FV9, respectively) at the
country level. This modified input file is shown in Figure 12.6.

Unfortunately, despite this reduction of estimated parameters at the
higher level of the model, the same error message appeared in the output,
although the analysis again terminated normally. An interesting comparison between these two models, however, was the substantial decrement
in model fit. Whereas goodness-of-fit statistics for Model 1 were $\chi^2_{(150)} =$
796.780, CFI = 0.993, RMSEA = 0.028, and SRMR (between) = 0.117, results
were $\chi^2_{(167)} = 1312.682$, CFI = 0.881, RMSEA = 0.035, and SRMR (between) =
0.335 for Model 2 (intercept and three residual variances fixed to 0.0). Thus,

```
VARIABLE:
NAMES ARE COUNTRY FV1 - FV18;
USEVARIABLES ARE COUNTRY FV1 FV2 FV3 FV4 FV5 FV6 FV8 FV9 FV10 FV11
       FV12 FV14 FV15 FV18;
CLUSTER IS COUNTRY;

ANALYSIS:
TYPE = GENERAL TWOLEVEL;

MODEL:
%BETWEEN%
BF1 by FV1 FV3 FV4 FV6 FV15 FV18;
BF2 by FV2 FV5 FV8 - FV12 FV14;
[FV1 - FV18@0];
FV5@0;
FV14@0;
FV9@0;

%WITHIN%
F1 by FV1 FV3 FV4 FV6 FV15 FV18 FV9 FV14;
F2 by FV2 FV5 FV8 - FV12 FV14;

OUTPUT: SAMPSTAT STDYX;
```

Figure 12.6. Mplus input file for test of multilevel model with reduction in number of estimated parameters.

although it seems evident that specifications pertinent to Model 1 are the more appropriate of the two, the smallness of the cluster size (of countries) is problematic when analyses are based on the MLR estimator.

Presented with these results, and in the sole interest of providing you with a window into the basics of MLV modeling, I consider it worthwhile to continue these MLV analyses based on the MUML rather than on the MLR estimator, albeit with the critically important caveat that whereas the MUML estimator assumes multivariate normality, our data here are nonnormally distributed. Thus, with the exception of the additional subcommand ESTIMATOR IS MUML, the input file shown in Figure 12.4 remains the same.

Importantly, analyses based on the MUML estimator terminated normally with no presentation of error messages. This information is particularly notable given results from two studies of MUML robustness (Hox & Maas, 2001; Yuan & Hayashi, 2005) in which results indicated the likelihood of increased occurrences of inadmissible solutions, particularly if the number of groups at the higher level was less than 50. On the other hand, presented with an admissible solution, Hox and Maas (2001) posited that the factor loadings are generally accurate, although the possibility remains that the residual variances may be underestimated and the standard errors small.

Table 12.3 M*plus* Output:
Estimated Intraclass Correlation Coefficients

Summary of Data	
Number of clusters	27
Quasi-average cluster size	201.354

Variable	Intraclass Correlation	Variable	Intraclass Correlation	Variable	Intraclass Correlation
FV1	0.412	FV2	0.136	FV3	0.346
FV4	0.411	FV5	0.073	FV6	0.378
FV8	0.215	FV9	0.071	FV10	0.184
FV11	0.328	FV12	0.334	FV14	0.130
FV15	0.403	FV18	0.471		

Intraclass Correlations

Initial information in the output file presents a "Summary of the Data" that includes the number of clusters in the analysis, the quasi-average cluster size, and the ICCs pertinent to each of the observed variables (the items). These results are reported in Table 12.3.

Of substantial interest here are the ICC values, which ranged from .071 to .471, with 12 of the 14 values being greater than 0.10 (see Muthén, 1997). In light of these ICC values, it is clear that the effects of culture are strongly impacting the FV Scale scores. Indeed, a review of the content related to FV Scale items yielding the six highest ICC values (FV18, FV1, FV4, FV15, FV6, and FV3; see Table 12.2) reveals all to bear on the perceived roles of mothers and fathers in the family, which I believe presents a pretty clear picture of why responses to the items should vary so widely across the 27 countries.

Model Fit

Tests of model fit for this MLV model, as reported in Table 12.4, reveal a fairly well-fitting two-level model in accordance with both the CFI and RMSEA goodness-of-fit values. Note, however, that two SRMR values are reported—one for the within (or individual) level (0.036) and one for the between (or country) level (0.112). As such, these results suggest that the model fits the data better at the individual than at the country level.

An interesting conundrum with respect to MLV modeling, however, is that these goodness-of-fit indices relate to the entire model. As such, they reflect the extent to which the model fits the data within the framework of the within-group model as well as the between-group model, a practice that Ryu and West (2009) equated with single-level SEM analyses. Given that, typically, sample size for the within-group is larger than that of

Table 12.4 M*plus* Output:
Selected Goodness-of-Fit Statistics

Tests of Model Fit	
Chi-Square Test of Model Fit	
Value	1245.684
Degrees of freedom	150
p-value	0.0000
CFI/TLI	
CFI	0.940
TLI	0.928
Root Mean Square Error of Approximation (RMSEA)	
Estimate	0.037
90 percent confidence interval (CI)	0.035 0.038
Probability RMSEA <= .05	1.000
Standardized Root Mean Square Residual (SRMR)	
Value for within	0.036
Value for between	0.112

the between-group, the former portion of the model tends to dictate these model fit values (Hox, 2002). Ideally, then, it would seem preferable that model fit be evaluated separately for each of the two levels. Unfortunately, preparation of these two matrices for separate model fit assessment is not a simple and straightforward process and, thus, is not included here. However, for readers who may be interested in performing these analyses, Hox (2002) suggested two possible approaches that can be taken. More recently, Ryu and West (2009), based on simulated data and ML estimation (thus assuming multivariate normality and balanced grouping), investigated two level-specific approaches to determining model fit in MLV models: one based on their proposed partially saturated model method, and the other on a segregating method proposed by Yuan and Bentler (2007). In both cases, these level-specific methods were successful in targeting evidence of misfit at the group level. Given the widely known limitations associated with the standard approach to assessment of fit in MLV modeling, it seems likely that researchers will increasingly seek out methods that allow them to detect misspecification specific to each level separately.

Parameter Estimates

Both the unstandardized and standardized estimates are presented in Table 12.5 for the individual (within-group) model and in Table 12.6 for

Table 12.5 M*plus* Output:
Selected Unstandardized and Standardized Estimates for Individual Level

				Model Results	

	Estimate	Standard Error (*SE*)	Estimate/ *SE*	Two-Tailed *p*-Value	Standardized Estimate
Within Level					
F1 BY					
FV1	1.000	0.000	999.000	999.000	0.684
FV3	0.957	0.026	36.372	0.000	0.580
FV4	0.808	0.025	32.497	0.000	0.511
FV6	1.009	0.024	41.837	0.000	0.687
FV15	0.901	0.023	39.217	0.000	0.634
FV18	0.960	0.024	40.726	0.000	0.664
FV9	−0.234	0.019	−12.470	0.000	−0.232
FV14	−0.130	0.016	−8.155	0.000	−0.141
F2 BY					
FV2	1.000	0.000	999.000	999.000	0.506
FV5	0.859	0.031	27.286	0.000	0.512
FV8	1.019	0.038	26.655	0.000	0.494
FV9	1.080	0.044	24.504	0.000	0.571
FV10	0.961	0.035	27.259	0.000	0.511
FV11	1.385	0.044	31.462	0.000	0.658
FV12	1.303	0.042	31.195	0.000	0.646
FV14	1.180	0.042	27.926	0.000	0.687
F2 WITH					
F1	0.304	0.014	21.861	0.000	0.533
Variances					
F1	1.067	0.041	26.049	0.000	1.000
F2	0.305	0.017	18.046	0.000	1.000
Residual Variances					
FV1	1.211	0.029	41.519	0.000	0.532
FV2	0.884	0.018	47.951	0.000	0.744
FV3	1.928	0.042	46.110	0.000	0.664
FV4	1.974	0.041	47.981	0.000	0.739
FV5	0.631	0.013	47.811	0.000	0.738
FV6	1.214	0.029	41.352	0.000	0.528
FV8	0.980	0.020	48.222	0.000	0.756

Table 12.5 Mplus Output:
Selected Unstandardized and Standardized Estimates for Individual Level
(*continued*)

	Estimate	Standard Error (*SE*)	Estimate/ *SE*	Two-Tailed *p*-Value	Standardized Estimate
Model Results					
FV9	0.830	0.018	46.092	0.000	0.761
FV10	0.795	0.017	47.830	0.000	0.739
FV11	0.767	0.018	42.677	0.000	0.568
FV12	0.720	0.017	43.235	0.000	0.582
FV14	0.550	0.013	41.990	0.000	0.612
FV15	1.290	0.029	44.098	0.000	0.598
FV18	1.248	0.029	42.662	0.000	0.559

the country (between-group) model. In reviewing the unstandardized estimates in these output files, you will quickly observe that all parameters estimates are statistically significant at both levels of the MLV model.

An overview of the standardized estimates reveals the factor loadings for all 14 items of the FV Scale to be larger for the country level than for the individual level. Indeed, presented with sufficient ICC values and, thus, stable loadings, it is typical for factor loadings to be larger at the between-group level than at the individual level. The reason for this common finding derives from the fact that analyses at the between-group level are based on the means, which, of course, are more reliable than raw scores, and thus much of the measurement error has been eliminated.

An important aspect of MLV modeling is that the factor loadings are standardized separately at the individual and group levels. As such, there is no relation in the proportion of variance accounted for in one level versus the other level. In a comparison of standardized loadings reported in Tables 12.5 and 12.6, for example, we can observe that whereas the loading of Item 3 (FV3) accounted for 33.6% (0.580^2) of the variability in F1 at the individual level, it accounted for 73.6% (0.858^2) at the country level. Likewise, there is no correspondence between interpretations of F1 at the individual versus the country levels.

The final piece of information provided in the output file relates to the multiple correlation (R^2) values at each level. In general terms, these values convey the strength of each item in measuring its target factor. Consistent with the standardized estimates reported in Tables 12.5 and 12.6, these R^2 values are substantially higher at the country level than at the individual level. Of interest here, however, is that whereas at the country level, the strongest factor loading was associated with the first item of the FV Scale

Table 12.6 Mplus Output:
Selected Unstandardized and Standardized Estimates for Country Level

Model Results

	Estimate	Standard Error (SE)	Estimate/ SE	Two-Tailed p-Value	Standardized (YX) Estimate
Between Level					
BF1 BY					
FV1	1.000	0.000	999.000	999.000	0.980
FV3	0.864	0.108	7.996	0.000	0.858
FV4	0.983	0.107	9.160	0.000	0.891
FV6	0.907	0.072	12.668	0.000	0.949
FV15	0.927	0.072	12.850	0.000	0.951
FV18	1.092	0.076	14.282	0.000	0.963
BF2 BY					
FV2	1.000	0.000	999.000	999.000	0.775
FV5	0.650	0.141	4.598	0.000	0.834
FV8	1.482	0.318	4.655	0.000	0.829
FV9	0.597	0.162	3.693	0.000	0.696
FV10	1.193	0.266	4.484	0.000	0.805
FV11	2.042	0.424	4.818	0.000	0.849
FV12	2.213	0.402	5.508	0.000	0.943
FV14	0.980	0.192	5.102	0.000	0.894
BF2 WITH					
BF1	0.331	0.117	2.837	0.005	0.816
Variances					
BF1	1.486	0.425	3.498	0.000	1.000
BF2	0.110	0.048	2.319	0.020	1.000
Residual Variances					
FV1	0.063	0.030	2.096	0.036	0.040
FV2	0.073	0.022	3.255	0.001	0.399
FV3	0.396	0.116	3.421	0.001	0.263
FV4	0.373	0.111	3.352	0.001	0.206
FV5	0.020	0.007	2.894	0.004	0.305
FV6	0.136	0.045	2.995	0.003	0.100
FV8	0.110	0.034	3.203	0.001	0.313
FV9	0.042	0.013	3.196	0.001	0.515

Table 12.6 M*plus* Output:
Selected Unstandardized and Standardized Estimates for Country Level
(*continued*)

				Model Results	
	Estimate	Standard Error (*SE*)	Estimate/ *SE*	Two-Tailed *p*-Value	Standardized (YX) Estimate
FV10	0.085	0.026	3.249	0.001	0.352
FV11	0.178	0.056	3.208	0.001	0.279
FV12	0.067	0.029	2.330	0.020	0.110
FV14	0.027	0.009	2.796	0.005	0.200
FV15	0.136	0.046	2.966	0.003	0.096
FV18	0.137	0.050	2.752	0.006	0.072

(FV1; 0.960), at the individual level it was associated with Item 6 (FV6; 0.472), with both items designed to measure Factor 1. These multiple correlations are presented in Table 12.7.

Potential Analytic Extensions

In my introduction of the model to be illustrated in this application, I noted that only the initial stages of testing for evidence of construct validity bearing on the FV Scale when used with hierarchically structured data would be included here. However, at that time, I stated that I would offer two suggestions on how this work might be meaningfully extended. I now address these potential extensions.

One very logical set of analyses that could contribute importantly to this construct validity work is that of testing for model invariance across individual and country levels. Indeed, given the relatively good fit of the MLV model to the data representing both structural levels, these proposed analyses would appear to be strongly justified. Recall again, however, that whereas the MUML estimator assumes multivariate normality, the data used here are nonnormally distributed. Thus, caution needs to be taken into account in any interpretation of results. Accordingly, analyses would focus on testing the equivalence of factorial structure for the FV Scale across levels. To assist you in initiating these analyses, the related M*plus* input file is shown in Figure 12.7.

This input file represents the initial test for equivalence of the commonly specified factor loadings across individual and country levels. I wish to draw your attention to several important features regarding these specifications. First, consistent with the specification of equality constraints involving single parameters across groups (see, e.g., Chapters

Table 12.7 Mplus Output:
Multiple Correlations for Individual and Country Levels

R-Square	
Within Level	
Observed Variable	*Estimate*
FV1	0.468
FV2	0.256
FV3	0.336
FV4	0.261
FV5	0.262
FV6	0.472
FV8	0.244
FV9	0.239
FV10	0.261
FV11	0.432
FV12	0.418
FV14	0.388
FV15	0.402
FV18	0.441
Between Level	
Observed Variable	*Estimate*
FV1	0.960
FV2	0.601
FV3	0.737
FV4	0.794
FV5	0.695
FV6	0.900
FV8	0.687
FV9	0.485
FV10	0.648
FV11	0.721
FV12	0.890
FV14	0.800
FV15	0.904
FV18	0.928

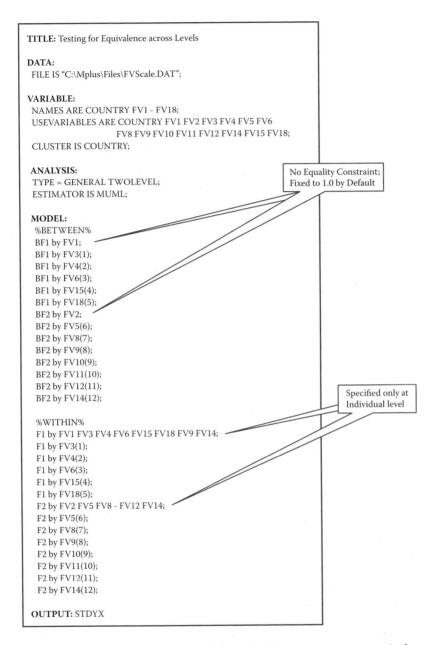

Figure 12.7. Mplus input file for test of factor-loading measurement equivalence across level.

7, 8, and 9), these constraints operate in the same way within the context of MLV modeling. That is, each equality constraint is accompanied by a parenthesized number that is identically assigned at the individual (within) and country (between) levels. Second, constraints have been specified for only the original target factor loadings. Thus, although the cross-loadings of FV9 and FV14 are specified as freely estimated parameters for the WITHIN model, they are not listed with parenthesized assigned numbers. Third, note that specification of the factor loadings is included only at the individual level (see the WITHIN model).[6] Finally, because the entire factor-loading pattern is not specified for the country-level model (see the BETWEEN model), it is necessary to identify the loading intended as the referent variable for purposes of model identification and latent variable scaling. Given that the first variable of each factor congeneric group (FV1, FV2) will be automatically fixed to 1.0 for the individual level, these same factor-loading parameters must be specified at the country level; consistent with the individual level, they will also be constrained to 1.0 by default.

Consistent with results in testing the unconstrained MLV model, those for the equivalence MLV model revealed a relatively good fit to the hierarchically structured data and minimal difference between the ad hoc fit indices ($\chi^2_{[62]}$ = 1300.563; CFI = 0.938; RMSEA = 0.036; SRMR [within] = 0.036; SRMR [between] = 0.214). Whereas the SRMR remained virtually the same at the individual level, it showed a decrement in fit at the country level (0.214 versus 0.112).

Of interest now, of course, is the extent to which this constrained MLV model differs from the unconstrained MLV model. Given that the constrained model is nested within the unconstrained model, we could take the difference between the MUML χ^2 values had these analyses been based on data that were normally distributed and minimally unbalanced (K. Yuan, personal communication, December 2010). Alternatively, had we been successful in our use of MLR estimation, we could have computed the corrected ΔMLR χ^2 value. However, given that neither of these options is relevant here, it is inappropriate to make any interpretations on a ΔMUML χ^2 value.

A second potential avenue of extended MLV analyses for these data is to consider the inclusion of possibly influential covariates. For example, given the substantial size of the ICCs evidenced in these analyses, we could consider what type of cultural phenomena might possibly contribute to the variability of FV Scale scores across these widely diverse 27 cultures. Indeed, two that come immediately to mind are those of affluence and religion. As such, these two covariates could be added to the model, and their impact on the two factors of Family Roles Hierarchy and Family/Kin Relations determined.

Notes

1. There are essentially two classes of MLV procedures: (a) latent variable MLV conducted within the framework of SEM, and (b) multiple regression MLV representing a multilevel version of the usual multiple regression model. As this chapter focuses only on SEM MLV modeling, readers interested in applications based on a multiple regression paradigm are referred to Bickel (2007), Heck and Thomas (2009), and Hox (2002, 2010).

2. Original data derived from a large project designed to measure family functioning across 30 cultures (Georgas et al., 2006). I am indebted to James Georgas for his generosity in permitting me to use a portion of these data as a means to illustrate the application of MLV modeling in this chapter.

3. Aggregated data derived through the summation of individual-level data have been termed an *ecological analysis*.

4. As noted by Kaplan et al. (2009), development of the EM algorithm for estimation (Dempster, Laird, & Rubin, 1977) was based on the premise of incomplete data.

5. In an effort to maximize ecocultural variation in known family-related context variables such as economic factors and religion, countries were selected from north, central, and south America; north, east, and south Europe; north, central, and south Africa; the Middle East; west and east Asia; and Oceania.

6. I don't want to leave the impression that it is incorrect to include specification of all factor loadings for the BETWEEN model as this is not so. However, if the full specification is included for the BETWEEN model, all factor-loading estimates, except for the referent variable loading, appear twice in the output file. For example, the loadings reported for F1 are FV1, FV3, FV4, FV6, FV15, FV18, *FV3, FV4, FV6, FV15,* and *FV18.*

References

Aikin, L. S., Stein, J. A., & Bentler, P. M. (1994). Structural equation analyses of clinical sub-population differences and comparative treatment outcomes: Characterizing the daily lives of drug addicts. *Journal of Consulting and Clinical Psychology, 62,* 488–499.

Aish, A. M., & Jöreskog, K. G. (1990). A panel model for political efficacy and responsiveness: An application of LISREL 7 with weighted least squares. *Quality and Quantity, 19,* 716–723.

Akaike, H. (1987). Factor analysis and AIC. *Psychometrika, 52,* 317–332.

American Psychological Association. (2010). *Publication manual of the American Psychological Association* (6th ed.). Washington, DC: Author.

American Psychologist. (1995). [Replies to Cohen (1994) article]. *50,* 1098–1103.

Anderson, J. C., & Gerbing, D. W. (1988). Structural equation modeling in practice: A review and recommended two-step approach. *Psychological Bulletin, 103,* 411–423.

Arbuckle, J. L. (1996). Full information estimation in the presence of incomplete data. In G. A. Marcoulides & R. E. Schumacker (Eds.), *Advanced structural equation modeling: Issues and techniques* (pp. 243–277). Mahwah, NJ: Erlbaum.

Arbuckle, J. L. (2007). *Amos™ 16 user's guide.* Chicago: SPSS.

Asparouov, T., & Muthén, B. (2010). Bayesian analysis of latent variable models using M*plus* (Technical Report, Version 4). Retrieved from http://www.statmodel.com

Atkinson, L. (1988). The measurement-statistics controversy: Factor analysis and subinterval data. *Bulletin of the Psychonomic Society, 26,* 361–364.

Austin, J. T., & Calderón, R. F. (1996). Theoretical and technical contributions to structural equation modeling: An updated bibliography. *Structural Equation Modeling, 3,* 105–175.

Babakus, E., Ferguson, C. E., Jr., & Jöreskog, K. G. (1987). The sensitivity of confirmatory maximum likelihood factor analysis to violations of measurement scale and distributional assumptions. *Journal of Marketing Research, 24,* 222–228.

Bacharach, S. B., Bauer, S. C., & Conley, S. (1986). Organizational analysis of stress: The case of elementary and secondary schools. *Work and Occupations, 13,* 7–32.

Bagozzi, R. P. (1993). Assessing construct validity in personality research: Applications to measures of self-esteem. *Journal of Research in Personality, 27,* 49–87.

Bagozzi, R. P., & Yi, Y. (1990). Assessing method variance in multitrait–multimethod matrices: The case of self-reported affect and perceptions at work. *Journal of Applied Psychology, 75,* 547–560.

Bandalos, D. L. (1993). Factors influencing cross-validation of confirmatory factor analysis models. *Multivariate Behavioral Research, 28,* 351–374.

Bandalos, D. L. (2002). The effects of item parceling on goodness-of-fit and parameter estimate bias in structural equation modeling. *Structural Equation Modeling Journal, 9,* 78–102.

Bandalos, D. L. (2008). Is parceling really necessary? A comparison of results from item parceling and categorical variable methodology. *Structural Equation Modeling, 15,* 211–240.

Bandalos, D. L., & Finney, S. J. (2001). Item parceling issues in structural equation modeling. In G. A. Marcoulides & R. E. Schumacker (Eds.), *New developments and techniques in structural equation modeling* (pp. 269–296). Mahwah, NJ: Erlbaum.

Baumler, E. R., Harrist, R. B., & Carvajal, S. (2003). Analysis of repeated measures data. In S. P. Reise & N. Duan (Eds.), *Multilevel modeling: Methodological advances, issues, and applications* (pp. 140–156). Mahwah, NJ: Erlbaum.

Beauducel, A., & Herzberg, P. Y. (2006). On the performance of maximum likelihood versus means and variance adjusted weighted least squares estimation in CFA. *Structural Equation Modeling, 13,* 186–203.

Beck, A., Steer, R., & Brown, G. (1996). *Beck Depression Inventory manual* (2nd ed.). San Antonio, TX: Psychological Association.

Beck, A. T., Ward, C. H., Mendelson, M., Mock, J., & Erbaugh, J. (1961). An inventory for measuring depression. *Archives of General Psychiatry, 4,* 561–571.

Benner, A. D., & Graham, S. (2009). The transition to high school as a developmental process among multiethnic urban youth. *Child Development, 80,* 356–376.

Benson, J., & Bandalos, D. L. (1992). Second-order confirmatory factor analysis of the Reactions to Tests Scale with cross-validation. *Multivariate Behavioral Research, 27,* 459–487.

Bentler, P. M. (1980). Multivariate analysis with latent variables: Causal modeling. *Annual Review of Psychology, 31,* 419–456.

Bentler, P. M. (1988). Causal modeling via structural equation systems. In J. R. Nesselroade & R. B. Cattell (Eds.), *Handbook of multivariate experimental psychology* (2nd ed., pp. 317–335). New York: Plenum.

Bentler, P. M. (1990). Comparative fit indexes in structural models. *Psychological Bulletin, 107,* 238–246.

Bentler, P. M. (1992). On the fit of models to covariances and methodology to the *Bulletin. Psychological Bulletin, 112,* 400–404.

Bentler, P. M. (2005). *EQS 6 structural equations program manual*. Encino, CA: Multivariate Software.

Bentler, P. M., & Bonett, D. G. (1980). Significance tests and goodness of fit in the analysis of covariance structures. *Psychological Bulletin, 88*, 588–606.

Bentler, P. M., & Chou, C-P. (1987). Practical issues in structural modeling. *Sociological Methods & Research, 16*, 78–117.

Bentler, P. M., & Yuan, K-H. (1999). Structural equation modeling with small samples: Test statistics. *Multivariate Behavioral Research, 34*, 181–197.

Bickel, R. (2007). *Multilevel analysis for applied research: It's just regression!* New York: Guilford.

Biddle, B. J., & Marlin, M. M. (1987). Causality, confirmation, credulity, and structural equation modeling. *Child Development, 58*, 4–17.

Biesanz, J. C., Deeb-Sossa, N., Papadakis, A. A., Bollen, K. A., & Curran, P. J. (2004). The role of coding time in estimating and interpreting growth curve models. *Psychological Methods, 9*, 30–52.

Blozis, S. A., & Cho, Y. I. (2008). Coding and centering of time in latent curve models in the presence of interindividual time heterogeneity. *Structural Equation Modeling, 15*, 413–433.

Bollen, K. A. (1989). *Structural equations with latent variables*. New York: Wiley.

Bollen, K. A., & Barb, K. H. (1981). Pearson's r and coursely categorized measures. *American Sociological Review, 46*, 232–239.

Bollen, K. A., & Davis, W. R. (2009). Two rules of identification for structural equation models. *Structural Equation Modeling, 16*, 523–536.

Bollen, K. A., & Long, J. S. (Eds.). (1993). *Testing structural equation models*. Newbury Park, CA: Sage.

Boomsma, A. (1982). The robustness of LISREL against small sample sizes in factor analysis models. In H. Wold & K. Jöreskog (Eds.), *Systems under indirect observation* (pp. 149–173). New York: Elsevier North Holland.

Boomsma, A. (1985). Nonconvergence, improper solutions, and starting values in LISREL maximum likelihood estimation. *Psychometrika, 50*, 229–242.

Boomsma, A. (1987). The robustness of maximum likelihood estimation in structural equation modeling. In P. Cuttance & R. Ecob (Eds.), *Structural equation modelling by example* (pp. 160–188). Cambridge: Cambridge University Press.

Boomsma, A., & Hoogland, J. J. (2001). The robustness of LISREL modeling revisited. In R. Cudeck, S. DuToit, & D. Sörbom (Eds.), *Structural equation modeling: Present and future*. Lincolnwood, IL: Scientific Software International.

Bovaird, J. A. (2007). Multilevel structural equation models for contextual factors. In T. D. Little, J. A. Bovaird, & N. A. Card (Eds.), *Modeling contextual effects in longitudinal studies* (pp. 149–182). Mahwah, NJ: Erlbaum.

Breckler, S. J. (1990). Applications of covariance structure modeling in psychology: Cause for concern? *Psychological Bulletin, 107*, 260–271.

Brown, T. A. (2006). *Confirmatory factor analysis for applied research*. New York: Guilford Press.

Browne, M. W. (1982). Covariance structures. In D. M.Hawkins (Ed.), *Topics in applied multivariate analysis* (pp. 72–141). Cambridge: Cambridge University Press.

Browne, M. W. (1984a). Asymptotically distribution-free methods for the analysis of covariance structures. *British Journal of Mathematical and Statistical Psychology, 37*, 62–83.

Browne, M. W. (1984b). The decomposition of multitrait–multimethod matrices. *British Journal of Mathematical and Statistical Psychology, 37*, 1–21.

Browne, M. W., & Cudeck, R. (1989). Single sample cross-validation indices for covariance structures. *Multivariate Behavioral Research, 24*, 445–455.

Browne, M. W., & Cudeck, R. (1993). Alternative ways of assessing model fit. In K. A. Bollen & J. S. Long (Eds.), *Testing structural equation models* (pp. 136–162). Newbury Park CA: Sage.

Browne, M. W., MacCallum, R. C., Kim, C-T., Andersen, B. L., & Glaser, R. (2002). When fit indices and residuals are incompatible. *Psychological Methods, 7*, 403–421.

Bryk, A. S., & Raudenbush, S. W. (1987). Applications of hierarchical linear models to assessing change. *Psychological Bulletin, 101*, 147–158.

Bryk, A. S., & Raudenbush, S. W. (1992). *Hierarchical linear models: Applications and data analysis methods.* Newbury Park, CA: Sage.

Byrne, B. M. (1988a). The Self-Description Questionnaire III: Testing for equivalent factorial validity across ability. *Educational and Psychological Measurement, 48*, 397–406.

Byrne, B. M. (1988b). Adolescent self-concept, ability grouping, and social comparison: Reexamining academic track differences in high school. *Youth and Society, 20*, 46–67.

Byrne, B. M. (1991). The Maslach Inventory: Validating factorial structure and invariance across intermediate, secondary, and university educators. *Multivariate Behavioral Research, 26*, 583–605.

Byrne, B. M. (1993). The Maslach Inventory: Testing for factorial validity and invariance across elementary, intermediate, and secondary teachers. *Journal of Occupational and Organizational Psychology, 66*, 197–212.

Byrne, B. M. (1994a). Testing for the factorial validity, replication, and invariance of a measuring instrument: A paradigmatic application based on the Maslach Burnout Inventory. *Multivariate Behavioral Research, 29*, 289–311.

Byrne, B. M. (1994b). Burnout: Testing for the validity, replication, and invariance of causal structure across elementary, intermediate, and secondary teachers. *American Educational Research Journal, 31*, 645–673.

Byrne, B. M. (1996). *Measuring self-concept across the lifespan: Issues and instrumentation.* Washington, DC: American Psychological Association.

Byrne, B. M. (1999). The nomological network of teacher burnout: A literature review and empirically validated model. In M. Huberman & R. Vandenberghe (Eds.), *Understanding and preventing teacher burnout: A sourcebook of international research and practice* (pp. 15–37). London: Cambridge University Press.

Byrne, B. M. (2003). Confirmatory factor analysis. In R. Fernández-Ballesteros (Ed.), *Encyclopedia of psychological assessment* (Vol. 1, pp. 399–402). Thousand Oaks, CA: Sage.

Byrne, B. M. (2004). Testing for multigroup invariance using AMOS Graphics: A road less travelled. *Structural Equation Modeling, 11*, 272–300.

Byrne, B. M. (2005a). Factor analytic models: Viewing the structure of an assessment instrument from three perspectives. *Journal of Personality Assessment, 85*, 17–30.

Byrne, B. M. (2005b). Factor analysis: Confirmatory. In B. S. Everitt & D. C. Howell (Eds.), *Encyclopedia of statistics in behavioural science* (pp. 599–606). London: Wiley.

Byrne, B. M. (2006). *Structural equation modeling with EQS: Basic concepts, applications, and programming* (2nd ed.). Mahwah, NJ: Erlbaum.

Byrne, B. M. (2008). Testing for multigroup equivalence of a measuring instrument: A walk through the process. *Psichothema, 20*, 872–882.

Byrne, B. M. (2009). *Structural equation modeling with AMOS: Basic concepts, applications, and programming* (2nd ed.). New York: Taylor & Francis/Routledge.

Byrne, B. M. (In press). Choosing SEM software: Snapshots of LISREL, EQS, AMOS, and M*plus*. In R. H. Hoyle (Ed.), *Handbook of structural equation modeling*. New York: Guilford.

Byrne, B. M., & Baron, P. (1993). The Beck Depression Inventory: Testing and cross validating an hierarchical structure for nonclinical adolescents. *Measurement and Evaluation in Counseling and Development, 26*, 164–178.

Byrne, B. M., & Baron, P. (1994). Measuring adolescent depression: Tests of equivalent factorial structure for English and French versions of the Beck Depression Inventory. *Applied Psychology: An International Review, 43*, 33–47.

Byrne, B. M., Baron, P., & Balev, J. (1996). The Beck Depression Inventory: Testing for its factorial validity and invariance across gender for Bulgarian adolescents. *Personality and Individual Differences, 21*, 641–651.

Byrne, B. M., Baron, P., & Balev, J. (1998). The Beck Depression Inventory: A cross-validated test of factorial structure for Bulgarian adolescents. *Educational and Psychological Measurement, 58*, 241–251.

Byrne, B. M., Baron, P., & Campbell, T. L. (1993). Measuring adolescent depression: Factorial validity and invariance of the Beck Depression Inventory across gender. *Journal of Research on Adolescence, 3*, 127–143.

Byrne, B. M., Baron, P., & Campbell, T. L. (1994). The Beck Depression Inventory (French Version): Testing for gender-invariant factorial structure for nonclinical adolescents. *Journal of Adolescent Research, 9*, 166–179.

Byrne, B. M., Baron, P., Larsson, B., & Melin, L. (1995). The Beck Depression Inventory: Testing and cross-validating a second-order factorial structure for Swedish nonclinical adolescents. *Behaviour Research and Therapy, 33*, 345–356.

Byrne, B. M., Baron, P., Larsson, B., & Melin, L. (1996). Measuring depression for Swedish nonclinical adolescents: Factorial validity and equivalence of the Beck Depression Inventory across gender. *Scandinavian Journal of Psychology, 37*, 37–45.

Byrne, B. M., & Bazana, P. G. (1996). Investigating the measurement of social and academic competencies for early/late preadolescents and adolescents: A multitrait–multimethod analysis. *Applied Measurement in Education, 9*, 113–132.

Byrne, B. M., & Campbell, T. L. (1999). Cross-cultural comparisons and the presumption of equivalent measurement and theoretical structure: A look beneath the surface. *Journal of Cross-Cultural Psychology, 30*, 557–576.

Byrne, B. M., & Crombie, G. (2003). Modeling and testing change over time: An introduction to the latent growth curve model. *Understanding Statistics: Statistical Issues in Psychology, Education, and the Social Sciences, 2*, 177–203.

Byrne, B. M., & Goffin, R. D. (1993). Modeling MTMM data from additive and multiplicative covariance structures: An audit of construct validity concordance. *Multivariate Behavioral Research, 28*, 67–96.

Byrne, B. M., Lam, W. W. T., & Fielding, R. (2008). Measuring patterns of change in personality assessments: An annotated application of latent growth curve modeling. *Journal of Personality Assessment, 90*, 1–11.

Byrne, B. M., Oakland, T., Leong, F. T. L., van de Vijver, F. J. R., Hambleton, R. K., Cheung, F. M., et al. (2009). A critical analysis of cross-cultural research and testing practices: Implications for improved education and training. *Training and Education in Professional Psychology, 3*, 94–105.

Byrne, B. M., & Shavelson, R. J. (1986). On the structure of adolescent self-concept. *Journal of Educational Psychology, 78*, 474–481.

Byrne, B. M., & Shavelson, R. J. (1996). On the structure of social self-concept for pre-, early, and late adolescents. *Journal of Personality and Social Psychology, 70*, 599–613.

Byrne, B. M., Shavelson, R. J., & Muthén, B. (1989). Testing for the equivalence of factor covariance and mean structures: The issue of partial measurement invariance. *Psychological Bulletin, 105*, 456–466.

Byrne, B. M., & Stewart, S. M. (2006). The MACS approach to testing for multigroup invariance of a second-order structure: A walk through the process. *Structural Equation Modeling, 13*, 287–321.

Byrne, B. M., Stewart, S. M., & Lee, P. W. H. (2004). Validating the Beck Depression Inventory-II for Hong Kong community adolescents. *International Journal of Testing, 4*, 199–216.

Byrne, B. M., & van de Vijver, F. J. R. (2010). Testing for measurement and structural equivalence in large-scale cross-cultural studies: Addressing the issue of nonequivalence. *International Journal of Testing, 10*, 107–132.

Byrne, B. M., & Watkins, D. (2003). The issue of measurement invariance revisited. *Journal of Cross-Cultural Psychology, 34*, 155–175.

Byrne, B. M., & Worth Gavin, D. A. (1996). The Shavelson model revisited: Testing for the structure of academic self-concept across pre-, early, and late adolescents. *Journal of Educational Psychology, 88*, 215–228.

Campbell, D. T., & Fiske, D. W. (1959). Convergent and discriminant validation by the multitrait–multimethod matrix. *Psychological Bulletin, 56*, 81–105.

Chen, Q., Kwok, O-M., Luo, W., & Willson, V. L. (2010). The impact of ignoring a level of nesting structure in multilevel growth mixture models: A Monte Carlo study. *Structural Equation Modeling, 17*, 570–589.

Cheng, T. A., & Williams, P. (1986). The design and development of a use in community studies of mental disorders in Taiwan. *Psychosomatic Medicine, 16*, 415–422.

Cheong, J. W., MacKinnon, D. P., & Khoo, S. T. (2003). Investigation of mediational processes using parallel process latent growth curve modeling. *Structural Equation Modeling, 10*, 238–262.

Cheung, G. W., & Rensvold, R. B. (2002). Evaluating goodness-of-fit indexes for testing measurement invariance. *Structural Equation Modeling, 9*, 233–255.

Cheung, M. W-L., & Au, K. (2005). Applications of multilevel structural equation modeling to cross-cultural research. *Structural Equation Modeling, 12*, 598–619.

Cheung, M. W-L., Leung, K., & Au, K. (2006). Evaluating multilevel models in cross-cultural research: An illustration with social axioms. *Journal of Cross-Cultural Psychology, 37*, 522–541.

Chinese Behavioral Sciences Society. (2000). *The Chinese version of the Beck Depression Inventory* (2nd ed., Licensed Chinese translation, Psychological Corporation). New York: Harcourt Brace.

Chou, C-P., & Bentler, P. M. (1990). Model modification in covariance structure modeling: A comparison among likelihood ratio, Lagrange multiplier, and Wald tests. *Multivariate Behavioral Research, 25*, 115–136.

Chou, C-P., Bentler, P. M., & Pentz, M. A. (1998). Comparisons of two statistical approaches to study growth curves: The multilevel model and the latent curve analysis. *Structural Equation Modeling, 5,* 247–266.

Chou, C-P., Bentler, P. M, & Pentz, M. A. (2000). A two-stage approach to multilevel structural equation models: Application to longitudinal data. In T. D. Little, K. U. Schnabel, & J. Baumert (Eds.), *Modeling longitudinal and multilevel data: Practical issues, applied approaches, and scientific examples* (pp. 33–49). Mahwah, NJ: Erlbaum.

Chou, C-P., Bentler, P. M., & Satorra, A. (1991). Scaled test statistics and robust standard errors for non-normal data in covariance structure analysis: A Monte Carlo study. *British Journal of Mathematical and Statistical Psychology, 44,* 347–357.

Cliff, N. (1983). Some cautions concerning the application of causal modeling methods. *Multivariate Behavioral Research, 18,* 115–126.

Coenders, G., & Saris, W. E. (2000). Testing nested additive, multiplicative, and general multitrait–multimethod models. *Structural Equation Modeling, 7,* 219–250.

Coenders, G., Satorra, A., & Saris, W. E. (1997). Alternative approaches to structural modeling of ordinal data: A Monte Carlo study. *Structural Equation Modeling, 4,* 261–282.

Cohen, J. (1994). The earth is round ($p < .05$). *American Psychologist, 49,* 997–1003.

Cole, D. A., Ciesla, J. A., & Steiger, J. (2007). The insidious effects of failing to include design-driven correlated residuals in latent-variable covariance structure analysis. *Psychological Methods, 12,* 381–398.

Collins, L. M., & Sayer, A. G. (2001). *New methods for the analysis of change.* Washington, DC: American Psychological Association.

Comrey, A. L. (1992). *A first course in factor analysis.* Hillsdale, NJ: Erlbaum.

Conway, J. M., Scullen, S. E., Lievens, F., & Lance, C. E. (2004). Bias in the correlated uniqueness model for MTMM data. *Structural Equation Modeling, 11,* 535–559.

Cooke, D. J., Kosson, D. S., & Michie, C. (2001). Psychopathy and ethnicity: Structural, item, and test generalizability of the Psychopathy Checklist-Revised (PCL-R) in Caucasian and African American participants. *Psychological Assessment, 13,* 531–542.

Corten, I. W., Saris, W. E., Coenders, G., van der Veld, W., Aalberts, C. E., & Kornelis, C. (2002). Fit of different models for multitrait-multimethod experiments. *Structural Equation Modeling, 9,* 213–232.

Courvoisier, D. S., Nussbeck, F. W., Eid, M., Geiser, C., & Cole, D. A. (2008). Analyzing the convergent and discriminant validity of states and traits: Development and applications of multimethod latent state-trait models. *Psychological Assessment, 20,* 270–280.

Cudeck, R. (1989). Analysis of correlation matrices using covariance structure models. *Psychological Bulletin, 105,* 317–327.

Cudeck, R., & Browne, M. W. (1983). Cross-validation of covariance structures. *Multivariate Behavioral Research, 18,* 147–167.

Cudeck, R., du Toit, S., & Sörbom, D. (2001). *Structural equation modeling: Present and future.* Lincolnwood IL: Scientific Software International.

Cudeck, R., & Henly, S. J. (1991). Model selection in covariance structures analysis and the "problem" of sample size: A clarification. *Psychological Bulletin, 109,* 512–519.

Cudeck, R., & MacCallum, R. C. (2007). *Factor analysis at 100: Historical developments and future directions.* Mahwah, NJ: Erlbaum.

Curran, P. J., Bauer, D. J., & Willoughby, M. T. (2004). Testing main effects and inter-actions in latent curve analysis. *Psychological Methods, 9*, 220–237.

Curran, P. J., & Hussong, A. M. (2003). The use of latent trajectory models in psy-chopathology research. *Journal of Abnormal Psychology, 112*, 526–544.

Curran, P. J., Muthén, B. O., & Harford, T. C. (1998). The influence of changes in marital status on developmental trajectories of alcohol use in young adults. *Journal of Studies on Alcohol, 59*, 647–658.

Curran, P. J., West. S. G., & Finch, J. F. (1996). The robustness of test statistics to nonnormality and specification error in confirmatory factor analysis. *Psychological Methods, 1*, 16–29.

DeCarlo, L. T. (1997). On the meaning and use of kurtosis. *Psychological Methods, 2*, 292–307.

Dedrick, R. F., & Greenbaum, P. E. (2010). Multilevel confirmatory factor analysis of a scale measuring interagency collaboration of children's mental health agencies. *Journal of Emotional and Behavioural Disorders, 10*, 1–14.

Dempster, A. P., Laird, N. M., & Rubin, D. B. (1977). Maximum likelihood from incomplete data via the EM algorithm. *Journal of the Royal Statistical Society (Series B), 39*, 1–38.

DiStefano, C. (2002). The impact of categorization with confirmatory factor analy-sis. *Structural Equation Modeling, 9*, 327–346.

Duncan, T. E., & Duncan, S. C. (1994). Modeling incomplete longitudinal sub-stance use data using latent variable growth curve methodology. *Multivariate Behavioral Research, 29*, 313–338.

Duncan, T. E., & Duncan, S. C. (1995). Modeling the processes of development via latent growth curve methodology. *Structural Equation Modeling, 3*, 187–205.

Duncan, T. E., Duncan, S. C., Okut, H., Stryker, L. A., & Li, F. (2002). An extension of the general latent variable growth modeling framework to four levels of the hierarchy. *Structural Equation Modeling, 9*, 303–326.

Duncan, T. E., Duncan, S. C., & Stryker, L. A. (2006). *An introduction to latent vari-able growth curve modeling: Concepts, issues, and applications* (2nd ed.). Mahwah, NJ: Erlbaum.

Ecob, R., & Der, G. (2003). An iterative method for the detection of outliers in longitudinal growth data using multilevel models. In S. P. Reise & N. Duan (Eds.), *Multilevel modeling: Methodological advances, issues, and applications* (pp. 229–254). Mahwah, NJ: Erlbaum.

Eid, M. (2000). A multitrait-multimethod model with minimal assumptions. *Psychometrika, 65*, 241–261.

Eid, M., Nussbeck, F. W., Geiser, C., Cole, D. A., Gollwitzer, M., & Lischetzke, T. (2008). Structural equation modeling of multitrait–multimethod data: Different models for different types of methods. *Psychological Methods, 13*, 230–253.

Enders, C. K. (2001). A primer on maximum likelihood algorithms available for use with missing data. *Structural Equation Modeling, 8*, 128–141.

Enders, C. K. (2010). *Applied missing data analysis.* New York: Guilford.

Enders, C. K., & Bandalos, D. L. (2001). The relative performance of full informa-tion likelihood estimation for missing data in structural equation models. *Structural Equation Modeling, 8*, 430–457.

Fabrigar, L. R., Wegener, D. T., MacCallum, R. C., & Strahan, E. J. (1999). Evaluating the use of exploratory factor analysis in psychological research. *Psychological Methods, 4*, 272–299.

Fan, X. (2003). Power of latent growth modeling for detecting group differences in linear growth trajectory parameters. *Structural Equation Modeling, 10,* 380–400.

Fan, X., & Sivo, S. A. (2005). Sensitivity of fit indexes to misspecified structural or measurement model components: Rationale for two-index strategy revisited. *Structural Equation Modeling, 12,* 343–367.

Fan, X., & Sivo, S. A. (2007). Sensitivity of fit indices to model misspecification and model types. *Multivariate Behavioural Research, 42,* 509–529.

Fan, X., Thompson, B., & Wang, L. (1999). Effects of sample size, estimation methods, and model specification on structural equation modeling fit indexes. *Structural Equation Modeling, 6,* 56–83.

Fielding, A. (2003). Ordered category responses and random effects in multilevel and other complex structures. In S. P. Reise & N. Duan (Eds.), *Multilevel modeling: Methodological advances, issues, and applications* (pp. 181–208). Mahwah, NJ: Erlbaum.

Finch, J. F., West, S. G., & MacKinnon, D. P. (1997). Effects of sample size and nonnormality on the estimation of mediated effects in latent variable models. *Structural Equation Modeling, 4,* 87–107.

Flora, D. B., & Curran, P. J. (2004). An empirical evaluation of alternative methods of estimation for confirmatory factor analysis with ordinal data. *Psychological Methods, 9,* 466–491.

Francis, D. J., Fletcher, J. M., & Rourke, B. P. (1988). Discriminant validity of lateral sensorimotor tests in children. *Journal of Clinical and Experimental Neuropsychology, 10,* 779–799.

Geiser, C., Eid, M., & Nussbeck, F. W. (2008). On the meaning of the latent variables in the CT-C(M-1) model: A comment on Maydeu-Olivares and Coffman (2006). *Psychological Methods, 13,* 49–57.

Georgas, J. (1999). Family as a context variable in cross-cultural psychology. In J. Adamopoulos & Y. Kashima (Eds.), *Social psychology and cultural context* (pp. 163–175). Beverly Hills, CA: Sage.

Georgas, J., Berry, J. W., van de Vijver, F. J. R., Kagitcibasi, C., & Poortinga, Y. H. (2006). *Families across cultures: A 30-nation psychological study.* Cambridge: Cambridge University Press.

Gerbing, D. W., & Anderson, J. C. (1993). Monte Carlo evaluations of goodness-of-fit indices for structural equation models. In K. A. Bollen & J. S. Long (Eds.), *Testing structural equation models* (pp. 40–65). Newbury Park, CA: Sage.

Gold, M. S., & Bentler, P. M. (2000). Treatments of missing data: A Monte Carlo comparison of RBHDI, iterative stochastic regression imputation, and expectation-maximization. *Structural Equation Modeling, 7,* 319–355.

Gonzalez, R., & Griffin, D. (2001). Testing parameters in structural equation modeling: Every "one" matters. *Psychological Methods, 6,* 258–269.

Gorsuch, R. L. (1983). *Factor analysis.* Hillsdale, NJ: Erlbaum.

Green, S. B., Akey, T. M., Fleming, K. K., Hershberger, S. L., & Marquis, J. G. (1997). Effect of the number of scale points on chi-square fit indices in confirmatory factor analysis. *Structural Equation Modeling, 4,* 108–120.

Green, S. B., & Babyak, M. A. (1997). Control of Type I errors with multiple tests of constraints in structural equation modeling. *Multivariate Behavioral Research, 32,* 39–51.

Green, S. B., Thompson, M. S., & Poirier, J. (1999). Exploratory analyses to improve fit: Errors due to misspecification and a strategy to reduce their occurrence. *Structural Equation Modeling, 6*, 113–126.

Green, S. B., Thompson, M. S., & Poirier, J. (2001). An adjusted Bonferroni method for elimination of parameters in specification addition searches. *Structural Equation Modeling, 8*, 18–39.

Grimm, K. J., Pianta, R. C., & Konold, T. (2009). Longitudinal multitrait–multitrait models for developmental research. *Multivariate Behavioural Research, 44*, 233–258.

Grimm, K. J., & Ramm, N. (2009). Nonlinear growth models in M*plus* and SAS. *Structural Equation Modeling, 16*, 676–701.

Hagtvet, K. A., & Nasser, F. M. (2004). How well do item parcels represent conceptually defined latent constructs? A two-facet approach. *Structural Equation Modeling, 11*, 168–193.

Hancock, G. R. (1999). A sequential Sheffé-type respecification for controlling Type I error in exploratory structural equation model modification. *Structural Equation Modeling, 6*, 158–168.

Hancock, G. R., Kuo, W-L., & Lawrence, F. R. (2001). An illustration of second-order latent growth models. *Structural Equation Modeling, 8*, 470–489.

Harlow, L. L., Mulaik, S. A., & Steiger, J. H. (Eds.). (1997). *What if there were no significance tests?* Mahwah, NJ: Erlbaum.

Harter, S. (1990). Causes, correlates, and the functional role of global self-worth: A lifespan perspective. In R. J. Sternberg & J. Kolligian (Eds.), *Competence considered* (pp. 67–97). New Haven, CT: Yale University Press.

Hau, K-T., & Marsh, H. W. (2004). The use of item parcels in structural equation modeling: Non-normal data and small sample sizes. *British Journal of Mathematical Statistical Psychology, 57*, 327–351.

Hayashi, K., & Marcoulides, G. A. (2006). Examining identification issues in factor analysis. *Structural Equation Modeling, 13*, 631–645.

Heck, R. H. (2001). Multilevel modeling with SEM. In G. A. Marcoulides & R. E. Schumacker (Eds.), *New developments and techniques in structural equation modeling.* Mahwah, NJ: Erlbaum.

Heck, R. H., & Thomas, S. L. (2009). *An introduction to multilevel modeling techniques* (2nd ed.). New York: Routledge.

Hernández, A., & González-Romá, V. (2002). Analysis of multitrait–multioccasion data: Additive versus multiplicative models. *Multivariate Behavioral Research, 37*, 59–87.

Hoffman, L. (2007). Multilevel models for examining individual differences in within-person variation and covariation over time. *Multivariate Behavioral Research, 42*, 609–629.

Horn, J. L., & McArdle, J. J. (1992). A practical and theoretical guide to measurement equivalence in aging research. *Experimental Aging Research, 18*, 117–144.

Hox, J. J. (2000). Multilevel analyses of grouped and longitudinal data. In T. D. Little, K. U. Schnabel, & J. Baumert (Eds.), *Modeling longitudinal and multilevel data: Practical issues, applied approaches, and scientific examples* (pp. 15–32). Mahwah, NJ: Erlbaum.

Hox, J. J. (2002). *Multilevel analysis: Techniques and applications.* Mahwah, NJ: Erlbaum.

Hox, J. J. (2010). *Multilevel analysis: Techniques and applications* (2nd ed.). New York: Routledge.

Hox, J. J., & de Leeuw, E. D. (2003). Multilevel models for meta-analyses. In S. P. Reise & N. Duan (Eds.), *Multilevel modeling: Methodological advances, issues, and applications* (pp. 90–111). Mahwah, NJ: Erlbaum.

Hox, J. J., & Kleiboer, A. M. (2007). Retrospective questions or a diary method? A two-level multitrait–multimethod analysis. *Structural Equation Modeling, 14,* 311–325.

Hox, J. J., & Maas, C. J. M. (2001). The accuracy of multilevel structural equation modeling with psuedobalanced groups and small samples. *Structural Equation Modeling, 8,* 157–174.

Hoyle, R. H. (Ed.). (1995). *Structural equation modeling: Concepts, issues, and applications.* Thousand Oaks, CA: Sage.

Hoyle, R. H. (In press). *Handbook of structural equation modeling.* New York: Guilford.

Hsieh, C-A., von Eye, A. A., & Maier, K. S. (2010). Using a multivariate multilevel polytomous item response theory model to study parallel processes of change: The dynamic association between adolescents' social isolation and engagement with delinquent peers in the National Youth Survey. *Multivariate Behavioral Research, 45,* 508–552.

Hu, L-T., & Bentler, P. M. (1995). Evaluating model fit. In R. H. Hoyle (Ed.), *Structural equation modeling: Concepts, issues, and applications* (pp. 76–99). Thousand Oaks, CA: Sage.

Hu, L-T., & Bentler, P. M. (1998). Fit indices in covariance structure modeling: Sensitivity to underparameterized model misspecification. *Psychological Methods, 3,* 424–453.

Hu, L-T., & Bentler, P. M. (1999). Cutoff criteria for fit indexes in covariance structure analysis: Conventional criteria versus new alternatives. *Structural Equation Modeling, 6,* 1–55.

Hu, L-T., Bentler, P. M., & Kano, Y. (1992). Can test statistics in covariance structure analysis be trusted? *Psychological Bulletin, 112,* 351–362.

Hung, L-F. (2010). The multigroup multilevel categorical latent growth curve models. *Multivariate Behavioral Research, 45,* 359–392.

Jo, B., & Muthén, B. O. (2003). Longitudinal studies with intervention and noncompliance: Estimation of causal effects in growth mixture modeling. In S. P. Reise & N. Duan (Eds.), *Multilevel modeling: Methodological advances, issues, and applications* (pp. 112–139). Mahwah, NJ: Erlbaum.

Jones, L. V., & Tukey, J. W. (2000). A sensible formulation of the significance test. *Psychological Methods, 5,* 411–414.

Jöreskog, K. G. (1971a). Statistical analysis of sets of congeneric tests. *Psychometrika, 36,* 109–133.

Jöreskog, K. G. (1971b). Simultaneous factor analysis in several populations. *Psychometrika, 36,* 409–426.

Jöreskog, K. G. (1990). New developments in LISREL: Analysis of ordinal variables using polychoric correlations and weighted least squares. *Quality and Quantity, 24,* 387–404.

Jöreskog, K. G. (1993). Testing structural equation models. In K. A. Bollen & J. S. Long (Eds.), *Testing structural equation models* (pp. 294–316). Newbury Park, CA: Sage.

Jöreskog, K. G. (1994). On the estimation of polychoric correlations and their asymptotic covariance matrix. *Psychometrika, 59,* 381–389.

Jöreskog, K. G., & Sörbom, D. (1989). *LISREL 7: User's reference guide.* Chicago: Scientific Software.

Jöreskog, K. G., & Sörbom, D. (1993). *LISREL 8: Structural equation modeling with the SIMPLIS command language.* Chicago: Scientific Software International.

Jöreskog, K. G., & Sörbom, D. (1996). *LISREL 8: User's reference guide.* Chicago: Scientific Software International.

Jöreskog, K. G., & van Thillo, M. (1972). *A general computer program for estimating a linear structural equation system involving multiple indicators of unmeasured variables* (Research Bulletin No. RB-72-56). Princeton, NJ: Educational Testing Service.

Julian, M. W. (2001). The consequences of ignoring multilevel data structures in nonhierarchical covariance modeling. *Structural Equation Modeling, 8,* 325–352.

Kaplan, D. (1989). Model modification in covariance structure analysis: Application of the expected parameter change statistic. *Multivariate Behavioral Research, 24,* 285–305.

Kaplan, D. (1998). Methods for multilevel data analysis. In G. A. Marcoulides (Ed.), *Modern methods for business research* (pp. 337–358). Mahwah, NJ: Erlbaum.

Kaplan, D. (2000). *Structural equation modeling: Foundations and extensions.* Thousand Oaks, CA: Sage.

Kaplan, D., & Elliott, P. R. (1997). A didactic example of multilevel structural equation modeling applicable to the study of organizations. *Structural Equation Modeling, 4,* 1–24.

Kaplan, D., & George, R. (1995). A study of power associated with testing factor mean differences under violations of factorial invariance. *Structural Equation Modeling, 2,* 101–118.

Kaplan, D., Kim, J-S., & Kim, S-Y. (2009). Multilevel latent variable modeling: Current research and recent developments. In R. E. Millsap & A. Maydeu-Olivares (Eds.), *The Sage handbook of quantitative methods in psychology* (pp. 592–613). Thousand Oaks, CA: Sage.

Kenny, D. A. (1976). An empirical application of confirmatory factor analysis to the multitrait–multimethod matrix. *Journal of Experimental Social Psychology, 12,* 247–252.

Kenny, D. A. (1979). *Correlation and causality.* New York: Wiley.

Kenny, D. A., & Kashy, D. A. (1992). Analysis of the multitrait–multimethod matrix by confirmatory factor analysis. *Psychological Bulletin, 112,* 165–172.

Kerlinger, F. N. (1984). *Liberalism and conservatism: The nature and structure of social attitudes.* Hillsdale, NJ: Erlbaum.

Kim, S., & Hagtvet, K. A. (2003). The impact of misspecified item parceling on representing latent variables in covariance structure modeling: A simulation study. *Structural Equation Modeling, 10,* 101–127.

Kirk, R. E. (1996). Practical significance: A concept whose time has come. *Educational and Psychological Measurement, 56,* 746–759.

Kishton, J. M., & Widaman, K. F. (1994). Unidimensional versus domain representative parceling of questionnaire items: An empirical example. *Educational and Psychological Measurement, 54,* 757–765.

Kline, R. B. (2004). *Beyond significance testing: Reforming data analysis methods in behavioural research.* Washington, DC: American Psychological Association.

Kline, R. B. (2011). *Principles and practice of structural equation modeling* (3rd ed.). New York: Guildford Press.

Kreft, I., & de Leeuw, J. (1998). *Introducing multilevel modeling*. Newbury Park, CA: Sage.

Kwok, O-M., West, S. G., & Green, S. B. (2007). The impact of misspecifying the within-subject covariance structure in multiwave longitudinal multilevel models: A Monte Carlo study. *Multivariate Behavioral Research, 42*, 557–592.

La Du, T. J., & Tanaka, J. S. (1989). Influence of sample size, estimation method, and model specification on goodness-of-fit assessments in structural equation modeling. *Journal of Applied Psychology, 74*, 625–636.

LaGrange, B., & Cole, D. A. (2008). An expansion of the trait–state–occasion model: Accounting for shared method variance. *Structural Equation Modeling, 15*, 241–271.

Lance, C. E., Noble, C. L., & Scullen, S. E. (2002). A critique of the correlated trait correlated method and correlated uniqueness models for multitrait–multimethod data. *Psychological Methods, 7*, 228–244.

Leiter, M. P. (1991). Coping patterns as predictors of burnout: The function of control and escapist coping patterns. *Journal of Organizational Behavior, 12*, 123–144.

Li, F., Duncan, T. E., Duncan, S. C., McAuley, E., Chaumeton, N. R., & Harmer, P. (2001). Enhancing the psychological well-being of elderly individuals through Tai Chi exercise: A latent growth curve analysis. *Structural Equation Modeling, 8*, 53–83.

Little, T. D. (1997). Mean and covariance structures (MACS) analyses of cross-cultural data: Practical and theoretical issues. *Multivariate Behavioral Research, 32*, 53–76.

Little, T. D. (In press). *Longitudinal structural equation modeling: Interindividual differences and panel models*. New York: Guilford Press.

Little, T. D., Card, N. A., Slegers, D. W., & Ledford, E. C. (2007). Representing contextual effects in multiple-group MACS models. In T. D. Little, J. A. Bovaird, & N. A. Card (Eds.), *Modeling contextual effects in longitudinal studies* (pp. 121–147). Mahwah, NJ: Erlbaum.

Little, T. D., Cunningham, W. A., Shahar, G., & Widaman, K. F. (2002). To parcel or not to parcel: Exploring the question, weighing the merits. *Structural Equation Modeling, 9*, 151–173.

Little, T. D., Lindenberger, U., & Nesselroade, J. R. (1999). On selecting indicators for multivariate measurement and modeling with latent variables: When "good" indicators are bad and "bad" indicators are good. *Psychological Methods, 4*, 192–211.

Little, T. D., Schnabel, K. U., & Baumert, J. (2000). *Modeling longitudinal and multilevel data: Practical issues, applied approaches, and scientific examples*. Mahwah, NJ: Erlbaum.

Little, T. D., Slegers, D. W., & Card, N. A. (2006). A non-arbitrary method of identifying and scaling latent variables in SEM and MACS models. *Structural Equation Modeling, 13*, 59–72.

Loehlin, J. C. (1992). *Latent variable models: An introduction to factor, path, and structural analyses*. Hillsdale, NJ: Erlbaum.

Long, J. S. (1983a). *Confirmatory factor analysis*. Beverly Hills, CA: Sage.

Long, J. S. (1983b). *Covariance structure models: An introduction to LISREL*. Beverly Hills, CA: Sage.

MacCallum, R. C. (1986). Specification searches in covariance structure modeling. *Psychological Bulletin, 100*, 107–120.

MacCallum, R. C. (1995). Model specification: Procedures, strategies, and related issues. In R. H. Hoyle (Ed.), *Structural equation modeling: Concepts, issues, and applications* (pp. 76–99). Newbury Park, CA: Sage.

MacCallum, R. C., & Austin, J. T. (2000). Applications of structural equation modeling in psychological research. *Annual Review of Psychology, 51,* 201–226.

MacCallum, R. C., Browne, M. W., & Cai, L. (2006). Testing differences between nested covariance structure models: Power analysis and null hypotheses. *Psychological Methods, 11,* 19–35.

MacCallum, R. C., Browne, M. W., & Sugawara, H. M. (1996). Power analysis and determination of sample size for covariance structure modeling. *Psychological Methods, 1,* 130–149.

MacCallum, R. C., & Kim, C. (2000). Modeling multivariate change. In T. D. Little, K. U. Schnabel, & J. Baumert (Eds.), *Modeling longitudinal and multilevel data: Practical issues, applied approaches, and scientific examples* (pp. 51–68). Mahwah, NJ: Erlbaum.

MacCallum, R. C., Kim, C., Malarkey, W., & Kiecolt-Glaser, J. (1997). Studying multivariate change using multilevel models and latent curve models. *Multivariate Behavioral Research, 32,* 215–253.

MacCallum, R. C., Roznowski, M., Mar, M., & Reith, J. V. (1994). Alternative strategies for cross-validation of covariance structure models. *Multivariate Behavioral Research, 29,* 1–32.

MacCallum, R. C., Roznowski, M., & Necowitz, L. B. (1992). Model modifications in covariance structure analysis: The problem of capitalization on chance. *Psychological Bulletin, 111,* 490–504.

MacCallum, R. C., Wegener, D. T., Uchino, B. N., & Fabrigar, L. R. (1993). The problem of equivalent models in applications of covariance structure analysis. *Psychological Bulletin, 114,* 185–199.

MacCallum, R. C., Widaman, K. F., Zhang, S., & Hong, S. (1999). Sample size in factor analysis. *Psychological Methods, 4,* 84–99.

Marcoulides, G. A., & Schumacker, R. E. (Eds.). (1996). *Advanced structural equation modeling: Issues and techniques.* Mahwah, NJ: Erlbaum.

Mardia, K. V. (1970). Measures of multivariate skewness and kurtosis with applications. *Biometrika, 57,* 519–530.

Mardia, K. V. (1974). Applications of some measures of multivariate skewness and kurtosis in testing normality and robustness studies. *Sankhya, B36,* 115–128.

Marsh, H. W. (1988). Multitrait–multimethod analyses. In J. P. Keeves (Ed.), *Educational research methodology, measurement, and evaluation: An international handbook* (pp. 570–578). Oxford: Pergamon.

Marsh, H. W. (1989). Confirmatory factor analyses of multitrait–multimethod data: Many problems and a few solutions. *Applied Psychological Measurement, 15,* 47–70.

Marsh, H. W. (1992). *Self Description Questionnaire (SDQ) I: A theoretical and empirical basis for the measurement of multiple dimensions of preadolescent self-concept: A test manual and research monograph.* Macarthur, NSW: Faculty of Education, University of Western Sydney.

Marsh, H. W. (1994). Confirmatory factor analysis models of factorial equivalence: A multifaceted approach. *Structural Equation Modeling, 1,* 5–34.

Marsh, H. W. (2007). Application of confirmatory factor analysis and structural equation modeling in sport/exercise psychology. In G. Tenenbaum & R. C. Eklund (Eds.), *Handbook of sport psychology* (3rd ed., pp. 774–798). New York: Wiley.

Marsh, H. W., & Bailey, M. (1991). Confirmatory factor analyses of multitrait mul-timethod data: A comparison of alternative models. *Applied Psychological Measurement*, *15*, 47–70.

Marsh, H. W., Balla, J. R., & McDonald, R. P. (1988). Goodness-of-fit indexes in confirmatory factor analysis: The effect of sample size. *Psychological Bulletin*, *103*, 391–410.

Marsh, H. W., Byrne, B. M., & Craven, R. (1992). Overcoming problems in confir-matory factor analyses of MTMM data: The correlated uniqueness model and factorial invariance. *Multivariate Behavioral Research*, *27*, 489–507.

Marsh, H. W., & Grayson, D. (1994). Longitudinal stability of means and individ-ual differences: A unified approach. *Structural Equation Modeling*, *1*, 317–359.

Marsh, H. W., & Grayson, D. (1995). Latent variable models of multitrait–mul-timethod data. In R. H. Hoyle (Ed.), *Structural equation modeling: Concepts, issues, and applications* (pp. 177–198). Thousand Oaks, CA: Sage.

Marsh, H. W., Hau, K-T., Artelt, C., Baumert, J., & Peschar, J. L. (2006). OECD's brief self-report measure of educational psychology's most useful affective constructs: Cross-cultural, psychometric comparisons across 25 countries. *International Journal of Testing*, *6*, 311–360.

Marsh, H. W., Hau, K-T., Balla, J. R., & Grayson, D. (1998). Is more ever too much? The number of indicators per factor in confirmatory factor analysis. *Multivariate Behavioral Research*, *33*, 181–220.

Marsh, H. W., Hey, J., & Roche, L. A. (1997). Structure of physical self-concept: Elite athletes and physical education students. *Journal of Educational Psychology*, *89*, 369–380.

Maslach, C., & Jackson, S. E. (1981). *Maslach Burnout Inventory manual*. Palo Alto, CA: Consulting Psychologists Press.

Maslach, C., & Jackson, S. E. (1986). *Maslach Burnout Inventory manual* (2nd ed.). Palo Alto, CA: Consulting Psychologists Press.

Maydeu-Olivares, A., & Coffman, D. L. (2006). Random intercept item factor anal-ysis. *Psychological Methods*, *11*, 344–362.

McArdle, J. J., & Epstein, D. (1987). Latent growth curves within developmental structural equation models. *Child Development*, *58*, 110–133.

McArdle, J. J., & Hamagami, F. (1996). Multilevel models from a multiple group structural equation perspective. In G. A. Marcoulides & R. E. Schumaker (Eds.), *Advanced structural equation modeling* (pp. 89–124). Mahwah, NJ: Erlbaum.

McDonald, R. P. (1985). *Factor analysis and related methods*. Hillsdale, NJ: Erlbaum.

McGaw, B., & Jöreskog, K. G. (1971). Factorial invariance of ability measures in groups differing in intelligence and socioeconomic status. *British Journal of Mathematical and Statistical Psychology*, *24*, 154–168.

Mehta, P. D., & Neale, M. C. (2005). People are variables too: Multilevel structural equation modeling. *Psychological Methods*, *10*, 259–284.

Meredith, W. (1993). Measurement invariance, factor analysis, and factorial invari-ance. *Psychometrika*, *58*, 525–543.

Meredith, W., & Tisak, J. (1990). Latent curve analysis. *Psychometrika*, *55*, 107–122.

Millsap, R. E., & Kwok, O-M. (2004). Evaluating the impact of partial factorial equivalence on selection in two populations. *Psychological Methods*, *9*, 93–115.

Millsap, R. E., & Yun-Tein, J. (2004). Assessing factorial invariance in ordered-cate-gorical measures. *Multivariate Behavioral Research*, *39*, 479–515.

Moustaki, I. (2001). A review of exploratory factor analysis for ordinal categorical data. In R. Cudeck, S. du Toit, & D. Sörbom (Eds.), *Structural equation modeling: Present and future* (pp. 461–480). Lincolnwood, IL: Scientific Software.

M*plus* Product Support. (2010, various dates). Retrieved from http://www.statmodel.com/support/index.shtml

Mulaik, S. A. (2009). *The foundations of factor analysis* (2nd ed.). London: CRC Press.

Mulaik, S. A., James, L. R., Van Altine, J., Bennett, N., Lind, S., & Stilwell, C. D. (1989). Evaluation of goodness-of-fit indices for structural equation models. *Psychological Bulletin, 105,* 430–445.

Muthén, B. (1978). Contributions to factor analysis of dichotomous variables. *Psychometrika, 43,* 551–560.

Muthén, B. (1983). Latent variable structural equation modeling with categorical data. *Journal of Econometrics, 22,* 48–65.

Muthén, B. (1984). A general structural equation model with dichotomous, ordered categorical, and continuous latent variable indicators. *Psychometrika, 49,* 115–132.

Muthén, B. (1987). *LISCOMP: Analysis of linear structural equations with a comprehensive measurement model: Theoretical integration and user's guide.* Mooresville, IN: Scientific Software.

Muthén, B. O. (1993). Goodness of fit with categorical and other nonnormal variables (pp. 205–234). In K. A. Bollen & J. S. Long (Eds.), *Testing structural equation models.* Newbury Park, CA: Sage.

Muthén, B. O. (1994). Multilevel covariance structure analysis. *Sociological Methods and Research, 22,* 376–398.

Muthén, B. O. (1997). Latent variable modeling of longitudinal and multilevel data. In A. E. Raftery (Ed.), *Sociological methodology 1997* (pp. 453–481). Washington, DC: American Sociological Association.

Muthén, B. (2004). Latent variable analysis: Growth mixture modeling and related techniques for longitudinal data. In D. Kaplan (Ed.), *Handbook of quantitative methodology for the social sciences* (pp. 345–368). Newbury Park, CA: Sage.

Muthén, B. (2010). Bayesian analysis in M*plus*: A brief introduction (Technical report, Version 3). Retrieved from http://www.statmodel.com/download/IntroBayesVersion%203.pdf

Muthén, B., & Asparouov, T. (2002). Latent variable analysis with categorical outcomes: Multiple-group and growth modeling in M*plus* (M*plus* Webnotes No. 4). Retrieved from http://www.statmodel.com/download/webnotes/CatMGLong.pdf

Muthén, B. O., & Curran, P. J. (1997). General longitudinal modelling of individual differences in experimental designs: A latent variable framework for analysis and power estimation. *Psychological Methods, 2,* 371–402.

Muthén, B. O., & Satorra, A. (1995). Complex sample data in structural equation modeling. In P. Marsden (Ed.), *Sociological Methodology 1995* (pp. 216–316). Boston: Blackwell.

Muthén, B., du Toit, S. H. C., & Spisic, D. (1997). *Robust inference using weighted least squares and quadratic estimating equations in latent variable modelling with categorical and continuous outcomes* (Technical Report). Los Angeles: University of California, Los Angeles.

Muthén, B., & Kaplan, D. (1985). A comparison of some methodologies for the factor analysis of non-normal Likert variables. *British Journal of Mathematical and Statistical Psychology, 38,* 171–189.

Muthén, B., Kaplan, D., & Hollis, M. (1987). On structural equation modeling with data that are not missing completely at random. *Psychometrika, 52,* 431–462.

Muthén, B., Khoo, S-T., Francis, D. J., & Boscardin, C. K. (2003). Analysis of reading skills development from kindergarten through first grade: An application of growth mixture modeling to sequential processes. In S. P. Reise & N. Duan (Eds.), *Multilevel modeling: Methodological advances, issues, and applications* (pp. 71–89). Mahwah, NJ: Erlbaum.

Muthén, L. K., & Muthén, B. O. (2000). The development of heavy drinking and alcohol-related problems from ages 18 to 37 in a U.S. national sample. *Journal of Studies on Alcohol, 61,* 290–300.

Muthén, L. K., & Muthén, B. O. (2007–2010). Mplus *user's guide* (6th ed.). Los Angeles: Authors.

Muthén, L. K., & Muthén, B. O. (2010). Mplus *short courses: Topic 3.* Los Angeles: Authors.

Nasser-Abu, F., & Wisenbaker, J. (2006). A Monte Carlo study investigating the impact of item parceling strategies on parameter estimates and their standard errors in CFA. *Structural Equation Modeling, 13,* 204–228.

O'Brien, R. M. (1985). The relationship between ordinal measures and their underlying values: Why all the disagreement? *Quality and Quantity, 19,* 265–277.

Pettegrew, L. S., & Wolf, G. E. (1982). Validating measures of teacher stress. *American Educational Research Journal, 19,* 373–396.

Pettit, G. S., Keiley, M. K., Laird, R. D., Bates, J. E., & Dodge, K. A. (2007). Predicting the developmental course of mother-reported monitoring across childhood and adolescence from early proactive parenting, child temperament, and parents' worries. *Journal of Family Psychology, 21,* 206–217.

Peugh, J. L., & Enders, C. K. (2010). Specification searches in multilevel structural equation modeling: A Monte Carlo investigation. *Structural Equation Modeling, 17,* 42–65.

Pohl, S., & Steyer, R. (2010). Modeling common traits and method effects in multitrait multimethod analysis. *Multivariate Behavioural Research, 45,* 45–72.

Pomplun, M., & Omar, M. H. (2003). Do minority representative reading passages provide factorially invariant scores for all students? *Structural Equation Modeling, 10,* 276–288.

Preacher, K. J., & MacCallum, R. C. (2003). Repairing Tom Swift's electric factor analysis machine. *Understanding Statistics, 2,* 13–43.

Preacher, K. J., Zyphur, M. J., & Zhang, Z. (2010). A general multilevel SEM framework for assessing multilevel mediation. *Psychological Methods, 15,* 209–233.

Raftery, A. E. (1993). Bayesian model selection in structural equation models. In K. A. Bollen & J. S. Long (Eds.), *Testing structural equation models* (pp. 163–180). Newbury Park, CA: Sage.

Raudenbush, S. W., & Bryk, A. S. (2002). *Hierarchical linear models: Applications and data analysis methods* (2nd ed.). Newbury Park, CA: Sage.

Raykov, T., & Marcoulides, G. A. (2000). *A first course in structural equation modeling.* Mahwah, NJ: Erlbaum.

Raykov, T., & Penev, S. (2010). Evaluation of reliability coefficients for two-level models via latent variable analysis. *Structural Equation Modeling, 17,* 629–641.

Raykov, T., & Widaman, K. F. (1995). Issues in structural equation modeling research. *Structural Equation Modeling, 2,* 289–318.

Reise, S. P. & Duan, N. (2003). Multilevel modeling: *Methodological advances, issues, and applications.* Mahwah, NJ: Erlbaum.

Reise, S. P., Widaman, K. F., & Pugh, P. H. (1993). Confirmatory factor analysis and item response theory: Two approaches for exploring measurement invariance. *Psychological Bulletin, 114,* 552–566.

Rigdon, E. E. (1996). CFI versus RMSEA: A comparison of two fit indexes for structural equation modeling. *Structural Equation Modeling, 3,* 369–379.

Rigdon, E. (1998). Structural equation models. In G. Marcoulides (Ed.), *Modern methods for business research* (pp. 251–294). Mahwah, NJ: Erlbaum.

Rindskopf, D., & Rose, T. (1988). Some theory and applications of confirmatory second-order factor analysis. *Multivariate Behavioral Research, 23,* 51–67.

Robinson, W. S. (1950). Ecological correlations and the behaviors of individuals. *American Sociological Review, 15,* 351–357.

Rodgers, J. L. (2010). The epistemology of mathematical and statistical modeling: A quiet methodological revolution. *American Psychologist, 65,* 1–12.

Rogers, W. M., & Schmitt, N. (2004). Parameter recovery and model fit using multidimensional composites: A comparison of four empirical parcelling algorithms. *Multivariate Behavioral Research, 39,* 379–412.

Rogosa, D. R., Brandt, D., & Zimowski, M. (1982). A growth curve approach to the measurement of change. *Psychological Bulletin, 90,* 726–748.

Rogosa, D. R., & Willett, J. B. (1985). Understanding correlates of change by modeling individual differences in growth. *Psychometrika, 50,* 203–228.

Rozeboom, W. W. (1960). The fallacy of the null hypothesis significance test. *Psychological Bulletin, 57,* 416–428.

Rubin, D. B. (1987). *Multiple imputation for nonresponse in surveys.* New York: Wiley.

Ryu, E., & West, S. G. (2009). Level-specific evaluation of model fit in multilevel structural equation modeling. *Structural Equation Modeling, 16,* 583–601.

Saris, W. E., & Aalberts, C. (2003). Different explanations for correlated disturbance terms in MTMM studies. *Structural Equation Modeling, 10,* 193–213.

Saris, W. E., Satorra, A., & Sörbom, D. (1987). The detection and correction of specification errors in structural equation models. *Sociological Methodology, 17,* 105–129.

Saris, W. E., Satorra, A., & van der Veld, W. M. (2009). Testing structural equation models or detection of misspecifications? *Structural Equation Modeling, 16,* 561–582.

Saris, W., & Stronkhorst, H. (1984). *Causal modeling: Nonexperimental research: An introduction to the LISREL approach.* Amsterdam: Sociometric Research Foundation.

Sass, D. A., & Smith, P. L. (2006). The effects of parceling unidimensional scales on structural parameter estimates in structural equation modeling. *Structural Equation Modeling, 13,* 566–586.

Satorra, A., & Bentler, P. M. (1986). Some robustness properties of goodness of fit statistics in covariance structure analysis. In *1986 American Statistical Association Proceedings of the Business and Economics Section* (pp. 549–554). Alexandria, VA: American Statistical Association.

Satorra, A., & Bentler, P. M. (1988). Scaling corrections for chi-square statistics in covariance structure analysis. In *1988 American Statistical Association Proceedings of the Business and Economics Section* (pp. 308–313). Alexandria VA: American Statistical Association.

Satorra, A., & Bentler, P. M. (1990). Model conditions for asymptotic robustness in the analysis of linear relations. *Computational Statistics and Data Analysis, 10*, 235–249.

Satorra, A., & Bentler, P. M. (2001). A scaled difference chi-square test statistic for moment structure analysis. *Psychometrika, 66*, 507–514.

Schafer, J. L., & Graham, J. W. (2002). Missing data: Our view of the state of the art. *Psychological Methods, 7*, 147–177.

Schmidt, F. L. (1996). Statistical significance testing and cumulative knowledge in psychology: Implications for training of researchers. *Psychological Methods, 1*, 115–129.

Schmitt, N., & Stults, D. M. (1986). Methodology review: Analysis of multitrait multimethod matrices. *Applied Psychological Measurement, 10*, 1–22.

Schnabel, K. U., Little, T. D., & Baumert, J. (2000). Modeling longitudinal and multilevel data. In T. D. Little, K. U. Schnabel, & J. Baumert (Eds.), *Modeling longitudinal and multilevel data: Practical issues, applied approaches, and scientific examples* (pp. 9–13). Mahwah, NJ: Erlbaum.

Schumacker, R. E., & Lomax, R. G. (2004). *A beginner's guide to structural equation modeling* (2nd ed.). Mahwah, NJ: Erlbaum.

Schwartz, G. (1978). Estimating the dimension of a model. *Annals of Statistics, 6*, 461–464.

Selig, J. P., Card, N. A., & Little, T. D. (2008). Latent variable structural equation modelling in cross-cultural research: Multigroup and multilevel approaches. In F. J. R. van de Vijver, D. A. van Hemert, & Y. H. Poortinga (Eds.), *Multilevel analysis of individuals and cultures* (pp. 93–119). Mahwah, NJ: Erlbaum.

Shafer, J. L. (1997). *Analysis of incomplete multivariate data.* London: Chapman & Hall.

Shavelson, R. J., Hubner, J. J., & Stanton, G. C. (1976). Self-concept: Validation of construct interpretations. *Review of Educational Research, 46*, 407–441.

Sobel, M. F., & Bohrnstedt, G. W. (1985). Use of null models in evaluating the fit of covariance structure models. In N. B. Tuma (Ed.), *Sociological methodology 1985* (pp. 152–178). San Francisco: Jossey-Bass.

Sörbom, D. (1974). A general method for studying differences in factor means and factor structures between groups. *British Journal of Mathematical and Statistical Psychology, 27*, 229–239.

Sörbom, D. (1989). Model modification. *Psychometrika, 54*, 371–384.

Sörbom, D. (2001). Karl Jöreskog and LISREL: A personal story. In R. Cudeck, S. du Toit, & D. Sörbom (Eds.), *Structural equation modeling: Present and future: A festschrift in honor of Karl Jöreskog.* Lincolnwood, IL: Scientific Software International.

Steiger, J. H. (1990). Structural model evaluation and modification: An interval estimation approach. *Multivariate Behavioral Research, 25*, 173–180.

Steiger, J. H. (1998). A note on multiple sample extensions of the RMSEA fit index. *Structural Equation Modeling, 5*, 411–419.

Steiger, J. H., & Lind, J. C. (1980, June). Statistically based tests for the number of common factors. Paper presented at the Psychometric Society annual meeting, Iowa City, IA.

Steiger, J. H., Shapiro, A., & Browne, M. W. (1985). On the multivariate asymptotic distribution of sequential chi-square statistics. *Psychometrika, 50,* 253–264.

Sugawara, H. M., & MacCallum, R. C. (1993). Effect of estimation method on incremental fit indexes for covariance structure models. *Applied Psychological Measurement, 17,* 365–377.

Tanaka, J. S. (1993). Multifaceted conceptions of fit in structural equation models. In J. A. Bollen & J. S. Long (Eds.), *Testing structural equation models* (pp. 10–39). Newbury Park, CA: Sage.

Tanaka, J. S., & Huba, G. J. (1984). Confirmatory hierarchical factor analysis of psychological distress measures. *Journal of Personality and Social Psychology, 46,* 621–635.

Thompson, B. (1996). AERA editorial policies regarding statistical significance testing: Three suggested reforms. *Educational Researcher, 25,* 26–30.

Tomarken, A. J., & Waller, N. G. (2005). Structural equation modeling: Strengths, limitations, and misconceptions. *Annual Review of Clinical Psychology, 1,* 2.1–2.35.

Tomás, J. M., Hontangas, P. M., & Oliver, A. (2000). Linear confirmatory factor models to evaluate multitrait–multimethod matrices: The effects of number of indicators and correlation among methods. *Multivariate Behavioral Research, 35,* 469–499.

Tucker, L. R., & Lewis, C. (1973). A reliability coefficient for maximum likelihood factor analysis. *Psychometrika, 38,* 1–10.

van de Vijver, F. J. R., Mylonas, K., Pavlopoulos, V., & Georgas, J. (2006). Results: Cross-cultural analyses of the family. In J. Georgas, J. W. Berry, F. J. R. van de Vijver, C. Kagitcibasi, & Y. H. Poortinga (Eds.), *Families across culture: A 30-nation psychological study* (pp. 126–185). Cambridge: Cambridge University Press.

Wang, S., Wang, N., & Hoadley, D. (2007). Construct equivalence of a national certification examination that uses dual languages and audio assistance. *International Journal of Testing, 7,* 255–268.

Welkenhuysen-Gybels, J., van de Vijver, F. J. R., & Cambré, B. (2007). A comparison of methods for the evaluation of construct equivalence in a multigroup setting. In G. Loosveldt, M. Swyngedouw, & B. Cambré (Eds.), *Measuring meaningful data in social research* (pp. 357–371). Leuven, Belgium: Acco.

Weng, L-J., & Cheng, C-P. (1997). Why might relative fit indices differ between estimators? *Structural Equation Modeling, 4,* 121–128.

West, S. G., Finch, J. F., & Curran, P. J. (1995). Structural equation models with nonnormal variables: Problems and remedies. In R. H. Hoyle (Ed.), *Structural equation modeling: Concepts, issues, and applications* (pp. 56–75). Thousand Oaks, CA: Sage.

Wheaton, B. (1987). Assessment of fit in overidentified models with latent variables. *Sociological Methods & Research, 16,* 118–154.

Whittaker, T. A., & Stapleton, L. M. (2006). The performance of cross-validation indices used to select among competing covariance structure models under multivariate nonnormality conditions. *Multivariate Behavioral Research, 41,* 295–335.

Widaman, K. F. (1985). Hierarchically tested covariance structure models for multitrait multimethod data. *Applied Psychological Measurement, 9*, 1–26.

Widaman, K. F., & Reise, S. P. (1997). Exploring the measurement equivalence of psychological instruments: Applications in the substance use domain. In K. J. Bryant, M. Windle, & S. G. West (Eds.), *The science of prevention* (pp. 281–324). Washington, DC: American Psychological Association.

Wilkinson, L., and the Task Force on Statistical Inference. (1999). Statistical methods in psychology journals: Guidelines and explanations. *American Psychologist, 54*, 594–604.

Willett, J. B. (1988). Questions and answers in the measurement of change. In E. Z. Rothkopf (Ed.), *Review of research in education* (Vol. 15, pp. 345–422). Washington, DC: American Educational Research Association.

Willett, J. B. (1989). Some results on reliability for the longitudinal measurement of change: Implications for the design of studies of individual growth. *Educational and Psychological Measurement, 49*, 587–602.

Willett, J. B., & Keiley, M. K. (2000). Using covariance structure analysis to model change over time. In H. E. A. Tinsley & S. D. Brown (Eds.), *Handbook of applied multivariate statistics and mathematical modeling* (pp. 665–694). San Diego, CA: Academic Press.

Willett, J. B., & Sayer, A. G. (1994). Using covariance structure analysis to detect correlates and predictors of individual change over time. *Psychological Bulletin, 116*, 363–381.

Willett, J. B., & Sayer, A. G. (1996). Cross-domain analyses of change over time: Combining growth modeling and covariance structural analysis. In G.A. Marcoulides & R.E. Schumacker (Eds.), *Advanced structural equation modeling: Issues and techniques* (pp. 125–157). Mahwah, NJ: Erlbaum.

Williams, L. J., & Holahan, P. J. (1994). Parsimony-based fit indices for multiple-indicator models: Do they work? *Structural Equation Modeling, 1*, 161–189.

Wolfle, L. M. (2003). The introduction of path analysis to the social sciences, and some emergent themes: An annotated bibliography. *Structural Equation Modeling, 10*, 1–34.

Wood, J. M., Tataryn, D. J., & Gorsuch, R. L. (1996). Effects of under- and overextraction on principal axis factor analysis with varimax rotation. *Psychological Methods, 1*, 354–365.

Wothke, W. (1993). Nonpositive definite matrices in structural modeling. In K. A. Bollen & J. S. Long (Eds.), *Testing structural equation models* (pp. 256–293). Newbury Park, CA: Sage.

Wothke, W. (1996). Models for multitrait–multimethod matrix analysis. In G. A. Marcoulides & R. E. Schumacker (Eds.), *Advanced structural equation modeling: Issues and techniques* (pp. 7–56). Mahwah, NJ: Erlbaum.

Wu, W., West, S. G., & Taylor, A. B. (2009). Evaluating model fit for growth curve models: Integration of fit indices from SEM and MLM frameworks. *Psychological Methods, 14*, 183–201.

Yoon, M., & Millsap, R. R. (2007). Detecting violations of factorial invariance using data-based specification searches: A Monte Carlo study. *Structural Equation Modeling, 14*, 435–463.

Yu, C-Y. (2002). *Evaluating cutoff criteria of model fit indices for latent variable models with binary and continuous outcomes.* (Doctoral dissertation, University of California, Los Angeles). Retrieved from http://www.statmodel.com/.

Yuan, K-H., & Bentler, P. M. (2000). Three likelihood-based methods for mean and covariance structure analysis with nonnormal missing data. *Sociological Methodology, 30,* 165–200.

Yuan, K-H., & Bentler, P. M. (2002). On normal theory based inference for multilevel models with distributional violations. *Psychometrika, 67,* 539–562.

Yuan, K-H., & Bentler, P. M. (2004a). On chi square difference and z-tests in mean and covariance structure analysis when the base model is misspecified. *Educational and Psychological Measurement, 64,* 737–757.

Yuan, K-H., & Bentler, P. M. (2004b). On the asymptotic distributions of two statistics for two-level covariance structure models within the class of elliptical distributions. *Psychometrika, 69,* 437–457.

Yuan, K-H., & Bentler, P. M. (2007). Multilevel covariance structure analysis by fitting multiple single-level models. *Sociological Methodology, 37,* 53–82.

Yuan, K-H., & Hayashi, K. (2005). On Muthén's maximum likelihood for two-level covariance structure models. *Psychometrika, 70,* 147–167.

Yuan, K-H., Lambert, P. L., & Fouladi, R. T. (2004). Mardia's multivariate kurtosis with missing data. *Multivariate Behavioral Research, 39,* 413–437.

Author Index

Subject Index